적중"100

영어 기출 문제집

중**3**

시사 | 박준언

Best Collection

구성과 특징

교과서의 주요 학습 내용을 중심으로 학습 영역별 특성에 맞춰 단계별로 다양한 학습 기회를 제공하여
단원별 학습능력 평가는 물론 중간 및 기말고사 시험 등에 완벽하게 대비할 수 있도록 내용을 구성

Words & Expressions

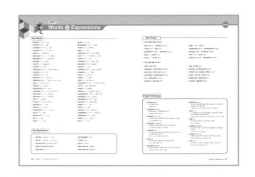

Step1 Key Words 단원별 핵심 단어 설명 및 풀이
Key Expression 단원별 핵심 숙어 및 관용어 설명
Word Power 반대 또는 비슷한 뜻 단어 배우기
English Dictionary 영어로 배우는 영어 단어

Step2 실력평가 단원별 수시평가 대비 주관식, 객관식 문제풀이

Step3 서술형 대비 학업성취도 및 수행능력평가 대비 서술형 문제풀이

Conversation

Step1 핵심 의사소통 소통에 필요한 주요 표현 방법 요약
핵심 Check 기본적인 표현 방법 및 활용능력 확인

Step2 대화문 익히기 교과서 대화문 심층 분석 및 확인

Step3 교과서 확인학습 빈칸 채우기를 통한 문장 완성 능력 확인

Step4 기본평가 시험대비 기초 학습 능력 평가

Step5 실력평가 단원별 수시평가 대비 주관식, 객관식 문제풀이

Step6 서술형 대비 학업성취도 및 수행능력평가 대비 서술형 문제풀이

Grammar

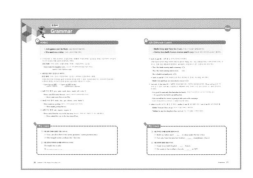

Step1 주요 문법 단원별 주요 문법 사항과 예문을 알기 쉽게 설명
핵심 Check 기본 문법사항에 대한 이해 여부 확인

Step2 기본평가 시험대비 기초 학습 능력 평가

Step3 실력평가 단원별 수시평가 대비 주관식, 객관식 문제풀이

Step4 서술형 대비 학업성취도 및 수행능력평가 대비 서술형 문제풀이

Reading

Step1 구문 분석 단원별로 제시된 문장에 대한 구문별 분석과 내용 설명
확인문제 문장에 대한 기본적인 이해와 인지능력 확인

Step2 확인학습A 빈칸 채우기를 통한 문장 완성 능력 확인

Step3 확인학습B 제시된 우리말을 영어로 완성하여 작문 능력 키우기

Step4 실력평가 단원별 수시평가 대비 주관식, 객관식 문제풀이

Step5 서술형 대비 학업성취도 및 수행능력평가 대비 서술형 문제풀이
교과서 구석구석 교과서에 나오는 기타 문장까지 완벽 학습

Composition

|영역별 핵심문제|

단어 및 어휘, 대화문, 문법, 독해 등 각 영역별 기출문제의 출제 유형을 분석하여 실전에 대비하고 연습할 수 있도록 문제를 배열

|단원별 예상문제|

기출문제를 분석한 후 새로운 시험 출제 경향을 더하여 새롭게 출제될 수 있는 문제를 포함하여 시험에 완벽하게 대비할 수 있도록 준비

|서술형 실전 및 창의사고력 문제|

학교 시험에서 점차 늘어나는 서술형 시험에 집중 대비하고 고득점을 취득하는데 만전을 기하기 위한 학습 코너

|단원별 모의고사|

영역별, 단계별 학습을 모두 마친 후 실전 연습을 위한 모의고사

교과서 파헤치기

- **단어Test1~3** 영어 단어 우리말 쓰기, 우리말을 영어 단어로 쓰기, 영영풀이에 해당하는 단어와 우리말 쓰기
- **대화문Test1~2** 대화문 빈칸 완성 및 전체 대화문 쓰기
- **본문Test1~5** 빈칸 완성, 우리말 쓰기, 문장 배열연습, 영어 작문하기 복습 등 단계별 반복 학습을 통해 교과서 지문에 대한 완벽한 습득
- **구석구석지문Test1~2** 지문 빈칸 완성 및 전문 영어로 쓰기

Lesson 8

Have Fun with Art!

 의사소통 기능

- 관심 표현하기
  I was fascinated by the colors in his paintings and his creativity.

- 만족이나 불만족에 대해 묻기
  How do you like this T-shirt?

언어 형식

- 분사구문
  Using common images, pop art looks plain.

- be동사+worth+동명사
  Pop art **is worth paying** attention to.

Words & Expressions

Key Words

- **ability** [əbíləti] 몡 능력
- **advertising** [ǽdvərtàiziŋ] 몡 광고
- **advice** [ædváis] 몡 충고, 조언
- **amazing** [əméiziŋ] 휑 놀라운
- **art museum** 미술관
- **art work** 예술 작품
- **artistic** [ɑːrtístik] 휑 예술적인
- **backpack** [bǽkpæk] 몡 가방, 배낭
- **boring** [bɔ́ːriŋ] 휑 지루한, 지겨운
- **cartoon** [kɑːrtúːn] 몡 만화
- **classical** [klǽsikəl] 휑 클래식의, 고전적인
- **colorful** [kʌ́lərfəl] 휑 화려한
- **common** [kámən] 휑 흔한, 평범한, 공통의
- **cone** [koun] 몡 원뿔, 원뿔형 물체
- **cool** [kuːl] 휑 멋진
- **copy** [kápi] 몡 복사본
- **create** [kriéit] 됭 만들다, 창조하다
- **creative** [kriéitiv] 휑 창의적인
- **creativity** [krìːeitívəti] 몡 창의력
- **decoration** [dèkəréiʃən] 몡 장식
- **exciting** [iksáitinŋ] 휑 신나는, 흥미진진한
- **exhibition** [èksəbíʃən] 몡 전시회
- **familiar** [fəmíljər] 휑 친숙한
- **fantastic** [fæntǽstik] 휑 환상적인, 멋진
- **favorite** [féivərit] 휑 가장 좋아하는
- **fever** [fíːvər] 몡 열, 발열
- **goods** [gudz] 몡 상품, 제품
- **huge** [hjuːdʒ] 휑 거대한, 큰
- **include** [inklúːd] 됭 포함하다, 넣다
- **lesson** [lésn] 몡 교훈
- **lively** [láivli] 휑 활기 넘치는, 생생한
- **main character** 주인공
- **mean** [miːn] 됭 의미하다
- **meaning** [míːniŋ] 몡 의미
- **musician** [mjuːzíʃən] 몡 음악가
- **object** [ábdʒikt] 몡 물건, 물체, 대상
- **outdoor** [áutdɔr] 휑 실외의
- **practice** [prǽktis] 됭 연습하다
- **performance** [pərfɔ́ːrməns] 몡 연기, 공연
- **plain** [plein] 휑 보통의, 평범한
- **plate** [pleit] 몡 접시
- **pop art** 팝 아트
- **popular** [pápjulər] 휑 대중적인, 인기 있는
- **probably** [prábəbli] 됭 아마
- **refreshing** [rifréʃiŋ] 휑 신선한, 참신한
- **run** [rʌn] 됭 운영하다
- **sculpture** [skʌ́lptʃər] 몡 조각품
- **special effects** 특수효과
- **speech balloon** 말풍선
- **subject** [sʌ́bdʒikt] 몡 주제, 과목, 실험대상자
- **toilet** [tɔ́ilit] 몡 변기, 화장실
- **traditional** [trədíʃənl] 휑 전통적인
- **truly** [trúːli] 됭 진심으로, 정말로
- **worth** [wəːrθ] 휑 ~의 가치가 있는

Key Expressions

- **as well** 또한, 역시
- **back then** 그 당시에
- **be able to** ~할 수 있다
- **be fascinated by** ~에 매료되다
- **be filled with** ~로 가득 차 있다
- **be made of** ~로 만들어지다
- **be made up of** ~로 구성되다
- **be regarded as** ~로 여겨지다
- **be short for** ~의 줄임말이다
- **be worth+동명사** ~할 가치가 있다
- **break down** ~을 부수다
- **by+-ing(동명사)** ~함으로써
- **change A into B** A를 B로 바꾸다
- **in other words** 다시 말해서, 즉
- **instead of** ~ 대신에
- **look like+명사(구)** ~처럼 보이다
- **no wonder** ~은 (별로) 놀랄 일이 아니다[~하는 것도 당연하다]
- **one of+복수 명사** ~ 중의 하나
- **pay attention to** ~에 주의를 기울이다
- **set up** 설치하다
- **the other day** 요전 날, 며칠 전
- **turn one's eyes to** ~로 눈길을 돌리다

Word Power

※ 서로 비슷한 뜻을 가진 어휘

□ **familiar** 친숙한 – **intimate** 친숙한, 친밀한
□ **as well** 또한 – **also** 또한
□ **lively** 활기 넘치는 – **animated** 생기가 있는
□ **common** 흔한, 평범한 – **ordinary** 평범한

□ **create** 만들다 – **produce** 제작하다
□ **advice** 조언, 충고 – **tip** 조언
□ **run** 운영하다 – **operate** 운영하다
□ **performance** 연기 – **acting** 연기

※ 서로 반대되는 뜻을 가진 어휘

□ **familiar** 친숙한 ↔ **unfamiliar** 낯선
□ **outdoor** 실외의 ↔ **indoor** 실내의
□ **colorful** 화려한 ↔ **colorless** 무색의
□ **huge** 거대한 ↔ **tiny** 아주 작은

□ **include** 포함하다 ↔ **exclude** 제외하다
□ **popular** 인기 있는 ↔ **unpopular** 인기 없는
□ **lively** 활기 넘치는 ↔ **dull** 활기 없는
□ **copy** 복사본 ↔ **original** 원형, 원본

※ 형용사 – 명사

□ **creative** 창의적인 – **creativity** 창의력
□ **traditional** 전통적인 – **tradition** 전통

□ **popular** 인기 있는 – **popularity** 인기
□ **familiar** 친밀한 – **familiarity** 친밀함

English Dictionary

□ **ability** 능력
→ the physical or mental power or skill needed to do something
뭔가를 하기 위해 필요한 신체적 또는 정신적 힘이나 기술

□ **advice** 충고
→ an opinion that someone offers you about what you should do or how you should act in a particular situation
어떤 사람이 특정한 상황에서 당신이 무엇을 해야 하는지 또는 어떻게 행동해야 하는지에 대해 당신에게 제안하는 의견

□ **boring** 지루한
→ not interesting or exciting
재미있거나 흥미롭지 않은

□ **classical** 클래식의, 고전적인
→ traditional in style or form, or based on methods developed over a long period of time, and considered to be of lasting value
전통적 스타일이나 형식, 또는 오랜 기간에 걸쳐 개발된 방법에 기초하고, 지속적인 가치가 있는 것으로 여겨지는

□ **cone** 원뿔
→ a shape with a flat, round or oval base and a top that becomes narrower until it forms a point
평평한, 둥근 또는 타원형의 기초와 점이 형성될 때까지 좁아지는 꼭대기를 가진 형태

□ **creativity** 창의력
→ the ability to produce or use original and unusual ideas
독창적이고 특이한 아이디어를 생산하거나 사용하는 능력

□ **exhibition** 전시회
→ an event at which objects such as paintings are shown to the public, a situation in which someone shows a particular skill or quality to the public, or the act of showing these things
그림과 같은 사물들이 대중에게 보여지는 경우, 누군가가 대중에게 특정한 기술이나 자질을 보여주는 상황, 또는 이러한 것들을 보여주는 행위

□ **familiar** 친숙한
→ easy to recognize because of being seen, met, heard, etc. before
이전에 보고, 만나고, 들었기 때문에 알아차리기 쉬운

□ **include** 포함하다
→ to contain something as a part of something else, or to make something part of something else
무언가를 다른 어떤 것의 일부로 포함하거나 어떤 것을 다른 어떤 것의 일부로 만들다

□ **plain** 평범한
→ not decorated in any way; with nothing added
어떤 식으로든 장식되지 않은; 아무것도 추가하지 않은

□ **popular** 대중적인, 인기 있는
→ liked, enjoyed, or supported by many people
많은 사람들이 좋아하거나, 즐기거나, 지지를 하는

□ **practice** 연습하다
→ to do or play something regularly or repeatedly in order to become skilled at it
어떤 것에 숙련되기 위해 그것을 규칙적으로 또는 반복적으로 하거나 연주하다

□ **traditional** 전통적인
→ following or belonging to the customs or ways of behaving that have continued in a group of people or society for a long time without changing
오랜 시간 동안 변화 없이 한 무리의 사람들 또는 사회에서 지속되어 온 관습이나 행동 방식을 따르거나 속해 있는

01 문장의 빈칸에 공통으로 들어갈 말로 가장 알맞은 것은?

- College is where we learn knowledge about a specific _____.
- Students had an argument for and against a given _____.

① object
② goods
③ sculpture
④ subject
⑤ musician

서답형

02 주어진 〈영영풀이〉를 읽고 빈칸에 冊을 이용하여 3 단어로 쓰시오.

Interestingly, the library will _____ _____ _____ e-books instead of paper books.

┤영영풀이├
to put a substance into an empty space

03 문장의 빈칸에 들어갈 말로 가장 알맞은 것은?

(A) It's _____ Athens is the birthplace of democracy!
(B) The name "Bulgaria" is _____ as the oldest country name in Europe.

	(A)	(B)
①	as well	regarded
②	as well	fascinated
③	no wonder	regarded
④	no wonder	made
⑤	no wonder	fascinated

[04~05] 다음 설명에 해당하는 단어를 고르시오.

04

following or belonging to the customs or ways of behaving that have continued in a group of people or society for a long time without changing

① traditional
② lively
③ classical
④ popular
⑤ artistic

05

not decorated in any way; with nothing added

① personal
② plain
③ proper
④ familiar
⑤ huge

서답형

06 다음 빈칸에 우리말에 맞게 주어진 단어를 활용하여 세 단어를 쓰시오.

이 영화는 두 번 볼 만한 가치가 있다. (watch)

➡ This movie _____ _____ _____ twice.

07 다음 짝지어진 단어의 관계가 나머지 넷과 다른 것은?

① create – produce
② lively – animated
③ common – ordinary
④ run – operate
⑤ include – exclude

01 다음 빈칸에 들어갈 말을 〈보기〉에서 찾아 쓰시오. (필요하면 어형을 변화시킬 것.)

┌── 보기 ──────────────┐
│ amaze   mean   create   goods │
└────────────────────────┘

(1) Prices are marked on the _____.

(2) There is so much history and _____ behind Taegeukgi.

(3) Horses are _____ animals. They are beautiful, strong, and smart.

(4) A _____ person has the ability to come up with interesting ideas.

02 다음 문장의 빈칸에 공통으로 들어갈 단어를 쓰시오.

┌────────────────────────┐
│ • Our luggage is brown and _____. │
│ • _____s and deserts stretched to the │
│   wooded coastal ranges and the Pacific │
│   Ocean. │
│ • They like to look at beautiful faces │
│   rather than _____ faces. │
└────────────────────────┘

03 다음 우리말과 같은 표현이 되도록 문장의 빈칸을 채우시오.

(1) 식이 시작되기 전, 여러 가지 문화 공연과 행사들이 있었습니다.
➡ Before the ceremony began, there were many cultural _____ and events.

(2) 그 당시만 해도 사람들은 지금보다 더 친환경적이지 않았다.
➡ _____ _____ people were not as environmentally conscious as they are now.

(3) 아이들은 컴퓨터가 있다면 선생님의 말에 귀를 기울이지 않을 것입니다.
➡ Kids will not _____ _____ _____ the teacher if they have a computer.

(4) 플라스틱 분자는 길고 단단한 탄소 골격으로 이루어져 있기 때문에 플라스틱 제품들은 시간이 지나도 쉽게 분해되지 않습니다.
➡ Plastic products don't _____ _____ easily over time because plastic molecules consist of long, sturdy carbon chains.

04 영영풀이에 해당하는 단어를 〈보기〉에서 찾아 첫 번째 빈칸에 쓰고, 두 번째 빈칸에는 우리말 뜻을 쓰시오.

┌── 보기 ──────────────┐
│ cone   practice   include   boring │
└────────────────────────┘

(1) _____ : not interesting or exciting: _____

(2) _____ : to do or play something regularly or repeatedly in order to become skilled at it: _____

(3) _____ : a shape with a flat, round or oval base and a top that becomes narrower until it forms a point: _____

Conversation

① 관심 표현하기

> **I was fascinated by the colors in his paintings and his creativity.** 나는 그의 작품에서 보이는 색감과 그의 창의성에 매료되었다.

- 'be fascinated by'는 '~에 매료되다'라는 의미로 어떤 것에 대해 깊은 관심이 있음을 나타낸다. by는 전치사이므로 뒤에 명사(구)나 동명사가 온다.

- 관심을 나타내는 다른 표현들
  상대방의 말에 관심을 나타낼 때 사용하는 표현으로는 'That interests me a lot.'이라고 표현한다. 이 표현은 '그것 참 재미있네요.' 또는 '그것 참 흥미롭네요.' 정도로 해석할 수 있다. 또는 I'm interested in ~.(나는 ~에 관심이 있다.) / I have an interest in ~.(나는 ~에 관심을 가지고 있다.) / I'm into ~.(나는 ~에 관심이 많다.) 등으로 나타낼 수 있다.
  - I'm fascinated by Korean traditional houses. 나는 한국의 전통 가옥에 매료되었다.
  - I'm into hip hop music. 나는 힙합 음악에 관심이 있다.
  - **A:** I'm really fascinated by musicals these days. 나는 요즘 뮤지컬에 정말 매료되었어.
    B: Are you sure? I have two tickets for the musical "*Cats.*" 정말? 나에게 뮤지컬 'Cats' 표 두 장이 있어.
  - I am interested in K-pop. 저는 K-pop에 관심이 있습니다.
    = I have an interest in K-pop.
    = I am fascinated by K-pop.
    = I'm into K-pop.

핵심 Check

1. 다음 대화의 빈칸에 들어가기에 <u>어색한</u> 말은?

> **A:** What movie do you like?
> **B:** I like *Fly to the Moon*.
> **A:** Why do you like it?
> **B:** _____

① I'm fascinated by its special effects.
② Yes. I read it in an article.
③ I'm into its story.
④ I'm interested in its scenes.
⑤ I have an interest in its characters.

2 만족이나 불만족에 대해 묻기

How do you like this T-shirt? 이 티셔츠 어때?

■ How do you like ~?'는 어떤 것에 대해 만족하는지 아니면 불만족하는지 묻는 표현이다.
만족이나 불만족에 대해 묻는 표현으로 'Is this what you wanted?'나 'Do you like it?' 등으로 물을 수 있다.
- **A:** Is this what you wanted? 이것 마음에 드시나요?
  B: Oh, no! That's not it at all. 오, 세상에! 그건 아니잖아요.
- **A:** How do you like your new phone, Sejin? 세진아, 새로 산 네 전화기 어떠니?
  B: I love it. 정말 좋아.

■ 만족이나 불만족을 나타내는 추가 표현
- Are you satisfied with this T-shirt?
- Are you happy with this T-shirt?
- Is this T-shirt what you want(ed)/have[had] in mind?

■ 만족 표현하기
- Good! / Fine! / Excellent! 좋아! / 훌륭해!
- I'm (very) satisfied. 나는 매우 만족해.
- That'll do. 그거면 충분해.

■ 불만족 표현하기
- I'm not satisfied/happy (with ~). 나는 (~에) 만족하지 않아.
- That won't do[work]. 그건 효과가 없을 거야.

핵심 Check

2. 다음 빈칸에 들어갈 말로 알맞은 것은?

> **A:** _____ this backpack?
> **B:** I like it. It's useful.

① Why do you like   ② When did you buy

③ Where did you get   ④ Do you have

⑤ How do you like

Listen & Speak 1 A-1

B: Sandy, you can listen to ❶many kinds of music in this music library.

G: That's cool, Bob. Can I listen to classical music?

B: Sure. Do you like classical music?

G: Yes, Beethoven is ❷one of my favorite musicians. How about you?

B: ❸I like pop music more than classical music.

G: I see. What do you like most about pop music?

B: ❹I'm really fascinated by its exciting rhythms.

B: Sandy, 너는 이 음악 도서관에서 많은 종류의 음악을 들을 수 있어.
G: 그거 멋지다, Bob. 클래식 음악도 들을 수 있어?
B: 물론이지. 너 클래식 음악 좋아하니?
G: 응. 베토벤이 내가 가장 좋아하는 음악가 중의 하나야. 너는 어때?
B: 나는 클래식보다는 대중음악이 더 좋아.
G: 그렇구나. 너는 대중음악의 어떤 점이 가장 마음에 들어?
B: 나는 대중음악의 신나는 리듬이 정말 좋아.

❶ 'many+복수 명사(kinds)'로 '많은 종류'라는 의미이다.
❷ 'one of the+복수명사' 형태로 '~ 중 하나'로 해석한다.
❸ '비교급 than' 구문으로 'I prefer pop music to classical music.'으로 바꾸어 쓸 수 있다. 'prefer A to B'는 'B보다 A를 더 좋아하다'라는 의미이다.
❹ 'be fascinated by'는 '~에 매료되다'라는 의미로 어떤 것에 대해 깊은 관심이 있음을 나타낸다. by는 전치사이므로 뒤에 명사(구)나 동명사가 온다.

Check(√) True or False

(1) Sandy likes classical music.　　　　　　　　　　　　　T ☐ F ☐

(2) Bob prefers classical music to pop music.　　　　　　　T ☐ F ☐

Listen & Speak 2 A-1

B: The other day I watched a play, *A Love Story in the War*.

G: Oh, ❶how did you like the play?

B: I liked the main characters. The actors' performances were fantastic.

G: Was the story good ❷as well?

B: No. It was a little boring, but the music was pretty good.

G: So, do you think I should see it?

B: ❸Only if you have a lot of time and money.

B: 며칠 전에 '전쟁 속의 사랑 이야기'라는 연극을 봤어.
G: 오, 그 연극 어땠어?
B: 주인공들이 좋았어. 배우들의 연기가 끝내줬거든.
G: 이야기도 좋았어?
B: 아니. 이야기는 조금 지루했는데, 음악은 꽤 괜찮았어.
G: 그럼, 너는 내가 그 연극을 보아야 한다고 생각하니?
B: 네가 돈과 시간이 많을 경우에만.

❶ 'How do you like ~?'는 어떤 것에 대해 만족하는지 아니면 불만족하는지 묻는 표현이다. 'Is this what you wanted?'나 'Do you like it?' 등으로 물을 수 있다.
❷ 'as well'은 문장 끝에서 '또한'의 의미로 사용된다.
❸ 'only if+주어+동사 ~'는 어떤 일이 가능한 유일한 상황을 진술할 때 사용하는 표현으로 '~해야만'의 의미를 갖고 있다.

Check(√) True or False

(3) The boy was satisfied with the story of the play.　　　T ☐ F ☐

(4) The girl will see the play if she has much time and money.　　　T ☐ F ☐

Listen & Speak 1 A-2

G: Jim, did you finish your art homework?

B: Yes. I drew the face of my role model on a plate.

G: ❶Sounds interesting. Who is your role model?

B: My dad. He always ❷gives me good advice. Who did you draw, Amy?

G: Well, I drew myself surfing in the sea.

B: Wonderful! ❸I'm fascinated by your drawing.

G: Thank you.

❶ 'sound+형용사': '~하게 들리다'의 의미이다.
❷ 4형식 문장으로 '~에게(간접목적어) …을(직접목적어) 주다'로 해석한다.
❸ 관심을 나타낼 때 사용하는 표현으로 'I'm interested in your drawing.', 'I'm into your drawing.' 등으로 쓸 수 있다.

 Listen & Speak 2 A-2

B: Claire, ❶how do you like your art class?

G: It's great. I learn a lot in the class.

B: What do you like most about it?

G: I ❷enjoy learning different drawing skills. What about you, Allen?

B: I also like the class. I learn good painting skills. I love painting with many colors.

G: Oh, I saw your work last time. I thought it was very creative.

B: Thanks. I practice a lot.

❶ 'How do you like ~?'는 어떤 것에 대해 만족하는지 아니면 불만족하는지 묻는 표현으로, 'Are you satisfied with your art class?', 'Are you happy with your art class?' 등으로 바꾸어 쓸 수 있다.
❷ 동사 'enjoy'는 동명사를 목적어로 취하는 동사로 'learning' 형태가 온다.

 Real Life Talk

Bora: Andy, ❶you went to the art museum, didn't you?

Andy: Yes. They had a special Chagall exhibition.

Bora: How did you like it?

Andy: It was fantastic! ❷I was fascinated by the colors in his paintings and his creativity.

Bora: No wonder. He was ❸one of the greatest painters ever. What else did you see in the museum?

Andy: I went to a gift shop and saw things like umbrellas, cups, and backpacks. Famous works of art were printed on them.

Bora: Did you buy anything?

Andy: Yes. I bought this T-shirt. How do you like it?

Bora: ❹It looks great on you.

Andy: Thank you.

❶ 사실을 확인하는 표현으로 'didn't you?'는 부가의문문으로 '그렇지 않니?'라고 해석한다.
❷ 상대방의 말에 관심을 나타낼 때 사용하는 표현으로는 'The colors in his paintings and his creativity interested me a lot.'으로 바꾸어 표현할 수 있다.
❸ 'one of the+최상급+복수명사' 형태로 '가장 ~한 것 중 하나'로 해석한다.
❹ '너에게 매우 잘 어울려.'라는 의미로 전치사 'on'은 '착용'의 의미가 있다.

 Wrap Up 1

B: Cindy, you went to the music festival, didn't you?

G: Yes. A lot of famous musicians performed there.

B: How did you like the festival?

G: It was fantastic! I really liked the special guest. Do you know the band ❶called *the Brothers*?

B: Oh, I've heard about them. The singer is famous.

G: Yes. His performance was great.

B: ❷No wonder.

❶ 'called'는 '~라 불리는'의 수동 의미를 가지는 과거분사이다.
❷ 'No wonder.'는 '당연해. 놀랄 일도 아니야'라는 의미를 가지고 있다.

● 다음 우리말과 일치하도록 빈칸에 알맞은 말을 쓰시오.

Listen & Speak 1 A

1. **B:** Sandy, you can _____ _____ many _____ of music in this _____ _____.

   G: That's _____, Bob. Can I listen to _____ music?

   B: _____. Do you like classical music?

   G: Yes, Beethoven is _____ _____ _____ _____ _____. How about you?

   B: I like pop music _____ _____ classical music.

   G: I see. _____ _____ _____ _____ most about pop music?

   B: I'm really _____ by its _____ rhythms.

2. **G:** Jim, did you _____ your art homework?

   B: Yes. I _____ the face of my role model on a _____.

   G: _____ _____. Who is your role model?

   B: My dad. He always gives me good _____. Who did you draw, Amy?

   G: Well, I drew _____ _____ in the sea.

   B: Wonderful! I'm _____ _____ your drawing.

   G: Thank you.

Listen & Speak 2 A

1. **B:** _____ _____ _____ _____ I watched a _____, *A Love Story in the War.*

   G: Oh, _____ _____ _____ _____ _____ the play?

   B: I liked the _____ _____. The actors' _____ were _____.

   G: Was the story good _____ _____?

   B: No. It was _____ _____ _____, but the music was pretty good.

   G: So, do you think I _____ _____ it?

   B: _____ _____ you have _____ _____ _____ time and money.

해석

1. B: Sandy, 너는 이 음악 도서관에서 많은 종류의 음악을 들을 수 있어.
   G: 그거 멋지다, Bob. 클래식 음악도 들을 수 있어?
   B: 물론이지. 너 클래식 음악 좋아하니?
   G: 응. 베토벤이 내가 가장 좋아하는 음악가 중의 하나야. 너는 어때?
   B: 나는 클래식보다는 대중음악이 더 좋아.
   G: 그렇구나. 너는 대중음악의 어떤 점이 가장 마음에 들어?
   B: 나는 대중음악의 신나는 리듬이 정말 좋아.

2. G: Jim, 미술 숙제 다 끝냈어?
   B: 응. 나는 접시에 나의 롤 모델을 그렸어.
   G: 그거 흥미롭구나. 너의 롤 모델은 누구야?
   B: 우리 아빠야. 아빠는 나에게 항상 좋은 조언을 해 주셔. 너는 누구를 그렸어, Amy?
   G: 음, 나는 내가 바다에서 서핑하는 것을 그렸어.
   B: 멋지다! 나는 네 그림에 푹 빠졌어.
   G: 고마워.

1. B: 며칠 전에 '전쟁 속의 사랑 이야기'라는 연극을 봤어.
   G: 오, 그 연극 어땠어?
   B: 주인공들이 좋았어. 배우들의 연기가 끝내줬거든.
   G: 이야기도 좋았어?
   B: 아니. 이야기는 조금 지루했는데, 음악은 꽤 괜찮았어.
   G: 그럼, 너는 내가 그 연극을 보러 가야 한다고 생각하니?
   B: 네가 돈과 시간이 많을 경우에만.

2. B: Caire, _____ _____ _____ your art class?

   G: It's great. I learn _____ _____ in the class.

   B: _____ _____ _____ _____ about it?

   G: I enjoy _____ _____ _____ _____. _____ about you, Allen?

   B: I also like the class. I learn good _____ _____. I love painting _____ many colors.

   G: Oh, I saw your _____ last time. I thought it was very _____.

   B: Thanks. I _____ _____ _____.

Real Life Talk

Bora: Andy, you went to the art museum, _____ _____?

Andy: Yes. They had a _____ Chagall exhibition.

Bora: _____ _____ _____ _____ it?

Andy: It was _____! I _____ _____ _____ the colors in his paintings and his _____.

Bora: _____ _____. He was _____ _____ _____ _____ ever. _____ _____ did you see in the museum?

Andy: I went to _____ _____ _____ and saw things like umbrellas, cups, and backpacks. Famous works of art _____ _____ on them.

Bora: Did you buy _____?

Andy: Yes. I bought this T-shirt. _____ _____ _____ it?

Bora: It _____ _____ you.

Andy: Thank you.

Wrap Up 1

B: Cindy, you went to the music _____, _____ you?

G: Yes. A lot of famous musicians _____ there.

B: _____ _____ _____ _____ the festival?

G: It was fantastic! I really liked the _____ _____. Do you know the band _____ *the Brothers*?

B: Oh, I've _____ about them. The singer is famous.

G: Yes. His _____ was great.

B: _____ _____.

해석

2. B: Claire, 미술 수업 어때?
   G: 훌륭해. 나는 그 수업에서 많은 것을 배워.
   B: 배우는 것 중에 어떤 것이 가장 좋아?
   G: 다양한 그림 기술 배우는 것이 재미있어. 너는 어때, Allen?
   B: 나도 미술 수업이 좋아. 괜찮은 색칠하기 기술들을 배우잖아. 나는 다양한 색깔을 사용해서 그림 그리는 것이 정말 좋아.
   G: 오, 지난번에 네 작품을 봤어. 나는 그게 굉장히 창의적이라고 생각했어.
   B: 고마워. 연습을 많이 했거든.

보라: Andy야, 너 미술관에 갔었지, 그렇지 않니?
Andy: 응. 샤갈 특별 전시회가 있었어.
보라: 그거 어땠니?
Andy: 멋졌어! 나는 그의 그림에 쓰인 색깔과 그의 창의성에 매료됐어.
보라: 당연해. 그는 가장 위대한 화가 중 한 명이었잖아. 너는 미술관에서 또 무엇을 봤니?
Andy: 기념품점에 갔었는데 우산, 컵, 가방 같은 것들을 봤어. 유명 예술 작품들이 그것들에 그려져 있었어.
보라: 구입한 게 있니?
Andy: 응. 나 이 티셔츠 샀어. 어때?
보라: 네게 잘 어울린다.
Andy: 고마워.

B: Cindy, 너 음악 축제에 갔었지, 그렇지 않니?
G: 응. 많은 유명 가수들이 거기서 공연을 했어.
B: 그 축제는 어땠어?
G: 아주 환상적이었어. 나는 특별 손님이 정말 좋았어. 너 '더 브라더스'라고 불리는 밴드를 아니?
B: 오, 들어본 적이 있어. 가수가 유명하잖아.
G: 맞아. 그의 공연은 굉장했어.
B: 놀랄 일도 아니지.

01 우리말에 맞도록 주어진 단어들을 이용하여 문장의 빈칸에 알맞은 말을 쓰시오.

> 이 재킷 어때? (how, do)

➡ _____ this jacket?

02 다음 대화의 빈칸에 들어갈 말로 알맞지 <u>않은</u> 것은?

> A: What movie do you like?
> B: I like *World Z*.
> A: Why do you like it?
> B: _____ its characters.

① I'm fascinated by   ② I'm into
③ I'm interested in   ④ I'm very satisfied
⑤ I have an interest in

03 다음 대화의 빈칸에 들어갈 말로 알맞은 표현은?

> B: Cindy, you went to the music festival, didn't you?
> G: Yes. A lot of famous musicians performed there.
> B: _____
> G: It was fantastic! I really liked the special guest.

① What about you?
② Which do you prefer, the music festival or the Chagall exhibition?
③ How did you like the festival?
④ Who is the special guest?
⑤ How do you like this song?

04 다음 대화의 밑줄 친 말의 의도로 알맞은 것은?

> A: <u>How do you like these shoes?</u>
> B: I like them. They are colorful.

① 권유하기   ② 만족이나 불만족에 대해 묻기
③ 관심 표현하기   ④ 제안하기
⑤ 안부 묻기

[01~02] 다음 대화를 읽고 물음에 답하시오.

Bora: Andy, you went to the art museum, didn't you?

Andy: Yes. They had a special Chagall exhibition.

Bora: (A)_____

Andy: It was fantastic! I was fascinated by the colors in his paintings and his creativity.

Bora: No wonder. He was one of the greatest painters ever. What else did you see in the museum?

Andy: I went to a gift shop and saw things like umbrellas, cups, and backpacks. Famous works of art were printed on them.

Bora: Did you buy anything?

Andy: Yes. I bought this T-shirt. How do you like it?

Bora: It looks great on you.

Andy: Thank you.

01 위 대화의 빈칸 (A)에 들어갈 말로 알맞은 것을 <u>모두</u> 고르시오.

① What are you interested in?

② Were you satisfied with it?

③ Why did you like it?

④ How did you like it?

⑤ Do you mind going to the art museum with me?

 위 대화의 내용과 일치하지 <u>않는</u> 것은?

① Andy went to the art museum with Bora.

② Andy was fascinated by the colors in Chagall's paintings and his creativity.

③ Andy bought a T-shirt at a gift shop.

④ Famous works of art were printed on things.

⑤ Chagall was one of the greatest painters ever.

 다음 대화의 (A)~(D)를 알맞은 순서로 배열한 것은?

B: The other day I watched a play, *A Love Story in the War*.

(A) Was the story good as well?

(B) No. It was a little boring, but the music was pretty good.

(C) Oh, how did you like the play?

(D) I liked the main characters. The actors' performances were fantastic.

G: So, do you think I should see it?

B: Only if you have a lot of time and money.

① (A) – (C) – (B) – (D)

② (B) – (A) – (D) – (C)

③ (C) – (B) – (A) – (D)

④ (C) – (D) – (A) – (B)

⑤ (D) – (C) – (A) – (B)

04 다음 대화의 빈칸에 들어갈 말로 가장 알맞은 것은?

A: How do you like this song?

B: I love it. It sounds exciting.

A: Yes, but I prefer this one, *The Phantom of the Opera*. _____

B: I like it, too.

① I'm fascinated by your drawing.

② I'm fascinated by its rhythms and melody.

③ Are you happy with this T-shirt?

④ I liked the story of the movie.

⑤ I'm interested in its special effects.

[05~06] 다음 대화를 읽고 물음에 답하시오.

B: Sandy, you can listen to many (a)kinds of music in this music library.

G: That's cool, Bob. Can I listen to classical music?

B: Sure. Do you like classical music?

G: Yes, Beethoven is one of my favorite (b) musician. How about you?

B: I like pop music (c)more than classical music.

G: I see. What do you like most about pop music?

B: I'm really (d)fascinated by its (e)exciting rhythms.

서답형

05 위 대화를 읽고 다음 물음에 영어로 답하시오.

Q: What kind of music does Sandy like? (4 단어로 답하시오.)

➡ _____

06 위 대화의 밑줄 친 (a)~(e) 중 어법상 어색한 것은?

① (a) ② (b) ③ (c) ④ (d) ⑤ (e)

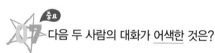

07 다음 두 사람의 대화가 어색한 것은?

① A: Why do you like the play?
   B: I'm fascinated by its characters.

② A: How do you like this song?
   B: I love it. It sounds exciting.

③ A: What do you want to make with these paper cups?
   B: I think we can make one of the world-famous bridges using paper cups.

④ A: How did you like the festival?
   B: Oh, I've heard about it. The singer is famous.

⑤ A: I bought this pencil case yesterday. How do you like it?
   B: It looks great. I like it.

[08~09] 다음 대화를 읽고 물음에 답하시오.

B: Claire, (A) _____

G: It's great. I learn a lot in the class.

B: What do you like most about it?

G: I enjoy learning different drawing skills. What about you, Allen?

B: I also like the class. I learn good painting skills. I love painting with many colors.

G: Oh, I saw your work last time. I thought it was very creative.

B: Thanks. I practice a lot.

서답형

08 위 대화의 빈칸 (A)에 알맞은 말을 주어진 〈조건〉에 맞게 쓰시오. (단어 하나를 추가할 것.)

조건

• 어떤 것에 대해 만족하는지 아니면 불만족하는지 묻는 표현을 쓸 것.

• you / like / your / do / ? / art class

➡ _____

서답형

09 위 대화를 읽고 다음 물음에 영어로 답하시오.

Q: What did Claire think about Allen's work?

➡ _____

서답형

10 다음 글의 빈칸에 들어갈 말을 주어진 〈조건〉에 맞게 영작하시오.

Our group liked the umbrella designed by Jinsu. He used the painting, *On White II*. We _____ its design. How do you like this umbrella?

조건

• 관심을 표현하는 문장을 쓸 것.

• fascinate를 활용할 것.

• 시제 일치를 맞출 것.

01 다음 대화를 읽고 밑줄 친 (A)를 구체적인 단어로 바꾸어 질문에 영어로 답하시오.

> G: Jim, did you finish your art homework?
> B: Yes. I drew the face of (A)my role model on a plate.
> G: Sounds interesting. Who is your role model?
> B: My dad. He always gives me good advice. Who did you draw, Amy?
> G: Well, I drew myself surfing in the sea.
> B: Wonderful! I'm fascinated by your drawing.
> G: Thank you.

> Q: What did Jim draw for his art homework?

➡ _____

[02~03] 다음 대화를 읽고 물음에 답하시오.

> Bora: Andy, you went to the art museum, didn't you?
> Andy: Yes. They had a special Chagall exhibition.
> Bora: (A)_____
> Andy: It was fantastic! I was fascinated by the colors in his paintings and his creativity.
> Bora: No wonder. He was one of the greatest painters ever. What else did you see in the museum?
> Andy: I went to a gift shop and saw things like umbrellas, cups, and backpacks. Famous works of art were printed on them.
> Bora: Did you buy anything?
> Andy: Yes. I bought this T-shirt. How do you like it?
> Bora: It looks great on you.

02 위 대화의 빈칸 (A)에 알맞은 말을 주어진 〈조건〉에 맞게 영어로 쓰시오.

> ┤ 조건 ├
> 'how'와 대명사 'it'을 사용할 것

➡ _____

03 위 대화를 읽고 다음 질문에 대한 답을 본문에 있는 문장을 그대로 사용하여 3 단어로 쓰시오.

> Q: How did Andy like the Chagall exhibition?

➡ _____

[04~05] 다음 대화를 읽고 물음에 답하시오.

> B: The other day I watched a play, A Love Story in the War.
> G: Oh, how did you like the play?
> B: I liked the main characters. The actors' performances were fantastic.
> G: Was the story good as well?
> B: No. It was a little boring, but the music was pretty good.
> G: So, do you think I should see it?
> B: 네가 돈과 시간이 많을 경우에만. (only / a lot of)

04 위 대화의 밑줄 친 우리말에 맞게 주어진 단어를 이용하여 쓰시오.

➡ _____

05 다음 질문에 영어로 답하시오.

> Q: What is the title of the play the boy watched?

➡ _____

Grammar

1 분사구문

> • **Using** common images, pop art looks plain. 흔한 이미지를 사용하기 때문에 팝 아트는 평범해 보인다.
> • I did my math homework, **listening** to classical music. 나는 클래식 음악을 들으며, 수학 숙제를 했다.

■ 분사구문은 종속접속사가 이끄는 부사절을 분사를 이용하여 간략한 부사구로 바꾼 것이다.

- **When I arrived** home, I saw my sister crying.
  = **Arriving** home, I saw my sister crying. 집에 도착했을 때, 나는 내 여동생이 울고 있는 것을 보았다.

■ 부사구와 주절의 관계에 따라 양보, 동시동작, 이유, 시간, 조건 등의 의미로 쓰인다.

(1) 양보: **Although he is** short, the player always scored best in the game.
  = **Being** short, the player always scored best in the game. 키가 작지만, 그 선수는 항상 경기에서 최고 득점을 했다.

(2) 동시동작(부대상황): **While she ate** her sandwich, she walked to work.
  = **Eating** her sandwich, she walked to work. 샌드위치를 먹으며, 그녀는 직장으로 걸었다.

(3) 이유: **Because I felt** satisfied with the machine, I ordered another one online.
  = **Feeling** satisfied with the machine, I ordered another one online. 그 기계에 만족해서, 나는 인터넷으로 또 한 대를 주문했다.

(4) 시간: **When she cleans** the room, she uses the special tools.
  = **Cleaning** the room, she uses the special tools. 청소할 때, 그녀는 특별 도구를 쓴다.

(5) 조건: **If you turn** left, you'll see the city hall.
  = **Turning** left, you'll see the city hall. 좌회전하면, 시청이 보일 것이다.

■ 종속절의 시제가 주절보다 앞선 경우, 완료분사구문을 사용한다.

- **As she had watched** the film before, Susan knew the complex relationships.
  = **Having watched** the film before, (그 영화를 전에 봤기 때문에 Susan은 그 복잡한 관계를 알았다.)

■ 주절과 종속절의 주어가 다를 경우, 분사구문의 주어를 남겨 두는 것을 독립분사구문이라고 하며, 일반인이 주어일 경우에는 생략이 가능하다. (비인칭 독립분사구문)

(1) 독립분사구문: **Since it is rainy**, we can't play baseball.
  = **It being** rainy, we can't play baseball. 비가 와서, 우리는 야구를 할 수 없다.

(2) 비인칭 독립분사구문: **generally speaking**(일반적으로 말해), **considering** ~(~를 고려하면)

(3) with+목적어+분사: The dog fell asleep **with its eyes closed**. (그 개는 눈을 감은 채로 잠이 들어 있었다.)

핵심 Check

1. 괄호 안에서 알맞은 말을 고르시오.

(1) (Feeling / Felt) tired, the old man took a rest under the tree.

(2) It (is / being) so snowy, the road got blocked with snow.

② be동사+worth+동명사

- Pop art **is worth paying** attention to. 팝 아트는 주목할 가치가 있다.
- Books about world history **are worth reading**. 세계사에 관한 책은 읽을 가치가 있다.

■ 'be동사+worth+동명사'는 동명사의 관용 표현으로 '~할 가치가 있다'는 뜻이다.

- The East Sea **is worth going** to. 동해는 가 볼 만한 가치가 있다.

■ worth의 의미

(1) 명사: '가치'

- You don't know the true **worth** of the book. 너는 그 책의 진정한 가치를 모른다.

(2) 형용사: '가치 있는, ~의 가치가 있는' (= worthy of)

- These books are **worth** 1,000 dollars. 이 책들은 1,000달러의 가치가 있다.
- These books are **worth** buying. 이 책들은 구매할 가치가 있다. 〈동명사 목적어〉

■ 의미는 '수동'이지만, '능동' 동명사를 쓴다.

- The book **is worth** [**reading** / being read(✗)]. 그 책은 읽을 가치가 있다.
- The project **was worth** [**working** / being worked(✗)] on. 그 프로젝트는 진행할 가치가 있었다.
- The movie **is worth watching**. 그 영화는 볼 만한 가치가 있다.

   = **It** is **worth watching** the movie. → 동명사만 가능(능동)

   = The movie is **worthy of watching[being watched]**. → 동명사만 (수동형이 일반적)

   = The movie is **worthy to watch[to be watched]**. → to부정사 (to be p.p.가 자주 쓰임)

   = It is **worthwhile[worth while] watching[to watch]** the movie. → 둘 다 가능

   = It is **worth your while to watch** the movie. → to부정사만 가능(능동형만)

■ 그밖의 동명사의 관용적 표현들

(1) can't help V-ing = can't but V '~하지 않을 수 없다'

- I **couldn't help laughing** when I saw him. 그를 봤을 때, 웃지 않을 수 없었다.

(2) spend 시간/돈 V-ing '~하느라 시간/돈을 쓰다'

- He **spent her whole weekend watching** dramas. 그는 드라마를 보느라 주말을 다 썼다.

(3) be busy V-ing '~하느라 바쁘다'

- The teacher **is busy checking** my homework. 선생님은 내 숙제 검사를 하시느라 바쁘다.

(4) feel like V-ing = feel inclined to V '~하고 싶다'

- She **felt like eating** pizza. 그녀는 피자를 먹고 싶었다.

(5) There is no V-ing = It is impossible to V '~하는 것은 불가능하다'

- **There is no knowing** what will happen tomorrow. 내일 무슨 일이 일어날지 알 수 없다.

(6) It is no use V-ing = It is useless[of no use] to V '~하는 것은 소용없다'

- **It is no use waiting** for her there. 거기에서 그녀를 기다려 봐야 소용없다.

핵심 Check

2. 괄호 안에서 알맞은 말을 고르시오.

   (1) The fish were worth (catching / being catched).

   (2) It is worth (to read / reading) the science paper.

01 다음 부사절을 분사구문으로 바꿔 쓸 때, 빈칸에 들어갈 말로 가장 적절한 것은?

> When Tom arrived home, he saw his sister reading a book.
> → _____ home, Tom saw his sister reading a book.

① As Tom arriving
② Tom arriving
③ Being arrived
④ Being arriving
⑤ Arriving

02 다음 우리말을 바르게 영작한 것을 고르시오.

> 샌프란시스코는 두 번 방문할 가치가 있었다.

① San Francisco was worthwhile visited twice.
② San Francisco was worth to be visited twice.
③ San Francisco was worth to visit twice.
④ San Francisco was worth visiting twice.
⑤ It was worth to visiting San Francisco twice.

03 다음 두 문장을 한 문장으로 바르게 연결한 것을 고르시오.

> • Billy watched the emotional scenes.
> • She was moved.

① Watched the emotional scenes, Billy was moved.
② Watching the emotional scenes, Billy was moved.
③ Being watched the emotional scenes, Billy was moved.
④ While she watching the emotional scenes, Billy was moved.
⑤ Though watching the emotional scenes, Billy was moved.

04 다음 괄호 속 동사의 알맞은 형태를 빈칸에 써 넣으시오.

(1) The project was worth _____(work) on because I could experience many things.

(2) Pop art is worth _____. (pay attention to)

(3) It is no use _____(cry) over poor grades.

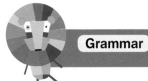
[01~02] 다음 중 어법상 알맞은 문장을 고르시오.

01
① Pop artists and their works are worth to be paid attention.
② Pop artists and their works have worth paying attention to.
③ Pop artists and their works are worthy being paid attention to.
④ Pop artists and their works are worth being paid attention to.
⑤ Pop artists and their works are worth paying attention to.

02
① I couldn't help falling in love with the beautiful song.
② I couldn't but falling in love with the beautiful song.
③ I couldn't help but falling in love with the beautiful song.
④ I couldn't but help falling in love with the beautiful song.
⑤ I couldn't help to falling in love with the beautiful song.

[03~04] 다음 주어진 우리말을 알맞게 영작한 것을 고르시오.

03
> 미술 전시회에서 친숙한 이미지들을 봤을 때 사람들은 그것들이 신선하다는 걸 알게 되었다.

① Seen familiar images in art exhibitions, people found them refreshing.
② Seeing familiar images in art exhibitions, people found them refreshing.
③ Being seen familiar images in art exhibitions, people found them refreshing.
④ When people seeing familiar images in art exhibitions, they found them refreshing.
⑤ Having seen familiar images in art exhibitions, people found them refreshing.

04
> 팝 아트가 평범해 보일지라도, 그것은 의미로 가득 차 있다.

① Pop art looking plain, it is filled with meaning.
② Being looked plain, pop art is filled with meaning.
③ Although pop art looking plain, it is filled with meaning.
④ Although looking plain, pop art is filled with meaning.
⑤ Although looked plain, pop art is filled with meaning.

05 다음 빈칸에 공통으로 들어갈 알맞은 말을 고르시오.

> (1) Books about world history and culture development are _____ reading.
> (2) The house must be _____ at least half a million dollars.

① value   ② worth   ③ price
④ expensive   ⑤ cost

서답형

06 다음 문장에서 어법상 어색한 단어 한 개를 찾아서 고치시오.

> Changed common objects into amazing art, the pop artists are creating the works of art for everyone in the world.

➡ _____

07 다음 밑줄 친 단어의 성격이 나머지 넷과 다른 하나를 고르시오.

① Those books written by the author are not worth knowing.
② There is no knowing what our lives in the future would be like.
③ Brian gave up the plan, knowing his friends were not going to join it.
④ We can't help knowing her since few Koreans live around here.
⑤ It was no use knowing that her problem came from anxiety

08 다음 밑줄 친 분사구문을 같은 의미의 부사절로 바꿔 쓸 때 적절하지 않은 것은?

① Making a lot of copies, Andy wanted to share arts with many people.
  → When he made a lot of copies,
② Playing drums, the member of the band sang the song.
  → While he was playing drums,
③ Using common objects, pop art looks plain.
  → Though they use common objects,
④ Taking a shower, Mr. Smith didn't receive the phone call.
  → As he was taking a shower,

⑤ Cartoons not being regarded as an art form, Roy Lichtenstein thought differently.
  → Though cartoons were not regarded as an art form,

09 다음 주어진 문장과 가장 가까운 의미의 문장으로 어법상 알맞은 것을 고르시오.

> It is worth seeing and collecting the works of many pop artists .

① The works of many pop artists are worth to see and collect.
② The works of many pop artists are worth being seen and collected.
③ The works of many pop artists are worth seeing and collecting.
④ The works of many pop artists are worth to be seen and collected.
⑤ The works of many pop artists are worth for seeing and collecting.

10 다음 중 밑줄 친 분사구문의 용법이 〈보기〉와 같은 것은?

> ┤ 보기 ├
> Looking a little plain and common, pop art is filled with a lot of meaning.

① Turning left at the next corner, you can face the shopping mall.
② Having lived in Madrid for 11 years, Angella still can't speak Spanish well.
③ Being honest, Jack is trusted by everyone.
④ Completing her team project, Alice went out to have some snacks.
⑤ Not knowing how rich David was, Railey was surprised at his luxury car.

[11~12] 우리말과 일치하도록 괄호 안에 주어진 단어들을 바르게 배열하되, 한 단어만 어법에 맞게 형태를 바꾸시오.

11

> 그 당시에, 만화는 예술의 형태로 간주되지 않았지만, Roy Lichtenstein은 다르게 생각했다.
> → (regard, cartoons, an art form, being, as, not, at that time), Roy Lichtenstein thought differently.

➡ _____

_____, Roy Lichtenstein thought differently.

12

> 모든 사람들이 그의 예술을 즐기기를 원해서, Oldenburg는 자신의 작품들을 옥외에 설치했다.
> → (everyone, to, his, want, art, enjoy), Oldenburg set up his works in outdoor places.

➡ _____,

Oldenburg set up his works in outdoor places.

[13~14] 다음 중 어법상 <u>어색한</u> 것을 고르시오.

13
① Pop art is worth paying attention.
② The city is worth visiting.
③ The idea was worth considering.
④ The works of pop artists were worth looking at.
⑤ The medicine was worth taking.

14
① Sean couldn't help falling in love with the girl he met yesterday.
② She felt like sleeping after swimming.
③ Mom spent all the money buying the jacket.
④ It is of no use crying over spilt milk.
⑤ Dad is busy preparing for the party.

[15~16] 다음의 같은 의미를 표현하는 문장들 중에서 어법 또는 의미상 <u>틀린</u> 것은?

15
① The bag made by the great craftsman is worth buying immediately.
② The bag made by the great craftsman is worthy of buying immediately.
③ The bag made by the great craftsman is worth to be bought immediately.
④ It is worth buying the bag immediately made by the great craftsman.
⑤ The bag made by the great craftsman is worth while buying immediately.

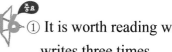

16
① It is worth reading what my favorite poet writes three times.
② It is worth while to read what my favorite poet writes three times.
③ What is written by my favorite poet is worth reading three times.
④ What my favorite poet writes is worth while to read three times.
⑤ My favorite poem is worth being read three times.

01 다음 문장의 괄호 안의 단어를 어법상 알맞은 형태로 바꿔 빈 칸에 쓰시오.

(1) A lot of small towns in the area are definitely worth _____(visit).

(2) It's worth _____(check) the details of the contract before you sign it.

(3) The film is worth _____(see).

(4) It's not worth _____(buy) a new phone as the one you have is just fine.

(5) Sammy couldn't help _____(laugh) at my face.

(6) Sammy couldn't but _____(laugh) at my face.

(7) Sammy couldn't help but _____ (laugh) when she saw my face.

(8) Sammy had no choice but _____ (laugh) when she saw my face.

(9) The cosmetic company spent 12 million dollars _____(advertise) its new product.

(10) There is no _____(know) what my teacher is thinking.

(11) It is impossible _____(know) what my teacher is thinking.

(12) The ants were busy _____(carry) food to their hill to store for the winter.

(13) It is of no use to _____(prepare) for the final exam.

(14) It is no use_____ (prepare) for the final exam.

02 다음 우리말과 일치하도록 괄호 안에 주어진 단어들을 바르게 배열하여 빈칸에 넣으시오.

(1) 평범한 사물을 놀라운 예술로 변모시킬 수 있게 되면서 팝 아티스트들은 예술에 대한 고정관념을 바꿔왔다. (turn, amazing, to, being, common, art, into, able, objects)

➡ _____

_____, pop artists have changed the stereotype of the art.

(2) 팝 아티스트들은 예술이 쉬워야 한다고 믿었기 때문에, 고급 예술과 대중문화 사이의 벽을 허물었다. (art, artists, that, should, believing, be, pop, broke, easy)

➡ _____

_____ the wall between high art and popular culture.

(3) 여기 주변에 남은 친구들이 없었기 때문에, 그 개는 외로움을 느꼈다. (friends, around, there, any, here, not, being, left)

➡ _____,

the dog felt lonely.

(4) 잡지와 상점에서 그의 주제를 찾으면서, Andy Warhol은 팝 아트 작품들을 만들었다. (magazines, stores, subjects, finding, in, his, and)

➡ _____,

Andy Warhol made a lot of pop art works.

03 다음 〈보기〉와 같이 각 문장의 밑줄 친 부분을 동명사로 바꿔서, 같은 의미를 표현할 수 있는 가장 짧은 형태의 문장을 영작하시오.

보기

It is worth <u>reading</u> this book.
→ The book is worth reading.

(1) Gloria's mom had no choice but <u>to drink</u> the sour beverage to save her.

➡ _____

_____

(2) It was worth while <u>to pay</u> for the expensive TV set.

➡ _____

(3) It was of no use <u>to fix</u> the ceiling unless the water problem is resolved.

➡ _____

_____

(4) Those men were busy because they were <u>preparing</u> for the awards ceremony.

➡ _____

_____

(5) It is worthwhile <u>to pay attention</u> to pop art.

➡ _____

04 다음 중 각 문장에서 어법상 어색한 단어를 한 개씩 찾아, 다른 한 단어로 고치거나 생략 또는 이동하여 옳은 문장으로 다시 쓰시오.

(1) As Andy Warhol wanting to show that art is something you see every day, he made many copies of his works.

➡ _____

_____

(2) Use daily images in a creative way, you can make a work of art for everyone.

➡ _____

_____

(3) When seen familiar images in art exhibitions, people found them refreshing.

➡ _____

_____

(4) Used common images and everyday items, pop art looks plain.

➡ _____

_____

(5) Because looking plain, pop art is filled with meaning that art should be easy to understand.

➡ _____

_____

_____

_____

(6) Wanting everyone to enjoy his art, a pop artist setting up his works in outdoor places.

➡ _____

_____

(7) Though cartoons being not regarded as an art form at that time, Roy Lichtenstein used them in making his works.

➡ _____

_____

_____

Reading

교과서

Pop Art: Art for Everyone

Welcome to the Pop Art Exhibition! What do you see? Paintings of soup cans? Big cartoons? Do they look like art works? Probably not, but think again. They are all famous works of pop art. Pop is short for popular. So pop art means popular art, or art for people. It began in the 1950s in America. Pop artists at that time wanted to create something fun and easy. Instead of difficult traditional art works, they turned their eyes to popular culture. They used images from TV, comic books, magazines, and advertising. When people saw familiar images in art exhibitions, they found them refreshing.

Since then, pop art has become truly popular. People thought that art was too difficult to understand. By using daily images and bright colors, pop artists changed that thought.

Using common images, pop art looks plain. In other words, it doesn't look artistic. But it is still worth paying attention to. Although it looks plain, it is filled with meaning. Let's learn about some famous pop artists. They became famous for their special artistic ability. They some famous pop artists were able to change common objects into amazing art.

Andy Warhol is called the King of Pop Art. He found his subjects in magazines and stores.

cartoon: 만화
pop art: 팝 아트
art work: 예술 작품
advertising: 광고
familiar: 친숙한
refreshing: 신선한, 참신한
turn one's eyes to: ~로 눈길을 돌리다
plain: 평범한
artistic: 예술적인
worth: ~의 가치가 있는
ability: 능력
object: 물건, 대상
in other words: 다시 말해서

 확인문제

● 다음 문장이 본문의 내용과 일치하면 T, 일치하지 않으면 F를 쓰시오.

1 Pop art is art for people. ☐

2 Pop artists want art to be fun and easy. ☐

3 People thought pop art was refreshing because of unfamiliar images. ☐

4 Andy Warhol went to stores to copy works of art. ☐

One of his famous works is made up of pictures of Marilyn Monroe,
_{one of 복수명사: 단수 취급}
the American actor. Another work shows cans of soup. He made many
_{Marilyn Monroe와 동격   another+단수명사}
copies of these works. Why did he make copies of his works? He

wanted to show that art is something you see every day.
_{명사절 접속사   something (that) you see ~ : 목적격 관계대명사 생략}

Claes Oldenburg is another pop artist who made art fun. He made
_{make+목적어+목적격보어(5형식)}
sculptures of everyday items, such as a hamburger, cookies, and a
_{~와 같은}
brush. In the beginning, he created soft sculptures. They were made of
_{soft sculptures 지칭}
plastic, paper, and other soft materials. For example, he used cloth to

make toilets. Later, he made huge sculptures of daily items, such as an
_{to부정사의 부사적 용법 중 목적(~하기 위해서)}
ice cream cone. Wanting everyone to enjoy his art, he set up his works
_{= As[Because] he wanted everyone to enjoy his art}
in outdoor places. He also ran a store inside his studio to sell his works.
_{to부정사의 부사적 용법 중 목적(~하기 위해서)}
For him, artistic works were fun goods for people.

Roy Lichtenstein used cartoons in his works. They were large and
_{cartoons 지칭}
painted in lively colors. He even included speech balloons in his
_{명사+ly: 형용사}
paintings. Back then, cartoons were not regarded as an art form.
_{be regarded as: ~로 여겨지다}
However, Roy Lichtenstein thought differently. He asked himself,
_{재귀대명사의 재귀적 용법}
'Why are they not?' Then Roy Lichtenstein broke down the wall

between high art and popular culture by adding cartoons to art.
_{by Ving: V함으로써}
Pop artists believed art should be easy. Anyone can create and enjoy
_{believed (that) ~: 명사절 접속사 that 생략}
art. How about creating a work of pop art today? By using daily images

in a creative way, you can make a work of art for everyone. This is the
_{'By using daily images in a creative way, you can make a work of art for everyone.'을 가리킴}
most important lesson from pop art.

be made up of: ~으로 구성되다
sculpture: 조각품
toilet: 변기, 화장실
cone: 원뿔, 원뿔형 물체
goods: 상품, 제품
set up: 설치하다
lively: 활기 넘치는, 생생한
speech balloon: 말풍선
break down: ~을 부수다

확인문제

● 다음 문장이 본문의 내용과 일치하면 T, 일치하지 <u>않으면</u> F를 쓰시오.

1   Marilyn Monroe's pictures were used as art works by Andy Warhol. ☐

2   Claes Oldenburg made toilets with clothes. ☐

3   Claes Oldenburg sold his works at a store inside his studio. ☐

4   Roy Lichtenstein set up the wall between hight art and popular culture. ☐

● 우리말을 참고하여 빈칸에 알맞은 말을 쓰시오.

Pop Art: Art for Everyone

1 _____ _____ the Pop Art Exhibition! _____ do you see? Paintings of soup cans? Big _____?

2 Do they _____ _____ art works? _____ not, but _____ again. They _____ all _____ _____ of pop art.

3 Pop _____ _____ _____ popular. So pop art means _____ _____, or art for people.

4 _____ _____ _____ the 1950s in America. Pop artists at that time _____ _____ create something fun and easy.

5 _____ _____ difficult _____ art works, they _____ their eyes _____ popular culture.

6 They _____ images _____ TV, comic books, magazines, and _____.

7 When people saw _____ _____ in art exhibitions, they found _____ _____.

8 Since then, pop art has _____ _____ _____.

9 People thought _____ art was _____ difficult _____ _____.

10 _____ _____ daily images and bright colors, pop artists _____ _____ _____.

11 _____ common images, pop art _____ _____. _____ _____ _____, it doesn't look _____.

12 But it is still _____ _____ _____ _____. Although it looks plain, it _____ _____ _____ meaning.

13 Let's learn about some _____ _____ _____.

14 They became _____ their special artistic _____. They were _____ _____ _____ common objects _____ _____ art.

15 Andy Warhol _____ _____ the King of Pop Art. He _____ his _____ _____ magazines and stores.

1 팝 아트 전시회에 온 것을 환영한다! 무엇이 보이는가? 수프 통조림들을 모아 놓은 그림? 커다란 만화 그림?

2 그것들이 예술 작품처럼 보이는가? 아마 그렇게 보이지 않겠지만, 다시 생각해 봐라. 그것들은 모두 유명한 팝 아트 작품들이다.

3 'pop'은 'popular(대중적인)'의 줄임말이다. 그래서 팝 아트는 대중 예술 또는 사람들을 위한 예술이라는 뜻이다.

4 팝 아트는 1950년대 미국에서 시작됐다. 그 당시 팝 아트 작가들은 재미있고 쉬운 것을 만들고 싶어 했다.

5 어려운 전통 예술 작품 대신 그들은 대중문화로 눈을 돌렸다.

6 그들은 텔레비전, 만화책, 잡지 및 광고에 나오는 이미지들을 사용했다.

7 미술 전시회에서 친숙한 이미지들을 봤을 때 사람들은 그것들이 신선하다는 걸 알게 되었다.

8 그때부터 팝 아트는 정말 유명해졌다.

9 사람들은 예술이 너무 어려워서 이해할 수 없는 것으로 생각했었다.

10 일상적인 이미지와 밝은 색을 씀으로써, 팝 아트 작가들은 그러한 관점을 바꿨다.

11 흔한 이미지를 사용하기 때문에 팝 아트는 평범해 보인다. 즉, 팝 아트는 예술적으로 보이지 않는다.

12 하지만 여전히 주목할 만한 가치가 있다. 평범해 보일지라도 그것은 의미로 가득 차 있다.

13 몇 명의 유명한 팝 아트 작가들에 대해 알아보자.

14 그들은 특별한 예술적인 능력으로 유명해졌다. 그들은 흔한 대상을 놀라운 예술로 바꿀 수 있었다.

15 Andy Warhol은 팝 아트의 왕이라 불린다. 그는 잡지와 상점에서 주제를 찾았다.

16 One of his famous works _____ _____ _____ of pictures of Marilyn Monroe, the American actor.

17 _____ _____ _____ cans of soup. He _____ many _____ of these works.

18 Why did he make _____ _____ _____ _____ _____? He wanted _____ _____ _____ art is something _____ _____ every day.

19 Claes Oldenburg is _____ pop artist _____ _____ art _____.

20 He made _____ _____ _____ _____ _____, such as a hamburger, cookies, and a brush.

21 _____ _____ _____, he _____ soft sculptures. They were _____ _____ plastic, paper, and other _____ _____.

22 _____, he used _____ _____ _____ toilets. Later, he made _____ _____ of daily items, _____ _____ an ice cream cone.

23 _____ everyone _____ _____ his art, he _____ his works in _____ places.

24 He also _____ a store _____ his studio _____ _____ his works. For him, artistic works _____ _____ for people.

25 Roy Lichtenstein _____ cartoons _____ _____ _____. They _____ large and _____ in _____ _____.

26 He even _____ speech balloons in his paintings. Back then, cartoons _____ not _____ _____ an art form.

27 _____, Roy Lichtenstein thought _____. He asked _____, '_____ are _____ _____?'

28 Then Roy Lichtenstein _____ _____ the wall _____ high art _____ popular culture _____ _____ cartoons to art.

29 Pop artists _____ art _____ _____ easy. _____ can _____ and _____ art.

30 How about _____ a work of _____ _____ today?

31 _____ _____ daily images _____ a creative way, you can _____ a work of art _____ everyone. This is _____ _____ _____ from pop art.

16 그의 유명 작품들 중 하나는 미국 배우인 Marilyn Monroe의 사진으로 구성되어 있다.

17 또 다른 작품은 수프 통조림들을 보여준다. 그는 이 작품들의 사본을 많이 만들었다.

18 그는 왜 작품의 복사본을 만들었나? 그는 예술은 여러분이 매일 보는 것임을 보여 주고 싶어 했다.

19 Claes Oldenburg는 예술을 재미있게 만들었던 또 다른 팝 아트 작가이다.

20 그는 햄버거와 쿠키, 붓 같은 일상적인 물품들의 조각품을 만들었다.

21 초기에 그는 부드러운 조각품을 만들었다. 그것들은 플라스틱, 종이, 그리고 다른 부드러운 재료들로 만들어졌다.

22 예를 들어서 그는 변기를 만들기 위해 천을 사용했다. 나중에 그는 아이스크림콘 같은 일상 물품의 거대한 조각품을 만들었다.

23 그는 모든 사람이 그의 작품을 보고 즐기기를 원했기 때문에 그의 작품들을 실외에 설치했다.

24 그는 작품 판매를 위해 그의 작업실 안에 상점을 운영하기도 했다. 그에게 예술적인 작품들은 사람들을 위한 재미있는 제품이었다.

25 Roy Lichtenstein은 그의 작품에 만화를 사용했다. 그것들은 크고 생기 넘치는 색들로 그려졌다.

26 그는 심지어 그의 작품에 말풍선을 넣었다. 그 당시에 만화는 예술 형식으로 여겨지지 않았다.

27 하지만 Roy Lichtenstein은 다르게 생각했다. 그는 스스로에게 '왜 만화는 예술로 간주되지 않을까?'라고 물었다.

28 만화를 예술에 첨가함으로써 Roy Lichtenstein은 순수 예술과 대중문화 사이의 벽을 허물었다.

29 팝 아트 작가들은 예술은 쉬워야 한다고 믿었다. 누구나 예술을 만들 수 있고, 즐길 수 있다.

30 오늘 팝 아트 작품 하나를 만들어 보는 것은 어떤가?

31 일상적인 이미지를 창의적인 방식으로 사용함으로써, 모든 사람을 위한 예술 작품을 만들 수 있다. 이것이 팝 아트의 가장 중요한 교훈이다.

● 우리말을 참고하여 본문을 영작하시오.

Pop Art: Art for Everyone

1 팝 아트 전시회에 온 것을 환영한다! 무엇이 보이는가? 수프 통조림들을 모아 놓은 그림? 커다란 만화 그림?

➡ _____

2 그것들이 예술 작품처럼 보이는가? 아마 그렇게 보이지 않겠지만, 다시 생각해 봐라. 그것들은 모두 유명한 팝 아트 작품들이다.

➡ _____

3 'pop'은 'popular(대중적인)'의 줄임말이다. 그래서 팝 아트는 대중 예술 또는 사람들을 위한 예술이라는 뜻이다.

➡ _____

4 팝 아트는 1950년대 미국에서 시작됐다. 그 당시 팝 아트 작가들은 재미있고 쉬운 것을 만들고 싶어 했다.

➡ _____

5 어려운 전통 예술 작품 대신 그들은 대중문화로 눈을 돌렸다.

➡ _____

6 그들은 텔레비전, 만화책, 잡지 및 광고에 나오는 이미지들을 사용했다.

➡ _____

7 미술 전시회에서 친숙한 이미지들을 봤을 때 사람들은 그것들이 신선하다는 걸 알게 되었다.

➡ _____

8 그때부터 팝 아트는 정말 유명해졌다.

➡ _____

9 사람들은 예술이 너무 어려워서 이해할 수 없는 것으로 생각했었다.

➡ _____

10 일상적인 이미지와 밝은 색을 씀으로써, 팝 아트 작가들은 그러한 관점을 바꿨다.

➡ _____

11 흔한 이미지를 사용하기 때문에 팝 아트는 평범해 보인다. 즉, 팝 아트는 예술적으로 보이지 않는다.

➡ _____

12 하지만 여전히 주목할 만한 가치가 있다. 평범해 보일지라도 그것은 의미로 가득 차 있다.

➡ _____

13 몇 명의 유명한 팝 아트 작가들에 대해 알아보자.

➡ _____

14 그들은 특별한 예술적인 능력으로 유명해졌다. 그들은 흔한 대상을 놀라운 예술로 바꿀 수 있었다.

➡ _____

_____

15 Andy Warhol은 팝 아트의 왕이라 불린다. 그는 잡지와 상점에서 주제를 찾았다.

➡ _____

16 그의 유명 작품들 중 하나는 미국 배우인 Marilyn Monroe의 사진으로 구성되어 있다.

➡ _____

17 또 다른 작품은 수프 통조림들을 보여준다. 그는 이 작품들의 사본을 많이 만들었다.

➡ _____

18 그는 왜 작품의 복사본을 만들었나? 그는 예술은 여러분이 매일 보는 것임을 보여 주고 싶어 했다.

➡ _____

19 Claes Oldenburg는 예술을 재미있게 만들었던 또 다른 팝 아트 작가이다.

➡ _____

20 그는 햄버거와 쿠키, 붓 같은 일상적인 물품들의 조각품을 만들었다.

➡ _____

21 초기에 그는 부드러운 조각품을 만들었다. 그것들은 플라스틱, 종이, 그리고 다른 부드러운 재료들로 만들어졌다.

➡ _____

_____

22 예를 들어서 그는 변기를 만들기 위해 천을 사용했다. 나중에 그는 아이스크림콘 같은 일상 물품의
거대한 조각품을 만들었다.

➡ _____

_____

23 그는 모든 사람이 그의 작품을 보고 즐기기를 원했기 때문에 그의 작품들을 실외에 설치했다.

➡ _____

24 그는 작품 판매를 위해 그의 작업실 안에 상점을 운영하기도 했다. 그에게 예술적인 작품들은 사람들을 위
한 재미있는 제품이었다.

➡ _____

_____

25 Roy Lichtenstein은 그의 작품에 만화를 사용했다. 그것들은 크고 생기 넘치는 색들로 그려졌다.

➡ _____

26 그는 심지어 그의 작품에 말풍선을 넣었다. 그 당시에 만화는 예술 형식으로 여겨지지 않았다.

➡ _____

_____

27 하지만 Roy Lichtenstein은 다르게 생각했다. 그는 스스로에게 '왜 만화는 예술로 간주되지 않을까?'라고 물
었다.

➡ _____

28 만화를 예술에 첨가함으로써 Roy Lichtenstein은 순수 예술과 대중문화 사이의 벽을 허물었다.

➡ _____

_____

29 팝 아트 작가들은 예술은 쉬워야 한다고 믿었다. 누구나 예술을 만들 수 있고, 즐길 수 있다.

➡ _____

30 오늘 팝 아트 작품 하나를 만들어 보는 것은 어떤가?

➡ _____

31 일상적인 이미지를 창의적인 방식으로 사용함으로써, 모든 사람을 위한 예술 작품을 만들 수 있다. 이것이
팝 아트의 가장 중요한 교훈이다.

➡ _____

_____

[01~03] 다음 글을 읽고 물음에 답하시오.

Welcome to the Pop Art Exhibition! What do you see? Paintings of soup cans? Big cartoons? Do they look like art works? Probably not, but think again. They are all famous works of pop art.

Pop is short for popular. So pop art means popular art, or art for people. It began in the 1950s in America. Pop artists at that time wanted to create something fun and easy. Instead of difficult traditional art works, they turned their eyes to popular culture. They used images from TV, comic books, magazines, and advertising. When people saw familiar images in art exhibitions, they found them refreshing. Since then, pop art has become truly popular. People thought that art was too difficult to understand. By using daily images and bright colors, pop artists changed that thought.

서답형
01 다음과 같이 풀이되는 말을 위 글에서 찾아 쓰시오.

a humorous drawing or series of drawings in a newspaper or magazine.

➡ _____

서답형
02 What images did pop artists use? Answer in English.

➡ _____
_____

중요
03 위 글을 읽고 답할 수 있는 것은?

① Who is the most famous pop artist?
② How many pop artists are there?
③ What did people think about art?
④ Why didn't pop artists use dark colors?
⑤ How many art exhibitions were held?

[04~06] 다음 글을 읽고 물음에 답하시오.

Using common images, pop art looks plain. In other words, it doesn't look artistic. But it is still worth paying attention to. Although it looks plain, it is filled with meaning. Let's learn about some famous pop artists. They became famous for their special artistic ability. They were able to change common objects into amazing art.

Andy Warhol is called the King of Pop Art. ① He found his subjects in magazines and stores. ② One of his famous works is made up of pictures of Marilyn Monroe, the American actor. ③ Another work shows cans of soup. ④ Why did he make copies of his works? ⑤ He wanted to show that art is something you see every day.

04 ①~⑤ 중 주어진 문장이 들어가기에 가장 적절한 곳은?

He made many copies of these works.

①   ②   ③   ④   ⑤

서답형
05 What is Andy Warhol called? Answer in English with a full sentence.

➡ _____

중요
06 위 글의 내용과 일치하는 것은?

① Pop art looks very special.
② Pop artists used uncommon images.
③ Pop art doesn't have any special meanings.
④ It is worth paying attention to works of pop artists.
⑤ Andy Warhol used to cooperate with Marilyn Monroe who was also an artist.

[07~09] 다음 글을 읽고 물음에 답하시오.

Claes Oldenburg is another pop artist who made art fun. He made sculptures of everyday items, such as a hamburger, cookies, and a brush. In the beginning, he created soft sculptures. They were made of plastic, paper, and other soft materials. (A)_____, he used cloth to make toilets. Later, he made huge sculptures of daily items, such as an ice cream cone. Wanting everyone to enjoy his art, he set up his works in outdoor places. He also ran a store inside his studio to sell his works. For him, artistic works were fun goods for people.

07 다음 중 빈칸 (A)에 들어갈 말로 가장 적절한 것은?

① On the other hand ② For example

③ In other words ④ Nevertheless

⑤ However

서답형

08 What did Claes Oldenburg want everyone to do? Answer in English.

➡ _____

중요

09 다음 중 Claes Oldenburg의 작품에 해당할 수 있는 것은?

① a detailed portrait of a king

② an expensive dish made with silver

③ a sandwich made with soft material

④ a huge spaceship made of iron, and plastic

⑤ the smallest doll which can be seen with a microscope

[10~13] 다음 글을 읽고 물음에 답하시오.

Roy Lichtenstein used cartoons in his works. They were large and painted in lively colors.

[A] Then Roy Lichtenstein broke down the wall between high art and popular culture by adding cartoons to art.

[B] However, Roy Lichtenstein thought differently. He asked himself, 'Why are they not?'

[C] He even included speech balloons in his paintings. Back then, cartoons were not regarded ⓐ_____ an art form.

Pop artists believed art should be easy. Anyone can ⓑ_____. How about creating a work of pop art today? By using daily images in a creative way, you can make a work of art for everyone. This is the most important lesson from pop art.

서답형

10 자연스러운 글이 되도록 [A]~[C]를 바르게 나열하시오.

➡ _____

11 빈칸 ⓐ에 들어갈 말로 가장 적절한 것은?

① to ② in ③ as ④ for ⑤ at

중요

12 빈칸 ⓑ에 들어갈 말로 가장 적절한 것은?

① express their emotions

② create and enjoy art

③ appreciate and judge art

④ talk about how they feel

⑤ understand what an art means

서답형

13 According to the passage, what did pop artists believe? Answer in English.

➡ _____

[14~17] 다음 글을 읽고 물음에 답하시오.

Welcome to the Pop Art Exhibition! What do you see? Paintings of soup cans? Big cartoons? Do they look like art works? Probably not, but think again. They are all famous (A)works of pop art.

Pop is short for popular. So pop art means popular art, or art for people. It began in the 1950s in America. Pop artists at that time wanted to create something fun and easy. Instead of difficult traditional art works, they turned their eyes to popular culture. They used images from TV, comic books, magazines, and advertising. When people saw familiar images in art exhibitions, they found them refreshing. Since then, pop art has become truly popular. People thought that art was too difficult to understand. By using daily images and bright colors, pop artists changed that thought.

14 밑줄 친 (A)와 그 의미가 같은 것은?

① I can't work if I catch a cold.

② The phone doesn't work at all.

③ She has been out of work for a year.

④ I think this is Picasso's greatest work.

⑤ The pill the doctor gave me works.

15 다음 중 위 글의 내용과 일치하는 것은?

① Pop art means art for geniuses.

② Pop artist used images only from books.

③ People thought that pop art was too difficult to understand.

④ Pop artists focused on examining traditional art works.

⑤ Daily images were used by pop artists.

서답형
16 When did pop art begin? Answer in English with a full sentence.

➡ _____

17 다음 중 팝 아트의 특징으로 알맞은 것을 <u>모두</u> 고르시오.

① dark images   ② daily items

③ unique images   ④ bright colors

⑤ few people enjoying it

[18~20] 다음 글을 읽고 물음에 답하시오.

Using common images, pop art looks plain. In other words, it doesn't look ①artistic. But it is still worth paying attention to. Although it looks ②plain, it is filled with meaning. Let's learn about some famous pop artists. They became famous for their ③special artistic ability. They were able to change ④special objects into amazing art.

Andy Warhol is called the King of Pop Art. He found his subjects in magazines and stores. One of his famous works is made up of pictures of Marilyn Monroe, the American actor. Another work shows cans of soup. He made many copies of these works. Why did he make copies of his works? He wanted to show that art is something you see ⑤every day.

18 ①~⑤ 중 글의 흐름상 <u>어색한</u> 것은?

①   ②   ③   ④   ⑤

19 위 글의 내용을 바르게 이해한 사람은?

① A: Pop art looks really special.

② B: I'm so sorry that pop art has no meaning.

③ C: I didn't know that Marilyn Monroe was one of pop artists.

④ D: It is surprising that cans of soup were turned into works of art.

⑤ E: It's so sorry that Andy Warhol always made only one work of art.

서답형

20 Where did Andy Warhol find his subjects? Answer in English.

➡ _____

[21~23] 다음 글을 읽고 물음에 답하시오.

Claes Oldenburg is another pop artist who made art fun. He made sculptures of (A)_____, such as a hamburger, cookies, and a brush. In the beginning, he created soft sculptures. They were made of plastic, paper, and other soft materials. For example, he used cloth to make toilets. Later, he made huge sculptures of daily items, such as an ice cream cone. Wanting everyone to enjoy his art, he set up his works in outdoor places. He also ran a store inside his studio to sell his works. For him, artistic works were fun goods for people.

 빈칸 (A)에 들어갈 말로 가장 적절한 것은?

① something uncommon   ② various foods
③ everyday items   ④ great works
⑤ people around the world

서답형

22 What did Claes Oldenburg create in the beginning?

➡ _____

23 위 글을 읽고 답할 수 있는 것은?

① When was Claes Oldenburg born?
② When did Claes Oldenburg start pop art?
③ How huge were the sculptures?
④ What did Claes Oldenburg use to make toilets?
⑤ How many works did Claes Oldenburg set up in outdoor places?

[24~27] 다음 글을 읽고 물음에 답하시오.

Roy Lichtenstein used cartoons in his works. They were large and painted in lively colors. He even included speech balloons in his paintings. Back then, cartoons were not regarded as an art form. However, Roy Lichtenstein thought differently. He asked (A)himself, 'Why are (B) they not?' Then Roy Lichtenstein broke down the wall between high art and popular culture by adding cartoons to art.

Pop artists believed art should be easy. Anyone can create and enjoy art. How about creating a work of pop art today? By using daily images in a creative way, you can make a work of art for everyone. This is the most important lesson from pop art.

24 밑줄 친 (A)와 쓰임이 다른 하나는?

① She enjoyed herself very much.
② Karl made himself famous.
③ The door opened in itself.
④ They got themselves ready.
⑤ Tom cooked the food himself.

서답형

25 밑줄 친 (B)가 가리키는 것을 위 글에서 찾아 쓰시오.

➡ _____

서답형

26 What did Roy Lichtenstein add to art? Answer in English with a full sentence.

➡ _____

서답형

27 ①~⑤ 중 위 글의 내용과 일치하지 않는 것은?

Roy Lichtenstein was one of ①pop artists who thought that cartoons could be ②an art form. So he used them in his works with ③lively colors and ④speech balloons. In this way, he ⑤built the huge wall between high art and popular culture.

[01~04] 다음 글을 읽고 물음에 답하시오.

Welcome to the Pop Art Exhibition! What do you see? Paintings of soup cans? Big cartoons? Do they look like art works? Probably not, but think again. They are all famous works of pop art.

Pop is short for popular. So pop art means popular art, or art for people. It began in the 1950s in America. Pop artists at that time wanted to create something fun and easy. Instead of difficult traditional art works, they turned their eyes to popular culture. They used images from TV, comic books, magazines, and advertising. When people saw familiar images in art exhibitions, they found them refreshing. Since (A)then, pop art has become truly popular. People thought that art was too difficult to understand. By using daily images and bright colors, pop artists changed that thought.

01 What does pop art mean? Answer in English with a full sentence.

➡ _____

02 위 글의 내용에 맞게 빈칸에 알맞은 말을 쓰시오.

> In 1950s, pop artists in America were interested in _____ _____ rather than _____ _____ _____ _____ .

03 밑줄 친 (A)가 의미하는 것을 우리말로 쓰시오.

➡ _____
_____

04 How did pop artists changed people's thought toward art? Answer in English with a full sentence.

➡ _____
_____

[05~07] 다음 글을 읽고 물음에 답하시오.

Using common images, pop art looks plain. In other words, it doesn't look artistic. But it is still worth paying attention to. Although it looks plain, it is filled with meaning. Let's learn about some famous pop artists. They became famous for their special artistic ability. They were able to change common objects into amazing art.

Andy Warhol is called the King of Pop Art. He found his subjects in magazines and stores. One of his famous works is made up of pictures of Marilyn Monroe, the American actor. Another work shows cans of soup. He made many copies of these works. Why did he make copies of his works? He wanted to show that art is something you see every day.

05 Write the reason why pop art looks plain. Use the phrase 'It's because.'

➡ _____

06 What were some famous pop artists able to do? Answer in English with ten words.

➡ _____
_____

07 위 글의 내용에 맞게 빈칸에 알맞은 말을 위 글에서 찾아 쓰시오.

> One of Andy Warhol's famous works is composed of _____ of Marilyn Monroe, who was _____ _____ _____.
> Besides the work, he produced many art works using _____ _____ which he could get with ease.

[08~10] 다음 글을 읽고 물음에 답하시오.

Claes Oldenburg is (A)예술을 재미있게 만들었던 또 다른 팝 아트 작가. He made sculptures of everyday items, such as a hamburger, cookies, and a brush. In the beginning, he created soft sculptures. They were made of plastic, paper, and other soft materials. For example, he used cloth to make toilets. Later, he made huge sculptures of daily items, such as an ice cream cone. (B)Wanting everyone to enjoy his art, he set up his works in outdoor places. He also ran a store inside his studio to sell his works. For him, artistic works were fun goods for people.

08 주어진 단어를 활용하여 밑줄 친 우리말 (A)를 영어로 쓰시오.

> (another / made / fun)

➡ _____

09 접속사를 이용하여 밑줄 친 (B)와 같은 의미의 절을 쓰시오.

➡ _____

10 What did Claes Oldenburg use to create soft sculptures? Answer in English.

➡ _____

[11~13] 다음 글을 읽고 물음에 답하시오.

Roy Lichtenstein used cartoons in his works. They were large and painted in lively colors. He even included speech balloons in his paintings. Back then, cartoons were not regarded as an art form. However, Roy Lichtenstein thought differently. He asked himself, '(A)Why are they not?' Then Roy Lichtenstein broke down the wall between high art and popular culture by adding cartoons to art.

Pop artists believed art should be easy. Anyone can create and enjoy art. How about creating a work of pop art today? By using daily images in a creative way, you can make a work of art for everyone. (B)This is the most important lesson from pop art.

11 How was Roy Lichtenstein's works painted? Answer in English with a full sentence.

➡ _____

12 밑줄 친 (A)의 의미를 일곱 단어로 이루어진 한 문장으로 쓰시오.

➡ _____

13 밑줄 친 (B)가 의미하는 것을 우리말로 쓰시오.

➡ _____

Project Step 1

A: What do you want to make with these paper cups?
    want는 목적어로 to부정사를 취한다.

B: Why don't we make a tower?
    '～하는 게 어때?'라고 제안을 하는 표현으로 'How[What] about making a tower?'로 바꿀 수 있다.

C: Wonderful! Let's build a tower like the Leaning Tower of Pisa.
    ～와 같은, 전치사

D: How about drawing something on the cups?
    '～하는 게 어때?'라는 제안을 하는 표현이다.

B: Sounds great. First, let's give everyone some paper cups.

구문해설 • tower: 탑 • build: 만들다 • like: ～와 같은

해석

A: 이 종이컵들로 무엇을 만 들고 싶어?

B: 탑을 만드는 게 어때?

C: 훌륭해! 피사의 사탑과 같 은 탑을 만들어 보자.

D: 종이컵에 뭔가를 그리는 게 어때?

B: 좋은 생각이야. 먼저 모두 에게 종이컵을 몇 개 나누 어 주자.

Enjoy Writing B

The Best Musical of My Life

Last Saturday I went to the concert hall to watch a musical. The title of
                                          to부정사–부사적 용법(목적)

the musical was *You and Me*. I watched it because my favorite actor was in

it. I liked the songs and dances of the musical. The story was about a girl
= the musical

who invited her best friends to her birthday party. They talked about their
관계대명사(주격)

friendship. The main character was Sophie. She sang many beautiful songs.

It was fantastic. Singing along to the songs during the performance, I was
                   분사구문(= As I sang)

excited. The musical was really worth watching.
과거분사 exciting(X)   형용사   동명사

구문해설 • main character: 주연, 주인공 • be worth V-ing: ～할 가치가 있다.

내 생애 최고의 뮤지컬

지난 토요일 나는 뮤지컬을 보러 콘서트홀에 갔다. 뮤지 컬 제목은 '너와 나'였다. 내 가 가장 좋아하는 배우가 그 뮤지컬에 나왔기 때문에 그 것을 보았다. 나는 공연의 노 래와 춤이 좋았다. 뮤지컬 의 내용은 가장 친한 친구들 을 자신의 생일 파티에 초대 했던 여자 아이에 관한 것이 었다. 그들은 자신들의 우정 에 대해 이야기했다. 주인공 은 Sophie였다. 그녀는 많 은 아름다운 노래들을 불렀 다. 그것은 환상적이었다. 공 연 중에 노래를 따라 부르며 매우 신났었다. 그 뮤지컬은 정말 볼 가치가 있었다.

Enjoy Writing B

A Movie That Moved Me

Last Saturday I went to my friend's house to watch a movie. The title of the
                                          to부정사의 부사적 용법 중 목적(～하기 위해서)

movie was *My Son*. I watched it because my friend recommended it. I liked the
                            이유를 이끄는 접속사

story of the movie. The story was about a brave man who tried to find his lost
                                              주격 관계대명사   아들을 잃어버린 것이므로 과거분사

son. The main character was John. He was played by the actor Roy Jones, who
                                                                관계대명사의 계속적 용법

was fantastic. It was touching. Watching the emotional scenes, I was moved.
                        감동을 유발하므로 현재분사   감동을 느낀 것이므로 과거분사

The movie was really worth watching.

구문해설 • title: 제목 • recommend: 추천하다 • brave: 용감한 • main character: 주인공
• fantastic: 멋진 • emotional: 감동적인 • scene: 장면 • be worth Ving: V할 가치가 있다

나에게 감동을 준 영화

지난 토요일 나는 영화를 보러 친 구 집에 갔다. 영화의 제목은 '나 의 아들'이었다. 나는 내 친구가 그 영화를 추천해서 봤다. 나는 그 영화의 이야기가 마음에 들었 다. 그것은 잃어버린 아들을 찾으 려 했던 용감한 남자에 관한 이 야기였다. 주인공은 John이었다. 그 역은 배우 Roy Jones가 연 기했는데 아주 멋졌다. 그 영화 는 감동적이었다. 나는 감동적인 장 면들을 보며 감동받았다. 그 영화 는 정말 볼 가치가 있었다.

01 다음 주어진 두 단어의 관계가 같도록 빈칸에 알맞은 단어를 쓰시오.

> dull – lively : familiar – _____

02 다음 문장의 빈칸 (A)와 (B)에 들어갈 단어로 바르게 짝지어진 것은?

> • I know a good spot to (A)_____ the tent.
> • They asked me to leave. (B)_____, I got fired.

① get into – For example
② look into – However
③ put into – On the other hand
④ set up – In other words
⑤ set for – Moreover

[03~04] 다음 영영풀이에 해당하는 것을 고르시오.

03

> the ability to produce or use original and unusual ideas

① purpose   ② creativity
③ advice   ④ performance
⑤ accident

04

> traditional in style or form, or based on methods developed over a long period of time, and considered to be of lasting value

① modern   ② familiar
③ popular   ④ refreshing
⑤ classical

05 다음 우리말에 맞게 주어진 문장의 빈칸을 네 단어로 채우시오.

> 그 위원회는 5명의 위원으로 구성될 것이다.
> The committee will _____ five members.

06 다음 밑줄 친 부분의 뜻이 잘못된 것은?

① His new work is a wooden sculpture. (조각품)
② I cleaned the toilet in the bathroom. (변기)
③ He had the ability to explain things clearly. (능력)
④ I went to an exhibition called *The World of Eric Carle*. (출구)
⑤ Computers can be expensive, but I think they are worth the money. (가치 있는)

07 다음 대화의 빈칸 (A)에 들어갈 말로 알맞은 것은?

> B: Do you like classical music?
> G: Yes, Beethoven is one of my favorite musicians. How about you?
> B: I like pop music more than classical music.
> G: I see. (A)_____
> B: I'm really fascinated by its exciting rhythms.

① Do you like pop music?
② How do you like classical music?
③ What do you like most about pop music?
④ How do you like this song?
⑤ Are you satisfied with classical music?

08 다음 그림에서 요리사가 할 말을 주어진 단어를 이용하여 영작하시오.

(how / your food)

➡ _____

[09~10] 다음 대화를 읽고 물음에 답하시오.

Bora: Andy, you went to the art museum, didn't you?
Andy: Yes. They had a special Chagall exhibition. (①)
Bora: How did you like it?
Andy: It was fantastic! I was fascinated by the colors in his paintings and his creativity. (②)
Bora: No wonder. He was one of the greatest painters ever. (③)
Andy: I went to a gift shop and saw things like umbrellas, cups, and backpacks. Famous works of art were printed on them. (④)
Bora: Did you buy anything?
Andy: Yes. I bought this T-shirt. How do you like it? (⑤)
Bora: It looks great on you.
Andy: Thank you.

09 위 대화의 (①)~(⑤) 중 주어진 문장이 들어갈 위치로 알맞은 것은?

> What else did you see in the museum?

①   ②   ③   ④   ⑤

10 위 대화를 읽고 답할 수 <u>없는</u> 질문은?

① What was Andy fascinated by?
② What did Andy buy at the gift shop?
③ How did Andy like the Chagall exhibition?
④ Why did Andy buy a T-shirt?
⑤ What did Andy see at the gift shop?

11 다음 대화의 (A)~(E)를 알맞은 순서로 나열한 것은?

> A: This is my treasure.
> (A) That's amazing.
> (B) Yes. I made it seven years ago. I've been using it every day since then.
> (C) How do you like it?
> (D) It's a mug, isn't it?
> (E) It looks great. I like the drawing of a little bear.

① (A) – (C) – (B) – (E) – (D)
② (B) – (C) – (D) – (A) – (E)
③ (C) – (E) – (D) – (B) – (A)
④ (D) – (B) – (A) – (C) – (E)
⑤ (D) – (A) – (E) – (C) – (B)

12 다음 대화의 밑줄 친 (A)와 같은 의미가 되도록 주어진 단어를 이용하여 쓰시오.

> G: Jim, did you finish your art homework?
> B: Yes. I drew the face of my role model on a plate.
> G: Sounds interesting. Who is your role model?
> B: My dad. He always gives me good advice. Who did you draw, Amy?
> G: Well, I drew myself surfing in the sea.
> B: Wonderful! (A)I'm fascinated by your drawing. (an interest)
> G: Thank you.

➡ _____

Grammar

13 다음 각 문장의 밑줄 친 부분이 나머지와 쓰임이 <u>다른</u> 하나를 고르시오.

① It was worth <u>meeting</u> your family.
② Jessica couldn't help <u>meeting</u> the strange man because her mother had arranged her schedule.
③ Don't you see the president <u>meeting</u> a lot of citizens without a minute's rest?
④ My parents were so busy <u>meeting</u> the teachers that I wanted to go out.
⑤ It was no use <u>meeting</u> Tom and Jack, as they couldn't help us.

14 다음 문장의 밑줄 친 분사구문을 부사절로 옳게 바꾼 것은?

There being a misconception that cartoons wouldn't belong to art, some pop artists made great works of art by using them.

① As a misconception was there that cartoons wouldn't belong to art,
② If there was a misconception that cartoons wouldn't belong to art,
③ Unless there was a misconception that cartoons wouldn't belong to art,
④ Though there was a misconception that cartoons wouldn't belong to art,
⑤ Because there was a misconception that cartoons wouldn't belong to art,

15 다음 그림을 보고 괄호 안의 단어를 배열하여 빈칸을 알맞게 채우되, 필요하다면 동사의 형태는 어법에 맞게 고치시오.

(1) (worth, see, works)

➡ The world famous pop artist Florentijn Hofman's _____.

(2) (busy, was, that, the show, so, watch)

➡ Minjun _____
he couldn't answer the phone.

16 다음 문장의 밑줄 친 부사절을 분사구문으로 알맞게 바꾼 것을 고르시오.

<u>As they didn't want people to think art should be difficult,</u> pop artists tried to change it by using daily images and bright colors.

① As they wanting people to think art shouldn't be difficult,
② There being people thinking that art shouldn't be difficult,
③ Wanting not people to think art should be difficult,
④ As wanting people to think art should be difficult,
⑤ Not wanting people to think that art should be difficult,

17 다음은 아래 주어진 문장의 내용과 같은 문장들이다. 어법상 **틀린** 문장 하나를 고르시오.

> The exhibition of Andy Warhol's Works of Art in New York last year was worth visiting.

① It was worth while to visit the exhibition of Andy Warhol's Works of Art in New York last year.

② The exhibition of Andy Warhol's Works of Art in New York last year was worthy of visiting.

③ The exhibition of Andy Warhol's Works of Art in New York last year was worth visiting it.

④ It was worthwhile visiting the exhibition of Andy Warhol's Works of Art in New York last year.

⑤ The exhibition of Andy Warhol's Works of Art in New York last year was worth visiting.

Reading

[18~21] 다음 글을 읽고 물음에 답하시오.

Pop is short for popular. So pop art means popular art, or art for people. It began in the 1950s in America. Pop artists at that time wanted to create something fun and easy. Instead of difficult traditional art works, ①they turned ②their eyes to popular culture. ③They used images from TV, comic books, magazines, and advertising. When people saw familiar images in art exhibitions, ④they found them refreshing. Since then, pop art has become truly popular. People thought that art was too difficult to understand. By using daily images and bright colors, ⑤pop artists changed that thought.

18 ①~⑤ 중 지칭하는 것이 **다른** 하나는?

①   ②   ③   ④   ⑤

19 What is pop short for? Answer in English with a full sentence.

➡ _____

20 위 글의 내용과 일치하는 것은?

① People in 1950s didn't like pop arts.

② Pop artists tried to stick to traditional art works.

③ Pop arts were created to be fun and easy.

④ There weren't any pop art exhibitions.

⑤ Pop artists were fond of using only one color.

21 What did people think about art? Answer in English.

➡ _____

_____

[22~24] 다음 글을 읽고 물음에 답하시오.

Roy Lichtenstein used cartoons in his works. ① They were large and painted in lively colors. ② He even included speech balloons in his paintings. ③ Back then, cartoons were not regarded as an art form. ④ He asked himself, 'Why are they not?' ⑤ Then Roy Lichtenstein broke down the wall between high art and popular culture by adding cartoons to art.

Pop artists believed art should be easy. Anyone can create and enjoy art. How about creating a work of pop art today? By using daily images in a creative way, you can make a work of art for everyone. This is the most important lesson from pop art.

22 ①~⑤ 중 주어진 문장이 들어가기에 가장 적절한 곳은?

> However, Roy Lichtenstein thought differently.

①   ②   ③   ④   ⑤

23 According to the passage, what is the most important lesson from pop art?

① making people in the world happy
② spreading American art works
③ using daily images as little as possible
④ building strong walls for pure art
⑤ employing everyday items creatively

24 What did Roy Lichtenstein include in his paintings? Answer in English.

➡ _____

[25~27] 다음 글을 읽고 물음에 답하시오.

A Movie That Moved Me
Last Saturday I went to my friend's house to watch a movie. The title of the movie was *My Son*. I watched it ①because my friend recommended it. I liked the story of the movie. The story was about a brave man ②who tried to find his lost son. The main character was John. He was played by the actor Roy Jones, ③that was fantastic. It was touching. ④Watching the emotional scenes, I was moved. The movie was really worth ⑤watching.

25 ①~⑤ 중 어법상 바르지 <u>않은</u> 것은?

①   ②   ③   ④   ⑤

26 What did the writer like about the movie? Answer in English.

➡ _____

27 다음 중 위 글을 읽고 답할 수 <u>없는</u> 것은?

① When did the writer go to the friend's house?
② What was the title of the movie?
③ Who recommended the movie?
④ Who played the main character?
⑤ How long did it take to watch the movie?

01 다음 짝지어진 단어의 관계가 같도록 빈칸에 알맞은 말을 쓰시오.

출제율 95%

> creative – creativity : popular – _____

02 다음 영영풀이에 해당하는 단어는?

출제율 90%

> an opinion that someone offers you about what you should do or how you should act in a particular situation

① suggestion   ② lesson

③ emotion   ④ advice

⑤ cartoon

[03~04] 다음 대화를 읽고 물음에 답하시오.

Bora: Andy, you went to the art museum, didn't you?

Andy: Yes. They had a special Chagall exhibition.

Bora: (a)What did you like it?

Andy: It was fantastic! (b)I was fascinated by the colors in his paintings and his creativity.

Bora: (c)No wonder. He was one of the greatest painters ever. What else did you see in the museum?

Andy: I went to a gift shop and saw things like umbrellas, cups, and backpacks. Famous works of art were printed on them.

Bora: Did you buy anything?

Andy: Yes. I bought this T-shirt. (d)How do you like it?

Bora: (d)It looks great on you.

Andy: Thank you.

03 위 대화의 밑줄 친 (a)~(e) 중 표현이 어색한 것은?

출제율 95%

① (a)   ② (b)   ③ (c)   ④ (d)   ⑤ (e)

04 위 대화의 내용과 일치하지 <u>않는</u> 것은?

출제율 100%

① The art museum had a special Chagall exhibition.

② Bora and Andy are talking in the art museum.

③ Andy also went to a gift shop and saw things like umbrellas, cups, and backpacks.

④ Bora acknowledges Chagall as one of the greatest painters.

⑤ The T-shirt Andy bought looks great on him.

[05~06] 다음 대화를 읽고 물음에 답하시오.

B: The other day I watched a play, *A Love Story in the War*.

G: Oh, how did you like the play?

B: I liked the main characters. The actors' performances were fantastic.

G: 이야기도 좋았어?

B: No. It was a little boring, but the music was pretty good.

G: So, do you think I should see it?

B: Only if you have a lot of time and money.

05 위 대화의 밑줄 친 우리말에 맞게 주어진 단어를 이용하여 영어로 쓰시오.

출제율 95%

> good, well

➡ _____

06 위 대화에서 다음 〈영영풀이〉가 설명하는 단어를 찾아 쓰시오.

출제율 90%

> not interesting or exciting

➡ _____

[07~08] 다음 대화를 읽고 물음에 답하시오.

B: Sandy, you can listen to many kinds of music in this music library.

G: That's cool, Bob. Can I listen to classical music?

B: Sure. Do you like classical music?

G: Yes, Beethoven is one of my favorite musicians. How about you?

B: (A)I like pop music more than classical music. (prefer / to)

G: I see. What do you like most about pop music?

B: I'm really fascinated by its exciting rhythms.

07 위 대화를 읽고 답할 수 <u>없는</u> 질문은?

① Where are Bob and Sandy now?

② What kind of music does Sandy like?

③ Who is one of Sandy's favorite musicians?

④ What kind of music does Bob like?

⑤ How many kinds of music can they hear in this music library?

08 위 대화의 밑줄 (A)와 같은 의미를 가진 문장이 되도록 주어진 단어를 활용하여 영작하시오.

➡ _____

09 다음 대화의 밑줄 친 (a)~(e) 중 어법상 <u>어색한</u> 것은?

G: Jim, did you finish your art homework?

B: Yes. I (a)<u>drew</u> the face of my role model on a plate.

G: Sounds (b)<u>interesting</u>. Who is your role model?

B: My dad. He (c)<u>always</u> gives me good advice. Who did you draw, Amy?

G: Well, I drew (d)<u>me</u> surfing in the sea.

B: Wonderful! I'm (e)<u>fascinated</u> by your drawing.

G: Thank you.

① (a) ② (b) ③ (c) ④ (d) ⑤ (e)

10 다음 주어진 문장의 부사절을 분사구문으로 적절히 전환한 문장을 고르시오.

Since he had not been invited to the awards ceremony, the actor watched it thorough the TV program.

① Having not been invited to the awards ceremony, the actor watched it thorough the TV program.

② As the actor not being invited to the awards ceremony, he watched it thorough the TV program.

③ As he being not invited to the awards ceremony, the actor watched it thorough the TV program.

④ Not having been invited to the awards ceremony, the actor watched it thorough the TV program.

⑤ Not having invited to the awards ceremony, the actor watched it thorough the TV program.

[11~12] 다음 주어진 우리말을 영작했을 때, 어법상 알맞지 <u>않은</u> 것을 고르시오.

11

그 고대 유적지를 찾아가기 위해 우리가 썼던 돈은 낼 만한 가치가 있었다.

① The money we spent visiting the ancient site was worth being paid for.

② The money that we spent visiting the ancient site was worth paying for.

③ The money that we spent visiting the ancient site was worthy of being paid for.

④ It was worth paying for the money that we spent visiting the ancient site.

⑤ It was worthwhile to pay for the money that we spent visiting the ancient site.

출제율 100%

12 그 부부는 그들의 잃어버린 강아지를 발견하고 울지 않을 수 없었다.

① The couple couldn't help crying to find their lost puppy.

② The couple couldn't help but crying to find their lost puppy.

③ The couple couldn't but cry to find their lost puppy.

④ The couple had no choice but to cry when they found their lost puppy.

⑤ The couple couldn't help but cry when they found their lost puppy.

출제율 95%

13 다음 중 어법상 어색한 문장을 모두 고르면? (정답 2개)

① Have you ever felt like going swimming on a cold day?

② The expensive jewelry she wore tonight was worth to buy.

③ The people attending the meeting were busy discussing the sensitive issues.

④ Incheon International Airport is worth of being visited.

⑤ The audience could not help laughing at the story the comedian told them.

[14~17] 다음 글을 읽고 물음에 답하시오.

Using common images, pop art looks plain. (A)_____, it doesn't look artistic. But it is still worth paying attention to. Although it looks plain, it is filled with meaning. Let's learn about some famous pop artists. They became famous for their special artistic ability. They were able to change common objects into amazing art.

Andy Warhol is called the King of Pop Art. He found his (B)subjects in magazines and stores. One of his famous works is made up of pictures of Marilyn Monroe, the American actor. Another work shows cans of soup. He made many copies of these works. Why did he make copies of his works? He wanted to show that art is something you see every day.

출제율 100%

14 다음 중 빈칸 (A)에 들어갈 말로 적절한 것을 모두 고르시오.

① In other words   ② However

③ On the other hand   ④ That is

⑤ Nevertheless

출제율 95%

15 다음 중 밑줄 친 (B)와 쓰임이 같은 것은?

① Biology is my favorite subject.

② We need male subjects who are healthy.

③ The chapter deals with serious subjects.

④ Flights are subject to delay because of the fog.

⑤ 'She' is the subject of the sentence.

출제율 90%

16 What are some pop artists famous for? Answer in English.

➡ _____

17 Which is right about Andy Warhol?

① He went out with Marilyn Monroe.

② He was famous for making common things.

③ He made an artwork with his friends.

④ He wanted art to be scarce and hard to see.

⑤ He made an artwork by using cans of soup.

[18~19] 다음 글을 읽고 물음에 답하시오.

Claes Oldenburg is another pop artist who made art fun. He made sculptures of everyday items, such as a hamburger, cookies, and a brush. In the beginning, he created soft sculptures. They were made of plastic, paper, and other soft materials. For example, he used cloth to make toilets. Later, he made huge sculptures of daily items, such as an ice cream cone. Wanting everyone to enjoy his art, he set up his works in outdoor places. He also ran a store inside his studio to sell his works. For him, artistic works were fun goods for people.

18 다음 중 Claes Oldenburg가 주제로 삼을 만한 소재가 <u>아닌</u> 것은?

① cake ② a bottle

③ a knife ④ a spoon

⑤ a waterfall

19 Where did Claes Oldenburg set up his works?

➡ _____

[20~21] 다음 글을 읽고 물음에 답하시오.

Q: (A)_____

A: Pop art means art for people. It began in the 1950s in America. Pop artists used daily images and bright colors.

Q: What did these pop artists create?

A: Andy Warhol found his subjects in magazines and stores. He made many copies of his works. In the beginning, Claes Oldenburg created soft sculptures. Later, he made huge sculptures and set up his works in outdoor places. Roy Lichtenstein used cartoons in his works and even included speech balloons in his paintings.

20 빈칸 (A)에 들어갈 말로 가장 적절한 것은?

① What kind of art do people like?

② What do you know about art?

③ What is pop art?

④ What kinds of art are there around us?

⑤ Why does pop art become famous?

21 위 글의 내용에 맞게 빈칸에 알맞은 말을 쓰시오.

Each pop artist has their own artistic ability. Andy Warhol liked to find his subjects in _____, Claes Oldenburg was an excellent _____, and Roy Lichtenstein was famous for using _____ in his paintings.

01 다음 대화의 괄호 안의 단어를 알맞은 형태로 바꾸어 쓰시오.

> Bora: Andy, you went to the art museum, didn't you?
> Andy: Yes. They had a special Chagall exhibition.
> Bora: How did you like it?
> Andy: It was fantastic! I was (A)(fasciate) by the colors in his paintings and his creativity.
> Bora: No wonder. He was one of the greatest (B)(painter) ever. What else did you see in the museum?
> Andy: I went to a gift shop and saw things like umbrellas, cups, and backpacks. Famous works of art (C)(be) printed on them.
> Bora: Did you buy anything?
> Andy: Yes. I bought this T-shirt. How do you like it?
> Bora: It looks great on you.
> Andy: Thank you.

➡ (A) _____ (B) _____ (C) _____

02 다음은 아래 왼쪽의 명화와 이를 이용해 디자인한 우산을 소개한 글이다. 이 글을 바탕으로 어색한 문장을 찾아 올바른 문장으로 고쳐 쓰시오.

On White II

> Our group liked the umbrella designed by Jinsu. He used the painting, *On White II*. He was fascinated by its design.

> A: Which painting did you choose?
> B: (1)I chose *On White II*.
> C: What did you like most about the painting?
> B: (2)I was fascinated by the bright colors.
> D: What did you design with the painting?
> B: (3)I designed an umbrella. (4)How do you like my umbrella?
> D: (5)I think it's beautiful.

➡ _____

03 다음 우리말에 맞도록 괄호 안에 주어진 어휘를 알맞게 배열하여 빈칸을 채우시오.

(1) 다른 사람들이 만화를 비웃고 있었지만, 팝 아티스트들은 그것들이 예술로 인정받도록 만들었다. (laughing, though, cartoons, at, people, other)

  ➡ _____
  pop artists made them recognized as art.

(2) 흔한 일상적 사물과 이미지를 사용했기 때문에, 팝 아트는 정말 유명해졌다. (and, using, images, objects, everyday, common)

  ➡ _____
  pop art has become really famous.

[04~05] 다음 우리말에 맞게 주어진 어구들을 알맞게 배열하여 빈칸을 채우시오.

04
> 동해의 섬, 독도는 우리가 일본으로부터 지켜야할 가치가 있다. (the island, is, in, protecting, the East Sea, worth)

➡ Dokdo, _____
from Japan.

05

지진이 얼마나 지속될지 아는 것은 불가능하다.
(the, no, how, knowing, there, long, is)

➡ _____ earthquake will last.

06 다음 각 밑줄 친 부분 중 어법상 어색한 것을 고쳐 다시 쓰시오.

(1) Having rained heavily the day before, some of the streets got flooded.

➡ _____

(2) People strictly speaking, you can buy the condition of happiness but you can't buy happiness.

➡ _____

(3) Exhausting from a series of overtime work, I slept right away without even having dinner.

➡ _____

(4) Found the kitty the old lady had lost, Bentley told her to come quickly.

➡ _____

[07~09] 다음 글을 읽고 물음에 답하시오.

Pop is short for popular. So pop art means popular art, or art for people. It began in the 1950s in America. (A)그 당시 팝 아트 작가들은 재미있고 쉬운 것을 만들고 싶어 했다. Instead of difficult traditional art works, they turned their eyes to popular culture. They used images from TV, comic books, magazines, and advertising. When people saw familiar images in art exhibitions, they found (B)them refreshing.

07 Where did pop art begin? Answer in English with a full sentence.

➡ _____

08 주어진 단어를 활용하여 밑줄 친 우리말 (A)를 영어로 쓰시오.

(at that time / something)

➡ _____
_____

09 밑줄 친 (B)가 가리키는 것을 위 글에서 찾아 쓰시오.

➡ _____

[10~11] 다음 글을 읽고 물음에 답하시오.

A Movie That Moved Me
Last Saturday I went to my friend's house to watch a movie. The title of the movie was My Son. I watched it because my friend recommended it. I liked the story of the movie. The story was about a brave man who tried to find his lost son. The main character was John. He was played by the actor Roy Jones, who was fantastic. It was (A)_____. (B)_____ the emotional scenes, I was (C)_____. The movie was really worth watching.

10 주어진 단어를 내용과 어법에 맞게 빈칸 (A)~(C)에 쓰시오.

(touch / move / watch)

➡ (A)_____ (B)_____ (C)_____

11 Write the reason why the writer went to his friend's house. Answer in English.

➡ _____

창의사고력 서술형 문제

01 다음 그림을 보고, 그림의 내용에 맞게 〈보기〉와 같이 분사구문이 포함된 문장을 자유롭게 영작하시오.

보기

- Sitting on the chair, she is playing the guitar.
- Having a fever, she stayed home.

---

① _____ ② _____

③ _____ ④ _____

02 다음 질의응답을 참고하여 감상문을 완성하시오.

Title: You and Me / Type: musical / When and Where: last Saturday, a concert hall

Q: Why did you watch the musical?

A: Because my favorite actor was in it.

Q: What did you like about it?

A: Songs and dances.

Q: What was it about?

A: It was about a girl who invited her best friends to her birthday party. They talked about their friendship.

Q: Talk about the main character.

A: The main character was Sophie. She sang many beautiful songs.

Q: How did you like it?

A: It was fantastic. Singing along to the songs during the performance, I was excited.

The Best Musical of My Life

_____ I went to _____ to watch _____. The title of the musical was _____. I watched it because _____. I liked _____ of the musical. The story was _____ _____. They talked _____. _____ Sophie. She _____. It was _____. _____ _____, I was _____. The musical was really worth watching.

단원별 모의고사

01 다음 단어에 대한 영어 설명이 <u>어색한</u> 것은?

① exhibition: an event at which objects such as paintings are shown to the public, a situation in which someone shows a particular skill or quality to the public, or the act of showing these things

② familiar: easy to recognize because of being seen, met, heard, etc. before

③ include: to contain something as a part of something else, or to make something part of something else

④ popular: liked, enjoyed, or supported by many people

⑤ copy: the first one made

02 다음 짝지어진 단어의 관계가 같도록 빈칸에 알맞은 말을 쓰시오.

advice – tip : intimate – _____

03 다음 영영풀이에 해당하는 어구를 고르시오.

in place of someone or something

① in spite of
② moreover
③ instead of
④ in other words
⑤ in the end

04 다음 중 짝지어진 대화가 <u>어색한</u> 것은?

① A: How do you like these shoes?
   B: I don't like them. They are too small.

② A: How do you like this movie?
   B: It looks great.

③ A: What was the story about?
   B: It was about the friendship between two friends.

④ A: I read the book, *The Wisdom*.
   B: I watched it alone.

⑤ A: What do you want to make with these paper cups?
   B: I think we can make one of the world-famous bridges using paper cups.

[05~06] 다음 대화를 읽고 물음에 답하시오.

Bora: Andy, you went to the art museum, didn't you?

Andy: Yes. They had a special Chagall exhibition.

Bora: (a)How did you like it?

Andy: It was fantastic! (b)I was fascinated by the colors in his paintings and his creativity.

Bora: (A)_____ He was (c)one of the greatest painters ever. What else did you see in the museum?

Andy: I went to a gift shop and saw things like umbrellas, cups, and backpacks. Famous works of art (d)were printed on them.

Bora: Did you buy anything?

Andy: Yes. I bought this T-shirt. How do you like it?

Bora: (e)It looks great on you.

Andy: Thank you.

05 위 대화의 빈칸 (A)에 들어갈 말로 알맞은 것은?

① Not at all.
② No problem.
③ No wonder.
④ Of course not.
⑤ Yes, I do.

06 위 대화의 밑줄 친 (a)~(e)에 대한 설명 중 잘못된 것은?

① (a): 어떤 것에 대해 만족하는지 아니면 불만족하는지 묻는 표현이다.

② (b): '~에 매료되었다'라는 의미로 어떤 것에 대해 깊은 관심이 있음을 나타내는 표현으로, I was into the colors로 바꾸어 표현할 수 있다.

③ (c): 'one of the 최상급+복수 명사' 형태로 '가장 ~한 것들 중 하나'의 뜻이다.

④ (d): 예술 작품들이 그려져 있다는 수동의 의미로 수동태를 사용하였고, them은 'gift shop'을 가리키는 대명사다.

⑤ (e): '너에게 잘 어울린다'라는 의미로 'It'은 'this T-shirt'를 가리킨다.

[07~08] 다음 대화를 읽고 물음에 답하시오.

G: Jim, did you finish your art homework?
B: Yes. I drew the face of my role model on a plate.
G: Sounds interesting. Who is your role model?
B: My dad. He always gives me good advice. Who did you draw, Amy?
G: Well, (a)나는 내가 바다에서 서핑하는 것을 그렸어.
B: Wonderful! (A)_____
G: Thank you.

07 위 대화의 빈칸 (A)에 들어갈 말로 알맞은 것은?

① I'm fascinated by its story.
② I'm fascinated by its characters.
③ I like its special effects.
④ I'm fascinated by your drawing.
⑤ I'm fascinated by its rhythms and melody.

08 위 대화의 밑줄 친 (a)의 우리말에 맞게 주어진 단어를 알맞은 순서로 배열하시오. (한 단어를 반드시 변형할 것)

(I / in / the / surfing / sea / drew / me)

➡ _____

09 다음 대화의 빈칸에 들어갈 알맞은 말은?

B: The other day I watched a play, *A Love Story in the War.*
G: Oh, _____?
B: I liked the main characters. The actors' performances were fantastic.
G: Was the story good as well?
B: No. It was a little boring, but the music was pretty good.
G: So, do you think I should see it?
B: Only if you have a lot of time and money.

① is this what you wanted
② how did you like the play
③ did you have fun
④ how did you like the song
⑤ how did you respond to the play

10 다음 대화의 밑줄 친 우리말에 맞게 주어진 단어를 이용하여 영작하시오.

A: I watched the musical, *Mom, You're My Angel.*
B: How did you like it?
A: It was fantastic. Watching the musical, 눈을 뗄 수가 없었어. (take / off / it)

➡ _____

11 다음 각 문장의 밑줄 친 부사절을 분사구문으로 바꾼 것 중 옳은 것은?

① While my sister was drawing some pop art pictures, the dogs fell asleep.
→ Drawing some pop art pictures,

② If you use daily images in a creative way, you can make a work of art for everyone.
→ Using daily images in a creative way,

③ When the structures are observed from a little higher position, they may look like a butterfly.
→ The structures observed from a little higher position,

④ If it doesn't snow next week, you can't go to ski school this year.
→ Not snowing next week,

⑤ As Maggy memorized the lines of the play, she went to bed as happily as ever.
→ Maggy memorizing the lines of the play,

[12~14] 다음 중 어법상 어색한 문장은?

12 ① What the professor wrote was not worth reading.
② The clothes and machines are worthy of being recycled.
③ The studio where the painter lived is worth being visited someday.
④ The time I shared with the girl was worth investing in.
⑤ It is worth while going to the concert.

13 ① I couldn't help being upset with her.
② Since my favorite actor shot the film, I cannot help going to watch the movie.
③ Robert could not help but crying when he saw his mom walking again.
④ The villagers couldn't help making smiles to see the missing baby coming back.
⑤ The prince couldn't help falling in love with the girl with long hair.

14 ① Being sensitive to the feedback, the pop artist was carefully making her works of cartoon art.
② Developed carelessly, the machine has been criticized as the worst of the 20th century.
③ It being hot and humid, all the outdoor games had to be cancelled.
④ Being no coins left, Mr. Collins gave up throwing them into the fountain.
⑤ Wanting to create something fun and easy, pop artists used familiar images and bright colors.

15 다음 각 분사구문을 접속사가 이끄는 부사절로 만들 때, 빈칸에 알맞은 말을 써 넣으시오.

(1) Using everyday items such as a hamburger, cookies, and a brush, Claes Oldenburg made pop art sculptures.
➡ As he ＿＿＿＿ ＿＿＿＿ ＿＿＿＿ such as a hamburger, cookies, and a brush, Claes Oldenburg made pop art sculptures.

(2) Watching the pop artist making the painting, they will understand the art is not difficult.

➡ _____ _____ _____ _____

_____ _____ _____ the painting, they will understand the art is not difficult.

(3) Getting interested in the film, she bought the movie ticket.

➡ Since _____ _____ _____

_____ _____ _____, she bought the movie ticket.

(4) Being unhealthy, the woman helped me carry the heavy boxes.

➡ _____ _____ _____ _____,

the woman helped me carry the heavy boxes.

[16~19] 다음 글을 읽고 물음에 답하시오.

Pop is short for popular. So pop art means popular art, or art for people. It began in the 1950s in America.

(A) Since then, pop art has become truly popular. People thought that art was too difficult to understand. By using daily images and bright colors, pop artists changed that thought.

(B) They used images from TV, comic books, magazines, and advertising. When people saw familiar images in art exhibitions, they found them refreshing.

(C) Pop artists at that time wanted to create something fun and easy. Instead of difficult traditional art works, they turned their eyes to popular culture.

Using common images, pop art looks plain. In other words, it doesn't look artistic. (D)하지만 여전히 주목할 만한 가치가 있다. Although it looks plain,

it is filled with meaning. Let's learn about some famous pop artists. They became famous for their special artistic ability. They were able to change common objects into amazing art.

16 다음 중 위 글의 제목으로 가장 적절한 것은?

① Pop Art: Unpopular Form of Art
② Pop Art: Art for Everyone
③ Unfortunate Art: Pop Art
④ Pop Art: Never Known to People
⑤ Enjoy the Bright Color of Art

17 자연스러운 글이 되도록 박스 안의 (A)~(C)를 바르게 나열하시오.

➡ _____

18 주어진 단어를 활용하여 밑줄 친 우리말 (D)를 영어로 쓰시오.

(but / still / worth / pay)

➡ _____

19 Choose one that is NOT true.

① Pop art is art for people.
② Pop artists wanted their works to be fun.
③ It is easy to say that pop art doesn't look artistic.
④ Pop art is meaningless because it looks plain.
⑤ People thought that it was refreshing to see familiar images in art exhibitions.

[20~21] 다음 글을 읽고 물음에 답하시오.

Andy Warhol is called the King of Pop Art. ①He found his subjects in magazines and stores. ②One of his famous works is made up of pictures of Marilyn Monroe, the American actor. ③She was the most beloved actor in America at that time but died young. ④ Another work shows cans of soup. ⑤He made many copies of these works. Why did he make copies of his works? He wanted to show that art is something you see every day.

20 밑줄 친 ①~⑤ 중 글의 흐름상 어색한 문장은?

① ② ③ ④ ⑤

21 Write the reason why Andy Warhol made many copies of his works. Use the phrase 'It's because.'

➡ _____

_____

[22~25] 다음 글을 읽고 물음에 답하시오.

ⓐClaes Oldenburg is other pop artist who made art fun. He made sculptures of everyday items, such as a hamburger, cookies, and a brush. In the beginning, he created soft sculptures. They were made of plastic, paper, and other soft materials. _____ⓑ_____, he used cloth (A)to make toilets. Later, he made huge sculptures of daily items, such as an ice cream cone. Wanting everyone to enjoy his art, he set up his works in outdoor places. He also ran a store inside his studio to sell his works. For him, artistic works were fun goods for people.

22 위 글의 밑줄 친 ⓐ에서 어법상 어색한 곳을 올바르게 고치시오.

_____ ➡ _____

23 위 글의 빈칸 ⓑ에 알맞은 것은?

① However ② Therefore
③ That is ④ For example
⑤ In the end

24 밑줄 친 (A)와 쓰임이 같은 것은?

① Is there someone to depend on?
② It is amazing to make her laugh.
③ There was no chance to get back the money.
④ I perfer to stay at home.
⑤ Jane waited there to visit me again.

25 Why did Claes Oldenburg run a store inside his studio? Answer in English.

➡ _____

_____

MEMO

Lesson 9

You Can Do It, Too

 의사소통 기능

- 가능성 정도 묻기

  A: Is it possible for you to read ten books in a month?

  B: Yes. I think it's possible.

- 바람 · 소원 말하기

  A: I wish I could have matches.

  B: What would you do with matches?

 언어 형식

- I wish 가정법 과거

  I wish she **had** a better robotic hand.

- 의문사가 없는 의문문의 간접의문문

  I wondered **if I could do something for those girls**.

Words & Expressions

Key Words

- **afford** [əfɔ́ːrd] 동 ~할 여유가 되다
- **business** [bíznis] 명 사업
- **coin** [kɔin] 명 동전
- **collect** [kəlékt] 동 수집하다
- **control** [kəntróul] 동 통제하다, 조절하다, 조정하다
- **corn** [kɔːrn] 명 옥수수
- **corn cob** 옥수수 속대
- **cost** [kɔːst] 동 값이 들다
- **countryside** [kʌ́ntrisaid] 명 시골
- **entrance fee** 입장료
- **failure** [féiljər] 명 실패
- **fair** [fɛər] 명 박람회
- **fee** [fiː] 명 요금
- **filter** [fíltər] 명 여과장치, 필터 동 여과하다, 거르다
- **headband** [hédbænd] 명 머리띠
- **invention** [invénʃən] 명 발명(품)
- **inventor** [invéntər] 명 발명가
- **knife** [naif] 명 칼
- **leaf** [liːf] 명 나뭇잎
- **match** [mætʃ] 명 성냥
- **pollute** [pəlúːt] 동 오염시키다
- **pollution** [pəlúːʃən] 명 오염
- **possible** [pásəbl] 형 가능한
- **president** [prézədənt] 명 대통령, 회장, 총재
- **raise** [reiz] 동 (자금을) 모으다

- **realize** [ríːəlàiz] 동 깨닫다, 인식하다
- **recommend** [rèkəménd] 동 추천하다
- **remove** [rimúːv] 동 제거하다
- **relaxed** [rilǽkst] 형 편안한, 여유 있는
- **robotic** [roubátik] 형 로봇식의
- **sew** [sou] 동 꿰매다, 바느질하다
- **sewing machine** 재봉틀
- **software** [sɔ́ːftweər] 명 소프트웨어
- **solve** [salv] 동 풀다, 해결하다
- **space** [speis] 명 우주
- **stay** [stei] 동 머무르다
- **step** [step] 명 단계
- **success** [səksés] 명 성공
- **surprised** [sərpráizd] 형 놀란
- **system** [sístəm] 명 체계, 장치
- **teenager** [tíːnèidʒer] 명 십 대(= **teen**)
- **town** [taun] 명 마을
- **triangle** [tráiæŋgl] 명 삼각형
- **useful** [júːsfəl] 형 유용한
- **useless** [júːslis] 형 쓸모없는, 소용없는
- **wish** [wiʃ] 명 소원 동 ~이면 좋겠다고 생각하다
- **whether** [hwéðər] 접 ~인지 (아닌지)
- **wonder** [wʌ́ndər] 동 궁금하다
- **wonderful** [wʌ́ndərfəl] 형 훌륭한

Key Expressions

- **by Ving** V함으로써
- **change A into B** A를 B로 바꾸다
- **come across** 우연히 마주치다
- **for free** 무료로
- **for oneself** 스스로
- **get together** 만나다

- **hit on** ~을 생각해 내다
- **look forward to Ving** V하기를 고대하다
- **not only A but also B** A 뿐만 아니라 B도
- **pay for** 지불하다
- **thanks to** ~ 덕분에
- **think to oneself** 마음속으로 생각하다

Word Power

※ 서로 비슷한 뜻을 가진 어휘
- □ **control** 조종하다 - **manage** 조종하다
- □ **fee** 요금 - **charge** 청구 금액, 요금
- □ **pollute** 오염시키다 - **contaminate** 오염시키다

- □ **remove** 제거하다 - **eliminate** 제거하다
- □ **useful** 유용한 - **helpful** 도움이 되는, 유용한
- □ **realize** 깨닫다 - **understand** 깨닫다

※ 서로 반대되는 뜻을 가진 어휘
- □ **failure** 실패 ↔ **success** 성공
- □ **useful** 유용한 ↔ **useless** 쓸모없는

- □ **possible** 가능한 ↔ **impossible** 불가능한
- □ **wonderful** 훌륭한 ↔ **terrible** 끔찍한

※ 접미사 -ful → 명사+ful
- □ **beauty** 아름다움 - **beautiful** 아름다운
- □ **harm** 해, 피해 - **harmful** 해로운
- □ **help** 도움 - **helpful** 도움이 되는

- □ **success** 성공 - **successful** 성공적인
- □ **use** 사용 - **useful** 유용한
- □ **wonder** 경이 - **wonderful** 훌륭한

※ 접미사 -tion → 동사+tion
- □ **communicate** 의사소통하다 - **communication** 의사소통
- □ **illuminate** 빛나다 - **illumination** 빛
- □ **invent** 발명하다 - **invention** 발명
- □ **invite** 초대하다 - **invitation** 초대

- □ **limit** 제한하다 - **limitation** 제한
- □ **pollute** 오염시키다 - **pollution** 오염
- □ **realize** 깨닫다 - **realization** 깨달음
- □ **transport** 수송하다 - **transportation** 운송, 수송

English Dictionary

□ **afford** ~할 여유가 되다
→ to be able to do something
어떤 것을 할 수 있다

□ **business** 사업
→ a work of producing, buying, and selling of goods and services
상품과 서비스를 생산하고 구매하고 파는 일

□ **coin** 동전
→ a round piece of metal used as money
돈으로 사용되는 동그란 금속 조각

□ **come across** 우연히 마주치다
→ to meet or find by chance
우연히 만나거나 발견하다

□ **control** 통제하다, 조정하다
→ to make an organization, person, or system do what you want or have in the way you want
당신이 원하는 대로 원하거나 갖고 있는 것을 조직, 사람 혹은 시스템이 하게 하다

□ **cost** 값이 들다
→ to be obtained at the price of
어떠한 가격으로 얻어지다

□ **fair** 박람회
→ a large public event where goods are bought and sold, usually from tables that have been specially arranged for the event
주로 행사를 위해 특별히 배열된 테이블에서 물건들이 구매되고 팔리는 큰 공공 행사

□ **for free** 무료로
→ without having to pay
지불할 필요가 없는

□ **headband** 머리띠
→ a narrow strip of material worn around the head, usually to keep your hair or sweat out of your eyes
머리에 두르는 좁은 금속 줄로 주로 머리카락이나 땀이 눈으로 들어가지 않게 하는 것

□ **hit on** ~을 생각해 내다
→ to think of a plan, a solution, etc. suddenly or by chance
계획, 해결책 등을 갑자기 혹은 우연히 생각하다

□ **pollute** 오염시키다
→ to damage the water, air, land, etc. by using harmful chemicals
유해한 화학물질을 이용함으로써 물, 공기, 땅을 손상시키다

□ **robotic** 로봇식의
→ relating to or like a robot
로봇과 같거나 혹은 로봇과 관련된

□ **sew** 꿰매다, 바느질하다
→ to stitch with thread
실로 꿰매다

□ **software** 소프트웨어
→ the operating applications programs that are used in a computer system
컴퓨터 시스템 내에서 사용되는 운영 응용 프로그램

□ **success** 성공
→ the achievement of an aim or purpose
목적 또는 목표의 성취

01 다음 짝지어진 단어의 관계가 같도록 빈칸에 알맞은 말은?

useful – useless : valuable – _____

① invaluable   ② precious
③ valueless   ④ priceless
⑤ pricy

02 주어진 영어 설명에 맞게 문장의 빈칸에 알맞은 말을 쓰시오.

My parents didn't _____ a new refrigerator.

┤영어 설명├
to be able to do something

03 밑줄 친 부분의 의미로 알맞지 않은 것은?

① The speaker ended by suggesting some serious topics for discussion. (제안함으로써)
② He hit on a new way of making people's lives more comfortable. (~을 명중하다)
③ Thanks to your effort, we could manage to finish this project. (~ 덕분에)
④ Every week they get together to make songs and perform together. (만나다)
⑤ You can hardly expect her to do it for free. (공짜로)

04 다음 〈보기〉의 단어를 사용하여 자연스러운 문장을 만들 수 없는 것은?

┤ 보기 ├
useless   control   whether   remove

① It is _____ for us to keep these things in the house.
② The government attempts to _____ immigration.
③ People _____ the environment with garbage.
④ Filters do not _____ all contaminants from water.
⑤ We don't know _____ he's alive or dead.

05 다음 빈칸에 공통으로 들어갈 말로 알맞은 것을 고르시오.

• Thanks _____ your advice, the problem can be solved with ease.
• We are looking forward _____ making another appointment with you.

① at   ② in   ③ by
④ with   ⑤ to

06 다음 중 두 단어의 관계가 어색한 것은?

① limit – limitation
② recommend – recommendation
③ invent – invention
④ consider – consideration
⑤ attempt – attemption

01 자연스러운 문장이 되도록 〈보기〉의 어구를 빈칸에 알맞게 쓰시오.

┌─ 보기 ├─
business / coin / for free / cost / control

(1) I have a _____ from China.
(2) You need to learn how to _____ your spending.
(3) She wants to have her own _____ someday.
(4) I can't believe it only _____ 5 dollars in total.
(5) You cannot expect people to work _____.

02 다음은 하나의 단어가 갖는 여러 가지 의미 중 일부이다. 해당하는 단어를 쓰시오.

• a large public event where goods are bought and sold, usually from tables that have been specially arranged for the event
• reasonable, right, and just

➡ _____

03 다음 짝지어진 두 단어의 관계가 같도록 빈칸에 알맞은 말을 쓰시오.

(1) inform – information : pollute – _____
(2) converse – conversation : limit – _____
(3) help – helpful : beauty – _____

04 우리말에 맞게 한 단어를 추가하여 주어진 어구를 알맞게 배열하시오.

(1) 우리는 사람들이 더 이상 필요로 하지 않는 신발과 옷 같은 것들을 모을 수 있습니다.
(we / things / no longer / can / shoes and clothes / that / need / like / people)
➡ _____
_____

(2) 어른들의 입장료는 10달러이다.
(for / the entrance / is / adults / $10)
➡ _____

(3) Sam은 공기를 오염시키지 않기 위해서 자전거를 탄다.
(the air / rides / Sam / to / not / a bike)
➡ _____

05 빈칸 (A)~(C)에 각각 공통으로 들어가는 전치사를 쓰시오.

(A) We are looking forward _____ seeing you again.
　'It can't be true,' he thought _____ himself.
(B) She became very smart _____ reading a lot of books.
　David made the cookies _____ himself.
(C) They lacked the money to pay _____ the repairs.
　Jennifer blamed me _____ being late for the meeting.

06 다음과 같이 풀이되는 말을 쓰시오.

the achievement of an aim or purpose

➡ _____

Conversation

교과서

가능성 정도 묻기

A: Is it possible for you to read ten books in a month? 네가 한 달에 책 열 권을 읽는 것이 가능하니?

B: Yes. I think it's possible. 응. 나는 가능하다고 생각해.

■ 어떤 일이 가능한지를 물을 때 'Is it possible ~?', 'Can you ~?', 'Are you likely to ~?' 등으로 물을 수 있다. 가주어 it에 진주어 to부정사를 쓸 경우 'for+목적격'을 이용하여 to부정사의 행위 주체를 나타낼 수 있다.

■ 이에 대한 대답으로 possible과 impossible을 이용하여 'Yes, I think it's possible.' 혹은 'No, I don't think it's possible.', 'No. I think it's impossible.'로 가능과 불가능에 대해 답할 수 있다.
(I'm) Sorry, but I can't ~. / Yes, I do[would]. / Sure. / Of course.

가능성 정도 묻기

- Is it possible for ~ to V …? (~가 V하는 것이 가능하니?) • Can S V …? (S가 V할 수 있니?)
- Is S likely to V …? (S가 V할 것 같니?) • Is it probable/likely that S can V …? (S가 V할 가능성이 있니?)
- Is it okay if I ~? (내가 ~한다면 괜찮겠니?)

가능성 정도 답하기

- Yes, I think it's possible. (응, 가능할 것 같아.) • No, I don't think it's possible. (아니, 가능할 것 같지 않아.)
- I'm not sure if I can. (내가 할 수 있는지 확신할 수 없어.) • Maybe you can. (아마도 넌 할 수 있을 거야.)

핵심 Check

1. 다음 괄호 안의 단어들을 이용해 밑줄 친 우리말을 영어로 쓰시오.

A: 그녀가 그것들을 통제하는 것도 가능하니? (too / control / possible / it / them / is / for / to / her)

B: Yes. I think it's possible.

➡ _____

2. 자연스러운 대화가 되도록 다음 빈칸에 알맞은 말을 쓰시오.

A: Is it probable that _____?

B: Yes. I think she can drive the truck.

② 바람 · 소원 말하기

> **A:** I wish I could have matches. 나는 성냥을 가졌으면 좋겠어.
>
> **B:** What would you do with matches? 성냥으로 무엇을 할 거야?

- 'I wish I could ~.'는 현재의 바람이나 소원을 나타내는 표현으로 'I wish' 가정법 과거이다. 이와 같은 표현으로는 'I want to V ~.', 'I'd like to V ~.', 'I look forward to Ving ~.', 'I'm looking forward to Ving ~.' 등이 있다.
  - I wish she loved me. 그녀가 나를 사랑한다면 좋을 텐데.

- 'I wish+주어+동사의 과거형'의 형태로 현재 사실을 말하지만 반드시 동사의 과거형을 써야 한다. 원칙적으로 가정법 과거에서 be동사는 'were'를 쓰지만 현대 영어에서는 1, 3인칭 단수일 때는 'was'를 쓰기도 한다.
  - I wish Sam spoke Korean. Sam이 한국말을 한다면 좋을 텐데. (실제 Sam은 한국말을 하지 못함)
  - I wish she were[was] a doctor. 그녀가 의사이면 좋을 텐데. (실제 그녀는 의사가 아님)
  - I wish I had my own room. 내가 내 방을 가진다면 좋을 텐데. (실제 내 방을 가지고 있지 않음)

- 'I wish I could ~.' 뒤에는 사실과 반대되거나 가능성이 거의 없는 일이 오고, 만약 가능성이 있거나 결과를 아직 모르는 것을 희망할 때는 'I hope ~'를 쓴다.
  - I wish I could live up to 200 years old. 내가 200살까지 살 수 있으면 좋을 텐데.
  - I hope I will be able to buy that car some day. 나는 언젠가 그 차를 살 수 있길 바라.

바람 · 소원 말하기

- I wish I could ~.: 내가 ~하면 좋겠어.
- I want to ~ .: 나는 ~하고 싶어.
- I'd like to ~.: 나는 ~하고 싶어.
- I look forward to Ving ~.: 나는 ~하는 것을 기대해.
- I am looking forward to Ving ~.: 나는 ~하는 것을 기대하고 있어.

핵심 Check

3. 주어진 단어를 이용하여 다음 대화의 밑줄 친 우리말을 영어로 쓰시오.

> **A:** 내가 대도시에 살면 좋을 텐데. (wish)
> **B:** Right. Living in a big city would be fantastic.

➡ _____

Listen & Speak 1 A-1

G: ❶Can you draw this on the paper?

B: Sure. From the middle point, I draw two triangles. Then I draw the circle, like this.

G: Good. Now, is it possible ❷for you to draw it without taking your pencil off the paper?

B: I'll try. Hmm... No, how is that possible?

G: Well, start at ❸one of the four red points.

B: Do you mean any of the red points?

G: Yes. Draw the circle first and then the two triangles like this. Or you can draw the triangles first, like this.

B: Oh, now ❹I get it.

G: 너 이걸 종이에 그릴 수 있겠니?

B: 물론이지. 가운데 지점으로부터 두 개의 삼각형을 그리면 돼. 그러고 나서 이렇게 원을 그리면 되지.

G: 좋아. 그럼 종이에서 연필을 떼지 않고 그것을 그리는 것이 가능하니?

B: 시도해 볼게. 흠… 아니, 그게 어떻게 가능하니?

G: 음, 네 개의 빨간 점 중 한 곳에서 시작하면 돼.

B: 빨간 점 중에 아무 점이나 말하는 거야?

G: 응. 원을 먼저 그리고, 그 다음에 삼각형 두 개를 이렇게 그려. 아니면 이렇게 삼각형을 먼저 그릴 수도 있어.

B: 오, 이제 알겠어.

❶ 가능한지 묻는 표현(= Is it possible for you to draw this on the paper?)
❷ to부정사의 의미상 주어는 'for+목적격' 형태로 to부정사 앞에서 의미상의 행위 주체를 나타낼 때 쓰인다.
❸ one of+복수명사: ~들 중 하나
❹ '이해한다'는 표현으로 'I understand it.'과 같다.

Check(√) True or False

(1) It is impossible for the girl to draw the picture without taking her pencil off the paper.　　T ☐ F ☐

(2) The picture has two triangles and a circle.　　T ☐ F ☐

Listen & Speak 2 A-1

B: Wendy, you ❶have been late for school a lot lately. What's wrong?

G: I want to wake up early, but I just can't.

B: Doesn't your mom ❷wake you up?

G: She does, but I don't get up right away. ❸I wish I could have an AI robot.

B: An AI robot?

G: Yes. I mean one that could make sure I got up and give me breakfast in the morning.

B: That sounds great.

B: Wendy, 너 요즘 계속 지각하네. 무슨 일 있어?

G: 일찍 일어나고 싶은데, 그게 안 돼.

B: 네 엄마가 널 깨워 주시지 않니?

G: 엄마가 깨워주시긴 하는데, 바로 일어나지 않아. 인공지능 로봇이 있으면 좋겠어.

B: 인공지능 로봇?

G: 응. 내가 아침에 꼭 일어나도록 확인해 주고, 아침밥을 가져다주는 그런 로봇 말이야.

B: 그거 좋은 생각이야.

❶ 현재완료 시제를 이용하여 최근의 상황을 표현한다.
❷ '타동사+부사'는 대명사 인칭목적어를 취할 때 '타동사+목적어+부사'의 어순을 취한다.
❸ 'I want to have an AI robot.'과 같은 의미이다.

Check(√) True or False

(3) Wendy has been late for school because her mom doesn't wake her up.　　T ☐ F ☐

(4) Wendy wants AI robot to make sure she did her homework.　　T ☐ F ☐

Listen & Speak 1 A-2

W: Hi. ❶I'm looking for a backpack for my son.

M: How old is your son?

W: He is five years old.

M: I want to recommend this ❷one.

W: Oh, it's so cute.

M: Yes, isn't it? It has a cap ❸that looks like a penguin, so kids love it.

W: ❹Is it possible for me to take the cap off for washing?

M: Sure. You can easily take it off and ❺put it back on.

W: That's wonderful. I'll take it.

❶ be looking for: ~을 찾는 중이다
❷ 정해지지 않은 하나를 가리킬 때 쓰는 부정대명사
❸ 주격 관계대명사
❹ 'Can I take the cap off for washing?'과 같은 뜻
❺ put A back on: A를 도로 끼다

 Listen & Speak 2 A-2

B: ❶I'm planning to visit my uncle in Mexico.

G: What are you going to do there, Mike?

B: I'll spend most of my time at his house because he has a big swimming pool.

G: That's great. ❷Can you swim well?

B: No, ❸I wish I could, but I can't. So I'll have fun with a water walking ball instead.

G: A water walking ball? What is that?

B: It's a large ball. We go inside ❹it and walk on the water.

G: That ❺must be fun.

❶ be planning to V: ~할 계획이다
❷ 'Is it likely that you can swim well?'과 같은 뜻
❸ 소망을 나타내는 말(수영을 잘하고 싶지만 그렇지 못함)
❹ a water walking ball 지칭
❺ '~임에 틀림없다'는 확신을 나타내는 표현

 Real Life Talk

Bora: What are you doing, Jessie?

Jessie: I'm drawing Dr. Rebecca, my favorite superhero.

Bora: Wow, that's great.

Jessie: Thanks. ❶I wish I could read people's minds like her.

Bora: Is it possible for her to control ❷them, too?

Jessie: Yes. She can control your mind ❸if she wants to.

Bora: That's very cool.

Jessie: What about you? Do you also have any favorite superheroes?

Bora: Sure. I love Sky X. I wish I could fly ❹like him.

Jessie: I like him, too. He can even breathe in space.

Bora: Yes. He can do ❺anything in space.

❶ 'I want to read people's minds like her.'와 같은 표현
❷ people's minds 지칭 ❸ 조건의 부사절을 이끄는 접속사(~라면)
❹ 전치사(~처럼) ❺ 긍정문에서 쓰일 때 '무엇이든'으로 해석

Wrap Up 1

W: Hi, Tom. What are you doing?

B: I'm flying my drone.

W: Cool! ❶Are you good at it?

B: No, I'm not very good right now, but I'm practicing ❷hard.

W: ❸As you know, I run a sandwich restaurant. Is it possible for you to deliver orders with your drone?

B: No, ❹it isn't. But I think it will be possible ❺in one or two years.

W: That will be great.

❶ be good at: ~을 잘하다 ❷ 부사(열심히) ❸ 너도 알다시피
❹ it is not possible for me to deliver orders with my drones
❺ 시간을 나타낼 때 '~ 후에'

● 다음 우리말과 일치하도록 빈칸에 알맞은 말을 쓰시오.

Listen & Speak 1 A-1

G: _____ _____ _____ this on the paper?

B: Sure. _____ the middle point, I draw _____ _____. Then I draw the circle, _____ _____.

G: Good. Now, is it _____ _____ _____ to draw it _____ _____ your pencil _____ the paper?

B: I'll try. Hmm... No, _____ _____ _____ possible?

G: Well, start _____ one of the _____ _____ _____.

B: Do you mean _____ _____ _____ _____ _____?

G: Yes. Draw the circle _____ and then _____ _____ _____ _____ _____. Or you can draw the _____ _____, like this.

B: Oh, now _____ _____ _____.

Listen & Speak 1 A-2

W: Hi. I'm _____ _____ a backpack _____ my son.

M: _____ _____ is your son?

W: He is _____ _____ _____.

M: I want _____ _____ this one.

W: Oh, it's _____ cute.

M: Yes, _____ _____? It has a cap _____ _____ _____ _____ a penguin, so kids _____ _____.

W: Is it possible _____ _____ _____ _____ _____ the cap _____ for washing?

M: Sure. You can easily _____ _____ _____ and _____ _____ _____ on.

W: That's _____. I'll _____ _____.

Listen & Speak 2 A-1

B: Wendy, _____ _____ _____ _____ _____ _____ school a lot lately. What's _____?

G: I want to _____ _____ _____, but I just _____.

B: Doesn't your mom _____ _____ _____?

G: She _____, but I don't get up _____. _____ I _____ have an AI robot.

B: _____ _____ _____?

G: Yes. I mean one _____ _____ _____ _____ I got up and _____ _____ _____ in the morning.

B: That sounds _____.

G: 너 이걸 종이에 그릴 수 있겠니?

B: 물론이지. 가운데 지점으로부터 두 개의 삼각형을 그리면 돼. 그러고 나서 이렇게 원을 그리면 되지.

G: 좋아. 그럼 종이에서 연필을 떼지 않고 그것을 그리는 것이 가능하니?

B: 시도해 볼게. 흠… 아니, 그게 어떻게 가능하니?

G: 음, 네 개의 빨간 점 중 한 곳에서 시작하면 돼.

B: 빨간 점 중에 아무 점이나 말하는 거야?

G: 응. 원을 먼저 그리고, 그 다음에 삼각형 두 개를 이렇게 그려. 아니면 이렇게 삼각형을 먼저 그릴 수도 있어.

B: 오, 이제 알겠어.

W: 안녕하세요. 아들을 위한 배낭을 찾고 있어요.

M: 아들이 몇 살인가요?

W: 아들은 다섯 살이에요.

M: 이것을 추천하고 싶네요.

W: 오, 이거 정말 귀엽네요.

M: 네, 그렇지 않나요? 펭귄과 같이 생긴 모자가 있어서 아이들이 좋아하죠.

W: 제가 세탁을 위해 모자를 분리하는 것도 가능한가요?

M: 물론이죠. 모자를 쉽게 분리했다가 다시 붙일 수도 있어요.

W: 훌륭해요. 이걸 살게요.

B: Wendy, 너 요즘 계속 지각하네. 무슨 일 있어?

G: 일찍 일어나고 싶은데, 그게 안 돼.

B: 네 엄마가 널 깨워 주시지 않니?

G: 엄마가 깨워주시긴 하는데, 바로 일어나지 않아. 인공지능 로봇이 있으면 좋겠어.

B: 인공지능 로봇?

G: 응. 내가 아침에 꼭 일어나도록 확인해 주고, 아침밥을 가져다주는 그런 로봇 말이야.

B: 그거 좋은 생각이야.

Listen & Talk 2 A-2

B: I'm _____ _____ _____ my uncle in Mexico.

G: What are you _____ _____ _____ _____, Mike?

B: I'll _____ _____ _____ _____ _____ at his house _____ he has a big _____ _____.

G: That's great. _____ you _____ _____ _____?

B: No, _____ _____ _____ _____, but I can't. So I'll _____ _____ _____ a water walking ball _____.

G: A water walking ball? _____ _____ _____?

B: _____ a large ball. We _____ _____ it and _____ _____ the water.

G: That _____ _____ fun.

Real Life Talk

Bora: What _____ you _____, Jessie?

Jessie: I'm _____ Dr. Rebecca, _____ _____ _____.

Bora: Wow, that's _____.

Jessie: Thanks. I wish I _____ _____ _____ _____ like her.

Bora: Is it possible _____ _____ _____ _____ _____ them, too?

Jessie: Yes. She can control your mind _____ _____ _____ _____.

Bora: That's very _____.

Jessie: What about you? Do you also _____ _____ _____ _____?

Bora: Sure. I love Sky X. I wish I _____ _____ _____ _____.

Jessie: I like him, too. He can _____ _____ _____ space.

Bora: Yes. He _____ _____ _____ in space.

Wrap Up 1

W: Hi, Tom. _____ _____ _____ _____ _____?

B: I'm _____ my drone.

W: Cool! _____ you _____ _____ it?

B: No, I'm not very good _____ _____, but I'm _____ _____.

W: _____ _____ _____, I _____ a sandwich restaurant. Is it possible _____ _____ _____ _____ _____ with your drone?

B: No, it _____. But I think _____ _____ _____ _____ _____ one or two years.

W: _____ will _____ _____.

해석

B: 나는 멕시코에 있는 삼촌을 방문할 계획이야.
G: 거기서 뭐 할 거야, Mike?
B: 삼촌이 큰 수영장을 가지고 계셔서 난 대부분의 시간을 삼촌 집에서 보낼 거야.
G: 멋지다. 너 수영 잘하니?
B: 아니, 잘했으면 좋겠는데, 못해. 그래서 대신 나는 물 위를 걷는 공을 가지고 놀 거야.
G: 물 위를 걷는 공? 그게 뭐야?
B: 그건 큰 공이야. 그 안에 들어가서 물 위를 걸으면 돼.
G: 그거 분명 재밌겠다.

Bora: Jessie야, 뭐 하고 있어?
Jessie: 내가 제일 좋아하는 슈퍼 영웅인 닥터 레베카를 그리고 있어.
Bora: 와, 훌륭해.
Jessie: 고마워. 나는 그녀처럼 사람들의 마음을 읽을 수 있으면 좋겠어.
Bora: 그녀가 사람들의 마음을 통제하는 것도 가능하니?
Jessie: 응. 그녀가 원하면 네 마음을 통제할 수 있어.
Bora: 그거 정말 멋지다.
Jessie: 너는 어때? 너도 좋아하는 슈퍼 영웅이 있니?
Bora: 물론. 나는 스카이 X를 좋아해. 스카이 X처럼 하늘을 날 수 있으면 좋겠어.
Jessie: 나도 그가 좋아. 그는 우주에서 숨 쉴 수도 있잖아.
Bora: 응. 그는 우주에서 뭐든 할 수 있어.

W: 안녕, Tom. 무엇을 하는 중이니?
B: 지금 드론을 날리고 있어요.
W: 멋지구나! 드론 조종을 잘하니?
B: 아니요, 전 지금은 별로 잘하지 못하지만 열심히 연습하고 있어요.
W: 네가 알다시피, 내가 샌드위치 가게를 운영하고 있잖아. 너는 네 드론으로 주문한 음식을 배달하는 것이 가능하니?
B: 아니요, 불가능해요. 하지만 1~2년 후에는 가능할 거라 생각해요.
W: 그러면 좋겠구나.

01 다음 대화의 빈칸 (A)와 (B)에 공통으로 들어갈 말을 쓰시오. (가주어 it을 쓸 것.)

> A: I'm Sky X. I can fly.
>
> B: Hi, Sky X. Nice to meet you.
>
> C: I wish I could fly like you. (A)_____ to fly to the moon?
>
> A: Sure.
>
> D: Then (B)_____ to travel to the sun?
>
> A: No. That's impossible.

02 다음 대화의 밑줄 친 부분과 바꾸어 쓸 수 있는 것은?

> A: Is it possible for us to arrive in 20 minutes?
>
> B: No. I don't think it's possible.

① Is it possible that you arrive in 20 minutes?

② Do you make sure you can arrive in 20 minutes?

③ Is it likely that we can arrive in 20 minutes?

④ Do you want us to arrive in 20 minutes?

⑤ Can you tell me how to get there in 20 minutes?

[03~04] 다음 대화를 읽고 물음에 답하시오.

> B: Wendy, you have been ①late for school a lot lately. What's wrong?
>
> G: I want to wake up ②early, but I just ③can.
>
> B: Doesn't your mom wake you up?
>
> G: She ④does, but I don't get up right away. I wish (A)_____
>
> B: An AI robot?
>
> G: Yes. I mean one that could make sure I got up and give me breakfast in the morning.
>
> B: That sounds ⑤great.

03 밑줄 친 ①~⑤ 중 대화의 흐름상 어색한 것은?

①   ②   ③   ④   ⑤

04 빈칸 (A)에 알맞은 말을 쓰시오. (6 words)

➡ _____

[01~02] 다음 대화를 읽고 물음에 답하시오.

G: Can you draw this on the paper?
B: (A)Sure. From the middle point, I draw two triangles. Then I draw the circle, like this.
G: Good. Now, is it possible for you to draw it without taking your pencil off the paper?
B: I'll try. Hmm... No, how is that possible?
G: Well, start at one of the four red points.
B: Do you mean any of the red points?
G: Yes. Draw the circle first and then the two triangles like this. Or you can draw the triangles first, like this.
B: Oh, now I get it.

01 밑줄 친 (A)를 대신하여 쓸 수 있는 것은?

① I'm not certain.
② That depends on you.
③ Yes. I think it's possible.
④ Don't be so negative.
⑤ Of course not.

02 Choose one that is TRUE.

① They are making something with paper.
② There are five red points on the paper.
③ The boy doesn't know how to draw the picture at all.
④ It doesn't matter which red point you choose.
⑤ It is impossible for them to draw the picture without taking a pencil off the paper.

[03~05] 다음 대화를 읽고 물음에 답하시오.

B: Wendy, you have been late for school a lot ⓐlately. What's wrong?

G: I want to wake up early, but I just can't.
(A) She does, but I don't get up right away. I wish I could have an AI robot.
(B) That sounds great.
(C) An AI robot?
(D) Doesn't your mom wake you up?
(E) Yes. I mean one that could make sure I got up and give me breakfast in the morning.

서답형
03 자연스러운 대화가 되도록 (A)~(E)를 바르게 나열하시오.

➡ _____

04 밑줄 친 ⓐ를 대신할 수 있는 것은?

① for a long time   ② recently
③ hardly   ④ behind time
⑤ frankly

서답형
05 Write the reason why Wendy has been late for school. Use the phrase 'It is because.'

➡ _____

서답형
06 주어진 단어를 활용하여 빈칸에 들어갈 말을 완성하시오.

A: _____
(wish / invent)
B: A time machine? What would you do with it?

07 다음 대화의 빈칸에 들어갈 말로 가장 적절한 것은?

> **A:** _____
> **B:** What would you do with it?
> **A:** I would send messages to my friends.

① I wish I had many friends.
② I want to have a watch.
③ I wish you could have a computer.
④ I'd like to have something to write.
⑤ I wish I could have a smartphone.

08 다음 대화의 밑줄 친 부분의 목적으로 가장 적절한 것은?

> **A:** <u>Is it possible for you to make a classmate laugh in 10 seconds?</u>
> **B:** Sure.

① asking for an opinion
② asking for possibility
③ saying hello to friends
④ making some suggestions
⑤ asking for help

09 다음 짝지어진 대화 중 어색한 것은?

① A: I wish I could fly like a bird.
  B: Why do you say so?
② A: Is it possible to visit the park on our second day?
  B: Sure. That sounds exciting.
③ A: Can we exchange this hat for a bigger one?
  B: Absolutely. It's not likely.
④ A: Is it likely that we can survive in Mars?
  B: No. I don't think it's possible.
⑤ A: I wish I could live on the water.
  B: Living on the water sounds interesting.

[10~12] 다음 대화를 읽고 물음에 답하시오.

> **W:** Hi, Tom. ①<u>무엇을 하는 중이니?</u>
> **B:** I'm flying my drone.
> **W:** Cool! ②<u>드론 조종을 잘하니?</u>
> **B:** No, I'm not very good right now, but ③<u>열심히 연습하고 있어요.</u>
> **W:** As you know, I run a sandwich restaurant. (A)<u>Is it possible for you to deliver orders with your drone?</u>
> **B:** ④<u>아니요, 불가능해요.</u> But I think it will be possible ⑤<u>1~2년 후에는.</u>
> **W:** That will be great.

10 밑줄 친 ①~⑤ 중 영어로 바르게 옮겨지지 <u>않은</u> 것은?

① What are you doing?
② Are you good at it?
③ I'm practicing hardly
④ No, it isn't.
⑤ in one or two years

11 Choose one that is TRUE.

① Tom is not interested in flying his drone.
② Tom doesn't know that the woman runs a restaurant.
③ Tom thinks he is skillful enough to deliver orders.
④ The woman wants Tom to deliver orders with his drone.
⑤ The woman wonders if Tom wants to work with his friends.

서답형
12 주어진 단어를 활용하여 밑줄 친 (A)와 같은 의미의 말을 쓰시오.

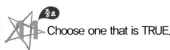

(can)

➡ _____

[01~03] 다음 대화를 읽고 물음에 답하시오.

G: (A)Can you draw this on the paper?

B: Sure. From the middle point, I draw two triangles. Then I draw the circle, like this.

G: Good. Now, is it possible for you to draw it without taking your pencil off the paper?

B: I'll try. Hmm... No, how is (B)that possible?

G: Well, start at one of the four red points.

B: Do you mean any of the red points?

G: Yes. Draw the circle first and then the two triangles like this. Or you can draw the triangles first, like this.

B: Oh, now I get it.

01 위 대화에 나오는 표현을 이용하여 밑줄 친 (A)와 같은 의미의 문장을 쓰시오.

➡ _____

02 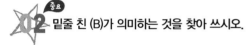 밑줄 친 (B)가 의미하는 것을 찾아 쓰시오.

➡ _____

03 Write the two ways how to draw the picture without taking off the pencil. Answer in Korean.

➡ _____

_____

04 다음은 Jane이 무인도에 홀로 남겨진다면 꼭 해야 할 일이라고 생각하는 것이다. 'I wish'를 이용하여 표현하시오.

• keep calm and pass the time
• create a shelter
• wait for help
• find food

➡ _____

_____

_____

_____

[05~06] 다음 대화를 읽고 물음에 답하시오.

Bora: What are you doing, Jessie?

Jessie: I'm drawing Dr. Rebecca, my favorite superhero.

Bora: Wow, that's great.

Jessie: Thanks. I wish I could read people's minds like her.

Bora: Is it possible for her to control them, too?

Jessie: Yes. She can control your mind if she wants to.

Bora: That's very cool.

Jessie: What about you? Do you also have any favorite superheroes?

Bora: Sure. I love Sky X. I wish I could fly like him.

Jessie: I like him, too. He can even breathe in space.

Bora: Yes. He can do anything in space.

05 According to the dialogue, what is it possible for Dr. Rebecca to do? Answer in English.

➡ _____

_____

06 Who is Bora's favorite superhero?

➡ _____

Grammar

① I wish 가정법 과거

> • **I wish** she had a better robotic hand. 그녀가 더 좋은 로봇 손을 가지면 좋을 텐데.
>
> • **I wish** Tony could live in this town so that we could easily get together. Tony가 이 마을에 살아서 우리가 쉽게 만날 수 있으면 좋을 텐데.

■ 'I wish' 가정법 과거는 현재 사실에 반대되는 소망 또는 현재 사실에 대한 유감을 나타낸다.

- **I wish** I **were** a great inventor like Edison. 내가 에디슨 같은 훌륭한 발명가라면 좋을 텐데.
  = In fact, I**'m not** a great inventor like Edison. (현재 사실 반대)
  = **I'm sorry that** I**'m not** a great inventor like Edison. (유감)

■ 가정법 과거: 현재 사실을 반대로 또는 실현 가능성이 없는 일을 가정. '**If**+주어+**동사 과거형** ~, 주어 +**would/could**+**동사원형** ….'의 형태, '만약 ~라면 …할 텐데.'의 뜻.

- **If** she **had** a car, she **would take** me to the airport. 그녀가 차가 있다면, 나를 공항까지 데려다 줄 텐데. (가 정법 과거, 현재 사실의 반대 가정)
  = **As** she **doesn't have** a car, she **won't take** me to the airport.
  cf. **If** she **has** a car, she **will take** me to the airport. 조건문(현재 또는 미래의 가능성)

■ 가정법 과거완료: 이미 일어난 과거 사실을 반대로 가정. '**If**+주어+**had**+**과거분사** ~, 주어+**would/ could**+**have**+**과거분사** ….'의 형태, '만약 ~했었더라면 …했을 텐데.'의 뜻.

- **If** they **had stopped** at the gas station, **they would not have run** out of gas. 그들이 주유소에 들렀더라면 기름이 떨어지지 않았을 텐데.

■ 'I wish' 가정법 과거완료: 과거 사실에 반대되는 소망 또는 과거 사실에 대한 유감을 나타낸다.

- **I wish** he **had not gone** there alone. 그가 그곳에 혼자 가지 않았더라면 좋을 텐데.
  = **I'm sorry that** he **went** there alone. (그가 혼자 갔던 것이 안타깝다.)

■ 가정법의 다양한 표현들

- **As** he **is** weak, he **can't** lift the box. 그는 약해서, 그 상자를 들 수 없다. (직설법)
  → **If** he **were not** weak, he **could** lift the box. 그가 약하지 않으면, 그 상자를 들 수 있을 텐데. (가정법)
  → **Were** he **not** weak, he **could** lift the box. (If 생략 후 be동사와 주어 도치)
  → **Without** his being weak, he **could** lift the box. (without 표현)
  → **If it were not for** his being weak, he **could** lift the box.
  → **Were it not for** his being weak, he **could** lift the box. (If 생략 후 be동사와 주어 도치)

핵심 Check

1. 다음 괄호 안의 단어를 활용하여 빈칸에 알맞은 단어를 써 넣으시오.

(1) I wish my uncle _____ with us. (live)

(2) I wish I _____ a doctor. (be) I want to cure my mom's heart.

(3) I wish Janet _____ sing well. (can) I can't stand it any more.

② 의문사가 없는 의문문의 간접의문문

- I wondered **if I could do something for those girls**. 나는 내가 그 소녀들을 위해서 어떤 것을 할 수 있을까 생각했다.

- I am not sure **whether the baby is hungry or sad**. 나는 그 아기가 배가 고픈 것인지 슬픈 것인지 모르겠다.

■ 간접의문문 만들기

(1) 의문사가 있을 때: '의문사+주어+동사' 어순
- She doesn't care. + Who is he? → She doesn't care **who he is**.
- Can he tell her? + What am I doing? → Can he tell her **what I am doing**?
- Nobody knows. + How did she come here? → Nobody knows **how she came here**.

cf. 주절의 동사가 think, believe, guess, suppose, imagine 등일 때, 의문사는 문두로 간다.
- Do you think? + Why is she upset? → **Why** do you <u>think</u> **she is upset**?
- Do you guess? + Who will be late? → **Who** do you <u>guess</u> **will be late**?

(2) 의문사가 없을 때: 'whether/if+주어+동사' 어순
- Does he know? + Is she upset? → Does he **know if she is upset**?
- I wonder. + Did she eat the cake? → I wonder **whether she ate the cake**.
- I'm not sure. + Is it going to rain? → I'm not sure **if it's going to rain**.
- I don't know. + Can anyone drink this? → I don't know **if anyone can drink this**.
- Do you know? + Does Paul speak Korean? → Do you know **whether Paul speaks Korean**?

■ whether와 if의 차이

(1) whether는 문두에서 주절을 이끌 수 있다. (if는 불가능)
- **Whether** he will join us (or not) is not certain. (그가 함께 할지는 확실하지 않다.)

(2) whether는 전치사 뒤에서 명사절 목적어 가능. (if는 불가능)
- There is an argument **about whether** cell phone use should be allowed in school. (학교에서 휴대전화 사용이 허용되어야 할지에 대한 논란이 있다.)

(3) whether는 to부정사와 붙여 쓸 수 있다. (if는 불가능)
- How can you decide **whether to use** 'that' or 'which'? (that을 쓸지, which를 쓸지 당신은 어떻게 결정합니까?)

(4) 'whether or not' 가능 (if는 불가능. 단, 'or not'을 뒤에 따로 쓰면 가능)
- I wonder **whether or not** it was true. (나는 그것이 사실이었는지 아닌지 궁금하다.)
- No one knows **whether[if]** she'll die **or not**. (아무도 그녀가 죽을 지 안 죽을지를 모른다.)

핵심 Check

2. 다음 괄호 안에서 알맞은 말을 고르시오.

(1) They wonder (if / that) Mike is sleeping on a sofa.

(2) Irene asked the expert (that / whether) her dog could be nice again.

01 다음 각 가정법 문장에서 어법상 어색한 단어를 한 개씩만 찾아 고치시오.

(1) I wish I can pay for the school fees for the African girls.

_____ ➡ _____

(2) I wish the girl has a better robotic hand.

_____ ➡ _____

(3) If we work together, we could build a better world.

_____ ➡ _____

(4) If the girl were not poor, she may go to school.

_____ _____

02 다음 각 문장의 빈칸에 공통으로 들어갈 말로 알맞은 것은? (대 · 소문자 구분 없음)

> • I wondered _____ I could solve the problem.
> • _____ it will rain tomorrow or not depends on the wind.
> • They asked _____ she could predict the result of the experiment.

① if   ② that   ③ what
④ whether   ⑤ which

03 다음 빈칸에 들어갈 말로 알맞은 것은?

> I wish the small holes in the corn cobs _____ dirty matter.

① filter   ② will filter   ③ has filtered
④ could filter   ⑤ are filtered

04 다음 중 밑줄 친 부분의 쓰임이 〈보기〉와 같은 것을 고르시오.

> ┤ 보기 ├
> I'm not sure if we could win the first prize.

① Why don't we take a taxi if your babies feel too tired?
② You will never miss the train if you leave now.
③ All the students wondered if what she said was true.
④ Nicole can use her phone if she finishes the math homework.
⑤ Mike will be in trouble if he keeps eating junk food.

[01~03] 다음 중 어법상 <u>어색한</u> 문장은?

01
① I wish many girls in Africa could go to school.
② I wish my mom weren't sick from food poisoning.
③ I wish his invention could clean up all the lakes in my village.
④ I wish someone will make her a better robotic hand.
⑤ I wish they made much cheaper and better tools for the poor people.

02
① If I were in California, I would never be safe from the disease.
② If her father were very rich, she might be allowed a car.
③ If it were not for his help, I would not be able to use the system.
④ If the boy knew the answer to the quiz, he would tell me.
⑤ If I pushed the doors hard, they can be broken.

03
① I wonder whether or not Brian heard of my broken heart.
② I wonder whether Brian heard of my broken heart or not.
③ I wonder if or not Brian heard of my broken heart.
④ I wonder if Brian heard of my broken heart.
⑤ I wonder if Brian heard of my broken heart or not.

서답형

[04~07] 다음 우리말과 일치하도록 괄호 안에 주어진 어구를 바르게 배열하시오.

04
당신이 나를 도와줄 수 있을지 모르겠지만, 그럴 수 있기를 바란다.
(help, I, me, you, know, if, don't, can), but I hope you can.

➡ _____

05
내가 미국의 대통령이라면 좋을 텐데.
(the President, I, I, of, were, wish, the United States).

➡ _____

06
David은 그 집에 화장실이 있는지 나에게 물어봤다.
(there, whether, asked, was, me, a bathroom, David) in the house.

➡ _____

07
내가 그 소녀라면, 포기할 텐데.
(give up, the girl, I, I, if, would, were).

➡ _____

[08~10] 다음 중 밑줄 친 부분의 쓰임이 나머지 넷과 다른 것은?

08
① I was wondering <u>if</u> the man would lend me some money.
② I wonder <u>if</u> the kids dancing under the sun ate lunch today.
③ Please tell me <u>if</u> your teacher will read the invitation card or not.
④ Let's go swimming in the sea <u>if</u> it is fine this weekend.
⑤ The queen of the tribe wanted to know <u>if</u> the visitor could help her.

09 중요
① I wish the boy who I met yesterday <u>could</u> eat Kimchi.
② I <u>could</u> not help but laugh at the funny dress my dad wore.
③ If my uncle were not ill, he <u>could</u> take me to the amusement park.
④ If Sandy got an A in the math test, her mom <u>would</u> buy her a new laptop.
⑤ If I had some money, I <u>could</u> buy you the mask you need.

10
① I'm wondering <u>if</u> Julie could help the kids in need.
② Karen was not sure <u>if</u> Jimin would come to the party.
③ Focus on the inner voice <u>if</u> you want to listen to your true self.
④ Do you know <u>if</u> she is going to study abroad or get married?
⑤ I'd like to know <u>if</u> my online fashion business will succeed.

11 다음 우리말을 영작할 때, 어법상 어색한 문장을 고르시오.

> 공기가 없다면, 지구에 생명체가 살 수 없을 것이다.

① Without air, lives on Earth would not be able to live.
② If there is no air, lives on Earth would not be able to live.
③ Were it not for air, lives on Earth would not be able to live.
④ If it were not for air, lives on Earth would not be able to live.
⑤ If there were no air, lives on Earth would not be able to live.

12 중요 다음 짝지어진 두 문장의 의미가 다른 것은?
① I wish my best friend Saya were a great musical actor.
 = In fact, my best friend Saya is not a great musical actor.
② If the boys studied harder, they could get good grades.
 = As the boys don't study harder, they can't get good grades.
③ I wish I could play all the musical instruments in the museum.
 = I am sorry that I can't play all the musical instruments in the museum.
④ If Susan told lies more often than now, I would not believe her.
 = As Susan doesn't tell lies more often than now, I believe her.
⑤ I wish I could make a much cheaper and better robotic hand.
 = I'm sorry that I couldn't make a much cheaper and better robotic hand.

13 다음 중 같은 뜻을 가진 문장으로 바르게 연결된 것은?

① Vannessa's sister doesn't have a cell phone, so she wants to get one.
= Vannessa's sister would get a cell phone if she wanted to have one.

② Nicky doesn't practice hard, so she can't show her parents what she wants.
= If Nicky practiced hard, she could show her parents what she wants.

③ Paul didn't have time, so he couldn't drive his daughter home.
= If Paul had time, he would drive his daughter home.

④ Grandma can't write a letter to my aunt as she doesn't know her address.
= Grandma couldn't write a letter to my aunt if she didn't know her address.

⑤ It rained cats and dogs, so all my family members stayed home.
= If it rained cats and dogs, all my family members wouldn't stay home.

[14~15] 다음 우리말을 어법상 알맞게 영작한 것을 고르시오.

14

그 어린 소녀는 그가 로봇 손을 만들 수 있는지 물었다.

① The little girl asked him to make the robotic hand.

② The little girl asked that he could make the robotic hand.

③ The little girl asked him that he could make the robotic hand.

④ The little girl asked him if he could make the robotic hand.

⑤ The little girl asked him whether he made the robotic hand.

15

나는 그가 수질 오염 문제를 해결할 수 있을지 궁금했다.

① I was wondering whether he can solve the problem of polluted water.

② I wondered whether the problem of polluted water can be solved by him.

③ I was curious about whether he will solve the problem of polluted water.

④ I wondered whether or not the problem of polluted water is solved by him.

⑤ I wondered whether he could solve the problem of polluted water.

16 다음 문장의 빈칸 (A)~(C)에 들어갈 말로 가장 적절한 것은?

- I wish I (A)_____ a mentor who could give me advice on my future job.
- Were it not for the sacrifice of the medical staff in our country, we (B)_____ be in trouble by the disease.
- I wish the girl (C)_____ a better and cheaper robotic hand and leg.

	(A)	(B)	(C)
①	had	will	has had
②	have	would	has
③	have	could	had
④	had	would	had
⑤	have had	will	has

01 다음 우리말과 일치하도록 괄호 안에 주어진 어구를 빈칸에 알맞게 배열하시오.

(1) 많은 가난한 소녀들이 학교에 갈 수 있도록 내가 수업료를 지불할 수 있으면 좋을 텐데.

➡ _____

_____ go to school. (could, I, pay, many, to, wish, the school fees, I, poor girls, for)

(2) 옥수수 솟대 안의 작은 구멍들이 오염된 물로부터 더러운 물질을 걸러낼 수 있으면 좋을 텐데.

➡ _____

_____ dirty matter out of the polluted water. (the small holes, could, in, wish, the corn cobs, filter, I)

(3) 과학 박람회에서 만났던 그 소녀가 더 나은 로봇 손을 가지면 좋을 텐데.

➡ _____

a better robotic hand. (met, had, a science fair, wish, I, I, at, the girl)

(4) 마을 사람들이 나를 도와주면, 여과 장치를 만들 수 있을 텐데.

➡ If _____

a filtering system. (me, could, the villagers, build, I, helped)

02 다음 문장에서 어법상 <u>어색한</u> 단어를 하나만 찾아 바르게 고쳐 다시 쓰시오.

(1) I asked myself that night if I can solve the problem of the polluted water.

➡ _____

_____

(2) Tony wasn't sure that he could make it but he decided to try.

➡ _____

_____

(3) If Jane will follow her heart or not is important in her life.

➡ _____

_____

(4) Even her closest friends doubted whether could she do something for the girls in Africa.

➡ _____

_____

(5) Most people in my town are wondering if it rains next week.

➡ _____

_____

(6) Sean couldn't decide if to reject the job offer or not.

➡ _____

_____

(7) The researchers want to know that my filtering system can clean up all the lakes not only in my village but also in other areas.

➡ _____

_____

_____

03 다음 〈보기〉의 문장과 같은 뜻이 되도록 괄호 안에 주어진 조건에 맞게 빈칸을 채우시오.

┌─ 보기 ├─
Without her invention, the town would suffer from the problem of polluted water.
└─

(1) _____ her invention, the town would suffer from the problem of polluted water. (2 단어)

(2) _____ her invention, the town would suffer from the problem of polluted water. (it, be동사 활용, 5 단어)

(3) _____ her invention, the town would suffer from the problem of polluted water. (it, be동사 활용, 4 단어)

(4) _____ not suffer from the problem of polluted water. (직설법, there, 접속사 as 활용, 8 단어)

04 다음 그림과 대화를 보고 우리말에 맞게 괄호 안의 어구를 알맞게 배열하시오.

Mrs. Forestier: What's the matter?
Matilda: Can I borrow something from you?
Mrs. Forestier: Sure. Choose whatever.
Matilda: This diamond necklace is beautiful! Will you lend me this?
Mrs. Forestier: Certainly! Go enjoy the ball!

(1) Matilda는 Mrs. Forestier로부터 뭔가를 빌릴 수 있을지 궁금해 했다.
(if, Mrs. Forestier, borrow, Matilda, she, could, something, wondered, from)

➡ _____

_____

(2) Matilda는 Mrs. Forestier에게 그 다이아몬드 목걸이를 빌려줄 것인지 물어봤다.
(if, Matilda, Mrs. Forestier, her, she, lend, would, that, asked, diamond necklace)

➡ _____

_____

[05~06] 다음 주어진 문장과 같은 뜻이 되도록 가정법을 이용하되, 글자 수 조건에 맞게 빈칸을 채우시오.

05
As the poor girls in Africa can't go to school, I feel sorry for it.
➡ I _____ to school. (8 단어)

06
I am sorry that I don't sing well like my grandfather who is a singer.
➡ I _____ my grandfather who is a singer. (5 단어)

[07~08] 다음 우리말을 if가 포함된 간접의문문을 사용하여 괄호 안에 주어진 조건과 글자 수에 맞게 영작하시오.

07
Susan이 한국말을 하는지 Mike에게 물어보아라.
(speak 활용, 변형 가능, 총 6 단어)

➡ _____

08
Gloria는 자신의 아기가 배가 고픈 것인지 슬픈 것인지 확신할 수 없었다.
(be sure 활용, 변형 가능, 축약형 불가, 총 11 단어)

➡ _____

Reading

Great Help with a Beautiful Mind

Who are the people who change the world? Do you think you are too
young to be one of these people? In the following stories you will meet
three teenagers who used their ideas to make the world a better place.

A Robotic Hand from a Helpful Mind (Easton LaChappelle)

One day, when I was fourteen, I came across a little girl at a science
fair. She had a robotic hand that could only open and close. I was
surprised that the hand had cost her 80,000 dollars! 'I wish she had a
better robotic hand,' I thought to myself. With that, I started to make a
much cheaper and better robotic hand.

After many failures, finally, by using 3D printing technology, I was
able to make a useful robotic hand for the price of only 300 dollars.

I decided to share the designs and software for my 3D robotic hand
with others for free. Maybe someone can take what I have done and do
something useful with it. No one person can change the world, but we
can build a better world by working together.

Headbands for Girls' Education (Mary Grace Henry)

'Why can't many girls in Africa go to school as I can? I wish they
could go to school, too.' I had this thought when I was twelve. I
realized that their families couldn't afford it. I wondered if I could do
something for those girls.

---

teenager: 십 대
robotic: 로봇식의
fair: 박람회
software: 소프트웨어
failure: 실패
come across: (우연히) 만나다
headband: 머리띠
realize: 깨닫다, 인식하다
afford: ~할 (금전적인) 여유가 되다

확인문제

- 다음 문장이 본문의 내용과 일치하면 T, 일치하지 않으면 F를 쓰시오.

1 At a science fair, Easton came across a girl who had a robotic hand. ☐

2 Easton succeeded in making a better robotic hand after many failures. ☐

3 The 3D printed robotic hand costs 80,000 dollars. ☐

Then I had an idea. For my birthday, I asked my parents to buy me
ask+목적어+to부정사: …가 ~하도록 요청하다
a sewing machine. They bought me one, and I learned how to make
= a sewing machine   *= how I can make*
headbands for myself. I created ten headbands and sold them at my
스스로
school. Soon, I raised enough money to send one girl in Africa to
school. I couldn't stop there.
열 개의 머리띠를 팔아 한 소녀의 학비를 모은 것을 뜻함
  I started a business to help girls in Africa who couldn't go to school.
to부정사의 부사적 용법 중 목적(~하기 위해서)   *주격 관계대명사*
Thanks to the success of my business, I can pay the school fees for
many poor girls in countries like Kenya and Uganda to go to school. I
also pay for their textbooks, uniforms, and pencils.
Isn't it amazing? My advice to you is to just do something. When you
놀라움을 유발하므로 현재분사
see a need, act. Start small, taking little steps. Your warm heart can
= Start small as you take little steps.
change lives.

Useless Corn Cobs as Useful Water Filters (Lalita Prasida)

  As a young girl living in the countryside in India, I often found that
현재분사가 a young girl을 뒤에서 수식   *명사절 접속사(find의 목적어를 이끎)*
the water around us was seriously polluted. I wondered how I could
solve this problem. Then I hit on the idea to use corn cobs.
간접의문문(의문사+주어+동사)
  Useless corn cobs were everywhere in my village. I thought that the
small holes in the corn cobs could filter dirty matter out of the polluted
water.
~에서
  One day, I picked up some dried cobs along the road, washed them,
and placed them in a bowl of dirty water. After a while, I checked the
picked. washed. and placed의 병렬 관계
water, and it looked much clearer. Then, using corn cobs that I had
the water 지칭   *= as I used*
collected from farmers, I built a filtering system.
여과 장치를 만들었던 것(built)보다 더 앞서 일어났으므로 과거완료가 쓰임
My system removed 70 to 80 percent of the dirty matter from the
water. I hope my filtering system can clean up all the lakes not only in
hope (that) ~   *not only A but also: B: A뿐만 아니라 B도*
my village but also in other areas.

---

raise: (자금을) 모으다
sewing machine: 재봉틀
business: 사업
success: 성공
fee: 요금
thanks to: ~ 덕분에
useless: 쓸모없는, 소용없는
filter: 필터, 여과 장치
countryside: 시골
pollute: 오염시키다
corn cob: 옥수수 속대
hit on: 불현듯 ~을 생각해 내다

 확인문제

● 다음 문장이 본문의 내용과 일치하면 T, 일치하지 <u>않으면</u> F를 쓰시오.

1   Mary made headbands for her friends with the sewing machine. ☐

2   Mary believes people's lives can be changed by warm heart. ☐

3   Lalita wants the filtering system to be used only in her town. ☐

● 우리말을 참고하여 빈칸에 알맞은 말을 쓰시오.

1 Who are the people _____ _____ the world? Do you think you are _____ _____ _____ _____ one of these people?

2 In the following stories you _____ _____ three teenagers who used their ideas _____ _____ the world a better place.

A Robotic Hand from a Helpful Mind (Easton LaChappelle)

3 One day, _____ I was fourteen, I _____ _____ a little girl _____ a science _____ .

4 She had a _____ hand _____ could only _____ and _____ .

5 I was _____ _____ the hand _____ _____ _____ 80,000 dollars!

6 'I _____ she _____ a better robotic hand,' I thought _____ _____ .

7 With that, I started to make _____ _____ _____ and _____ robotic hand.

8 After many _____ , finally, _____ _____ 3D printing technology, I _____ _____ _____ make a useful robotic hand _____ the price _____ only 300 dollars.

9 I decided _____ _____ the designs and software _____ my 3D robotic hand _____ _____ _____ _____ .

10 Maybe someone can _____ _____ _____ _____ _____ and do _____ _____ with it.

11 _____ _____ person can _____ the world, but we can _____ a better world _____ _____ together.

Headbands for Girls' Education (Mary Grace Henry)

12 'Why _____ many girls in Africa _____ _____ _____ as I can? I wish they _____ _____ to school, too.'

13 I _____ _____ _____ when I was twelve. I _____ _____ their families couldn't _____ it.

14 I wondered _____ _____ _____ _____ _____ for those girls. Then I _____ an idea.

---

1 세상을 바꾸는 사람들은 누구인 가? 여러분은 너무 어려서 이런 사람들 중 하나가 될 수 없다고 생각하나요?

2 다음 이야기에서 여러분은 세상 을 더 나은 곳으로 만들기 위해 자신들의 아이디어를 사용한 세 명의 십 대들을 만날 겁니다.

돕는 마음으로부터 탄생한 로봇 손 (Easton LaChappelle)

3 내가 열네 살이었을 때, 어느 날 한 과학 박람회에서 어린 소녀를 우연히 만났다.

4 그녀는 겨우 접었다 펴지기만 하 는 로봇 손을 가지고 있었다.

5 나는 그녀가 그 손에 8만 달러를 지불했다는 데 놀랐다!

6 '나는 그녀가 더 나은 로봇 손을 가질 수 있으면 좋겠어.'라고 마음 속으로 생각했다.

7 나는 이런 생각을 가지고 더 싸고 좋은 로봇 손을 만들기 시작했다.

8 많은 실패 뒤 마침내 3D 프린트 기술을 사용해서 나는 단 300달 러짜리의 유용한 로봇 손을 만들 수 있었다.

9 나는 내 3D 로봇 손의 디자인과 소프트웨어를 다른 사람들과 무 료로 공유하기로 결심했다.

10 아마도 누군가는 내가 만든 것을 이용해 다른 유용한 것을 할 수 있을 것이다.

11 혼자 세상을 바꿀 수는 없지만, 함께 일 하면서 더 나은 세상을 만들 수 있다.

여학생 교육을 위한 머리띠 (Mary Grace Henry)

12 '아프리카의 많은 소녀들은 왜 나 처럼 학교에 갈 수 없지? 나는 그 들도 학교에 갈 수 있으면 좋을 텐데.'

13 내가 12살 때, 이런 생각을 했었 다. 나는 그들의 가족이 그럴 금 전적 여유가 없다는 것을 깨달았 다.

14 나는 내가 그 소녀들을 위해서 어 떤 것을 할 수 있을까 생각했다. 그때 아이디어가 떠올랐다.

15 For my birthday, I _____ my parents to _____ _____
_____ _____.

16 They _____ _____ _____, and I learned _____
_____ _____ headbands for myself.

17 I created _____ _____ and sold _____ at my school.

18 Soon, I _____ _____ _____ _____ to send one girl in Africa
to school. I couldn't _____ there.

19 I started _____ _____ to help girls in Africa _____
couldn't _____ to school.

20 Thanks _____ _____ _____ of my business, I can pay
the school _____ _____ many poor girls in countries
_____ Kenya and Uganda _____ _____ _____
_____.

21 I also _____ _____ their _____, _____, and
pencils. Isn't it _____?

22 My _____ to you _____ to just _____ _____.
When you see _____ _____, _____.

23 Start _____, _____ little steps. Your warm heart can
change _____.

Useless Corn Cobs as Useful Water Filters (Lalita Prasida)

24 _____ a young girl _____ in the countryside in India, I
_____ _____ _____ the water around us was _____
_____.

25 I wondered _____ _____ _____ _____ this
problem. Then I _____ _____ the idea _____
_____ corn cobs.

26 _____ corn cobs _____ everywhere _____ my village.

27 I thought that _____ _____ _____ in the corn cobs
_____ _____ _____ _____ out of the _____
water.

28 One day, I _____ up some dried cobs along the road,
_____ _____, and _____ them _____ _____
_____ _____ dirty water.

29 _____ _____ _____ _____, I checked the water, and
_____ looked _____ _____.

30 Then, _____ corn cobs _____ I had _____
farmers, I built a _____ system.

31 My system _____ 70 to 80 percent of _____ _____
_____ from the water.

32 I hope my _____ _____ can _____ _____ all the
lakes _____ _____ in my village _____ _____ in
other areas.

---

15 나는 내 생일에 부모님께 재봉틀을 사 달라고 부탁드렸다.

16 그들은 재봉틀을 사 주셨고 나는 머리띠 만드는 법을 혼자 배웠다.

17 10개의 머리띠를 만들어 학교에서 팔았다.

18 나는 곧 아프리카에 있는 한 명의 소녀를 학교에 보낼 수 있는 충분한 자금을 모았다. 나는 거기서 멈출 수 없었다.

19 나는 학교에 갈 수 없는 아프리카의 소녀들을 돕기 위해 사업을 시작했다.

20 내 사업의 성공 덕분에 나는 케냐와 우간다 같은 나라에 있는 많은 가난한 소녀들이 학교에 갈 수 있게 수업료를 지불할 수 있다.

21 나는 또한 그들의 교과서와 교복, 연필을 위한 비용도 지불한다. 놀랍지 않은가?

22 나의 조언은 그냥 무엇이든 하라는 것이다. 필요성이 보인다면 행동하라.

23 작은 단계를 밟아가면서 작은 것부터 시작하라. 너의 따뜻한 마음이 삶을 바꿀 수 있다.

유용한 물 여과 장치로 쓰인 쓸모없는 옥수수 속대 (Lalita Prasida)

24 인도의 시골에 살고 있었던 어린 소녀인 나는 종종 내 주변에 있는 물이 심각하게 오염되어 있는 것을 발견했다.

25 나는 이 문제를 어떻게 해결할 수 있을지 궁금했다. 그때 나는 옥수수 속대를 이용해야겠다는 생각이 불현듯 떠올랐다.

26 내가 사는 마을에는 쓸모없는 옥수수 속대가 곳곳에 널려 있다.

27 나는 옥수수 속대의 작은 구멍들이 더러운 물질을 오염된 물 밖으로 걸러 낼 수 있을 거라고 생각했다.

28 어느 날 나는 길을 따라 마른 옥수수 속대를 주운 뒤, 그것들을 씻어서 더러운 물이 담긴 그릇에 넣었다.

29 잠시 뒤 물을 확인했는데 훨씬 더 맑게 보였다.

30 그리고 나서 나는 농부들로부터 모은 옥수수 속대를 이용하여 여과 장치를 만들었다.

31 내 장치는 물에서 70~80%의 더러운 물질을 제거했다.

32 나는 내 여과 장치가 내 마을뿐만 아니라 다른 지역에 있는 모든 호수를 깨끗하게 해 줄 수 있기를 희망한다.

● 우리말을 참고하여 본문을 영작하시오.

1 세상을 바꾸는 사람들은 누구인가? 여러분은 너무 어려서 이런 사람들 중 하나가 될 수 없다고 생각하나요?

➡ _____

_____

2 다음 이야기에서 여러분은 세상을 더 나은 곳으로 만들기 위해 자신들의 아이디어를 사용한 세 명의 십 대들을 만날 겁니다

➡ _____

_____

A Robotic Hand from a Helpful Mind (Easton LaChappelle)

3 내가 열네 살이었을 때, 어느 날 한 과학 박람회에서 어린 소녀를 우연히 만났다.

➡ _____

4 그녀는 겨우 접었다 펴지기만 하는 로봇 손을 가지고 있었다.

➡ _____

5 나는 그녀가 그 손에 8만 달러를 지불했다는 데 놀랐다!

➡ _____

6 '나는 그녀가 더 나은 로봇 손을 가질 수 있으면 좋겠어.'라고 마음속으로 생각했다.

➡ _____

7 나는 이런 생각을 가지고 더 싸고 좋은 로봇 손을 만들기 시작했다.

➡ _____

8 많은 실패 뒤 마침내 3D 프린트 기술을 사용해서 나는 단 300달러짜리의 유용한 로봇 손을 만들 수 있었다.

➡ _____

_____

9 나는 내 3D 로봇 손의 디자인과 소프트웨어를 다른 사람들과 무료로 공유하기로 결심했다.

➡ _____

10 아마도 누군가는 내가 만든 것을 이용해 다른 유용한 것을 할 수 있을 것이다.

➡ _____

11 혼자 세상을 바꿀 수는 없지만, 함께 일 하면서 더 나은 세상을 만들 수 있다.

➡ _____

Headbands for Girls' Education (Mary Grace Henry)

12 '아프리카의 많은 소녀들은 왜 나처럼 학교에 갈 수 없지? 나는 그들도 학교에 갈 수 있으면 좋을 텐데.'

➡ _____

13 내가 12살 때, 이런 생각을 했었다. 나는 그들의 가족이 그럴 금전적 여유가 없다는 것을 깨달았다.

➡ _____

14 나는 내가 그 소녀들을 위해서 어떤 것을 할 수 있을까 생각했다. 그때 아이디어가 떠올랐다.

➡ _____

15 나는 내 생일에 부모님께 재봉틀을 사 달라고 부탁드렸다.

➡ _____

16 그들은 재봉틀을 사 주셨고 나는 머리띠 만드는 법을 혼자 배웠다.

➡ _____

17 10개의 머리띠를 만들어 학교에서 팔았다.

➡ _____

18 나는 곧 아프리카에 있는 한 명의 소녀를 학교에 보낼 수 있는 충분한 자금을 모았다. 나는 거기서 멈출 수 없었다.

➡ _____

19 나는 학교에 갈 수 없는 아프리카의 소녀들을 돕기 위해 사업을 시작했다.

➡ _____

20 내 사업의 성공 덕분에 나는 케냐와 우간다 같은 나라에 있는 많은 가난한 소녀들이 학교에 갈 수 있게 수업료를 지불할 수 있다.

➡ _____

➡ _____

21 나는 또한 그들의 교과서와 교복, 연필을 위한 비용도 지불한다. 놀랍지 않은가?

➡ _____

22 나의 조언은 그냥 무엇이든 하라는 것이다. 필요성이 보인다면 행동하라.

➡ _____

23 작은 단계를 밟아가면서 작은 것부터 시작하라. 너의 따뜻한 마음이 삶을 바꿀 수 있다.

➡ _____

Useless Corn Cobs as Useful Water Filters (Lalita Prasida)

24 인도의 시골에 살고 있었던 어린 소녀인 나는 종종 내 주변에 있는 물이 심각하게 오염되어 있는 것을 발견했다.

➡ _____

25 나는 이 문제를 어떻게 해결할 수 있을지 궁금했다. 그때 나는 옥수수 속대를 이용해야겠다는 생각이 불현듯 떠올랐다.

➡ _____

26 내가 사는 마을에는 쓸모없는 옥수수 속대가 곳곳에 널려 있다.

➡ _____

27 나는 옥수수 속대의 작은 구멍들이 더러운 물질을 오염된 물 밖으로 걸러 낼 수 있을 거라고 생각했다.

➡ _____

28 어느 날 나는 길을 따라 마른 옥수수 속대를 주운 뒤, 그것들을 씻어서 더러운 물이 담긴 그릇에 넣었다.

➡ _____

29 잠시 뒤 물을 확인했는데 훨씬 더 맑게 보였다.

➡ _____

30 그러고 나서 나는 농부들로부터 모은 옥수수 속대를 이용하여 여과 장치를 만들었다.

➡ _____

31 내 장치는 물에서 70~80%의 더러운 물질을 제거했다.

➡ _____

32 나는 내 여과 장치가 내 마을뿐만 아니라 다른 지역에 있는 모든 호수를 깨끗하게 해 줄 수 있기를 희망한다.

➡ _____

[01~02] 다음 글을 읽고 물음에 답하시오.

Who are the people who change the world? Do you think you are too young to be one of (A)these people? In the following stories you will meet three teenagers who used their ideas to make the world a better place.

서답형

01 밑줄 친 (A)가 의미하는 것을 위 글에서 찾아 쓰시오.

➡ _____

중요

02 다음 중 위 글에 이어질 내용으로 가장 적절한 것은?

① some great ideas for teenagers

② some teens who helped world with their ideas

③ people who are good at telling stories

④ some creative people who get their ideas from teenagers

⑤ tips for making the world a better place to live in

[03~05] 다음 글을 읽고 물음에 답하시오.

A Robotic Hand from a Helpful Mind (Easton LaChappelle)

One day, when I was fourteen, I came across a little girl at a science fair. She had ①a robotic hand that could only open and close. I was ②surprised that the hand had cost her 80,000 dollars! 'I wish she had a better robotic hand,' I thought to myself. With that, I started to make a much ③cheaper and better robotic hand. After many ④failures, finally, by using 3D printing technology, I was able to make a ⑤useless robotic hand for the price of only 300 dollars. I decided

to share the designs and software for my 3D robotic hand with others for free. Maybe someone can take what I have done and do something useful with it. No one person can change the world, but we can build a better world by (A)_____.

03 빈칸 (A)에 들어갈 말로 가장 적절한 것은?

① living alone

② working on our own

③ being careful

④ working together

⑤ being creative

중요

04 밑줄 친 ①~⑤ 중 글의 흐름상 어색한 것은?

①   ②   ③   ④   ⑤

서답형

05 What did the writer use to make the robotic hand? Answer in English.

➡ _____

[06~09] 다음 글을 읽고 물음에 답하시오.

Headbands for Girls' Education (Mary Grace Henry)

'Why can't many girls in Africa go to school as I can? I wish they could go to school, too.' (①) I had this thought when I was twelve. I realized that their families couldn't afford it. (②) I wondered if I could do something for those girls. Then I had an idea. (③) They bought me one, and I learned how to make headbands for myself. (④) I created ten headbands and sold them at my school. (⑤) Soon, I raised enough money to send one girl in Africa to school. I couldn't stop there.

I started a business to help girls in Africa who couldn't go to school. Thanks to the success of my business, I can pay the school fees for many poor girls in countries like Kenya and Uganda to go to school. I also pay for their textbooks, uniforms, and pencils.

Isn't it amazing? My advice to you is to just do something. When you see a need, act. Start small, taking little steps. Your warm heart can change lives.

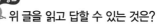

06 (①)~(⑤) 중 주어진 문장이 들어가기에 가장 적절한 곳은?

> For my birthday, I asked my parents to buy me a sewing machine.

①   ②   ③   ④   ⑤

서답형

07 Write the reason why many girls in Africa couldn't go to school. Answer in English. (6 words)

➡ _____

서답형

08 다음과 같이 풀이되는 말을 위 글에서 찾아 쓰시오.

> to have enough money to pay for something

➡ _____

09 위 글을 읽고 답할 수 있는 것은?

① How many African girls can't go to school?
② How much did the writer charge for a headband?
③ When did the writer start the business to help girls in Africa?
④ How do the writer's friends think about her business?
⑤ Where did the writer sell ten headbands?

[10~12] 다음 글을 읽고 물음에 답하시오.

(A)_____ (Lalita Prasida)

As a young girl living in the countryside in India, I often found ①that the water around us was seriously ②polluted. I wondered how I could solve this problem. Then I hit on the idea ③to use corn cobs. Useless corn cobs were everywhere in my village. I thought that the small holes in the corn cobs could filter dirty matter out of the polluted water.

One day, I picked up some dried cobs along the road, washed them, and ④place them in a bowl of dirty water. After a while, I checked the water, and it looked ⑤much clearer. Then, using corn cobs that I had collected from farmers, I built a filtering system. My system removed 70 to 80 percent of the dirty matter from the water. I hope my filtering system can clean up all the lakes not only in my village but also in other areas.

서답형

10 주어진 단어를 바르게 나열하여 빈칸 (A)에 들어갈 위 글의 제목을 쓰시오.

> (Useful / Useless / Filters / Corn Cobs / Water / as)

➡ _____

11 밑줄 친 ①~⑤ 중 어법상 바르지 않은 것은?

①   ②   ③   ④   ⑤

12 위 글의 내용과 일치하는 것은?

① Lalita lived in a city in India.
② No small holes can be found in corn cobs.
③ The filtering system that Lalita made can make 100 percent pure water.
④ Lalita got corn cobs from farmers.
⑤ Lalita saw someone using corn cobs to filter polluted water.

[13~16] 다음 글을 읽고 물음에 답하시오.

A Robotic Hand from a Helpful Mind (Easton LaChappelle)

One day, when I was fourteen, I came across a little girl at a science fair. She had a robotic hand that could only open and close. I was surprised that the hand had cost her 80,000 dollars! 'I wish she had a better robotic hand,' I thought to myself. With that, I started to make a (A)_____ cheaper and better robotic hand.

After many failures, finally, by using 3D printing technology, I was able to make a useful robotic hand for the price of only 300 dollars. I decided to share the designs and software for my 3D robotic hand with others for free. Maybe someone can take (B)<u>what I have done</u> and do something useful with it. No one person can change the world, but we can build a better world by working together.

13 다음 중 빈칸 (A)에 알맞지 <u>않은</u> 것은?

① much   ② a lot   ③ far
④ still   ⑤ very

14 밑줄 친 (B)의 의미로 가장 적절한 것은?

① the software of the 3D printer
② the designs and software for the robotic hand
③ the designs and software that the robotic hand made
④ the free product of 3D printing technology
⑤ making useful hands for a low price

서답형
15 Write the reason why Easton was surprised. Use the phrase 'It's because.'

➡ _____

_____

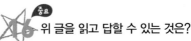

16 위 글을 읽고 답할 수 있는 것은?

① With whom did Easton go to the fair?
② How old was Easton when he invented the robotic hand?
③ How long did it take for the little girl to make a robotic hand?
④ Why did Easton start to make a robotic hand?
⑤ What did the little girl think about what Easton invented?

[17~20] 다음 글을 읽고 물음에 답하시오.

Headbands for Girls' Education (Mary Grace Henry)

(A) They bought me one, and I learned how to make headbands for myself. I created ten headbands and sold them at my school. Soon, I raised enough money to send one girl in Africa to school. I couldn't stop there.

(B) I realized that their families couldn't afford it. I wondered if I could do something for those girls. Then I had an idea. For my birthday, I asked my parents to buy me a sewing machine.

(C) I started a business to help girls in Africa who couldn't go to school. Thanks to the success of my business, I can pay the school fees for many poor girls in countries like Kenya and Uganda ⓐ_____ to school. I also pay for their textbooks, uniforms, and pencils.

(D) 'Why can't many girls in Africa go to school as I can? I wish they could go to school, too.' I had this thought when I was twelve.

Isn't it amazing? My advice to you is to just do something. When you see a need, ⓑ_____. Start small, taking little steps. Your warm heart can change lives.

서답형
17 동사 go를 어법에 맞게 빈칸 ⓐ에 쓰시오.

➡ _____

18 빈칸 ⓑ에 들어갈 말로 가장 적절한 것은?

① wait   ② act

③ calm down   ④ ignore it

⑤ pay attention to it

19 자연스러운 글이 되도록 (A)~(D)를 바르게 나열하시오.

➡ _____

20 위 글의 내용과 일치하는 것은?

① Mary bought headbands to collect them.

② Mary's parents gave her headbands as her birthday present.

③ Mary didn't succeed in sending one girl in Africa to school.

④ Mary started a business to make money to spend on her clothes.

⑤ Mary came up with an idea to help poor girls in Africa.

[21~25] 다음 글을 읽고 물음에 답하시오.

Useless Corn Cobs as Useful Water Filters (Lalita Prasida)

(A)As a young girl living in the countryside in India, I often found that the water around us was seriously polluted. (①) I wondered how I could solve (B)this problem. Then I hit on the idea to use corn cobs. (②) Useless corn cobs were everywhere in my village. I thought that the small holes in the corn cobs could filter dirty matter out of the polluted water. (③) One day, I picked up some dried cobs along the road, washed them, and placed them in a bowl of dirty water. (④) Then, using corn cobs that I had collected from farmers, I built a filtering system. My system removed 70 to 80 percent of the dirty matter from the water. (⑤) I hope my filtering system can clean up all the lakes not only in my village but also in other areas.

21 (①)~(⑤) 중 주어진 문장이 들어가기에 가장 적절한 곳은?

> After a while, I checked the water, and it looked much clearer.

①   ②   ③   ④   ⑤

22 What could filter dirty matter out of the polluted water? Answer in English.

➡ _____

_____

23 밑줄 친 (A)와 쓰임이 같은 것은?

① As you were out, I waited for a while.

② They were all dressed as clowns.

③ He works as a counselor.

④ We did as they told us to do.

⑤ As you know, I don't like her.

24 밑줄 친 (B)가 의미하는 것을 우리말로 쓰시오.

➡ _____

25 Choose one that is NOT true.

① Lalita tried to clean the polluted water.

② Corn cobs could be easily found in the village.

③ Corn cobs have a narrow hole.

④ Lalita made a filtering system by herself.

⑤ The filtering system is made of corn cobs.

[01~05] 다음 글을 읽고 물음에 답하시오.

A Robotic Hand from a Helpful Mind (Easton LaChappelle)

One day, when I was fourteen, I came across a little girl at a science fair. She had a robotic hand that could only open and close. I was surprised that the hand had cost her 80,000 dollars! 'I wish she had a better robotic hand,' I thought to myself. With (A)that, I started to make a much cheaper and better robotic hand.

After many failures, finally, by using 3D printing technology, I was able to make a useful robotic hand for the price of only 300 dollars. I decided to share the designs and software for my 3D robotic hand with others for free. Maybe someone can take what I have done and do something useful with it. No one person can change the world, but we can build a better world by working together.

01 Where did Easton meet the little girl? Answer in English with a full sentence.

➡ _____

02 밑줄 친 (A)가 의미하는 것을 우리말로 쓰시오.

➡ _____

03 What was Easton able to do by using 3D printing technology? Answer in English.

➡ _____
_____

04 According to Easton, how can we build a better world? Answer in English.

➡ _____

05 다음 중 위 글의 내용과 일치하지 않는 부분을 세 군데 찾아 바르게 고쳐 쓰시오.

> Easton was surprised at a girl's cheap robotic foot and wanted to make a cheaper and better one. Finally he made one and decided to sell his designs and software for free.

➡ _____

[06~08] 다음 글을 읽고 물음에 답하시오.

Headbands for Girls' Education (Mary Grace Henry)

'Why can't many girls in Africa go to school as I can? I wish they could go to school, too.' I had this thought when I was twelve. I realized that their families couldn't afford it. I wondered if I could do something for those girls. Then I had an idea. For my birthday, I asked my parents to buy me a sewing machine. They bought me one, and I learned how to make headbands for myself. I created ten headbands and sold them at my school. Soon, I raised enough money to send one girl in Africa to school. I couldn't stop there.

I started a business to help girls in Africa who couldn't go to school. Thanks to the success of my business, I can pay the school fees for many poor girls in countries like Kenya and Uganda to go to school. I also pay for their textbooks, uniforms, and pencils.

Isn't it amazing? (A)나의 조언은 그냥 무엇이든 하라는 것이다. When you see a need, act. Start small, taking little steps. Your warm heart can change lives.

06 What did Mary ask her parents to do for her birthday? Answer in English with a full sentence.

➡ _____

_____

07 위 글의 내용에 맞게 빈칸에 알맞은 말을 쓰시오.

> Thanks to the success of her business, Mary can pay for not only _____ _____ _____ but also _____ _____, _____, _____ _____ for many poor girls in countries like Kenya and Uganda _____ _____ _____ _____.

08 주어진 단어를 바르게 배열하여 밑줄 친 우리말 (A)를 영어로 쓰시오. 하나의 단어를 두 번 사용하시오.

> (do / is / advice / something / to / my / just / you)

➡ _____

[09~12] 다음 글을 읽고 물음에 답하시오.

> **Useless Corn Cobs as Useful Water Filters (Lalita Prasida)**
>
> As a young girl living in the countryside in India, I often found that the water around us was seriously polluted. I wondered how I could solve this problem. Then I hit on the idea to use corn cobs. Useless corn cobs were everywhere in my village. I thought that the small holes in the corn cobs could filter dirty matter out of the polluted water.
>
> One day, I picked up some dried cobs along the road, washed them, and placed them in a bowl of dirty water. After a while, I checked the water, and it looked much (A)_____. Then, using corn cobs that I had collected from farmers, I built a filtering system. My system removed 70 to 80 percent of the dirty matter from the water. I hope my filtering system can clean up all the lakes not only in my village but also in other areas.

09 위 글의 흐름상 빈칸 (A)에 들어갈 말로 가장 적절한 것을 쓰시오.

➡ _____

10 Where did Lalita Prasida live? Answer in English.

➡ _____

11 What did Lalita decide to use to filter water? Answer in English.

➡ _____

12 How much dirty matter did Lalita's system remove from the water? Answer in English with a full sentence.

➡ _____

_____

구석구석

Communication Task

A: I'm Sky X. I can fly.
B: Hi, Sky X. Nice to meet you.
C: I wish I could fly like you. Is it possible for you to fly to the moon?
　　소망을 나타내는 표현(I wish+주어+과거동사)　　　　to부정사의 의미상 주어
A: Sure.
D: Then is it possible for you to travel to the sun?
　　　　가능성을 묻는 표현(= can you travel to the sun?)
A: No. That's impossible.
　　　to travel to the sun

구문해설 ・possible: 가능한 ・travel: 여행하다, 이동하다

Enjoy Writing

To Genie,

I have three wishes. I wonder if you can make my wishes come true. First, I
　　　　　　　　명사절 접속사(~인지 아닌지) = whether　　make+목적어+동사원형
wish I lived in Hawaii. Then I could swim at a beautiful beach. Second, I wish
I wish 가정법(~이라면 좋을 텐데)　조동사 과거(가정법 과거시제의 주절)　　　　　가정법
every Wednesday were a holiday. Then, I could be more relaxed. Finally, I
　　　　　　　　과거형 is(X)　　　　　　　　조동사 과거　　　보어(과거분사)
wish I were the president of Korea. Then I would try hard to make my country
가정법 과거　　　　　　　　　　　　　　　조동사 과거　　부사　　　5형식
a happier place to live in. I don't know if you can help me, but I hope you can.
　　　　　to부정사의 형용사적 용법　　(= whether)　　　　　　　　can (help me)

Best Wishes,
Sohee

구문해설 ・come true: 실현되다 ・relaxed: 편안한 ・president: 대통령 ・Best Wishes: 행운을 빌며
(편지의 끝 인사말)

After You Read

Creative Teens!

Easton was surprised at a girl's expensive robotic hand and wanted to make a
　　　　~에 놀랐다
cheaper and better one. Finally he made one for only 300 dollars and decided
　　　　　　　　　　　　　　　　　a cheaper and better robotic hand
to share his designs and software for free.
Mary wished she could send girls in Africa to school. She made and sold
　　　현재의 사실과 반대되는 상황을 가정할 때(wish+주어+과거동사)
headbands. Now she pays for the school fees, textbooks, uniforms, and pencils
of many poor school girls in Africa.
Lalita wondered how she could clean the water. Using corn cobs, she made
　　　　　　　　간접의문문(의문사+주어+동사)　　　　분사구문
a filtering system. It removed 70 to 80 percent of the dirty matter from the
water.

구문해설 ・surprised: 놀란 ・expensive: 비싼 ・decide: 결정하다 ・for free: 무료로 ・headband: 머리띠
・remove: 없애다 ・matter: 물질

해석

A: 나는 스카이 X야. 나는 하늘을 날 수 있어.
B: 안녕, 스카이 X. 만나서 반가워.
C: 나는 너처럼 하늘을 날 수 있으면 좋겠어. 너는 달까지 날아가는 것이 가능하니?
A: 물론이지.
D: 그럼 너는 태양으로 여행하는 것이 가능하니?
A: 아니. 그건 불가능해.

Genie에게

나는 세 가지 소원이 있다. 네가 나의 소원들을 모두 이루어 줄 수 있을지 궁금하다. 첫 번째로, 나는 하와이에 살았으면 좋겠다. 그럼 하와이의 아름다운 해변에서 수영할 수 있을 것이다. 두 번째로, 나는 모든 수요일이 휴일이었으면 좋겠다. 그럼 나는 더 편히 쉴 수 있을 것이다. 마지막으로, 나는 한국의 대통령이었으면 좋겠다. 그럼 나는 이 나라를 살기에 더 행복한 곳으로 만들기 위해 열심히 노력할 것이다. 나는 네가 나를 도와줄 수 있을지 모르겠지만, 네가 할 수 있길 바란다. 행운을 빌며, 소희가

창의적인 십 대들!

Easton은 어떤 소녀의 비싼 로봇 손을 보고 놀라서, 더 싸고 좋은 로봇 손을 만들고 싶었다. 마침내 그는 단 300달러짜리 로봇 손을 만들었고 그의 디자인과 소프트웨어를 무료로 나누기로 결심했다.

Mary는 아프리카 소녀들을 학교에 보낼 수 있기를 바랐다. 그녀는 머리띠를 만들어 팔았다. 이제 그녀는 아프리카의 많은 가난한 소녀들의 학비와 교과서, 교복 그리고 연필의 비용을 지불한다.

Lalita는 어떻게 물을 깨끗하게 할 수 있을지 궁금했다. 그녀는 옥수수 속대를 이용해서 정수 장치를 만들었다. 그 정수 장치는 오염된 물에서 70~80퍼센트의 더러운 물질을 제거했다.

Words & Expressions

01 다음 중 짝지어진 단어들의 관계가 나머지와 <u>다른</u> 것은?

① participate – participation
② sense – sensation
③ illuminate – illumination
④ inform – information
⑤ ment – mention

02 다음 빈칸에 들어갈 말로 가장 적절한 것은?

> I can't _____ to buy a new air conditioner.
> (나는 새 에어컨을 살 여유가 없어.)

① control
② manage
③ use
④ afford
⑤ spend

03 다음 빈칸 (A)~(C)에 들어갈 말이 바르게 짝지어진 것은?

> • She hits (A)_____ a new idea for her cafe.
> • I came (B)_____ one of my friends in the restaurant. It made me really surprised.
> • (C)_____ visiting schools, the actors hope to inspire children to realize their dream.

① by – across – On
② on – across – By
③ upon – up – By
④ on – with – In
⑤ by – across – About

04 〈보기〉의 밑줄 친 단어와 같은 의미로 쓰인 것은?

> ┤ 보기 ├
> The <u>fair</u> includes works by Impressionists.

① It was a pretty <u>fair</u> election.
② A <u>fair</u> number of people came along.
③ It is not <u>fair</u> to ask for the money.
④ I visited a world trade <u>fair</u> last weekend.
⑤ It is a <u>fair</u> and breezy day today.

Conversation

05 다음 대화의 빈칸에 들어갈 말로 적절하지 <u>않은</u> 것은?

> A: _____
> B: Why not? You can be anything you want.

① Can I become a world-famous singer?
② Is it possible for me to be a dentist?
③ Is it likely that I can be a super model?
④ Is it okay if you become a doctor?
⑤ Is it probable that I can be a dancer?

06 다음 중 어색한 대화를 고르시오.

① A: I wish I could float around like an astronaut.
   B: Really? I don't. It looks uncomfortable.
② A: Is is possible for us to make delicious pie?
   B: Sure, why not?
③ A: I wish I could travel abroad alone.
   B: I'm with you. I'm sure that's every teenager's wish.
④ A: Can you speak French well?
   B: No. I don't think I can, but I'm practicing really hard.
⑤ A: I wish I could live in the desert.
   B: Me, too. It seems very dangerous.

[07~10] 다음 대화를 읽고 물음에 답하시오.

B: I'm planning to visit my uncle in Mexico.
G: What are you going to do there, Mike? (①)
B: I'll spend most of my time at his house because he has a big swimming pool. (②)
G: That's great. (A)Can you swim well?
B: No, I wish I could, but I can't. (③)
G: A water walking ball? What is that? (④)
B: It's a large ball. (⑤) We go inside it and walk on the water.
G: That must be fun.

07 단어 possible을 이용하여 밑줄 친 (A)와 같은 의미의 문장을 쓰시오.

➡ _____

08 Write the reason why Mike will spend most of his time at his uncle's house. Use the word 'Because.'

➡ _____

09 (①)~(⑤) 중 주어진 말이 들어가기에 가장 적절한 곳은?

> So I'll have fun with a water walking ball instead.

① ② ③ ④ ⑤

10 다음 중 위 대화를 읽고 답할 수 없는 것은?

① Where does Mike's uncle live?
② What does Mike's uncle have in his house?
③ How can Mike enjoy the pool with a water walking ball?
④ How long is Mike going to stay in his uncle's house?
⑤ What is Mike planning to do?

11 주어진 문장에서 어법상 어색한 부분을 찾아, 바르게 고친 것을 고르시오.

> Mom asked me that or not I could succeed in making the filter with corn cobs.

① Mom asked me if or not I could succeed in making the filter with corn cobs.
② Mom asked me however I could succeed in making the filter with corn cobs.
③ Mom asked me whether or not I could succeed in making the filter with corn cobs.
④ Mom asked me if could I succeed in making the filter with corn cobs.
⑤ Mom asked me whether I succeeded in making the filter with corn cobs or not.

12 다음 빈칸에 들어갈 말로 알맞은 것은?

> _____ the student gets an A doesn't matter. How hard he prepared for the test is much more important.

① Though   ② As   ③ If
④ Whether   ⑤ Whatever

13 다음 〈보기〉와 같이 직설법 문장을 가정법으로 고치시오.

> ┌─ 보기 ─┐
> As he is not rich, he can't buy the boat.
> ➡ If he were rich, he could buy the boat.

(1) As I am not an inventor, I can't make cheaper and more convenient robotic arms.

➡ _____
_____

(2) Since Jake is wearing the skirt, he looks like a school girl.

➡ _____

_____

(3) As there is no pen, I can't write or draw a thing right now.

➡ _____

_____

(4) Because Henry doesn't have the violin, it is not easy for him to perform the songs.

➡ _____

_____

14 다음 그림을 보고 괄호 안의 단어를 배열하여 빈칸을 알맞게 채우시오.

➡ Yunho couldn't decide _____

_____.

(Canada, England, study, to, in, whether, or)

15 다음 중 밑줄 친 단어의 쓰임이 나머지와 <u>다른</u> 하나는?

① Any boy can use my bat and balls <u>if</u> he wants to play softball.

② Dave's mom asked me <u>if</u> he had done my homework for me.

③ The police will ask Robert <u>if</u> it's all right to live as before.

④ Kevin was wondering <u>if</u> his sister had breakfast that morning.

⑤ Kathy asked me <u>if</u> I had been to Spain.

[16~17] 다음 주어진 우리말을 어법에 맞게 바르게 영작한 것은?

16

옥수수 숏대를 오염된 물에 대한 여과기로 쓸 수 있으면 좋을 텐데.

① I wished I could use corn cobs as a filter for the polluted water.

② I wish I could use corn cobs as a filter for the polluted water.

③ I wish could I use as a filter through corn cobs for the polluted water.

④ I wish I can use corn cobs as a filter for the polluted water.

⑤ I wish I could use the filter as corn cobs for the polluted water.

17

비가 충분히 온다면 곡식들이 전보다 더 잘 자랄 수 있을 텐데.

① If it didn't rain enough, the crops would grow better than before.

② If it had rained enough, the crops would have grown better than before.

③ Had it rained enough, the crops would grow better than before.

④ Did it rain enough, the crops will grow better than before.

⑤ If it rained enough, the crops would grow better than before.

18 다음 주어진 문장의 밑줄 친 if와 같은 용법으로 쓰인 문장은?

> I would be a dead person if it were not for my brother.

① Newton used to wonder if all the things would pull each other.

② They don't know if the game will be put off because of the rain.

③ My friends are wondering if my wife is going to her mother's house today.

④ The African girls would be happy if there were helping hands somewhere.

⑤ The reporter asked the medical staff if she was in good condition.

Reading

[19~22] 다음 글을 읽고 물음에 답하시오.

Who are the people who change the world? ⓐDo you think you are too young to be one of these people? In the following stories you will meet three teenagers who used their ideas to make the world a better place.

A Robotic Hand from a Helpful Mind (Easton LaChappelle)

(A) 'I wish she had a better robotic hand,' I thought to myself. With that, I started to make a much cheaper and better robotic hand. After many failures, finally, by using 3D printing technology, I was able to make a useful robotic hand for the price of only 300 dollars.

(B) One day, when I was fourteen, I came across a little girl at a science fair. She had a robotic hand that could only open and close. I was surprised that the hand had cost her 80,000 dollars!

(C) I decided to share the designs and software for my 3D robotic hand with others for free. Maybe someone can take what I have done and do something useful with it. No one person can change the world, but we can build a better world by working together.

19 자연스러운 글이 되도록 (A)~(C)를 바르게 나열한 것은?

① (A)–(C)–(B)　　② (B)–(A)–(C)

③ (B)–(C)–(A)　　④ (C)–(A)–(B)

⑤ (C)–(B)–(A)

20 주어진 단어를 활용하여 밑줄 친 ⓐ와 같은 의미의 문장을 쓰시오.

> (so / that)

➡ _____

_____

21 How much did the girl pay for her robotic hand? Answer in English.

➡ _____

22 다음 중 위 글의 내용과 일치하는 것은?

① Easton gave the girl what he had made.

② Easton planned to meet the girl at a science fair.

③ The girl's robotic hand had so many functions.

④ Easton made a 3D printer with the robotic hand.

⑤ The designs and software for the 3D robotic hand are shared without cost.

[23~25] 다음 글을 읽고 물음에 답하시오.

Useless Corn Cobs as Useful Water Filters
(Lalita Prasida)

  As a young girl living in the countryside in India, I often found that the water around us was seriously polluted. (①) I wondered how I could solve this problem. Then I hit on the idea to use corn cobs. (②) Useless corn cobs were everywhere in my village. I thought that the small holes in the corn cobs could filter dirty matter out of the polluted water. (③) One day, I picked up some dried cobs along the road, washed them, and placed them in a bowl of dirty water. (④) After a while, I checked the water, and it looked much clearer. (⑤) My system removed 70 to 80 percent of the dirty matter from the water. I hope my filtering system can clean up all the lakes not only in my village but also in other areas.

23 (①)~(⑤) 중 주어진 문장이 들어가기에 가장 적절한 곳은?

> Then, using corn cobs that I had collected from farmers, I built a filtering system.

①   ②   ③   ④   ⑤

24 According to Lalita, what could filter dirty matter out of the polluted water? Answer in English with a full sentence.

➡ _____

_____

25 위 글을 읽고 답할 수 있는 것은?

① When did Lalita make the filtering system?
② Who wanted Lalita to build the filtering system?
③ What did Lalita use to make the filtering system?
④ What did people in India think about what Lalita had made?
⑤ How long did it take for Lalita to build the filtering system?

[26~27] 다음 글을 읽고 물음에 답하시오.

To Genie,
  I have three wishes. I wonder ①if you can make my wishes ②come true. First, I wish I ③lived in Hawaii. Then, I could swim at a beautiful beach. Second, I wish every Wednesday ④were a holiday. Then, I could be more relaxed. Finally, I wish I were the president of Korea. Then, I would try hard to make my country a happier place ⑤to live. (A)나는 네가 나를 도와줄 수 있을지 모르겠지만, 네가 할 수 있길 바란다.

Best Wishes,
Sohee

26 밑줄 친 ①~⑤ 중 어법상 바르지 않은 것은?

①   ②   ③   ④   ⑤

27 주어진 단어를 활용하여 밑줄 친 우리말 (A)를 영어로 쓰시오.

> (know / can / help / hope)

➡ _____

_____

01 출제율 90%

다음과 같이 풀이되는 단어로 가장 적절한 것은?

> to stitch with thread

① manage　　② collect　　③ coin
④ realize　　⑤ sew

02 출제율 100%

다음 중 밑줄 친 단어의 우리말 의미가 바르지 않은 것은?

① She was clearly relaxed and in a good mood. (편안한)
② The system can filter dirty matter. (여과하다)
③ We should get together to discuss the issue. (협조하다)
④ He got to the place for himself. (스스로)
⑤ Filters do not remove all bad things from water. (없애다)

03 출제율 95%

주어진 단어를 적절히 활용하여 빈칸에 알맞은 말을 쓰시오.

(1) She tried her best, but it was _____. But she didn't give up. (use)
(2) Sue bought a _____ vacuum cleaner recently. It looks terrific. (robot)

04 출제율 90%

주어진 단어를 활용하여 다음 우리말을 아홉 단어로 이루어진 한 문장의 영어로 쓰시오.

> 네가 이 퍼즐을 푸는 것이 가능하니? (possible / the puzzle)

➡ _____

05 출제율 90%

자연스러운 대화가 되도록 (A)~(E)를 바르게 나열하시오.

W: Hi, Tom. What are you doing?
(A) No, I'm not very good right now, but I'm practicing hard.
(B) Cool! Are you good at it?
(C) As you know, I run a sandwich restaurant. Is it possible for you to deliver orders with your drone?
(D) No, it isn't. But I think it will be possible in one or two years.
(E) I'm flying my drone.
W: That will be great.

➡ _____

[06~08] 다음 대화를 읽고 물음에 답하시오.

W: Hi. I'm looking for a backpack for my son.
M: How old is your son?
W: He is five years old.
M: I want to recommend this one.
W: Oh, ①it's so cute.
M: Yes, isn't it? ②It has a cap that looks like a penguin, so kids love ③it.
W: Is ④it possible for me to take the cap off for washing?
M: Sure. You can easily take it off and put it back on.
W: That's wonderful. I'll take ⑤it.

06 출제율 95%

Where is this conversation likely to take place?

① at a grocery store　　② at the library
③ at a mall　　④ in a house
⑤ at the bus stop

07 밑줄 친 ①~⑤ 중 가리키는 것이 나머지 넷과 <u>다른</u> 하나는?

①　　　②　　　③　　　④　　　⑤

08 Choose one that is NOT true.

① The woman has a five-year-old son.

② The woman buys the backpack that the man recommends to her.

③ It is impossible for her to wash the cap.

④ The backpack is popular among kids.

⑤ The backpack has a cap that looks like a penguin on it.

[09~10] 다음 대화를 읽고 물음에 답하시오.

Bora: What are you doing, Jessie?

Jessie: I'm drawing Dr. Rebecca, my favorite superhero.

Bora: Wow, that's great.

Jessie: Thanks. I wish I could read people's minds like her.

Bora: (A)Is it possible for her to control them, too?

Jessie: Yes. She can control your mind if she wants to.

Bora: That's very cool.

Jessie: What about you? Do you also have any favorite superheroes?

Bora: Sure. I love Sky X. (B)I wish I could fly like him.

Jessie: I like him, too. He can even breathe in space.

09 주어진 단어를 활용하여 밑줄 친 (B)와 같은 의미의 문장을 쓰시오.

(would like)

➡ _____

10 밑줄 친 (A)를 대신하여 쓸 수 있는 것은?

① Can you control them, too?

② Is it likely that she can control them, too?

③ Are you sure she can control them, too?

④ Do you think it is possible to control them, too?

⑤ Is it probable that you can control them, too?

11 다음 중 어법상 올바른 문장을 <u>모두</u> 고르면?

① The owner of the shop asked her whether she liked the rosemary flavor.

② All the children at the kindergarten want to know if it is fine next Monday.

③ The P.E. teacher couldn't tell if the girl was lying or telling the truth.

④ I wonder whether your sister will come to the library last weekend.

⑤ I'm not quite sure if or not there is a grocery store around my house.

12 다음 문장을 'I wish 가정법' 구문으로 알맞게 전환한 것은?

I'm sorry that I can't pay the school fees for many poor girls in Africa.

① I wish I can't pay the school fees for many poor girls in Africa.

② I wish I can pay the school fees for many poor girls in Africa.

③ I wish I couldn't pay the school fees for many poor girls in Africa.

④ I wish I could pay the school fees for many poor girls in Africa.

⑤ I wish could I pay the school fees for many poor girls in Africa.

13 다음 주어진 문장을 가정법으로 바르게 고친 것은?

> As I am not smart enough, I won't be one of those who changed the world.

① If I am smart enough, I will be one of those who changed the world.

② If I'm not smart enough, I will be one of those who changed the world.

③ If I weren't smart enough, I would be one of those who changed the world.

④ If I were smart enough, I would be one of those who changed the world.

⑤ If I were smart enough, I wouldn't be one of those who changed the world.

14 다음 〈보기〉와 같이 if를 사용하여 주어진 문장을 완성하시오.

> ┤ 보기 ├
>
> Can I make a cheaper robotic hand?
> ➡ I'm not sure if I can make a cheaper robotic hand.

(1) Is he going to come back here?
→ I wonder _____.

(2) Did she have breakfast with the man?
→ I want to know _____
_____.

(3) Has anyone seen my teacher's book on the bench?
→ I don't know _____
_____.

(4) Can the professor and her students come on time for dinner?
→ I'm not sure _____
_____.

(5) Are there any clothes for us to give out to the poor villagers?
→ I want to know _____
_____.

(6) Will it be cloudy the day after tomorrow?
→ I have no idea _____
_____.

[15~16] 다음 각 가정법 과거 문장에서 어법상 옳은 것을 고르시오.

15 ① I wish their younger brother doesn't live far from New York.

② I wish I can see the concert of the idol band this coming Saturday.

③ I wish I knew a lot about the Great King Sejong.

④ I wish my daddy can speak English so well that he could be promoted.

⑤ I wish Sunny follows your advice when she is in trouble.

16 ① If we work together, we could build a better world.

② I wish the small holes in the corn cobs could filter dirty matter out of the polluted water.

③ If the farmers had helped me, I can make the filtering system using the corn cobs.

④ I wish they know the solution to the problem of the polluted water.

⑤ I wish my filtering system will remove all the dirty matter from the water.

17 다음 간접의문문이 사용된 문장들 중 어법상 옳은 것을 고르시오.

① I don't know whether is the rumor true or not.

② Whether my daughter will join them or not depend on you.

③ It doesn't matter whether did Mr. Parker make a mistake or not.

④ I wonder if what you broke at the museum is an expensive item.

⑤ I have no idea that or not the boss will attend the meeting.

[18~20] 다음에 주어진 두 문장을 합쳐서 가정법의 한 문장으로 영작하되, 주어진 단어로 시작하시오.

18

> • I'm sorry that I'm not as tall as Jordan.
> • I want to be as tall as Jordan.

➡ I _____.

19

> • Bob doesn't know Judy's SNS address.
> • He wants to visit her SNS.

➡ If _____
_____.

20

> • I was able to make a useful robotic hand for the price of only 300 dollars.
> • That was due to 3D printing technology.

➡ Had _____
_____
_____.

21 다음 그림과 각 캐릭터의 생각이나 대화를 기록한 〈보기〉를 읽고, 내용에 맞게 빈칸에 들어갈 알맞은 말을 쓰시오. (단, whether는 쓸 수 없으며, 모든 캐릭터는 여성으로 간주할 것.)

┤ 보기 ├
> **Aunt Mary:** Is it going to rain today?
> **Becky:** Can I wash the parrot?
> **Parrot:** Did she get a cleaner's license?
> **Snake:** Will anyone come to see me?
> **Kitty:** Is there anything left to eat?
> **Tree:** Has Becky washed me before?

(1) Aunt Mary wonders _____
_____.

(2) Becky asks _____.

(3) Parrot doubts _____.

(4) Snake wants to know _____
_____.

(5) Kitty has no idea _____
_____.

(6) Tree doesn't know _____
_____.

22 다음 각 가정법 문장에서 어법상 어색한 단어를 한 개씩만 찾아 바르게 고치시오. (고친 부분은 두 단어라도 상관 없음.)

(1) I wish my wife is strong enough to move the rock.

_____ ➡ _____

(2) If you are in her situation, you would understand how much the girls in Africa want to go to school.

_____ ➡ _____

(3) I wish I have a lot of robotic hands so that I can take care of my little sisters.

_____ ➡ _____

(4) I wish my girl friend is the president of the company.

_____ ➡ _____

(5) Tony wouldn't be late for the meeting yesterday if his bike had not been broken.

_____ ➡ _____

(6) I wish someone can take what I have done and do something useful with it.

_____ ➡ _____

출제율 90%

23 다음 각 문장을 읽고, 괄호 안에 주어진 동사와 if를 이용한 간접의문문을 사용하여 같은 내용이 되도록 만드시오.

(1) Peter's girl friend said to him, "Do you really love me?" (ask)

➡ _____

(2) Easton thought to himself, "Can I make her a better dress?" (be sure)

➡ _____

(3) Mary said to her parents, "Will you buy me a sewing machine for my birthday?" (ask)

➡ _____

_____

[24~28] 다음 글을 읽고 물음에 답하시오.

Headbands for (A)_____ (Mary Grace Henry)

'Why can't many girls in Africa go to school as I can? I wish they could go to school, too.' I had this thought when I was twelve. I realized that their families couldn't ①afford it. I wondered if I could do something for those girls. Then I had an idea. For my birthday, I asked my parents to buy me a sewing machine. They bought me one, and I learned how to make headbands for myself. I created ten headbands and ②sold them at my school. Soon, I ③raised enough money to send one girl in Africa to school. I couldn't stop there. I started a business to help girls in Africa who couldn't go to school. Thanks to the ④success of my business, I can pay the school fees for many poor girls in countries like Kenya and Uganda to go to school. I also pay (B)_____ their textbooks, uniforms, and pencils.

Isn't (C)it amazing? My advice to you is to just do something. When you see a need, act. Start small, taking little steps. Your ⑤cold heart can change lives.

출제율 100%

24 빈칸 (A)에 들어갈 말로 가장 적절한 것은?

① My Fortune ② Girls' Education
③ Girls' Clothes ④ Enough Food
⑤ Poor Pets

출제율 95%

25 다음 중 빈칸 (B)에 들어갈 말과 같은 말이 들어가는 것은?

① It is rude _____ him to reject the offer.
② How kind _____ you to say so!
③ It was careless _____ me to behave like that.
④ We stepped aside _____ her to pass.
⑤ Isn't it generous _____ them to give this information?

26 밑줄 친 (C)의 의미로 가장 적절한 것은?
출제율 100%

① making so many headbands
② helping friends with a sewing machine
③ helping many poor girls go to school
④ giving food to girls in Africa
⑤ helping poor girls in Africa stand on their own feet

27 Write the reason why Mary started a business. Answer in English.
출제율 90%

➡ _____

_____

28 ①~⑤ 중 글의 흐름상 어색한 것을 찾아 바르게 고쳐 쓰시오.
출제율 95%

➡ _____

[29~31] 다음 글을 읽고 물음에 답하시오.

Useless Corn Cobs as Useful Water Filters (Lalita Prasida)

As a young girl living in the countryside in India, I often found that the water around us was seriously polluted. I wondered how I could solve this problem. Then I hit on the idea to use corn cobs. Useless corn cobs were everywhere in my village. I thought that the small holes in the corn cobs could filter dirty matter into the polluted water.

One day, I picked up some dried cobs along the road, washed them, and placed them in a bowl of dirty water. After a while, I checked the water, and it looked much clearer. Then, using corn cobs (A)that I had collected from farmers, I built a filtering system. My system removed 70 to 80

percent of the dirty matter from the water. I hope my filtering system can clean up all the lakes not only in my village but also in other areas.

29 밑줄 친 (A)와 쓰임이 같은 것은?
출제율 95%

① Did you say that I stole the money?
② The news that he came back spread.
③ Who is the man that she is looking at?
④ The problem was that I couldn't afford it.
⑤ We didn't know that he wasn't satisfied with our service.

30 What does Lalita hope? Answer in English with a full sentence.
출제율 90%

➡ _____

_____

_____

31 위 글의 내용과 일치하는 것은?
출제율 100%

① Lalita collected wet corn cobs to make the filtering system.
② Lalita didn't wash cobs before placing them in a bowl of dirty water.
③ Farmers didn't give corn cobs to Lalita for free.
④ The filtering system couldn't make entirely clear water.
⑤ Lalita wasn't interested in water around her.

[01~03] 다음 대화를 읽고 물음에 답하시오.

Bora: What are you doing, Jessie?

Jessie: I'm drawing Dr. Rebecca, my favorite superhero.

Bora: Wow, that's great.

Jessie: Thanks. (A)I wish I could read people's minds like her.

Bora: Is it possible for her to control them, too?

Jessie: Yes. She can control your mind if she wants to.

Bora: That's very cool.

Jessie: What about you? Do you also have any favorite superheroes?

Bora: Sure. I love Sky X. I wish I could fly like him.

Jessie: I like him, too. He can even breathe in space.

Bora: Yes. He can do anything in space.

01 다음은 밑줄 친 문장 (A)의 의미이다. 빈칸에 알맞은 말을 쓰시오.

Jessie can't _____, but Dr. Rebecca can.

02 Who is Jessie's favorite superhero? Answer in English.

➡ _____

03 According to the dialogue, what can Sky X do? Answer in English.

➡ _____

04 다음 주어진 〈보기〉와 같이 각 그림과 설명을 보고 해당하는 문장을 'I wish 가정법' 형태로 영작하시오.

┌─ 보기 ─┐

The math teacher likes me.

➡ I wish the math teacher liked me.

(1) I live in Hawaii.

(2) I am the president of Korea.

(3) I have a million dollars.

(4) Every Wednesday were[was] a holiday.

(1) I wish _____.

(2) I wish _____.

(3) I wish _____.

(4) I wish _____.

05 다음 중에서 틀린 문장을 찾아 기호를 쓰고, 바르게 고쳐 문장을 다시 쓰시오.

① Andy wondered if he really enjoyed the job of guarding the entrance.

② Father asked me if I wanted to get a chance to go abroad.

③ Parker didn't know if watching stars and taking pictures could lead to a job.

④ I don't know if that the professor wrote is worth reading.

⑤ I wonder if I have courage to make decisions that will change my life.

➡ _____

_____

Useless Corn Cobs as Useful Water Filters (Lalita Prasida)

As a young girl living in the countryside in India, I often found that the water around us was seriously polluted. I wondered (A)_____. Then I hit on the idea to use corn cobs. Useless corn cobs were everywhere in my village. I thought that the small holes in the corn cobs could filter dirty matter out of the polluted water.

One day, I picked up some dried cobs along the road, washed them, and placed them in a bowl of dirty water. After a while, I checked the water, and it looked much clearer. Then, using corn cobs that I had collected from farmers, I built a filtering system. My system removed 70 to 80 percent of the dirty matter from the water. I hope my filtering system can clean up all the lakes not only in my village but also in other areas.

06 주어진 단어를 바르게 배열하여 빈칸 (A)에 들어갈 말을 완성하시오.

(this / solve / how / could / I / problem)

➡ _____

07 What was the idea that Lalita came up with to clear the polluted water? Answer in English with six words.

➡ _____

08 What was everywhere in Lalita's village? Answer in English with a full sentence.

➡ _____

09 다음은 위 글을 요약한 것이다. 위 글의 내용과 일치하지 <u>않는</u> 곳을 세 군데 찾아 바르게 고쳐 쓰시오.

Lalita wondered how she could clean the air. Using corn leaves, she made a filtering system. It moved 70 to 80 percent of the dirty matter from the water.

➡ _____

[10~11] 다음 글을 읽고 물음에 답하시오.

To Genie,

I have three wishes. I wonder (A)_____ you can make my wishes come true. First, (B)나는 하와이에 살았으면 좋겠다. Then, I could swim at a beautiful beach. Second, I wish every Wednesday were a holiday. Then, I could be more relaxed. Finally, I wish I were the president of Korea. Then, I would try hard to make my country a happier place to live in. I don't know (C)_____ you can help me, but I hope you can.

Best Wishes,
Sohee

10 빈칸 (A)와 (C)에 공통으로 들어갈 말을 쓰시오.

➡ _____

11 동사 wish를 활용하여 밑줄 친 우리말 (B)를 영어로 쓰시오. (6 words)

➡ _____

01 다음은 슈퍼 영웅 SKY X의 능력이다. 빈칸에 알맞은 말을 써서 대화를 완성하시오.

> • What he can do: fly to the moon
> • What he can't do: travel to the sun

A: I'm Sky X. I can fly.

B: Hi, Sky X. Nice to meet you.

C: I wish I could fly like you. Is it possible _____?

A: Sure.

D: Then is it possible _____?

A: No. That's impossible.

02 다음 〈보기〉와 같이 원하는 번호의 그림을 골라, 그림에 맞게 가정법 과거 시제의 조건문과 주절을 영작하시오.

┃ 보기 ┃

　① If I knew his phone number, I would call him.

➡ _____

➡ _____

➡ _____

03 다음 소원과, 소원이 이루어진다면 하고 싶은 일을 참고하여 램프의 요정에게 쓰는 편지를 완성하시오.

> I have a million dollars. — I can help all the children who can't afford to go to school.
> I am a famous singer. — I will be on TV and my grandma will be happy.
> I am a bird. — I can fly all around the world.

> To Genie,
> I have three wishes. I wonder if you can make my wishes come true. First, I wish _____. Then, I could _____. Second, I wish _____. Then, _____. Finally, I wish _____. Then, _____. I don't know if you can help me, but I hope you can.
>
> 　　　　　　　　　　　　　　　　　　　　　Best Wishes,
> 　　　　　　　　　　　　　　　　　　　　　Sohee

단원별 모의고사

01 다음 중 빈칸에 들어갈 말이 다른 하나는?

① Did you pay _____ each item?
② Thank you _____ understanding me.
③ She has built a house _____ herself.
④ He hit _____ creative ideas to make the situation better.
⑤ She has used the machines _____ free since last year.

02 다음 대화의 밑줄 친 부분과 의미가 가장 가까운 것은?

> A: What are you doing here?
> B: I'm looking at the club poster. I'd like to play the drums.

① I want you to play the drums.
② I wish I could play the drums.
③ I'm sure I can play the drums.
④ It is possible for me to play the drums.
⑤ I think I have to learn how to play the drums.

03 짝지어진 두 단어의 관계가 같도록 빈칸에 알맞은 말을 쓰시오.

> fee – charge : contaminate – _____

04 주어진 단어를 활용하여 다음 우리말을 7단어로 이루어진 한 문장의 영어로 쓰시오.

> 그녀는 내일 너를 만나기를 고대하고 있어.
> (look / to)

➡ _____

05 다음 중 단어의 영영 풀이가 바르지 않은 것은?

① business: a work of producing, buying, and selling of goods and services
② coin: a round piece of metal used as money
③ headband: a narrow strip of material worn around the head, usually to keep your hair or sweat out of your eyes
④ come across: to pass by someone
⑤ software: the operating applications programs that are used in a computer system

06 자연스러운 대화가 되도록 (A)~(D)를 바르게 나열하시오.

> (A) Yes, but I'm not good at speaking yet.
> (B) I've been learning it for a month.
> (C) Is it possible for you to read Korean now?
> (D) How long have you been learning Korean?

➡ _____

[07~08] 다음 대화를 읽고 물음에 답하시오.

> W: Hi. I'm looking for a backpack for my son.
> M: How old is your son?
> W: He is five years old.
> M: I want to recommend this one.
> W: Oh, it's so cute.
> M: Yes, isn't it? It has a cap that looks like a penguin, so kids love it.
> W: (A)Is it possible for me to take the cap off for washing?
> M: Sure. You can easily take it off and put it back on.
> W: That's wonderful. I'll take it.

07 주어진 단어를 활용하여 밑줄 친 (A)와 같은 의미의 문장을 쓰시오.

(can)

➡ _____

08 위 대화를 읽고 답할 수 <u>없는</u> 것은?

① What is the woman looking for?
② How old is the woman's son?
③ What does the man recommend?
④ What is the backpack made with?
⑤ Can the woman wash the cap?

09 다음 대화의 빈칸에 알맞은 말을 세 단어로 쓰시오.

A: Can you swim well?
B: No, I _____ , but I can't.

[10~12] 다음 대화를 읽고 물음에 답하시오.

B: Wendy, you have been late for school a lot ①lately. ②What's wrong?
G: (A)_____ , but I just can't.
B: Doesn't your mom wake you up?
G: She does, but I don't get up ③right away. ④ I wish I could have an AI robot.
B: An AI robot?
G: Yes. I mean one that could make sure I ⑤got up and give me breakfast in the morning.
B: That sounds great.

10 빈칸 (A)에 들어갈 말로 적절하지 <u>않은</u> 것을 <u>모두</u> 고르시오.

① I want to wake up early
② I'd like to wake up early
③ I wish I could wake up early
④ I can't wait to wake up early
⑤ I always wake up early

11 What does Wendy's mother do? Answer in English.

➡ _____

12 ①~⑤ 중 주어진 말로 바꾸어 쓸 수 <u>없는</u> 것은?

① recently
② What's the matter with you?
③ at once
④ It is possible for me to have an AI robot.
⑤ woke up

13 다음 빈칸 ⓐ, ⓑ, ⓒ에 공통으로 들어갈 말로 가장 적절한 것은?

• Lalita wanted to know ⓐ_____ she could help her village with the filter she made using corn cobs.
• You can make your dream come true ⓑ_____ you dream it specifically.
• Fabien is asking the man ⓒ_____ there is an art museum near the building.

① when   ② that   ③ how
④ if   ⑤ whether

14 다음 중 어법상 <u>어색한</u> 것은?

① If Minsu got up earlier this morning, he wouldn't miss the bus.
② If Jay had put on his glasses, he would have noticed her.
③ If Mary missed the bus, she would not have been late for work.
④ If the organization could be awarded the prize, I would be proud of it.
⑤ If Bruce told the truth to his mom, she would be impressed with what he did for her.

15 다음 중 〈보기〉의 문장과 의미가 가장 가까운 것을 고르시오.

> 보기
>
> If Yeon-kyoung were in good condition, she would make twice as many attacks of spikes as any other players.

① As Yeon-kyoung is not in good condition, she didn't make as many attacks of spikes as any other players.

② As Yeon-kyoung is not in good condition, she doesn't make as many attacks of spikes as any other players.

③ Though Yeon-kyoung were not in good condition, she made as many attacks of spikes as any other players.

④ As Yeon-kyoung was not in good condition, she didn't make as many attacks of spikes as any other players.

⑤ As Yeon-kyoung was in good condition, she made twice as many attacks of spikes as any other players.

[16~17] 다음 〈보기〉의 밑줄 친 부분과 쓰임이 다른 하나는?

16

> I wish I could please my mother.

① I wish the visitor could speak Korean.

② She could get freedom if you told the truth to the police.

③ I wish I could make as many foreign friends as possible.

④ Could you find me a job suitable for my age?

⑤ If he knew her number, he could make a phone call.

17

> I wonder if my filter will completely remove the dirty matter in the water.

① Sean asked his cousins if the game titles would look interesting.

② I'm not sure if the actress will come to my city tomorrow or not.

③ My teacher wondered if the war broke out in 1904 or in 1905.

④ The player wasn't sure if the girl in first row was seeing him or not.

⑤ David won't attend the meeting if his friend Tom appears this evening.

[18~21] 다음 글을 읽고 물음에 답하시오.

**A Robotic Hand from a Helpful Mind
(Easton LaChappelle)**

One day, when I was fourteen, I came across a little girl at a science fair. (①) She had a robotic hand that could only open and close. I was surprised that the hand had cost her 80,000 dollars! (②) 'I wish she had a better robotic hand,' I thought to myself. (③) After many failures, finally, by using 3D printing technology, I was able to make a useful robotic hand for the price of only 300 dollars. (④) I decided to share the designs and software for my 3D robotic hand with others for free. (⑤) Maybe someone can take what I have done and do something useful with it. (A) No one person can change the world, but we can build a better world by working together.

18 (①)~(⑤) 중 주어진 문장이 들어가기에 가장 적절한 곳은?

> With that, I started to make a much cheaper and better robotic hand.

　　　　　　④　　⑤

19 According to the passage, what did Easton decide to do after inventing the robotic hand with 3D printing technology? Answer in English.

➡ _____

_____

20 밑줄 친 (A)의 의미로 가장 적절한 것은?

① No one can change the world.

② None of us change the world.

③ Not all of us can change the world.

④ The world can be changed by one person.

⑤ The world can't be changed by a single person.

21 위 글을 읽고 답할 수 있는 것은?

① How old was the little girl who had a robotic hand?

② Who did Easton meet at a science fair?

③ How did Easton get the 3D printer?

④ How many times did Easton fail to invent the robotic hand?

⑤ What brought Easton to the science fair?

[22~25] 다음 글을 읽고 물음에 답하시오.

Headbands for Girls' Education (Mary Grace Henry)

'Why can't many girls in Africa go to school as I can? (A)나는 그들도 학교에 갈 수 있으면 좋을 텐데.' I had this thought when I was twelve. I realized ①that their families couldn't afford it. I wondered ②that I could do something for those girls. Then I had an idea. For my birthday, I asked my parents to buy me a sewing machine. They bought me one, and I learned how to make headbands ③for myself. I created ten headbands and sold them at my school. Soon, I raised enough money ④to send one girl in Africa to school. I couldn't stop there. I started a business to help girls in Africa who couldn't go to school. Thanks to the success of my business, I can pay the school fees for many poor girls in countries like Kenya and Uganda to go to school. I also pay for their textbooks, uniforms, and pencils.

Isn't it amazing? My advice to you ⑤is to just do something. When you see a need, act. Start small, taking little steps. Your warm heart can change lives.

22 주어진 단어를 활용하여 밑줄 친 우리말 (A)를 영어로 쓰시오.

(wish / go / too) (8 words)

➡ _____

23 밑줄 친 ①~⑤ 중 어법상 바르지 <u>않은</u> 것은?

①   ②   ③   ④   ⑤

24 What did Mary start to help girls in Africa who couldn't go to school? Answer in English with seven words.

➡ _____

25 위 글의 내용과 일치하지 <u>않는</u> 것은?

① Mary wanted the poor girls in Africa to go to school like her.

② Mary taught herself how to make headbands.

③ Mary's parents bought her a sewing machine as she asked them.

④ Mary also helps the poor girls in her neighborhood.

⑤ Mary thinks our warm heart can change lives of people.

Lesson

Special

The Necklace

Key Words

- **admire** [ədmáiər] 동 존경하다, 칭찬하다, 감탄하며 바라보다
- **ambassador** [æmbǽsədər] 명 대사
- **amount** [əmáunt] 명 양, 액수
- **ball** [bɔːl] 명 무도회
- **beauty** [bjúːtj] 명 아름다움, 미
- **borrow** [bɑːrou] 동 빌리다
- **certainly** [sə́ːrtnli] 부 확실히, 틀림없이
- **couple** [kʌ́pl] 명 부부
- **cry** [krai] 동 울다
- **diamond** [dáiəmənd] 명 다이아몬드
- **fancy** [fǽnsi] 형 화려한
- **franc** [fræŋ] 명 프랑 (프랑스, 스위스 등의 화폐 단위)
- **huge** [hjuːdʒ] 형 거대한, 엄청난
- **invitation** [invitéiʃən] 명 초대, 초대장
- **jeweler** [dʒúːələr] 명 보석 상인

- **jewelry** [dʒúːəlri] 명 보석류
- **lend** [lend] 동 빌려주다
- **lie** [lai] 명 거짓말
- **look** [luk] 명 보기, 눈길
- **nearly** [níərli] 부 거의
- **necklace** [néklis] 명 목걸이
- **piece** [piːs] 명 한 개, 한 부분, 조각
- **replace** [ripléis] 동 (다른 사람·사물을) 대신하다
- **second job** 부업
- **shocked** [ʃakt] 형 충격을 받은
- **similar** [símələr] 형 비슷한, 유사한
- **whatever** [hwʌtévər] 대 ~이든지, ~한 어떤 것이든
- **whisper** [hwíspər] 동 속삭이다, 귓속말을 하다
- **worth** [wəːrθ] 형 ~의 가치가 있는
- **worn** [wɔːrn] 형 지친

Key Expressions

- **at once** 즉시, 당장
- **call on** ~에게 청하다, 부탁하다
- **Do I know you**? 절 아시나요?
- **It takes**+목적어+시간+**to**부정사 (목적어)가 ~하는 데 (시간)이 걸리다

- **pay back** 갚다, 돌려주다
- **run into** ~을 우연히 만나다
- **spend**+시간+동명사 ~하는 데 (시간)을 소비하다

Word Power

※ 서로 비슷한 뜻을 가진 어휘
- □ **admire** 존경하다 – **respect** 존경하다
- □ **amount** 양, 액수 – **quantity** 양
- □ **huge** 거대한, 엄청난 – **vast** 광대한, 거대한
- □ **replace** ~을 대신하다 – **substitute** ~을 대신하다, 대리하다
- □ **similar** 비슷한, 유사한 – **alike** 비슷한
- □ **whisper** 속삭이다, 귓속말을 하다 – **murmur** 속삭이다

※ 서로 반대되는 뜻을 가진 어휘
- □ **borrow** 빌리다 ↔ **lend** 빌려주다
- □ **huge** 거대한, 엄청난 ↔ **tiny** 아주 작은
- □ **similar** 비슷한, 유사한 ↔ **different** 다른, 상이한
- □ **whisper** 속삭이다, 귓속말을 하다 ↔ **shout** 큰소리를 내다, 외치다, 소리[고함]치다

English Dictionary

- □ **admire** 존경하다, 칭찬하다, 감탄하며 바라보다
  → to like and respect someone or something very much
  누군가 또는 어떤 것을 매우 좋아하고 존경하다

- □ **ambassador** 대사
  → a diplomat of the highest rank who is the official representative of his or her country in another country
  다른 나라에서 자신의 나라의 공식적인 대표인 가장 높은 지위의 외교관

- □ **amount** 양, 액수
  → a quantity of something 어떤 것의 양

- □ **ball** 무도회
  → a large formal place where people dance
  사람들이 춤추는 큰 정식의 장소

- □ **certainly** 확실히, 틀림없이
  → surely; without doubt
  확실히, 의심 없이

- □ **couple** 부부
  → two people who are married
  결혼한 두 사람

- □ **cry** 울다
  → to let tears come from the eyes because of sadness, hurt, etc.
  슬픔, 아픔 등 때문에 눈에서 눈물이 나오게 하다

- □ **diamond** 다이아몬드
  → a hard, bright, precious stone which is clear and colorless
  깨끗하고 무색인 단단하고 밝고 귀중한 돌

- □ **invitation** 초대, 초대장
  → a request to come to an event or somewhere
  행사나 어느 곳으로 오라는 요청

- □ **jeweler** 보석 상인
  → a person who makes, sells, and repairs jewelry and watches
  보석류나 시계를 만들고, 팔고, 수리하는 사람

- □ **jewelry** 보석류
  → decorative objects worn on clothes or on the body, such as rings and necklaces
  반지나 목걸이 같은 옷이나 몸에 걸치는 장식물

- □ **lie** 거짓말
  → a statement which you know is not true
  진실이 아님을 아는 언급

- □ **nearly** 거의
  → almost but not quite
  거의 그러나 완전히는 아닌

- □ **replace** ~을 대신하다
  → to take a place of
  ~을 대신하다

- □ **shocked** 충격을 받은
  → feeling very upset or surprised
  매우 혼란하거나 놀란 느낌

- □ **similar** 비슷한, 유사한
  → alike in many ways
  여러 방식으로 비슷한

- □ **whisper** 속삭이다, 귓속말을 하다
  → to speak or say something very softly and low
  무언가를 매우 부드럽고 낮게 말하다

- □ **worn** 지친
  → very tired
  매우 피곤한

Reading

The Necklace
Scene 1

 This is Mr. and Mrs. Loisel's home in Paris. Although the home is
<u>양보의 부사절을 이끄는 접속사(비록 ~일지라도)</u>
nice, Mrs. Loisel is not happy. She is young and pretty, and wants a

fancier life.

Mrs. Loisel: (*to herself*) Same old house and same <u>boring</u> dinners. I
<u>to oneself: 혼잣말로</u>   <u>감정을 유발할 때: 현재분사</u>

       hate <u>living</u> here!
       <u>(= to live)</u>

Mrs. Loisel: Matilda, I am home. Look <u>what</u> I have got for you!
       <u>관계대명사(~하는 것)</u>

Mrs. Loisel: What is that?

Mrs. Loisel: An invitation to the Ambassador's Ball. I <u>had to</u> fight <u>to get</u>
       <u>must의 과거</u>   <u>to부정사의 부사적 용법 중 목적(하기 위해서)</u>

       it. Everybody wanted it.

Mrs. Loisel: *crying*) Why would I want it?

Mrs. Loisel: Matilda. What is wrong?

Mrs. Loisel: I have nothing <u>to wear</u> to <u>such a fancy party</u>. I cannot go.
       <u>to부정사의 형용사적 용법(nothing 수식)</u>   <u>such+a(n)+형용사+명사</u>

Mrs. Loisel: Don't be sad. Here, I will give you 400 francs. Get <u>yourself</u>
       <u>재귀대명사의 재귀적 용법</u>

       a beautiful new dress.

Scene 2

Mrs. Loisel: (*looking at Matilda's new dress*) <u>Amazing</u>, Matilda.
       <u>감정을 유발할 때: 현재분사</u>

       Beautiful!

Mrs. Loisel: Something is not right.

Mrs. Loisel: What could be wrong?

Mrs. Loisel: (*crying*) Oh, no. What am I going to do?

Mrs. Loisel: What is it, Matilda?

---

necklace: 목걸이
invitation: 초대장, 초청장
ambassador: 대사
ball: 무도회
franc: 프랑 (스위스 등의 화폐 단위)

🖇 **확인문제**

● 다음 문장이 본문의 내용과 일치하면 T, 일치하지 <u>않으면</u> F를 쓰시오.

1 The Loisels live in Paris. ☐

2 What Mr. Loisel wants is a fancier life. ☐

3 Mrs. Loisel is not happy with the invitation because she doesn't have beautiful

    clothes to wear. ☐

4 Mrs. Loisel will buy a jewel with **400** francs. ☐

Mrs. Loisel: I have no jewelry to wear with my beautiful dress. I
to부정사의 형용사적 용법(jewelry 수식)
will look so poor!
look+형용사(~하게 보이다)

Mrs. Loisel: Call on your friend, Mrs. Forestier. I am sure she will
your friend와 동격
lend you some of her jewelry.

Mrs. Loisel: That is a good idea! Let me go at once.
즉시

Scene 3

Mrs. Forestier: Matilda, it is so nice to see you! What brings you here?
가주어

Mrs. Loisel: We are invited to the Ambassador's Ball.
수동태(초대되다)

Mrs. Forestier: The Ambassador's Ball! That is wonderful! You must
must be: ~임에 틀림없다
be excited.
감정을 느낄 때 과거분사

Mrs. Loisel: Yes… And no. I am sad to say I have no jewelry. May
to부정사의 부사적 용법 중 감정의 원인
I borrow something from you?

Mrs. Forestier: Sure! Here is my case.

Mrs. Loisel: Wow, you have so many wonderful pieces!

Mrs. Forestier: Choose whatever you like.
복합관계대명사(= anything which): choose의 목적어를 이끎

Mrs. Loisel: Would you lend me this diamond necklace? It is beautiful!

Mrs. Forestier: Certainly! Now go enjoy the ball.
= go and enjoy

Scene 4

Matilda has a perfect evening. Everybody at the ball admires her
everybody: 단수 취급
beauty. It is very late when the Loisels leave the ball.
비인칭주어   the+사람의 성 복수형: ~ 부부, ~ 가족

Mrs. Loisel: It was such a long night. I am so tired.

Mrs. Loisel: But it was worth it. Do you know I danced with the
Ambassador?

---

jewelry: 보석 장식, 장신구
call on: ~에게 청하다, 부탁하다
piece: 한 개, 한 부분, 조각
whatever: ~한 어떤 것이든
diamond: 다이아몬드
certainly: 틀림없이, 분명히
admire: ~에 감탄하다, 칭찬하다
beauty: 아름다움, 미
worth: ~의 가치가 있는

📎 **확인문제**

● 다음 문장이 본문의 내용과 일치하면 T, 일치하지 <u>않으면</u> F를 쓰시오.

1 Mrs. Loisel is satisfied with her dress and wants nothing more. ☐

2 Mrs. Loisel sends her husband to borrow a necklace from her friend. ☐

3 Mrs. Forestier willingly lends her necklace to Matilda. ☐

Mrs. Loisel: I am glad you <u>enjoyed yourself</u>, but I have to go to

enjoy oneself: 즐기다

work in the morning.

Mrs. Loisel: (*looking in the mirror*) Just one more look.

(*shocked*) The necklace… It is gone!

Mrs. Loisel: What? Did you have it <u>when</u> we left the ball?

부사절을 이끄는 접속사(~할 때)

Mrs. Loisel: Yes, I surely <u>did</u>. Please go find it!

had it when we left the ball

Mr. Loisel searches the streets. He returns to the ball and then goes

to the police. When the necklace is not found, Mr. Loisel <u>tells Matilda</u>

tell+목적어+to부정사: 목적어에게 …하라고 말하다

<u>to lie</u> to her friend. Matilda tells Mrs. Forestier she broke the necklace

and would fix it before returning it. The couple needs time <u>to find</u> a

to부정사의 형용사적 용법(time 수식)

similar <u>one</u>.

necklace를 가리키는 부정대명사

Scene 5

Mrs. Loisel: (*to the jeweler*) Excuse me? <u>May</u> we look at that

정중히 요청할 때

diamond necklace?

Mrs. Loisel: (*whispering*) It is nearly the same. We <u>must</u> have it!

필요성이나 중요성을 나타낼 때

Mrs. Loisel: How much is it?

Jeweler: 40,000 francs.

Mrs. Loisel: How about 36,000?

Mrs. Loisel: Please, we really need it.

Jeweler: Well, then… 36,000 it is.

They do not have 36,000 francs. It is a huge amount of money. So

they borrow <u>it</u>. After <u>buying</u> the necklace <u>for</u> Mrs. Forestier, the couple

a huge amount of money 지칭   4형식을 3형식으로 전환할 때 간접목적어에 전치사 for

<u>spends</u> ten years paying back the money.

spend+시간/돈+Ving: V하느라 시간이나 돈을 쓰다

---

look: 보기, 눈길

surely: 확실히, 분명히

couple: 남녀, 커플, 부부

similar: 비슷한, 유사한

jewler: 보석상

whisper: 속삭이다

huge: 거대한, 엄청난

amount: 금액, 액수, 양

pay back: 갚다, 돌려주다

📎 **확인문제**

● 다음 문장이 본문의 내용과 일치하면 T, 일치하지 <u>않으면</u> F를 쓰시오.

1   Mr. Loisel has to go to work the next day of the party. ☐

2   Matilda is sure that she lost her necklace at the ball. ☐

3   The Loisels manage to find just the same necklace as Mrs. Forestier's. ☐

4   The Loisels borrow money from the jeweler. ☐

5   It took a decade for the couple to pay back the money. ☐

They move to a very small place. Mr. Loisel gets a second job. Matilda washes clothes for others. Ten years of hard work makes Matilda old and worn. After ten years, Matilda runs into Mrs. Forestier on the street.

make+목적어+목적격보어(목적어를 ~하게 만들다)

worn: 몹시 지친, 수척한

second job: 부업

run into: ~를 우연히 만나다, 마주치다

replace: 대신하다

tell ~ the truth: ~에게 진실을 말하다

Scene 6

Mrs. Loisel: Mrs. Forestier, good morning.

Mrs. Forestier: Do I know you?

Mrs. Loisel: Yes, it is me, Matilda.

Mrs. Forestier: Oh, I cannot believe it! You have changed so much.

Mrs. Loisel: I have had some difficult times because of you.

현재완료(계속 용법)　　　　　　전치사(+명사)

Mrs. Forestier: Because of me? What do you mean?

~ 때문에

Mrs. Loisel: Do you remember the diamond necklace you lent me?

목적격 관계대명사 that 생략 (that) you lent me

Well, I lost it.

Mrs. Forestier: But you returned it to me.

Mrs. Loisel: No, I returned another one just like it. It took us ten

= necklace

years to pay for it.

It takes 사람 시간 to V: 사람이 V하느라 ~만큼의 시간이 걸리다

Mrs. Forestier: You bought a diamond necklace to replace mine?

to부정사의 부사적 용법 중 목적(~하기 위해서)

Mrs. Loisel: Yes.

Mrs. Forestier: Oh, my poor Matilda. Why didn't you come to me

Why didn't you+동사원형 ~?: 왜 ~하지 않았니?

and tell me the truth? My diamond necklace was not real.

It was worth only 500 francs!

확인문제

● 다음 문장이 본문의 내용과 일치하면 T, 일치하지 않으면 F를 쓰시오.

1 Matilda washes clothes for others to pay back the money. ☐

2 Matilda becomes old and worn because of the ten years of hard work. ☐

3 Mrs. Forestier recognizes Matilda as soon as she sees her. ☐

4 The necklace that Matilda returned to Mrs. Forestier wasn't what she had borrowed

   from Mrs. Forestier. ☐

5 The necklace Matilda borrowed from Mrs. Forestier was real. ☐

6 Mrs. Forestier didn't know the truth that Matilda lost her necklace. ☐

● 우리말을 참고하여 빈칸에 알맞은 말을 쓰시오.

Scene 1

1 _____ _____ Mr. and Mrs. Loisel's home _____ _____.

2 _____ the home is _____, Mrs. Loisel is _____ _____.

3 She is young and pretty, _____ _____ a _____ life.

4 Mrs. Loisel: (_____ _____) Same _____ _____ and same _____ dinners. I hate _____ here!

5 Mr. Loisel: Matilda, I _____ _____. Look _____ I _____ _____ for you!

6 Mrs. Loisel: What is _____?

7 Mr. Loisel: An _____ _____ the Ambassador's Ball. I _____ _____ _____ _____ _____ _____. Everybody wanted it.

8 Mrs. Loisel: (crying) _____ _____ I want it?

9 Mr. Loisel: Matilda. What _____ _____?

10 Mrs. Loisel: I have _____ _____ _____ to _____ _____ _____ _____. I cannot go.

11 Mr. Loisel: _____ _____ sad. Here, I will _____ 400 francs. _____ _____ a beautiful new dress.

Scene 2

12 Mr. Loisel: (_____ _____ *Matilda's new dress*) _____, Matilda. Beautiful!

13 Mrs. Loisel: Something is _____ _____.

14 Mr. Loisel: _____ _____ _____ _____ _____?

15 Mrs. Loisel: (crying) Oh, no. What am I _____ _____ _____?

1 이곳은 파리의 Loisel 부부의 집이다.

2 그들의 집은 멋지지만, Loisel 부인은 행복하지 않다.

3 그녀는 젊고 예뻐서 더 화려하고 고급스러운 삶을 원한다.

4 Mrs. Loisel: (혼잣말로) 똑같은 낡은 집과 매일 같이 똑같은 지겨운 저녁 식사. 여기서 사는 게 너무 싫어!

5 Mr. Loisel: Matilda, 나 집에 왔어요. 내가 당신을 위해 무엇을 가져왔는지 봐요!

6 Mrs. Loisel: 뭐예요?

7 Mr. Loisel: 대사님이 여는 무도회 초대장이에요. 이걸 얻기 위해 엄청난 노력을 했단 말이에요. 모두가 갖고 싶어 했거든요.

8 Mrs. Loisel: (울면서) 내가 그걸 왜 갖고 싶겠어요?

9 Mr. Loisel: Matilda. 무슨 문제 있어요?

10 Mrs. Loisel: 그런 고급스러운 파티에 입고 갈 옷이 하나도 없는걸요. 못가요.

11 Mr. Loisel: 슬퍼하지 말아요. 자, 여기 400프랑을 줄게요. 아름다운 새 드레스를 사요.

12 Mr. Loisel: (Matilda의 새 드레스를 보며) 멋져요, Matilda. 아름답군요!

13 Mrs. Loisel: 뭔가 제대로 맞지 않아요.

14 Mr. Loisel: 뭐가 안 맞을 수 있죠?

15 Mrs. Loisel: (울면서) 오, 안 돼. 어쩌면 좋아요?

16 Mr. Loisel: _____ _____ _____, Matilda?

17 Mrs. Loisel: I have _____ _____ _____ _____ with my beautiful dress. I will look _____ _____!

18 Mr. Loisel: _____ _____ your friend, Mrs. Forestier. I am sure _____ _____ _____ _____ some of her jewelry.

19 Mrs. Loisel: That is a good idea! _____ _____ _____ at once.

Scene 3

20 Mrs. Forestier: Matilda, it is so nice _____ _____ you! _____ _____ _____ _____?

21 Mrs. Loisel: We are _____ _____ the Ambassador's Ball.

22 Mrs. Forestier: The Ambassador's Ball! That is _____! You must be _____.

23 Mrs. Loisel: Yes… And no. I am sad _____ _____ I have _____ _____. May I _____ _____ _____ _____ _____?

24 Mrs. Forestier: Sure! _____ _____ my case.

25 Mrs. Loisel: Wow, you have _____ _____ _____ _____!

26 Mrs. Forestier: Choose _____ _____ _____.

27 Mrs. Loisel: Would you _____ _____ _____ _____ _____? It is beautiful!

28 Mrs. Forestier: _____! Now _____ _____ _____ the ball.

Scene 4

29 Matilda has _____ _____ _____. Everybody at the ball _____ _____.

30 _____ _____ very late _____ _____ _____ _____ the ball.

31 Mr. Loisel: It was _____ _____ _____ _____ _____. I am so tired.

---

16 Mr. Loisel: 뭐예요, 부인?

17 Mrs. Loisel: 이 아름다운 드레스에 어울릴 보석이 하나도 없어요. 내가 너무 불쌍해 보일 거예요!

18 Mr. Loisel: 당신 친구 Forestier 부인에게 부탁해 봐요. 그녀는 자신이 가진 보석을 분명히 빌려줄 거예요.

19 Mrs. Loisel: 그거 좋은 생각이에요! 지금 당장 가봐야겠어요.

장면 3

20 Mrs. Forestier: Matilda, 이렇게 보게 되어서 정말 좋아요! 무슨 일로 왔어요?

21 Mrs. Loisel: 우리 부부가 대사의 무도회에 초대되었어요.

22 Mrs. Forestier: 대사의 무도회라! 멋지네요! 당신은 분명 신났겠군요.

23 Mrs. Loisel: 네… 그리고 아니기도 해요. 말하기 슬프지만 난 보석이 없어요. 부인에게서 좀 빌릴 수 있을까요?

24 Mrs. Forestier: 물론이죠! 여기 내 보석함이에요.

25 Mrs. Loisel: 와, 부인은 정말 멋진 보석들이 많네요!

26 Mrs. Forestier: 원하는 것 아무거나 골라요.

27 Mrs. Loisel: 이 다이아몬드 목걸이를 빌려줄 수 있나요? 이거 정말 아름다워요!

28 Mrs. Forestier: 당연하죠! 자, 이제 가서 무도회를 즐겨요.

장면 4

29 Matilda는 완벽한 저녁을 보낸다. 무도회장에 있는 모든 사람들이 아름다운 그녀를 감탄하며 바라본다.

30 Loisel 부부는 아주 늦은 시간이 되어서야 무도회를 떠났다.

31 Mr. Loisel: 정말 길고 긴 밤이었어요. 정말 피곤해요.

32 Mrs. Loisel: But _____ _____ _____ _____. Do you know I _____ _____ the Ambassador?

33 Mr. Loisel: I am glad _____ _____ _____, but I have to go to work in the morning.

34 Mrs. Loisel: (_____ _____ *the mirror*) Just one _____ _____. (*shocked*) The necklace… It is gone!

35 Mr. Loisel: What? Did you have it _____ _____ _____ _____ _____?

36 Mrs. Loisel: Yes, I surely _____. Please _____ _____ it!

37 Mr. Loisel _____ the streets.

38 He _____ _____ the ball and then _____ _____ the police.

39 When the necklace _____ _____ _____, Mr. Loisel tells Matilda _____ _____ _____ her friend.

40 Matilda tells Mrs. Forestier she _____ the necklace and would _____ _____ before _____ _____.

41 The couple needs time _____ _____ _____ _____ _____.

Scene 5

42 Mr. Loisel: (*to the jeweler*) Excuse me? _____ _____ _____ _____ that diamond necklace?

43 Mrs. Loisel: (_____) It is _____ _____ _____. We must have it!

44 Mr. Loisel: _____ _____ is it?

45 Jeweler: 40,000 _____.

46 Mr. Loisel: _____ _____ 36,000?

47 Mrs. Loisel: Please, we _____ _____ _____ _____.

48 Jeweler: Well, then… 36,000 _____ _____.

49 They _____ _____ _____ 36,000 francs. It is _____ _____ _____ _____ money.

50 So they _____ _____.

32 Mrs. Loisel: 그렇지만 충분히 가치가 있었어요. 당신, 제가 대사님과 춤춘 것을 아나요?

33 Mr. Loisel: 당신이 즐거웠다니 기쁘지만 나 아침에 출근해야 해요.

34 Mrs. Loisel: (거울을 보며) 한 번만 더 볼게요. (충격을 받고) 목걸이… 목걸이가 없어졌어요!

35 Mr. Loisel: 뭐라고요? 무도회를 떠날 때 걸고 있었소?

36 Mrs. Loisel: 네, 분명히 하고 있었는데. 가서 찾아 줘요!

37 Loisel 씨는 길거리를 수색한다.

38 그는 무도회장으로 되돌아가 본 다음 경찰서에도 간다.

39 목걸이가 발견되지 않자, Loisel 씨는 Matilda에게 그녀의 친구에게 거짓말을 하라고 한다.

40 Matilda는 Forestier 부인에게 목걸이를 망가뜨려서 돌려주기 전에 고쳐 주겠다고 말한다.

41 부부는 비슷한 것을 찾을 시간이 필요하다.

장면 5

42 Mr. Loisel: (보석상에게) 실례합니다. 저 다이아몬드 목걸이가 좀 볼 수 있을까요?

43 Mrs. Loisel: (속삭이며) 거의 똑같아요. 저걸 꼭 사야만 해요!

44 Mr. Loisel: 이거 얼마인가요?

45 Jeweler: 40,000프랑이에요.

46 Mr. Loisel: 36,000에 안 될까요?

47 Mrs. Loisel: 부탁드려요. 우린 이게 정말 필요하거든요.

48 Jeweler: 음, 그럼… 36,000프랑에 하시죠.

49 그들은 36,000프랑이 없다. 그건 큰돈이다.

50 그래서 그들은 돈을 빌린다.

51 After _____ the necklace _____ Mrs. Forestier, the couple _____ ten years _____ back the money.

52 They _____ _____ a very small place.

53 Mr. Loisel _____ _____ _____ _____ . Matilda _____ clothes _____ others.

54 Ten years of hard work _____ Matilda _____ and _____ .

55 After ten years, Matilda _____ _____ Mrs. Forestier _____ the street.

Scene 6

56 Mrs. Loisel: Mrs. Forestier, _____ _____ .

57 Mrs. Forestier: _____ _____ _____ _____ ?

58 Mrs. Loisel: Yes, _____ _____ _____ , Matilda.

59 Mrs. Forestier: Oh, I cannot _____ _____ ! You _____ so much.

60 Mrs. Loisel: I _____ _____ some _____ because of you.

61 Mrs. Forestier: Because of me? _____ _____ _____ _____ ?

62 Mrs. Loisel: Do you remember the diamond necklace _____ _____ _____ ? Well, I _____ _____ .

63 Mrs. Forestier: But you _____ _____ to me.

64 Mrs. Loisel: No, I returned _____ _____ just _____ _____ . _____ took us ten years _____ _____ _____ .

65 Mrs. Forestier: You _____ a diamond necklace _____ _____ mine?

66 Mrs. Loisel: Yes.

67 Mrs. Forestier: Oh, my poor Matilda. _____ _____ _____ to me and _____ _____ _____ the truth? My diamond necklace _____ _____ _____ . It was _____ only 500 francs!

51 부부는 Forestier 부인에게 돌려줄 목걸이를 산 후 돈을 갚는 데 십 년이 걸린다.

52 그들은 아주 작은 곳으로 이사한다.

53 Loisel 씨는 부업을 구한다. Matilda는 다른 사람들을 위해 빨래를 해 준다.

54 10년 동안의 고된 일로 Matilda는 늙고 지쳤다.

55 십 년 후, Matilda는 Forestier 부인과 거리에서 마주친다.

56 Mrs. Loisel: Forestier 부인, 좋은 아침이에요.

57 Mrs. Forestier: 제가 당신을 아나요?

58 Mrs. Loisel: 네, 저예요, Matilda.

59 Mrs. Forestier: 오, 믿을 수 없어요! 당신 너무 많이 변했어요.

60 Mrs. Loisel: 저는 당신 때문에 힘든 시간을 보냈거든요.

61 Mrs. Forestier: 나 때문에요? 무슨 말이에요?

62 Mrs. Loisel: 당신이 빌려준 목걸이 기억하죠? 음, 제가 그걸 잃어버렸어요.

63 Mrs. Forestier: 그런데 그거 나한테 돌려줬잖아요.

64 Mrs. Loisel: 아니요, 나는 당신 것과 똑같은 다른 목걸이를 돌려줬어요. 그 값을 치르느라 십 년이 걸렸어요.

65 Mrs. Forestier: 내 것을 대체하려고 다이아몬드 목걸이를 샀다고요?

66 Mrs. Loisel: 네, 맞아요.

67 Mrs. Forestier: 오, 가엾은 Matilda. 왜 내게 와서 사실을 말하지 않았어요? 그 다이아몬드 목걸이는 진품이 아니었어요. 그건 단돈 오백 프랑짜리였다고요!

● 우리말을 참고하여 본문을 영작하시오.

Scene 1

1 이곳은 파리의 Loisel 부부의 집이다.

➡ _____

2 그들의 집은 멋지지만, Loisel 부인은 행복하지 않다.

➡ _____

3 그녀는 젊고 예뻐서 더 화려하고 고급스러운 삶을 원한다.

➡ _____

4 Mrs. Loisel: (혼잣말로) 똑같은 낡은 집과 매일 같이 똑같은 지겨운 저녁 식사. 여기서 사는 게 너무 싫어!

➡ _____

5 Mr. Loisel: Matilda, 나 집에 왔어요. 내가 당신을 위해 무엇을 가져왔는지 봐요!

➡ _____

6 Mrs. Loisel: 뭐예요?.

➡ _____

7 Mr. Loisel: 대사님이 여는 무도회 초대장이에요. 이걸 얻기 위해 엄청난 노력을 했단 말이에요. 모두가 갖고 싶어 했거든요.

➡ _____

8 Mrs. Loisel: (울면서) 내가 그걸 왜 갖고 싶겠어요?

➡ _____

9 Mr. Loisel: Matilda. 무슨 문제 있어요?

➡ _____

10 Mrs. Loisel: 그런 고급스러운 파티에 입고 갈 옷이 하나도 없는걸요. 못가요.

➡ _____

11 Mr. Loisel: 슬퍼하지 말아요. 자, 여기 400프랑을 줄게요. 아름다운 새 드레스를 사요.

➡ _____

Scene 2

12 Mr. Loisel: (Matilda의 새 드레스를 보며) 멋져요, Matilda. 아름답군요!

➡ _____

13 Mrs. Loisel: 뭔가 제대로 맞지 않아요.

➡ _____

14 Mr. Loisel: 뭐가 안 맞을 수 있죠?

➡ _____

15 Mrs. Loisel: (울면서) 오, 안 돼. 어쩌면 좋아요?

➡ _____

16 Mr. Loisel: 뭐예요, 부인?

➡ _____

17 Mrs. Loisel: 이 아름다운 드레스에 어울릴 보석이 하나도 없어요. 내가 너무 불쌍해 보일 거예요!

➡ _____

18 Mr. Loisel: 당신 친구 Forestier 부인에게 부탁해 봐요. 그녀는 자신이 가진 보석을 분명히 빌려줄 거예요.

➡ _____

19 Mrs. Loisel: 그거 좋은 생각이에요! 지금 당장 가봐야겠어요.

➡ _____

Scene 3

20 Mrs. Forestier: Matilda, 이렇게 보게 되어서 정말 좋아요! 무슨 일로 왔어요?

➡ _____

21 Mrs. Loisel: 우리 부부가 대사의 무도회에 초대되었어요.

➡ _____

22 Mrs. Forestier: 대사의 무도회라! 멋지네요! 당신은 분명 신났겠군요.

➡ _____

23 Mrs. Loisel: 네… 그리고 아니기도 해요. 말하기 슬프지만 난 보석이 없어요. 부인에게서 좀 빌릴 수 있을까요?

➡ _____

24 Mrs. Forestier: 물론이죠! 여기 내 보석함이에요.

➡ _____

25 Mrs. Loisel: 와, 부인은 정말 멋진 보석들이 많네요!

➡ _____

26 Mrs. Forestier: 원하는 것 아무거나 골라요.

➡ _____

27 Mrs. Loisel: 이 다이아몬드 목걸이를 빌려줄 수 있나요? 이거 정말 아름다워요!

➡ _____

28 Mrs. Forestier: 당연하죠! 자, 이제 가서 무도회를 즐겨요.

➡ _____

Scene 4

29 Matilda는 완벽한 저녁을 보낸다. 무도회장에 있는 모든 사람들이 아름다운 그녀를 감탄하며 바라본다.

➡ _____

30 Loisel 부부는 아주 늦은 시간이 되어서야 무도회를 떠났다.

➡ _____

31 Mr. Loisel: 정말 길고 긴 밤이었어요. 정말 피곤해요.

➡ _____

32 Mrs. Loisel: 그렇지만 충분히 가치가 있었어요. 당신, 제가 대사님과 춤춘 것을 아나요?
➡ _____

33 Mr. Loisel: 당신이 즐거웠다니 기쁘지만 나 아침에 출근해야 해요.
➡ _____

34 Mrs. Loisel: (거울을 보며) 한 번만 더 볼게요. (충격을 받고) 목걸이… 목걸이가 없어졌어요!
➡ _____

35 Mr. Loisel: 뭐라고요? 무도회를 떠날 때 걸고 있었소?
➡ _____

36 Mrs. Loisel: 네, 분명히 하고 있었는데. 가서 찾아 줘요!
➡ _____

37 Loisel 씨는 길거리를 수색한다.
➡ _____

38 그는 무도회장으로 되돌아가 본 다음 경찰서에도 간다.
➡ _____

39 목걸이가 발견되지 않자, Loisel 씨는 Matilda에게 그녀의 친구에게 거짓말을 하라고 한다.
➡ _____

40 Matilda는 Forestier 부인에게 목걸이를 망가뜨려서 돌려주기 전에 고쳐 주겠다고 말한다.
➡ _____

41 부부는 비슷한 것을 찾을 시간이 필요하다.
➡ _____

Scene 5

42 Mr. Loisel: (보석상에게) 실례합니다. 저 다이아몬드 목걸이 좀 볼 수 있을까요?
➡ _____

43 Mrs. Loisel: (속삭이며) 거의 똑같아요. 저걸 꼭 사야만 해요!
➡ _____

44 Mr. Loisel: 이거 얼마인가요?
➡ _____

45 Jewler: 40,000프랑이에요.
➡ _____

46 Mr. Loisel: 36,000에 안 될까요?
➡ _____

47 Mrs. Loisel: 부탁드려요, 우린 이게 정말 필요하거든요.
➡ _____

48 Jewler: 음, 그럼… 36,000프랑에 하시죠.
➡ _____

49 그들은 36,000프랑이 없다. 그건 큰돈이다.
➡ _____

50 그래서 그들은 돈을 빌린다.
➡ _____

51 부부는 Forestier 부인에게 돌려줄 목걸이를 산 후 돈을 갚는 데 십 년이 걸린다.
➡ _____

52 그들은 아주 작은 곳으로 이사한다.
➡ _____

53 Loisel 씨는 부업을 구한다. Matilda는 다른 사람들을 위해 빨래를 해 준다.
➡ _____

54 10년 동안의 고된 일로 Matilda는 늙고 지쳤다.
➡ _____

55 십 년 후, Matilda는 Forestier 부인과 거리에서 마주친다.
➡ _____

Scene 6

56 Mrs. Loisel: Forestier 부인, 좋은 아침이에요.
➡ _____

57 Mrs. Forestier: 제가 당신을 아나요?
➡ _____

58 Mrs. Loisel: 네, 저예요, Matilda.
➡ _____

59 Mrs. Forestier: 오, 믿을 수 없어요! 당신 너무 많이 변했어요.
➡ _____

60 Mrs. Loisel: 저는 당신 때문에 힘든 시간을 보냈거든요.
➡ _____

61 Mrs. Forestier: 나 때문에요? 무슨 말이에요?
➡ _____

62 Mrs. Loisel: 당신이 빌려준 목걸이 기억하죠? 음, 제가 그걸 잃어버렸어요.
➡ _____

63 Mrs. Forestier: 그런데 그거 나한테 돌려줬잖아요.
➡ _____

64 Mrs. Loisel: 아니요, 나는 당신 것과 똑같은 다른 목걸이를 돌려줬어요. 그 값을 치르느라 십 년이 걸렸어요.
➡ _____

65 Mrs. Forestier: 내 것을 대체하려고 다이아몬드 목걸이를 샀다고요?
➡ _____

66 Mrs. Loisel: 네, 맞아요.
➡ _____

67 Mrs. Forestier: 오, 가엾은 Matilda. 왜 내게 와서 사실을 말하지 않았어요? 그 다이아몬드 목걸이는 진품이 아니었어요. 그건 단돈 오백 프랑짜리였다고요!
➡ _____

_____

서술형 실전문제

01 다음 빈칸에 알맞은 단어를 〈보기〉에서 골라 쓰시오

┌─ 보기 ─
│ ball   invitation   admire   replace
└

(1) You have to _____ the way he handled the situation.
(2) He goes to the _____, wearing a mask.
(3) Machines have _____d human labour in many industries.
(4) I regret that I am unable to accept your kind _____.

02 다음 주어진 단어의 영영풀이가 **잘못된** 것을 고르시오.

① certainly: surely; without doubt
② amount: an essential and distinguishing attribute of something or someone
③ jewelry: decorative objects worn on clothes or on the body, such as rings and necklaces
④ cry: to let tears come from the eyes because of sadness, hurt, etc.
⑤ ambassador: a diplomat of the highest rank who is the official representative of his or her country in another country

03 밑줄 친 부분과 바꿔 쓸 수 있는 말을 고르시오.

The UN has called on both sides to start peace talks.

① respected   ② delayed
③ recommended   ④ invited
⑤ asked

04 다음 우리말에 맞도록 빈칸에 알맞은 말을 쓰시오. (철자가 주어진 것도 있음.)

(1) 이것이 우리에게 엄청난 문제가 될 것이다.
   ➡ This is going to be a h_____ problem for us.
(2) 변화에 대한 반대로 그 산업이 거의 파괴되었다.
   ➡ Resistance to change has n_____ destroyed the industry.
(3) 내가 한 번 봐도 될까?
   ➡ Do you mind if I have a _____?

05 빈칸 (A)와 (B)에 들어갈 알맞은 말이 바르게 짝지어진 것을 고르시오.

• It (A)_____ on Japan to withdraw the plan.
• I can't (B)_____ back the debt by next year.

(A)   (B)
① took   pay
② took   keep
③ called   take
④ called   pay
⑤ called   take

06 다음 우리말에 맞게 주어진 어휘를 알맞게 배열하시오.

(1) 나는 대사님의 무도회 초대장을 얻기 위해 싸워야만 했다. (to get, had to, to, the Ambassador's Ball, the invitation, I, fight)

➡ _____
_____

(2) 나는 그렇게나 화려한 파티에 입고 갈 것이 없다. (to wear, nothing, such, to, a fancy party, have, I)

➡ _____

(3) 나는 보석이 없다는 말을 하기가 슬프다. (to say, jewelry, am, no, I, I, sad, have)

➡ _____

(4) Matilda는 그녀의 친구에게 거짓말을 하게 되어 미안했다. (to lie, sorry, her friend, Matilda, to, was)

➡ _____

(5) 그 부부가 비슷한 목걸이를 찾을 시간이 필요하다. (to find, similar, the couple, time, a, needs, necklace)

➡ _____

(6) 우리가 그 목걸이 값을 치르느라 10년이 걸렸다. (to pay, ten years, took, for, us, the necklace, it)

➡ _____

07 다음 문장에서 어법상 어색한 부분을 찾아 바르게 고치시오.

After buying the necklace for Mrs. Forestier, the couple spends ten years to pay back the money.

➡ _____

08 다음 그림을 보고, 우리말에 맞게 괄호 안의 단어를 배열하여 빈칸을 채우시오.

그 목걸이는 겨우 5백 프랑짜리였어!
➡ _____ francs!
(only, worth, 500, was, the necklace)

[09~11] 다음 글을 읽고 물음에 답하시오.

Scene 1

This is Mr. and Mrs. Loisel's home in Paris. Although the home is nice, Mrs. Loisel is not happy. She is young and pretty, and wants a fancier life.

Mrs. Loisel: (*to herself*) Same old house and same boring dinners. I hate living here!

Mr. Loisel: Matilda, I am home. Look what I have got for you!

Mrs. Loisel: What is that?

Mr. Loisel: An invitation to the Ambassador's Ball. I had to fight to get it. Everybody wanted it.

Mrs. Loisel: (*crying*) Why would I want it?

Mr. Loisel: Matilda. What is wrong?

Mrs. Loisel: I have nothing to wear to such a fancy party. I cannot go.

Mr. Loisel: Don't be sad. Here, I will give you 400 francs. Get yourself a beautiful new dress.

09 What has Mr. Loisel got for Matilda? Answer in English.

➡ _____

10 Write the reason why Mrs. Loisel says that she can't go to the Ambassador's Ball. Use the phrase 'It is because.'

➡ _____

_____

11 How much money does Mr. Loisel give to his wife? Answer in English.

➡ _____

[12~13] 다음 글을 읽고 물음에 답하시오.

Scene 2

Mr. Loisel: (*looking at Matilda's new dress*) Amazing, Matilda. Beautiful!

Mrs. Loisel: Something is not right.

Mr. Loisel: What could be wrong?

Mrs. Loisel: (*crying*) Oh, no. What am I going to do?

Mr. Loisel: What is it, Matilda?

Mrs. Loisel: I have no jewelry to wear with my beautiful dress. I will look so poor!

Mr. Loisel: Call on your friend, Mrs. Forestier. (A)그녀가 틀림없이 보석을 빌려줄 거요.

Mrs. Loisel: That is a good idea! Let me go at once.

12 주어진 단어를 활용하여 밑줄 친 우리말 (A)를 영어로 쓰시오.

(I / sure / she / some of)

➡ _____

13 위 대화의 내용과 일치하도록 빈칸에 알맞은 말을 쓰시오.

Although Matilda has got _____, she still doesn't feel satisfied because she doesn't have _____ with it.

[14~16] 다음 글을 읽고 물음에 답하시오.

Scene 3

Mrs. Forestier: Matilda, it is so nice to see you! What brings you here?

Mrs. Loisel: We are invited to the Ambassador's Ball.

Mrs. Forestier: The Ambassador's Ball! That is wonderful! You must be excited.

Mrs. Loisel: Yes⋯ And no. I am sad to say I have no jewelry. May I borrow (A)something from you?

Mrs. Forestier: Sure! Here is my case.

Mrs. Loisel: Wow, you have so many wonderful pieces!

Mrs. Forestier: ⓐ_____

Mrs. Loisel: Would you lend me this diamond necklace? It is beautiful!

Mrs. Forestier: Certainly! Now go enjoy the ball.

14 주어진 단어를 바르게 배열하여 빈칸 ⓐ에 들어갈 말을 쓰시오.

(like / whatever / choose / you)

➡ _____

15 밑줄 친 (A)가 의미하는 것을 위 글에서 찾아 쓰시오.

➡ _____

16 Why is Mrs. Loisel visiting Mrs. Forestier now? Answer in English.

➡ _____

_____

19 What does Mr. Loisel tell Matilda to do when the necklace is not found? Answer in English.

➡ _____

[17~19] 다음 글을 읽고 물음에 답하시오.

Scene 4

Matilda has a perfect evening. Everybody at the ball admires her beauty. It is very late when the Loisels leave the ball.

Mr. Loisel: It was such a long night. I am so tired.

Mrs. Loisel: But it was worth it. Do you know I danced with the Ambassador?

Mr. Loisel: I am glad you enjoyed (A)you, but I have to go to work in the morning.

Mrs. Loisel: (looking in the mirror) Just one more look. (shocked) The necklace... It is gone!

Mr. Loisel: What? Did you have it when we left the ball?

Mrs. Loisel: Yes, I surely did. Please go find it!

Mr. Loisel searches the streets. He returns to the ball and then goes to the police. When the necklace is not found, Mr. Loisel tells Matilda to lie to her friend. Matilda tells Mrs. Forestier she broke the necklace and would fix it before returning it. The couple needs time to find a similar one.

17 밑줄 친 (A)you를 어법에 맞게 쓰시오.

➡ _____

18 What is admired at the ball? Answer in English.

➡ _____

[20~22] 다음 글을 읽고 물음에 답하시오.

Scene 5

Mr. Loisel: (to the jeweler) Excuse me? May we look at that diamond necklace?

Mrs. Loisel: (whispering) It is nearly the same. We must have it!

Mr. Loisel: How much is it?

Jeweler: 40,000 francs.

Mr. Loisel: How about 36,000?

Mrs. Loisel: Please, we really need it.

Jeweler: Well, then... 36,000 it is.

They do not have 36,000 francs. It is a huge amount of money. So they borrow it. After buying the necklace for Mrs. Forestier, the couple spends ten years paying back the money. They move to a very small place. Mr. Loisel gets a second job. Matilda washes clothes for others. Ten years of hard work makes Matilda old and worn. After ten years, Matilda runs into Mrs. Forestier on the street.

20 What do Mr. and Mrs. Loisel do to pay back the money? Answer in English.

➡ _____

_____

21 How does ten years of hard work make Matilda look? Answer in English.

➡ _____

_____

22 How much does they pay for the diamond necklace?

➡ _____

[01~02] 다음 빈칸에 공통으로 들어갈 말을 쓰시오.

출제율 90%

01

• Very few of his books are worth _____.
• I spend almost every day _____ a book in the library.

출제율 95%

02

• I ran _____ an old friend of mine.
• Dolphins can't fall _____ a deep sleep.

출제율 100%

03 다음 빈칸에 알맞은 단어를 〈보기〉에서 골라 쓰시오.

┌─── 보기 ───┐
shocked   worn   similar   once
└────────────┘

(1) Can we sit down? I'm _____ out.
(2) It is a good plan to go at _____.
(3) Others have met _____ problems.
(4) I was _____ when I heard the news.

출제율 95%

04 다음 짝지어진 단어의 관계가 같도록 빈칸에 알맞은 말을 주어진 철자로 시작하여 쓰시오.

(1) borrow – lend : similar – d_____
(2) deep – shallow : tiny – h_____
(3) replace – substitute : respect – a_____

출제율 95%

05 다음 영영풀이를 보고 빈칸에 알맞은 단어를 주어진 철자로 시작하여 쓰시오.

┌────────────────────────┐
to take a place of
└────────────────────────┘

┌────────────────────────┐
Can anything r_____ a mother's love and care?
└────────────────────────┘

출제율 90%

06 다음 괄호 안의 어휘를 우리말에 맞게 배열하시오.

┌────────────────────────────────┐
내가 거기까지 걸어갔다가 돌아오는 데 1시간이 걸린다. (it, an hour, me, and, there, takes, walk, back, to)
└────────────────────────────────┘

➡ _____

출제율 90%

07 다음 그림을 보고, 우리말에 맞게 괄호 안의 단어를 배열하여 빈칸을 채우시오.

┌────────────────────────────────┐
10년 동안의 고된 일로 Matilda는 늙고 수척해진다.
➡ Ten _____
_____. (make, wear, hard, year, work, old, Matilda, of, and, 3 단어의 어형을 변화시킬 것.)
└────────────────────────────────┘

08 다음 중 〈보기〉의 밑줄 친 to부정사와 쓰임이 같은 것은?

┌─ 보기 ─┐
She complained that she had no jewelry to wear with her beautiful dress.
└─────┘

① Jane was disappointed to have lost the luxury bag.
② Mr. Loisel had to fight to get the invitation to the King's Ball.
③ The couple had to work hard to pay back the money for the new necklace.
④ The fake diamond necklace was too cheap to replace the real one.
⑤ Matilda has nothing to wear to such a fancy party.

09 다음 밑줄 친 부분 중 어법상 어색한 것을 고르시오.

① Ten years of hard work has made Matilda old and worn.
② I have had some difficult times because of you.
③ You and your husband have changed so much for the past 10 years.
④ Have you had the necklace when we left the ball?
⑤ Have you bought a diamond necklace to replace mine?

10 다음 중 〈보기〉의 밑줄 친 to부정사와 쓰임이 다른 것은?

┌─ 보기 ─┐
Matilda is sad to tell her friend that she has no jewelry.
└─────┘

① Have you come here to buy the diamond necklace?
② Mrs. Frostier feels sorry to hear her friend had difficulty paying back money.
③ He determined to pay for the ring he had lost.
④ Matilda went to her friend's office to return the ring she had borrowed.
⑤ The Loisels must be crazy to buy the real diamond necklace without checking.

11 다음 〈보기〉와 같이 빈칸에 알맞은 단어를 넣어 같은 의미의 문장을 완성하시오.

┌─ 보기 ─┐
Choose anything that you like.
→ Choose whatever you like.
└─────┘

(1) Anyone who comes to this village will be welcomed.
   ➡ _____ will be welcomed.

(2) I hate anyone that tries to make fool of good people.
   ➡ I hate _____ _____.

(3) The boy always throws any things that he has in his hands.
   ➡ The boy always throws _____ _____.

12 다음 중 밑줄 친 부분의 성격이 다른 하나를 고르시오.

① The prince left the girl <u>crying</u> over the torn dress.

② Matilda tells her friend that she would fix the necklace before <u>returning</u> it.

③ The couple spent ten years <u>paying</u> back the money.

④ They have had a difficult time <u>doing</u> so many kinds of works.

⑤ After <u>buying</u> the necklace for the lady, the man visited her.

13 다음 주어진 우리말에 맞게 괄호 안의 단어만을 사용하여, The couple을 포함한 총 10 단어로 영작하시오. (어법에 맞게 단어의 형태 변화 가능.)

> 그 부부는 비슷한 다이아몬드 목걸이를 찾을 시간이 필요하다.
> (find, similar, necklace, time, need, a, to, diamond)

➡ The couple _____

_____.

14 다음 각 문장의 밑줄 친 that 중 생략할 수 없는 것은?

① I am sure <u>that</u> she will lend you some of her jewelry.

② It is very late <u>that</u> the Loisels leave the ball.

③ Do you remember the diamond necklace <u>that</u> you lent me?

④ I have nothing <u>that</u> I would wear to such a fancy party.

⑤ I am sad to say <u>that</u> I have no jewelry to put on.

[15~18] 다음 글을 읽고 물음에 답하시오.

Scene 1

This is Mr. and Mrs. Loisel's home in Paris. Although the home is nice, Mrs. Loisel is not happy. She is young and pretty, and wants a fancier life.

Mrs. Loisel: (*to herself*) Same old house and same boring dinners. I hate living here!

Mr. Loisel: Matilda, I am home. Look (A)_____ I have got for you!

Mrs. Loisel: What is that?

Mr. Loisel: An invitation to the Ambassador's Ball. I had to fight to get it. Everybody wanted it.

Mrs. Loisel: (*crying*) Why would I want it?

Mr. Loisel: Matilda. What is wrong?

Mrs. Loisel: I have nothing (B)_____. I cannot go.

Mr. Loisel: Don't be sad. Here, I will give you 400 francs. Get yourself a beautiful new dress.

15 빈칸 (A)에 들어갈 말과 다른 말이 들어가는 것은?

① I don't understand _____ she is saying.

② I think _____ he wants doesn't matter to us.

③ Can you please tell me _____ you are doing now?

④ The reason is _____ I don't believe they are our friends.

⑤ Watching you enjoy your work is _____ I want most.

16 What did Mrs. Loisel have to do to get the invitation? Answer in English.

➡ _____

17 대화의 흐름상 빈칸 (B)에 들어갈 말로 가장 적절한 것은?

① to eat for the great life
② to see at the boring party
③ to wear to such a fancy party
④ to talk with such a fancy people
⑤ to buy for such a great place

18 대화의 내용과 일치하는 것은?

① The Loisels' house is humble.
② Mrs. Loisel feels happy about her life.
③ Mrs. Loise tells her husband she hates living in the house.
④ Matilda thinks her life is boring and is not enjoyable.
⑤ Mr. Loisel will give some money to his wife in order that she can get some jewelry.

[19~24] 다음 글을 읽고 물음에 답하시오.

Scene 4

Matilda has a perfect evening. Everybody at the ball ①admires her beauty. It is very late ②when the Loisels leave the ball.

Mr. Loisel: It was such a long night. I am so tired.

Mrs. Loisel: But it was worth ③it. Do you know I danced with the Ambassador?

Mr. Loisel: I am glad you enjoyed yourself, but I have to go to work in the morning.

Mrs. Loisel: (*looking in the mirror*) Just one ④more look. (*shocked*) The necklace... It is gone!

Mr. Loisel: What? Did you have it when we left the ball?

Mrs. Loisel: Yes, I surely ⑤was. Please go find it!

Mr. Loisel searches the streets. He returns to the ball and then goes to the police. When the necklace is not found, Mr. Loisel tells Matilda to lie to her friend. Matilda tells Mrs. Forestier she broke the necklace and would ⓐfix it before returning it. The couple needs time to find a similar one.

19 ①~⑤ 중 어법상 바르지 <u>않은</u> 것을 바르게 고쳐 쓰시오.

_____ ➡ _____

20 다음 중 밑줄 친 ⓐ와 같은 의미로 쓰인 것은?

① She'll <u>fix</u> a meeting.
② I always <u>fix</u> dinner for you.
③ You need to <u>fix</u> the picture on the wall.
④ Let's <u>fix</u> the date of the next meeting.
⑤ My car won't start. Can you <u>fix</u> it?

21 Choose one that is TRUE.

① Nobody cares about Matilda's presence.
② The Loisels leave the ball as early as possible.
③ Mrs. Loisel thinks it wasn't a good idea to go to the party.
④ Mr. Loisel feels great because his wife enjoyed herself.
⑤ Matilda goes out to find the necklace by herself.

22 위 장면에서 Matilda의 심경 변화로 가장 적절한 것은?

출제율 100%

① excited → happy
② embarrassed → sad
③ pleased → anxious
④ bored → embarrassed
⑤ delighted → threatened

23 What does the couple need? Answer in English.

출제율 95%

➡ _____

24 What does Matilda tell Mrs. Forestier? Answer in English.

출제율 95%

➡ _____

_____

[25~28] 다음 글을 읽고 물음에 답하시오.

Scene 3

Mrs. Forestier: Matilda, it is so nice to see you! @무슨 일로 왔어요?

Mrs. Loisel: We are invited to the Ambassador's Ball.

Mrs. Forestier: The Ambassador's Ball! That is wonderful! You must be (A)_____.

Mrs. Loisel: Yes... And no. I am sad to say I have no jewelry. (B)_____

Mrs. Forestier: Sure! Here is my case.

Mrs. Loisel: Wow, you have so many wonderful pieces!

Mrs. Forestier: Choose whatever you like.

Mrs. Loisel: Would you lend me this diamond necklace? It is beautiful!

Mrs. Forestier: Certainly! Now go enjoy the ball.

25 빈칸 (A)에 동사 excite를 어법에 맞게 쓰시오.

출제율 95%

➡ _____

26 빈칸 (B)에 들어갈 말로 가장 적절한 것은?

출제율 90%

① May I look around here?
② Can I use your bathroom?
③ May I lend you jewelry?
④ Can you buy me a new one?
⑤ May I borrow something from you?

27 주어진 단어를 활용하여 밑줄 친 우리말 @를 영어로 쓰시오.

출제율 95%

| (bring) (4 words) |

➡ _____

28 Choose one that is TRUE.

출제율 100%

① Matilda is Mrs. Loisel's relative.
② Mrs. Forestier was invited to the Ambassador's Ball.
③ Unlike Mrs. Loisel, Mrs. Forestier has many pieces of jewelry.
④ Mrs. Forestier chose the diamond necklace for Mrs. Loisel.
⑤ The beautiful diamond necklace is given to Mrs. Loisel as a gift.

[29~31] 다음 글을 읽고 물음에 답하시오.

Scene 2

Mr. Loisel: (*looking at Matilda's new dress*) Amazing, Matilda. Beautiful!

Mrs. Loisel: Something is not right.

Mr. Loisel: What could be wrong?

Mrs. Loisel: (*crying*) Oh, no. What am I going to do?

Mr. Loisel: What is it, Matilda?

Mrs. Loisel: I have no jewelry to wear with my beautiful dress. I will look so poor!

Mr. Loisel: Call on your friend, Mrs. Forestier. I am sure she will lend you some of her jewelry.

Mrs. Loisel: That is a good idea! Let me (A)_____ at once.

출제율 90%

29 빈칸 (A)에 동사 go를 어법에 맞게 쓰시오.

➡ _____

출제율 95%

30 Write the reason why Matilda thinks she will look so poor despite of her new dress. Use the phrase 'It is because.'

➡ _____

_____

출제율 100%

31 다음 중 위 장면에 이어질 내용으로 가장 적절한 것은?

① making Mr. Loisel go to Mrs. Forestier to lend jewelry

② Mr. Loisel going to work to make money for buying beautiful jewelry

③ forcing Mrs. Forestier to give up her jewelry for Mrs. Loisel

④ Mrs. Loisel buying more dresses for herself

⑤ asking Mrs. Forestier to lend her jewelry to Matilda

[32~35] 다음 글을 읽고 물음에 답하시오.

Scene 5

Mr. Loisel: (*to the jeweler*) Excuse me? May we look at that diamond necklace?

Mrs. Loisel: (*whispering*) It is nearly the same. We must have it!

Mr. Loisel: How much is it?

Jeweler: 40,000 francs.

Mr. Loisel: How about 36,000?

Mrs. Loisel: Please, we really need it.

Jeweler: Well, then… 36,000 it is.

They do not have 36,000 francs. It is a huge amount of money. So they borrow it. After buying the necklace for Mrs. Forestier, the couple spends ten years paying back the money. They move to a very small place. Mr. Loisel gets a second job. Matilda washes clothes for others. Ten years of hard work makes Matilda old and worn. After ten years, Matilda runs into Mrs. Forestier on the street.

출제율 95%

32 Wirte the reason why Mr. and Mrs. Loisel move to a very small place. Use the phrase 'It is because.'

➡ _____

_____

출제율 100%

33 위 글을 읽고 답할 수 있는 것은?

① How many diamond necklaces does the jeweler have?

② Why did Matilda borrow a necklace from Mrs. Forestier?

③ How much is the necklace that Matilda borrowed?

④ Where did Matilda lose Mrs. Forestier's necklace?

⑤ What makes Matilda look old and worn?

출제율 95%

34 How long does it take for the couple to pay back the money? Answer in English with a full sentence.

➡ _____

_____

출제율 95%

35 위 글의 내용과 일치하지 <u>않는</u> 곳을 한 군데 찾아 바르게 고쳐 쓰시오.

> The Loisels go to the jeweler to buy a necklace which looks like the one Matilda borrowed from Mrs. Forestier. After buying the necklace with borrowed money, they have to work hard to pay back the money. Ten years have passed and Matilda meets Mrs. Forestier on purpose.

➡ _____

[36~40] 다음 글을 읽고 물음에 답하시오.

Scene 6

Mrs. Loisel: Mrs. Forestier, good morning.

Mrs. Forestier: Do I know you?

Mrs. Loisel: Yes, it is me, Matilda.

Mrs. Forestier: Oh, I cannot believe it! (A)_____

Mrs. Loisel: I have had some difficult times because of you.

Mrs. Forestier: Because of me? What do you mean?

Mrs. Loisel: Do you remember the diamond necklace you lent me? Well, I lost ①it.

Mrs. Forestier: But you returned ②it to me.

Mrs. Loisel: No, I returned another one just like ③it. It took us ten years to pay for ④it.

Mrs. Forestier: You bought a diamond necklace (B)<u>to replace</u> mine?

Mrs. Loisel: Yes.

Mrs. Forestier: Oh, my poor Matilda. Why didn't you come to me and tell me (C)<u>the truth</u>? My diamond necklace was not real. ⑤It was worth only 500 francs!

출제율 100%

36 대화의 흐름상 빈칸 (A)에 들어갈 말로 가장 적절한 것은?

① What makes you so happy?

② You have changed so much.

③ I don't remember who you are.

④ You finally made it!

⑤ How come you are here?

출제율 95%

37 ①~⑤ 중 지칭하는 것이 <u>다른</u> 하나는?

①   ②   ③   ④   ⑤

출제율 90%

38 다음 중 밑줄 친 (B)와 쓰임이 같은 것은?

① There is a chance <u>to talk</u> with her.

② It was nice <u>to feel</u> proud of myself.

③ <u>To make</u> him do his best matters.

④ He promised <u>to trust</u> us again.

⑤ She went out <u>to find</u> something to drink.

출제율 95%

39 How much was Mrs. Forestier's necklace worth? Answer in English.

➡ _____

출제율 95%

40 밑줄 친 (C)가 의미하는 것을 우리말로 쓰시오.

➡ _____

INSIGHT
on the textbook

교과서 파헤치기

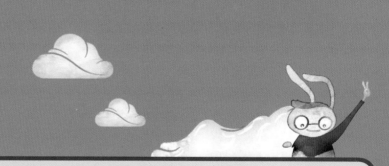

※ 다음 영어를 우리말로 쓰시오.

01 goods _____

02 probably _____

03 subject _____

04 huge _____

05 popular _____

06 include _____

07 ability _____

08 traditional _____

09 plain _____

10 lively _____

11 cone _____

12 main character _____

13 exhibition _____

14 plate _____

15 outdoor _____

16 fever _____

17 advertising _____

18 performance _____

19 common _____

20 creativity _____

21 familiar _____

22 art work _____

23 special effects _____

24 creative _____

25 lesson _____

26 artistic _____

27 copy _____

28 run _____

29 colorful _____

30 classical _____

31 refreshing _____

32 sculpture _____

33 decoration _____

34 worth _____

35 be made up of _____

36 set up _____

37 the other day _____

38 be regarded as _____

39 in other words _____

40 instead of _____

41 pay attention to _____

42 break down _____

43 turn one's eyes to _____

※ 다음 우리말을 영어로 쓰시오.

01	대중적인, 인기 있는	_____	22	거대한, 큰	_____
02	예술적인	_____	23	포함하다, 넣다	_____
03	지루한, 지겨운	_____	24	아마	_____
04	접시	_____	25	신선한, 참신한	_____
05	광고	_____	26	교훈	_____
06	전시회	_____	27	주인공	_____
07	화려한	_____	28	전통적인	_____
08	친숙한	_____	29	실외의	_____
09	조각품	_____	30	장식	_____
10	연기, 공연	_____	31	보통의, 평범한	_____
11	창의적인	_____	32	운영하다	_____
12	활기 넘치는, 생생한	_____	33	원뿔, 원뿔형 물체	_____
13	열, 발열	_____	34	특수효과	_____
14	창의력	_____	35	~로 만들어지다	_____
15	진심으로, 정말로	_____	36	다시 말해서, 즉	_____
16	~의 가치가 있는	_____	37	~을 부수다	_____
17	흔한, 평범한, 공통의	_____	38	~로 여겨지다	_____
18	변기, 화장실	_____	39	~에 주의를 기울이다	_____
19	상품, 제품	_____	40	A를 B로 바꾸다	_____
20	능력	_____	41	~의 줄임말이다	_____
21	예술 작품	_____	42	~로 구성되다	_____
			43	요전 날, 며칠 전	_____

※ 다음 영영풀이에 알맞은 단어를 <보기>에서 골라 쓴 후, 우리말 뜻을 쓰시오.

1 _____ : not interesting or exciting: _____

2 _____ : not decorated in any way; with nothing added: _____

3 _____ : liked, enjoyed, or supported by many people: _____

4 _____ : the way an actor performs a part in a play, movie, etc.: _____

5 _____ : the physical or mental power or skill needed to do something: _____

6 _____ : the ability to produce or use original and unusual ideas: _____

7 _____ : a thing that makes something look more attractive on special occasions: _____

8 _____ : to do or play something regularly or repeatedly in order to become skilled at it: _____

9 _____ : easy to recognize because of being seen, met, heard, etc. before: _____

10 _____ : a shape with a flat, round or oval base and a top that becomes narrower until it forms a point: _____

11 _____ : an opinion that someone offers you about what you should do or how you should act in a particular situation: _____

12 _____ : traditional in style or form, or based on methods developed over a long period of time, and considered to be of lasting value: _____

13 _____ : to contain something as a part of something else, or to make something part of something else: _____

14 _____ : a work of art that is a solid figure or object made by carving or shaping wood, stone, clay, metal, etc.: _____

15 _____ : following or belonging to the customs or ways of behaving that have continued in a group of people or society for a long time without changing: _____

16 _____ : an event at which objects such as paintings are shown to the public, a situation in which someone shows a particular skill or quality to the public, or the act of showing these things: _____

보기			
traditional	creativity	exhibition	ability
cone	boring	classical	popular
include	practice	sculpture	decoration
advice	performance	familiar	plain

※ 다음 우리말과 일치하도록 빈칸에 알맞은 말을 쓰시오.

해석

Listen & Speak 1 A

1. B: Sandy, you can _____ _____ many _____ of music in this _____ _____ .

   G: That's _____ , Bob. Can I _____ _____ _____ music?

   B: _____ . Do you like _____ _____ ?

   G: Yes, Beethoven is _____ _____ _____ _____ _____ . How _____ you?

   B: I like pop music _____ _____ _____ _____ .

   G: I see. _____ _____ _____ _____ most about pop music?

   B: I'm really _____ _____ its _____ rhythms.

2. G: Jim, did you _____ your _____ _____ ?

   B: Yes. I _____ the face of my role model on a _____ .

   G: _____ _____ . Who is your role model?

   B: My dad. He always gives me good _____ . Who _____ you _____ , Amy?

   G: Well, I drew _____ _____ in the sea.

   B: Wonderful! I'm _____ _____ _____ _____ .

   G: Thank you.

Listen & Speak 2 A

1. B: _____ _____ _____ I watched a _____ , *A Love Story in the War.*

   G: Oh, _____ _____ _____ _____ the play?

   B: I liked the _____ . The _____ _____ were _____ .

   G: Was the story good _____ _____ ?

   B: No. It was _____ _____ _____ , but the music was _____ _____ .

   G: So, do you think I _____ _____ it?

   B: _____ _____ you have _____ _____ _____ time and money.

2. B: Caire, _____ _____ _____ _____ your art class?

G: It's great. I learn _____ _____ in the _____.

B: _____ _____ _____ _____ _____ about it?

G: I enjoy _____ _____ _____ _____. _____ about you, Allen?

B: I also like the class. I learn good _____ _____. I love painting _____ many colors.

G: Oh, I saw your _____ _____ _____. I _____ it was very _____.

B: Thanks. I _____ _____ _____.

Real Life Talk

Bora: Andy, you went to the art museum, _____ _____?

Andy: Yes. They had a _____ Chagall exhibition.

Bora: _____ _____ _____ _____ it?

Andy: It was _____! I _____ _____ _____ the colors in his _____ and his _____.

Bora: _____. He was _____ _____ _____ _____ _____ ever. _____ _____ did you see in the museum?

Andy: I went to _____ _____ _____ and saw things like umbrellas, cups, and backpacks. _____ _____ of art _____ _____ on them.

Bora: Did you buy _____?

Andy: Yes. I bought this T-shirt. _____ _____ _____ _____ it?

Bora: It _____ _____ _____ you.

Andy: Thank you.

Wrap Up 1

B: Cindy, you went to the music _____, _____ you?

G: Yes. _____ _____ _____ famous musicians _____ there.

B: _____ _____ _____ _____ _____ the festival?

G: It was fantastic! I really liked the _____ _____. Do you know the band _____ the Brothers?

B: Oh, I've _____ about them. The singer is _____.

G: Yes. His _____ was great.

B: _____ _____.

2. B: Claire, 미술 수업 어때?
  G: 훌륭해. 나는 그 수업에서 많은 것을 배워.
  B: 배우는 것 중에 어떤 것이 가장 좋아?
  G: 다양한 그림 기술 배우는 것이 재미있어. 너는 어때, Allen?
  B: 나도 미술 수업이 좋아. 괜찮은 색칠하기 기술들을 배우잖아. 나는 다양한 색깔을 사용해서 그림 그리는 것이 정말 좋아.
  G: 오, 지난번에 네 작품을 봤어. 나는 그게 굉장히 창의적이라고 생각했어.
  B: 고마워. 연습을 많이 했거든.

보라: Andy야, 너 미술관에 갔었지, 그렇지 않니?
Andy: 응. 샤갈 특별 전시회가 있었어.
보라: 그거 어땠니?
Andy: 멋졌어! 나는 그의 그림에 쓰인 색깔과 그의 창의성에 매료됐어.
보라: 당연해. 그는 가장 위대한 화가 중 한 명이었잖아. 너는 미술에서 또 무엇을 봤니?
Andy: 기념품점에 갔었는데 우산, 컵, 가방 같은 것들을 봤어. 유명 예술 작품들이 그것들에 그려져 있었어.
보라: 구입한 게 있니?
Andy: 응. 나 이 티셔츠 샀어. 어때?
보라: 네게 잘 어울린다.
Andy: 고마워.

B: Cindy, 너 음악 축제에 갔었지, 그렇지 않니?
G: 응. 많은 유명 가수들이 거기서 공연을 했어.
B: 그 축제는 어땠어?
G: 아주 환상적이었어. 나는 특별 손님이 정말 좋았어. 너 '더 브라더스'라고 불리는 밴드를 아니?
B: 오, 들어본 적이 있어. 가수가 유명하잖아.
G: 맞아. 그의 공연은 굉장했어.
B: 놀랄 일도 아니지.

※ 다음 우리말에 맞도록 대화를 영어로 쓰시오.

Listen & Speak 1 A

1. B: _____

   G: _____

   B: _____

   G: _____

   B: _____

   G: _____

   B: _____

2. G: _____

   B: _____

   G: _____

   B: _____

   G: _____

   B: _____

   G: _____

1. B: Sandy, 너는 이 음악 도서관에서 많은 종류의 음악을 들을 수 있어.
   G: 그거 멋지다, Bob. 클래식 음악도 들을 수 있어?
   B: 물론이지. 너 클래식 음악 좋아하니?
   G: 응. 베토벤이 내가 가장 좋아하는 음악가 중의 하나야. 너는 어때?
   B: 나는 클래식보다는 대중음악이 더 좋아.
   G: 그렇구나. 너는 대중음악의 어떤 점이 가장 마음에 들어?
   B: 나는 대중음악의 신나는 리듬이 정말 좋아.

2. G: Jim, 미술 숙제 다 끝냈어?
   B: 응. 나는 접시에 나의 롤 모델을 그렸어.
   G: 그거 흥미롭구나. 너의 롤 모델은 누구야?
   B: 우리 아빠야. 아빠는 나에게 항상 좋은 조언을 해 주셔. 너는 누구를 그렸어, Amy?
   G: 음, 나는 내가 바다에서 서핑하는 것을 그렸어.
   B: 멋지다! 나는 네 그림에 푹 빠졌어.
   G: 고마워.

Listen & Speak 2 A

1. B: _____

   G: _____

   B: _____

   G: _____

   B: _____

   G: _____

   B: _____

1. B: 며칠 전에 '전쟁 속의 사랑 이야기'라는 연극을 봤어.
   G: 오, 그 연극 어땠어?
   B: 주인공들이 좋았어. 배우들의 연기가 끝내줬거든.
   G: 이야기도 좋았어?
   B: 아니. 이야기는 조금 지루했는데, 음악은 꽤 괜찮았어.
   G: 그럼, 너는 내가 그 연극을 보러 가야 한다고 생각하니?
   B: 네가 돈과 시간이 많을 경우에만.

2. B: _____

G: _____

B: _____

G: _____

B: _____

G: _____

B: _____

2. B: Claire, 미술 수업 어때?

G: 훌륭해. 나는 그 수업에서 많은 것을 배워.

B: 배우는 것 중에 어떤 것이 가장 좋아?

G: 다양한 그림 기술 배우는 것이 재미있어. 너는 어때, Allen?

B: 나도 미술 수업이 좋아. 괜찮은 색칠하기 기술들을 배우잖아. 나는 다양한 색깔을 사용해서 그림 그리는 것이 정말 좋아.

G: 오, 지난번에 네 작품을 봤어. 나는 그게 굉장히 창의적이라고 생각했어.

B: 고마워. 연습을 많이 했거든.

Real Life Talk

Bora: _____

Andy: _____

Bora: _____

Andy: _____

Bora: _____

Andy: _____

Bora: _____

Andy: _____

Bora: _____

Andy: _____

보라: Andy야, 너 미술관에 갔었지, 그렇지 않니?

Andy: 응. 샤갈 특별 전시회가 있었어.

보라: 그거 어땠니?

Andy: 멋졌어! 나는 그의 그림에 쓰인 색깔과 그의 창의성에 매료됐어.

보라: 당연해. 그는 가장 위대한 화가 중한 명이었잖아. 너는 미술관에서 또 무엇을 봤니?

Andy: 기념품점에 갔었는데 우산, 컵, 가방 같은 것들을 봤어. 유명 예술 작품들이 그것들에 그려져 있었어.

보라: 구입한 게 있니?

Andy: 응. 나 이 티셔츠 샀어. 어때?

보라: 네게 잘 어울린다.

Andy: 고마워.

Wrap Up 1

B: _____

G: _____

B: _____

G: _____

B: _____

G: _____

B: _____

B: Cindy, 너 음악 축제에 갔었지, 그렇지 않니?

G: 응. 많은 유명 가수들이 거기서 공연을 했어.

B: 그 축제는 어땠어?

G: 아주 환상적이었어. 나는 특별 손님이 정말 좋았어. 너 '더 브라더스'라고 불리는 밴드를 아니?

B: 오, 들어본 적이 있어. 가수가 유명하잖아.

G: 맞아. 그의 공연은 굉장했어.

B: 놀랄 일도 아니지.

※ 다음 우리말과 일치하도록 빈칸에 알맞은 것을 골라 쓰시오.

Pop Art: Art for Everyone

1 _____ to the Pop Art _____! What do you see? _____ of soup cans? Big _____?

   A. cartoons   B. Welcome   C. paintings   D. Exhibition

2 Do they look like art works? _____ not, but _____ again. They are all _____ _____ of pop art.

   A. works   B. probably   C. think   D. famous

3 Pop is _____ for popular. _____ pop art means _____ _____, or art for people.

   A. art   B. short   C. popular   D. so

4 It _____ in the 1950s in America. Pop artists at that time wanted to _____ _____ fun and _____.

   A. create   B. began   C. easy   D. something

5 _____ of difficult _____ art _____, they _____ their eyes to popular culture.

   A. traditional   B. turned   C. instead   D. works

6 They _____ images _____ TV, comic books, _____, and _____.

   A. from   B. magazines   C. used   D. advertising

7 When people saw _____ _____ in art _____, they found them _____.

   A. images   B. refreshing   C. exhibitions   D. familiar

8 _____ then, pop art has _____ _____ _____.

   A. become   B. since   C. popular   D. truly

9 People thought _____ art was _____ difficult _____.

   A. too   B. understand   C. that   D. to

10 By _____ daily images and _____ colors, pop artists _____ that _____.

   A. changed   B. using   C. thought   D. bright

11 Using _____ images, pop art looks _____. In other _____, it doesn't look _____.

   A. words   B. common   C. artistic   D. plain

12 But it is still _____ _____ _____ to. Although it looks plain, it is _____ with meaning.

   A. attention   B. filled   C. paying   D. worth

13 _____ _____ about some _____ pop _____.

   A. famous   B. let's   C. artists   D. learn

14 They became _____ for their special artistic _____. They were able to _____ common _____ into amazing art.

   A. ability   B. objects   C. famous   D. change

15 Andy Warhol is _____ the King of Pop Art. He _____ his _____ magazines and stores.

   A. found   B. called   C. in   D. subjects

1 팝 아트 전시회에 온 것을 환영한다! 무엇이 보이는가? 수프 통조림들을 모아 놓은 그림? 커다란 만화 그림?

2 그것들이 예술 작품처럼 보이는가? 아마 그렇게 보이지 않겠지만, 다시 생각해 봐라. 그것들은 모두 유명한 팝 아트 작품들이다.

3 'pop'은 'popular(대중적인)'의 줄임말이다. 그래서 팝 아트는 대중 예술 또는 사람들을 위한 예술이라는 뜻이다.

4 팝 아트는 1950년대 미국에서 시작됐다. 그 당시 팝 아트 작가들은 재미있고 쉬운 것을 만들고 싶어 했다.

5 어려운 전통 예술 작품 대신 그들은 대중문화로 눈을 돌렸다.

6 그들은 텔레비전, 만화책, 잡지 및 광고에 나오는 이미지들을 사용했다.

7 미술 전시회에서 친숙한 이미지들을 봤을 때 사람들은 그것들이 신선하다는 걸 알게 되었다.

8 그때부터 팝 아트는 정말 유명해졌다.

9 사람들은 예술이 너무 어려워서 이해할 수 없는 것으로 생각했었다.

10 일상적인 이미지와 밝은 색을 씀으로써, 팝 아트 작가들은 그러한 관점을 바꿨다.

11 흔한 이미지를 사용하기 때문에 팝 아트는 평범해 보인다. 즉, 팝 아트는 예술적으로 보이지 않는다.

12 하지만 여전히 주목할 만한 가치가 있다. 평범해 보일지라도 그것은 의미로 가득 차 있다.

13 몇 명의 유명한 팝 아트 작가들에 대해 알아보자.

14 그들은 특별한 예술적인 능력으로 유명해졌다. 그들은 흔한 대상을 놀라운 예술로 바꿀 수 있었다.

15 Andy Warhol은 팝 아트의 왕이라 불린다. 그는 잡지와 상점에서 주제를 찾았다.

16 One of his _____ works is _____ _____ of pictures of Marilyn Monroe, the American _____.

    A. made   B. actor   C. famous   D. up

17 _____ work shows cans of soup. He _____ many _____ of these _____.

    A. works   B. another   C. made   D. copies

18 Why did he make _____ of his _____? He wanted to _____ that art is _____ you see every day.

    A. works   B. show   C. copies   D. something

19 Claes Oldenburg is _____ pop artist _____ _____ art _____.

    A. made   B. another   C. fun   D. who

20 He made _____ of _____ _____, such as a hamburger, cookies, and a _____.

    A. brush   B. sculptures   C. items   D. everyday

21 In the _____, he _____ soft sculptures. They were _____ of plastic, paper, and other soft _____.

    A. made   B. beginning   C. materials   D. created

22 For example, he used _____ to make toilets. Later, he made _____ _____ of daily items, such _____ an ice cream cone.

    A. sculptures   B. cloth   C. as   D. huge

23 _____ everyone to enjoy his art, he _____ _____ his works in _____ places.

    A. set   B. outdoor   C. wanting   D. up

24 He also _____ a store _____ his studio to _____ his works. For him, artistic works were funs _____ for people.

    A. inside   B. ran   C. goods   D. sell

25 Roy Lichtenstein _____ cartoons in his _____. They were large and _____ in _____ colors.

    A. works   B. lively   C. used   D. painted

26 He even _____ speech balloons in his paintings. Back then, cartoons _____ not _____ _____ an art form.

    A. regarded   B. included   C. were   D. as

27 _____, Roy Lichtenstein thought _____. He asked _____, '_____ are they not?'

    A. differently   B. however   C. himself   D. why

28 Then Roy Lichtenstein _____ _____ the wall _____ high art and popular culture by _____ cartoons to art.

    A. down   B. between   C. broke   D. adding

29 Pop artists _____ art _____ be easy. _____ can _____ and enjoy art.

    A. create   B. believed   C. anyone   D. should

30 How about _____ a _____ of _____ _____ today?

    A. work   B. creating   C. art   D. pop

31 By _____ daily images in a _____ way, you can make a work of art for everyone. This is the most _____ _____ from pop art.

    A. lesson   B. creative   C. important   D. using

---

16 그의 유명 작품들 중 하나는 미국 배우인 Marilyn Monroe의 사진으로 구성되어 있다.

17 또 다른 작품은 수프 통조림들을 보여준다. 그는 이 작품들의 사본을 많이 만들었다.

18 그는 왜 작품의 복사본을 만들었나? 그는 예술은 여러분이 매일 보는 것임을 보여 주고 싶어 했다.

19 Claes Oldenburg는 예술을 재미있게 만들었던 또 다른 팝 아트 작가이다.

20 그는 햄버거와 쿠키, 붓 같은 일상적인 물품들의 조각품을 만들었다.

21 초기에 그는 부드러운 조각품을 만들었다. 그것들은 플라스틱, 종이, 그리고 다른 부드러운 재료들로 만들어졌다.

22 예를 들어서 그는 변기를 만들기 위해 천을 사용했다. 나중에 그는 아이스크림콘 같은 일상 물품의 거대한 조각품을 만들었다.

23 그는 모든 사람이 그의 작품을 보고 즐기기를 원했기 때문에 그의 작품들을 실외에 설치했다.

24 그는 작품 판매를 위해 그의 작업실 안에 상점을 운영하기도 했다. 그에게 예술적인 작품들은 사람들을 위한 재미있는 제품이었다.

25 Roy Lichtenstein은 그의 작품에 만화를 사용했다. 그것들은 크고 생기 넘치는 색으로 그려졌다.

26 그는 심지어 그의 작품에 말풍선을 넣었다. 그 당시에 만화는 예술 형식으로 여겨지지 않았다.

27 하지만 Roy Lichtenstein은 다르게 생각했다. 그는 스스로에게 '왜 만화는 예술로 간주되지 않을까?'라고 물었다.

28 만화를 예술에 첨가함으로써 Roy Lichtenstein은 순수 예술과 대중문화 사이의 벽을 허물었다.

29 팝 아트 작가들은 예술은 쉬워야 한다고 믿었다. 누구나 예술을 만들 수 있고, 즐길 수 있다.

30 오늘 팝 아트 작품 하나를 만들어 보는 것은 어떤가?

31 일상적인 이미지를 창의적인 방식으로 사용함으로써, 모든 사람을 위한 예술 작품을 만들 수 있다. 이것이 팝 아트의 가장 중요한 교훈이다.

※ 다음 우리말과 일치하도록 빈칸에 알맞은 것을 골라 쓰시오.

Pop Art: Art for Everyone

1 _____ _____ the Pop Art _____! _____ do you see? Paintings of soup cans? Big _____?

2 Do they _____ _____ art works? _____ not, but _____ again. They _____ all _____ _____ of pop art.

3 Pop _____ _____ _____. So pop art means _____ _____, or art for people.

4 _____ _____ _____ the 1950s in America. Pop artists at that time _____ _____ create _____ _____ and easy.

5 _____ _____ difficult _____ art works, they _____ their eyes _____ _____ _____.

6 They _____ images _____ TV, comic books, magazines, and _____.

7 When people saw _____ _____ in _____ _____, they found _____ _____.

8 _____ then, pop art has _____ _____ _____.

9 People thought _____ art was _____ difficult _____ _____.

10 _____ _____ daily images and _____ _____, pop artists _____ _____ _____.

11 _____ common images, pop art _____ _____. _____ _____ _____, it doesn't look _____.

12 But it is still _____ _____ _____ _____. Although it _____ _____, it _____ _____ _____ meaning.

13 _____ learn about some _____ _____ _____.

14 They became _____ their special artistic _____. They were _____ _____ _____ _____ _____ _____ _____ art.

15 Andy Warhol _____ _____ the King of Pop Art. He _____ his _____ _____ magazines and stores.

1 팝 아트 전시회에 온 것을 환영한다! 무엇이 보이는가? 수프 통조림들을 모아 놓은 그림? 커다란 만화 그림?

2 그것들이 예술 작품처럼 보이는가? 아마 그렇게 보이지 않겠지만, 다시 생각해 봐라. 그것들은 모두 유명한 팝 아트 작품들이다.

3 'pop'은 'popular(대중적인)'의 줄임말이다. 그래서 팝 아트는 대중 예술 또는 사람들을 위한 예술이라는 뜻이다.

4 팝 아트는 1950년대 미국에서 시작됐다. 그 당시 팝 아트 작가들은 재미있고 쉬운 것을 만들고 싶어 했다.

5 어려운 전통 예술 작품 대신 그들은 대중문화로 눈을 돌렸다.

6 그들은 텔레비전, 만화책, 잡지 및 광고에 나오는 이미지들을 사용했다.

7 미술 전시회에서 친숙한 이미지들을 봤을 때 사람들은 그것들이 신선하다는 걸 알게 되었다.

8 그때부터 팝 아트는 정말 유명해졌다.

9 사람들은 예술이 너무 어려워서 이해할 수 없는 것으로 생각했었다.

10 일상적인 이미지와 밝은 색을 씀으로써, 팝 아트 작가들은 그러한 관점을 바꿨다.

11 흔한 이미지를 사용하기 때문에 팝 아트는 평범해 보인다. 즉, 팝 아트는 예술적으로 보이지 않는다.

12 하지만 여전히 주목할 만한 가치가 있다. 평범해 보일지라도 그것은 의미로 가득 차 있다.

13 몇 명의 유명한 팝 아트 작가들에 대해 알아보자.

14 그들은 특별한 예술적인 능력으로 유명해졌다. 그들은 흔한 대상을 놀라운 예술로 바꿀 수 있었다.

15 Andy Warhol은 팝 아트의 왕이라 불린다. 그는 잡지와 상점에서 주제를 찾았다.

16 One of his famous works _____ _____ _____ of pictures of Marilyn Monroe, the American actor.

17 _____ _____ cans of soup. He _____ many _____ of these _____.

18 Why did he make _____ _____ _____ _____? He wanted _____ _____ _____ art is something _____ _____ every day.

19 Claes Oldenburg is _____ pop artist _____ _____ art _____.

20 He made _____ _____ _____ _____, _____ _____ a hamburger, cookies, and a _____.

21 _____ _____ _____, he _____ _____ _____. They were _____ _____ plastic, paper, and other _____ _____.

22 _____ _____, he used _____ _____ _____ toilets. Later, he made _____ _____ of _____ _____, _____ _____ an ice cream cone.

23 _____ everyone _____ _____ his art, he _____ his works in _____ places.

24 He also _____ a store _____ his studio _____ _____ his works. For him, artistic works _____ _____ _____ for people.

25 Roy Lichtenstein _____ cartoons _____ _____. They _____ large and _____ in _____ _____.

26 He even _____ speech balloons in his paintings. _____ _____, cartoons _____ not _____ _____ an art form.

27 _____, Roy Lichtenstein thought _____. He asked _____, '_____ are _____ _____?'

28 Then Roy Lichtenstein _____ _____ the wall _____ high art _____ popular culture _____ _____ cartoons to art.

29 Pop artists _____ art _____ _____ easy. _____ can _____ and _____ art.

30 How about _____ a work of _____ _____ today?

31 _____ _____ daily images _____ a _____ _____ _____, you can _____ a work of art _____ everyone. This is _____ _____ _____ _____ _____ from pop art.

---

16 그의 유명 작품들 중 하나는 미국 배우인 Marilyn Monroe의 사진으로 구성되어 있다.

17 또 다른 작품은 수프 통조림들을 보여준다. 그는 이 작품들의 사본을 많이 만들었다.

18 그는 왜 작품의 복사본을 만들었나? 그는 예술은 여러분이 매일 보는 것임을 보여 주고 싶어 했다.

19 Claes Oldenburg는 예술을 재미있게 만들었던 또 다른 팝 아트 작가이다.

20 그는 햄버거와 쿠키, 붓 같은 일상적인 물품들의 조각품을 만들었다.

21 초기에 그는 부드러운 조각품을 만들었다. 그것들은 플라스틱, 종이, 그리고 다른 부드러운 재료들로 만들어졌다.

22 예를 들어서 그는 변기를 만들기 위해 천을 사용했다. 나중에 그는 아이스크림콘 같은 일상 물품의 거대한 조각품을 만들었다.

23 그는 모든 사람이 그의 작품을 보고 즐기기를 원했기 때문에 그의 작품들을 실외에 설치했다.

24 그는 작품 판매를 위해 그의 작업실 안에 상점을 운영하기도 했다. 그에게 예술적인 작품들은 사람들을 위한 재미있는 제품이었다.

25 Roy Lichtenstein은 그의 작품에 만화를 사용했다. 그것들은 크고 생기 넘치는 색으로 그려졌다.

26 그는 심지어 그의 작품에 말풍선을 넣었다. 그 당시에 만화는 예술 형식으로 여겨지지 않았다.

27 하지만 Roy Lichtenstein은 다르게 생각했다. 그는 스스로에게 '왜 만화는 예술로 간주되지 않을까?'라고 물었다.

28 만화를 예술에 첨가함으로써 Roy Lichtenstein은 순수 예술과 대중문화 사이의 벽을 허물었다.

29 팝 아트 작가들은 예술은 쉬워야 한다고 믿었다. 누구나 예술을 만들 수 있고, 즐길 수 있다.

30 오늘 팝 아트 작품 하나를 만들어 보는 것은 어떤가?

31 일상적인 이미지를 창의적인 방식으로 사용함으로써, 모든 사람을 위한 예술 작품을 만들 수 있다. 이것이 팝 아트의 가장 중요한 교훈이다.

※ 다음 문장을 우리말로 쓰시오.

Pop Art: Art for Everyone

1 Welcome to the Pop Art Exhibition! What do you see? Paintings of soup cans? Big cartoons?

➡ _____

2 Do they look like art works? Probably not, but think again. They are all famous works of pop art.

➡ _____

3 Pop is short for popular. So pop art means popular art, or art for people.

➡ _____

4 It began in the 1950s in America. Pop artists at that time wanted to create something fun and easy.

➡ _____

5 Instead of difficult traditional art works, they turned their eyes to popular culture.

➡ _____

6 They used images from TV, comic books, magazines, and advertising.

➡ _____

7 When people saw familiar images in art exhibitions, they found them refreshing.

➡ _____

8 Since then, pop art has become truly popular.

➡ _____

9 People thought that art was too difficult to understand.

➡ _____

10 By using daily images and bright colors, pop artists changed that thought.

➡ _____

11 Using common images, pop art looks plain. In other words, it doesn't look artistic.

➡ _____

12 But it is still worth paying attention to. Although it looks plain, it is filled with meaning.

➡ _____

13 Let's learn about some famous pop artists.

➡ _____

14 They became famous for their special artistic ability. They were able to change common objects into amazing art.

➡ _____

15 Andy Warhol is called the King of Pop Art. He found his subjects in magazines and stores.

➡ _____

16 One of his famous works is made up of pictures of Marilyn Monroe, the American actor.

➡ _____

17 Another work shows cans of soup. He made many copies of these works.

➡ _____

18 Why did he make copies of his works? He wanted to show that art is something you see every day.

➡ _____

19 Claes Oldenburg is another pop artist who made art fun.

➡ _____

20 He made sculptures of everyday items, such as a hamburger, cookies, and a brush.

➡ _____

21 In the beginning, he created soft sculptures. They were made of plastic, paper, and other soft materials.

➡ _____

22 For example, he used cloth to make toilets. Later, he made huge sculptures of daily items, such as an ice cream cone.

➡ _____

_____

23 Wanting everyone to enjoy his art, he set up his works in outdoor places.

➡ _____

24 He also ran a store inside his studio to sell his works. For him, artistic works were fun goods for people.

➡ _____

_____

25 Roy Lichtenstein used cartoons in his works. They were large and painted in lively colors.

➡ _____

26 He even included speech balloons in his paintings. Back then, cartoons were not regarded as an art form.

➡ _____

27 However, Roy Lichtenstein thought differently. He asked himself, 'Why are they not?'

➡ _____

28 Then Roy Lichtenstein broke down the wall between high art and popular culture by adding cartoons to art.

➡ _____

29 Pop artists believed art should be easy. Anyone can create and enjoy art.

➡ _____

30 How about creating a work of pop art today?

➡ _____

31 By using daily images in a creative way, you can make a work of art for everyone. This is the most important lesson from pop art.

➡ _____

_____

※ 다음 괄호 안의 단어들을 우리말에 맞도록 바르게 배열하시오.

Pop Art: Art for Everyone

1 (to / Welcome / the / Art / Pop / Exhibition! // do / what / see? / you // of / paintings / cans? / soup // cartoons? / big)
➡ _____

2 (they / do / like / look / works? / art // not, / probably / think / but / again. // are / they / famous / all / of / works / art. / pop)
➡ _____

3 (is / pop / for / short / popular. // pop / so / means / art / art, / popular / art / or / people. / for)
➡ _____

4 (began / it / the / in / 1950s / America. / in // artists / pop / that / at / wanted / time / to / something / create / easy. / and / fun)
➡ _____

5 (of / instead / traditional / difficult / works, / art / turned / they / eyes / their / popular / to / culture.)
➡ _____

6 (used / they / from / images / TV, / books, / comic / advertising. / and / magazines,)
➡ _____

7 (people / when / familiar / saw / in / images / art / they / exhibitions, / found / refreshing. / them)
➡ _____

8 (then, / since / art / pop / become / has / popular. / truly)
➡ _____

9 (thought / people / art / that / too / was / to / understand. / difficult)
➡ _____

10 (using / by / images / daily / and / colors, / bright / artists / pop / changed / thought. / that)
➡ _____

11 (common / using / pop / images, / looks / art / plain. // other / in / words, / doesn't / it / artistic. / look)
➡ _____

12 (it / but / is / worth / is / still / attention / paying / to. // it / although / plain, / looks / is / it / with / filled / meaning.)
➡ _____

13 (learn / let's / some / about / pop / famous / artists.)
➡ _____

14 (became / they / for / famous / special / their / ability. / artistic // were / they / to / able / common / change / into / objects / art. / amazing)
➡ _____

15 (Warhol / Andy / called / is / King / the / Pop / of / Art. // found / he / subjects / his / magazines / in / stores. / and)
➡ _____

1 팝 아트 전시회에 온 것을 환영한다! 무엇이 보이는가? 수프 통조림들을 모아 놓은 그림? 커다란 만화 그림?

2 그것들이 예술 작품처럼 보이는가? 아마 그렇게 보이지 않겠지만, 다시 생각해 봐라. 그것들은 모두 유명한 팝 아트 작품들이다.

3 'pop'은 'popular(대중적인)'의 줄임말이다. 그래서 팝 아트는 대중예술 또는 사람들을 위한 예술이라는 뜻이다.

4 팝 아트는 1950년대 미국에서 시작됐다. 그 당시 팝 아트 작가들은 재미있고 쉬운 것을 만들고 싶어 했다.

5 어려운 전통 예술 작품 대신 그들은 대중문화로 눈을 돌렸다.

6 그들은 텔레비전, 만화책, 잡지 및 광고에 나오는 이미지들을 사용했다.

7 미술 전시회에서 친숙한 이미지들을 봤을 때 사람들은 그것들이 신선하다는 걸 알게 되었다.

8 그때부터 팝 아트는 정말 유명해졌다.

9 사람들은 예술이 너무 어려워서 이해할 수 없는 것으로 생각했었다.

10 일상적인 이미지와 밝은 색을 씀으로써, 팝 아트 작가들은 그러한 관점을 바꿨다.

11 흔한 이미지를 사용하기 때문에 팝 아트는 평범해 보인다. 즉, 팝 아트는 예술적으로 보이지 않는다.

12 하지만 여전히 주목할 만한 가치가 있다. 평범해 보일지라도 그것은 의미로 가득 차 있다.

13 몇 명의 유명한 팝 아트 작가들에 대해 알아보자.

14 그들은 특별한 예술적인 능력으로 유명해졌다. 그들은 흔한 대상을 놀라운 예술로 바꿀 수 있었다.

15 Andy Warhol은 팝 아트의 왕이라 불린다. 그는 잡지와 상점에서 주제를 찾았다.

16 (of / one / famous / his / is / works / up / made / of / pictures / Marilyn / of / Monroe, / the / actor. / American)
➡ _____
_____

17 (work / another / cans / shows / soup. / of // he / many / made / copies / these / of / works.)
➡ _____
_____

18 (did / why / make / he / of / copies / works? / his // wanted / he / show / that / to / art / something / is / see / you / day. / every)
➡ _____
_____

19 (Oldenburg / Claes / is / pop / another / who / artist / art / made / fun.)
➡ _____

20 (made / he / of / sculptures / everyday / such / items, / as / hamburger, / a / cookies, / and / brush. / a)
➡ _____
_____

21 (the / in / beginning, / created / he / sculptures. / soft // were / they / of / made / plastic, / and / paper, / soft / other / materials.)
➡ _____
_____

22 (example, / for / used / he / to / cloth / toilets. / make // he / later, / huge / made / of / sculptures / items, / daily / as / such / ice / an / cone. / cream)
➡ _____
_____

23 (everyone / wanting / enjoy / to / art, / his / set / he / up / works / his / outdoor / in / places.)
➡ _____
_____

24 (also / he / a / ran / inside / store / studio / his / sell / to / works. / his // him, / for / works / artistic / were / goods / fun / people. / for)
➡ _____
_____

25 (Lichtenstein / Roy / cartoons / used / his / in / works. // were / they / and / large / in / painted / colors. / lively)
➡ _____
_____

26 (even / he / speech / included / balloons / his / in / paintings. // then, / back / were / cartoons / regarded / not / an / as / form. / art)
➡ _____
_____

27 (however, / Lichtenstein / Roy / differently. / thought // asked / he / himself, / are / 'why / not?' / they)
➡ _____
_____

28 (Roy / then / broke / Lichtenstein / down / the / between / wall / art / high / and / culture / popular / by / cartoons / adding / art. / to)
➡ _____
_____

29 (artists / pop / art / believed / be / should / easy. // can / anyone / enjoy / and / create / art.)
➡ _____

30 (about / how / a / creating / of / work / art / pop / today?)
➡ _____

31 (using / by / images / daily / a / in / way, / creative / can / you / a / make / work / art / of / everyone. / for // is / this / the / important / most / from / lesson / art. / pop)
➡ _____
_____

16 그의 유명 작품들 중 하나는 미국 배우인 Marilyn Monroe의 사진으로 구성되어 있다.

17 또 다른 작품은 수프 통조림들을 보여준다. 그는 이 작품들의 사본을 많이 만들었다.

18 그는 왜 작품의 복사본을 만들었나? 그는 예술은 여러분이 매일 보는 것임을 보여 주고 싶어 했다.

19 Claes Oldenburg는 예술을 재미있게 만들었던 또 다른 팝 아트 작가이다.

20 그는 햄버거와 쿠키, 붓 같은 일상적인 물품들의 조각품을 만들었다.

21 초기에 그는 부드러운 조각품을 만들었다. 그것들은 플라스틱, 종이, 그리고 다른 부드러운 재료들로 만들어졌다.

22 예를 들어서 그는 변기를 만들기 위해 천을 사용했다. 나중에 그는 아이스크림콘 같은 일상 물품의 거대한 조각품을 만들었다.

23 그는 모든 사람이 그의 작품을 보고 즐기기를 원했기 때문에 그의 작품들을 실외에 설치했다.

24 그는 작품 판매를 위해 그의 작업실 안에 상점을 운영하기도 했다. 그에게 예술적인 작품들은 사람들을 위한 재미있는 제품이었다.

25 Roy Lichtenstein은 그의 작품에 만화를 사용했다. 그것들은 크고 생기 넘치는 색들로 그려졌다.

26 그는 심지어 그의 작품에 말풍선을 넣었다. 그 당시에 만화는 예술 형식으로 여겨지지 않았다.

27 하지만 Roy Lichtenstein은 다르게 생각했다. 그는 스스로에게 '왜 만화는 예술로 간주되지 않을까?'라고 물었다.

28 만화를 예술에 첨가함으로써 Roy Lichtenstein은 순수 예술과 대중문화 사이의 벽을 허물었다.

29 팝 아트 작가들은 예술은 쉬워야 한다고 믿었다. 누구나 예술을 만들 수 있고, 즐길 수 있다.

30 오늘 팝 아트 작품 하나를 만들어 보는 것은 어떤가?

31 일상적인 이미지를 창의적인 방식으로 사용함으로써, 모든 사람을 위한 예술 작품을 만들 수 있다. 이것이 팝 아트의 가장 중요한 교훈이다.

※ 다음 우리말을 영어로 쓰시오.

Pop Art: Art for Everyone

1 팝 아트 전시회에 온 것을 환영한다! 무엇이 보이는가? 수프 통조림들을 모아 놓은 그림? 커다란 만화 그림?

➡ _____

2 그것들이 예술 작품처럼 보이는가? 아마 그렇게 보이지 않겠지만, 다시 생각해 봐라. 그것들은 모두 유명한 팝 아트 작품들이다.

➡ _____

3 'pop'은 'popular(대중적인)'의 줄임말이다. 그래서 팝 아트는 대중 예술 또는 사람들을 위한 예술이라는 뜻이다.

➡ _____

4 팝 아트는 1950년대 미국에서 시작됐다. 그 당시 팝 아트 작가들은 재미있고 쉬운 것을 만들고 싶어 했다.

➡ _____

5 어려운 전통 예술 작품 대신 그들은 대중문화로 눈을 돌렸다.

➡ _____

6 그들은 텔레비전, 만화책, 잡지 및 광고에 나오는 이미지들을 사용했다.

➡ _____

7 미술 전시회에서 친숙한 이미지들을 봤을 때 사람들은 그것들이 신선하다는 걸 알게 되었다.

➡ _____

8 그때부터 팝 아트는 정말 유명해졌다.

➡ _____

9 사람들은 예술이 너무 어려워서 이해할 수 없는 것으로 생각했었다.

➡ _____

10 일상적인 이미지와 밝은 색을 씀으로써, 팝 아트 작가들은 그러한 관점을 바꿨다.

➡ _____

11 흔한 이미지를 사용하기 때문에 팝 아트는 평범해 보인다. 즉, 팝 아트는 예술적으로 보이지 않는다.

➡ _____

12 하지만 여전히 주목할 만한 가치가 있다. 평범해 보일지라도 그것은 의미로 가득 차 있다.

➡ _____

13 몇 명의 유명한 팝 아트 작가들에 대해 알아보자.

➡ _____

14 그들은 특별한 예술적인 능력으로 유명해졌다. 그들은 흔한 대상을 놀라운 예술로 바꿀 수 있었다.

➡ _____

_____

15 Andy Warhol은 팝 아트의 왕이라 불린다. 그는 잡지와 상점에서 주제를 찾았다.

➡ _____

16 그의 유명 작품들 중 하나는 미국 배우인 Marilyn Monroe의 사진으로 구성되어 있다.

➡ _____

17 또 다른 작품은 수프 통조림들을 보여준다. 그는 이 작품들의 사본을 많이 만들었다.
➡ _____

18 그는 왜 작품의 복사본을 만들었나? 그는 예술은 여러분이 매일 보는 것임을 보여 주고 싶어 했다.
➡ _____

19 Claes Oldenburg는 예술을 재미있게 만들었던 또 다른 팝 아트 작가이다.
➡ _____

20 그는 햄버거와 쿠키, 붓 같은 일상적인 물품들의 조각품을 만들었다.
➡ _____

21 초기에 그는 부드러운 조각품을 만들었다. 그것들은 플라스틱, 종이, 그리고 다른 부드러운 재료들로 만들어졌다.
➡ _____
_____

22 예를 들어서 그는 변기를 만들기 위해 천을 사용했다. 나중에 그는 아이스크림콘 같은 일상 물품의
거대한 조각품을 만들었다.
➡ _____
_____

23 그는 모든 사람이 그의 작품을 보고 즐기기를 원했기 때문에 그의 작품들을 실외에 설치했다.
➡ _____

24 그는 작품 판매를 위해 그의 작업실 안에 상점을 운영하기도 했다. 그에게 예술적인 작품들은 사람들을 위한
재미있는 제품이었다.
➡ _____
_____

25 Roy Lichtenstein은 그의 작품에 만화를 사용했다. 그것들은 크고 생기 넘치는 색들로 그려졌다.
➡ _____

26 그는 심지어 그의 작품에 말풍선을 넣었다. 그 당시에 만화는 예술 형식으로 여겨지지 않았다.
➡ _____

27 하지만 Roy Lichtenstein은 다르게 생각했다. 그는 스스로에게 '왜 만화는 예술로 간주되지 않을까?'라고 물었다.
➡ _____

28 만화를 예술에 첨가함으로써 Roy Lichtenstein은 순수 예술과 대중문화 사이의 벽을 허물었다.
➡ _____

29 팝 아트 작가들은 예술은 쉬워야 한다고 믿었다. 누구나 예술을 만들 수 있고, 즐길 수 있다.
➡ _____

30 오늘 팝 아트 작품 하나를 만들어 보는 것은 어떤가?
➡ _____

31 일상적인 이미지를 창의적인 방식으로 사용함으로써, 모든 사람을 위한 예술 작품을 만들 수 있다. 이것이
팝 아트의 가장 중요한 교훈이다.
➡ _____
_____

※ 다음 우리말과 일치하도록 빈칸에 알맞은 말을 쓰시오.

Project Step 1

1. A: What do you _____ _____ _____ _____ these paper cups?

2. B: _____ _____ _____ make a tower?

3. C: Wonderful! _____ _____ a tower _____ the Leaning Tower of Pisa.

4. D: _____ _____ _____ something on the cups?

5. B: Sounds great. First, _____ _____ everyone _____ _____ _____.

1. A: 이 종이컵들로 무엇을 만들고 싶어?
2. B: 우리 탑을 만드는 게 어때?
3. C: 훌륭해! 피사의 사탑과 같은 탑을 만들어 보자.
4. D: 종이컵에 뭔가를 그리는 게 어때?
5. B: 좋은 생각이야. 먼저 모두에게 종이컵을 몇 개 나누어 주자.

Enjoy Writing B

1. _____ _____ _____ of _____ _____

2. _____ _____ I went to the concert hall _____ _____ _____ _____.

3. _____ _____ _____ _____ _____ was *You and Me*.

4. I watched it _____ my favorite actor was _____ _____.

5. I liked the _____ and _____ _____ _____ _____.

6. The story was about _____ _____ _____ _____ _____ _____ to her birthday party.

7. They _____ _____ _____ _____ _____.

8. The _____ _____ was Sophie. She sang _____ _____ _____. It was fantastic.

9. _____ _____ _____ the songs _____ _____ _____, I was _____.

10. The musical was really _____ _____.

1. 내 생애 최고의 뮤지컬
2. 지난 토요일 나는 뮤지컬을 보러 콘서트홀에 갔다.
3. 뮤지컬 제목은 '너와 나'였다.
4. 내가 가장 좋아하는 배우가 그 뮤지컬에 나왔기 때문에 그것을 보았다.
5. 나는 공연의 노래와 춤이 좋았다.
6. 뮤지컬의 내용은 가장 친한 친구들을 자신의 생일 파티에 초대했던 여자 아이에 관한 것이었다.
7. 그들은 자신들의 우정에 대해 이야기했다.
8. 주인공은 Sophie였다. 그녀는 많은 아름다운 노래들을 불렀다. 그것은 환상적이었다.
9. 공연 중에 노래를 따라 부르며 매우 신났었다.
10. 그 뮤지컬은 정말 볼 가치가 있었다.

Enjoy Writing B

1. A _____ _____ _____ Me

2. Last Saturday I _____ _____ my friend's house _____ _____ _____ _____.

3. _____ _____ _____ _____ _____ _____ was *My Son*. I watched it _____ _____ it.

4. I liked the _____ _____ _____ _____. The story was about _____ _____ _____ _____ _____ _____ his lost son.

5. _____ _____ _____ was John. He _____ _____ _____ the actor Roy Jones, _____ was fantastic.

6. It was touching. Watching the _____ _____, I was _____.

7. The movie _____ _____ _____ _____ _____.

1. 나에게 감동을 준 영화
2. 지난 토요일 나는 영화를 보러 친구 집에 갔다.
3. 영화의 제목은 '나의 아들'이었다. 나는 내 친구가 그 영화를 추천해서 봤다.
4. 나는 그 영화의 이야기가 마음에 들었다. 그것은 잃어버린 아들을 찾으려 했던 용감한 남자에 관한 이야기였다.
5. 주인공은 John이었다. 그 역은 배우 Roy Jones가 연기했는데 아주 멋졌다.
6. 그 영화는 감동적이었다. 나는 감동적인 장면들을 보며 감동받았다.
7. 그 영화는 정말 볼 가치가 있었다.

※ 다음 우리말을 영어로 쓰시오.

Project Step 1

1. A: 이 종이컵들로 무엇을 만들고 싶어?
➡

2. B: 우리 탑을 만드는 게 어때?
➡

3. C: 훌륭해! 피사의 사탑과 같은 탑을 만들어 보자.
➡

4. D: 종이컵에 뭔가를 그리는 게 어때?
➡

5. B: 좋은 생각이야. 먼저 모두에게 종이컵을 몇 개 나누어 주자.
➡

Enjoy Writing B

1. 내 생애 최고의 뮤지컬
➡

2. 지난 토요일 나는 뮤지컬을 보러 콘서트홀에 갔다.
➡

3. 뮤지컬 제목은 '너와 나'였다.
➡

4. 내가 가장 좋아하는 배우가 그 뮤지컬에 나왔기 때문에 그것을 보았다.
➡

5. 나는 공연의 노래와 춤이 좋았다.
➡

6. 뮤지컬의 내용은 가장 친한 친구들을 자신의 생일 파티에 초대했던 여자 아이에 관한 것이었다.
➡

7. 그들은 자신들의 우정에 대해 이야기했다.
➡

8. 주인공은 Sophie였다. 그녀는 많은 아름다운 노래들을 불렀다. 그것은 환상적이었다.
➡

9. 공연 중에 노래를 따라 부르며 매우 신났었다.
➡

10. 그 뮤지컬은 정말 볼 가치가 있었다.
➡

Enjoy Writing B

1. 나에게 감동을 준 영화
➡

2. 지난 토요일 나는 영화를 보러 친구 집에 갔다.
➡

3. 영화의 제목은 '나의 아들'이었다. 나는 내 친구가 그 영화를 추천해서 봤다.
➡

4. 나는 그 영화의 이야기가 마음에 들었다. 그것은 잃어버린 아들을 찾으려 했던 용감한 남자에 관한 이야기였다.
➡

5. 주인공은 John이었다. 그 역은 배우 Roy Jones가 연기했는데 아주 멋졌다.
➡

6. 그 영화는 감동적이었다. 나는 감동적인 장면들을 보며 감동받았다.
➡

7. 그 영화는 정말 볼 가치가 있었다.
➡

※ 다음 영어를 우리말로 쓰시오.

01 afford _____

02 business _____

03 corn cob _____

04 filter _____

05 collect _____

06 invention _____

07 useful _____

08 relaxed _____

09 sew _____

10 control _____

11 sewing machine _____

12 useless _____

13 system _____

14 match _____

15 cost _____

16 countryside _____

17 pollute _____

18 entrance fee _____

19 triangle _____

20 stay _____

21 failure _____

22 fair _____

23 raise _____

24 fee _____

25 remove _____

26 success _____

27 president _____

28 whether _____

29 step _____

30 recommend _____

31 pollution _____

32 realize _____

33 teenager _____

34 headband _____

35 hit on _____

36 come across _____

37 thanks to _____

38 for oneself _____

39 change A into B _____

40 for free _____

41 pay for _____

42 think to oneself _____

43 not only A but also B _____

※ 다음 우리말을 영어로 쓰시오.

01	오염	
02	~할 여유가 되다	
03	깨닫다, 인식하다	
04	머무르다	
05	사업	
06	수집하다	
07	성공	
08	제거하다	
09	값이 들다	
10	편안한, 여유 있는	
11	박람회	
12	재봉틀	
13	요금	
14	시골	
15	입장료	
16	여과장치; 여과하다	
17	옥수수 속대	
18	쓸모없는, 소용없는	
19	실패	
20	~인지 (아닌지)	
21	성냥	

22	꿰매다, 바느질하다	
23	오염시키다	
24	(자금을) 모으다	
25	통제하다, 조절하다, 조정하다	
26	십 대	
27	추천하다	
28	삼각형	
29	유용한	
30	발명(품)	
31	대통령, 회장	
32	체계, 장치	
33	발명가	
34	단계	
35	지불하다	
36	~ 덕분에	
37	스스로	
38	마음속으로 생각하다	
39	A를 B로 바꾸다	
40	우연히 마주치다	
41	무료로	
42	만나다	
43	A 뿐만 아니라 B도	

※ 다음 영영풀이에 알맞은 단어를 <보기>에서 골라 쓴 후, 우리말 뜻을 쓰시오.

1 _____ : relating to or like a robot: _____

2 _____ : to stitch with thread: _____

3 _____ : to be able to do something: _____

4 _____ : to be obtained at the price of: _____

5 _____ : the achievement of an aim or purpose: _____

6 _____ : without having to pay: _____

7 _____ : a round piece of metal used as money: _____

8 _____ : to meet or find by chance: _____

9 _____ : to think of a plan, a solution, etc. suddenly or by chance: _____

10 _____ : a work of producing, buying, and selling of goods and services: _____

11 _____ : to damage the water, air, land, etc. by using harmful chemicals: _____

12 _____ : the operating applications programs that are used in a computer system: _____

13 _____ : a large public event where goods are bought and sold, usually from tables that have been specially arranged for the event: _____

14 _____ : a narrow strip of material worn around the head, usually to keep your hair or sweat out of your eyes: _____

15 _____ : to make an organization, person, or system do what you want or have in the way you want: _____

16 _____ : a short, thin piece of wood or thick paper with a special tip that produces fire when it is scratched against something else: _____

보기			
fair	success	headband	coin
hit on	cost	pollute	robotic
match	come across	control	for free
software	sew	business	afford

※ 다음 우리말과 일치하도록 빈칸에 알맞은 말을 쓰시오.

Listen & Speak 1 A-1

G: _____ _____ _____ this _____ the paper?

B: Sure. _____ the middle point, I draw _____ _____. Then I _____ the _____, _____ _____.

G: Good. Now, is it _____ _____ _____ to draw it _____ _____ your pencil _____ the paper?

B: I'll try. Hmm... No, _____ _____ _____ _____?

G: Well, start _____ one of the _____ _____.

B: Do you mean _____ _____ _____ _____ _____ _____?

G: Yes. Draw the circle _____ and then _____ _____ _____ _____ _____. Or you can draw the _____ _____, like this.

B: Oh, now _____ _____ _____.

Listen & Speak 1 A-2

W: Hi. I'm _____ _____ a backpack _____ my son.

M: _____ _____ is your son?

W: He is _____ _____ _____.

M: I want _____ _____ this one.

W: Oh, it's _____ _____.

M: Yes, _____ _____? It has a cap _____ _____ _____ _____ a penguin, _____ kids _____ _____.

W: Is it possible _____ _____ _____ _____ _____ the cap _____ for _____?

M: Sure. You can easily _____ _____ _____ and _____ _____ _____ on.

W: That's _____. I'll _____ _____ _____.

Listen & Speak 2 A-1

B: Wendy, _____ _____ _____ _____ _____ school a lot _____. What's _____?

G: I want to _____ _____ _____, but I just _____.

B: Doesn't your mom _____ _____ _____?

G: She _____, but I don't get up _____ _____ _____. _____ I _____ have an AI robot.

B: _____ _____ _____?

G: Yes. I mean one _____ _____ _____ _____ I _____ and _____ _____ _____ in the morning.

B: That sounds _____.

G: 너 이걸 종이에 그릴 수 있겠니?
B: 물론이지. 가운데 지점으로부터 두 개의 삼각형을 그리면 돼. 그러고 나서 이렇게 원을 그리면 되지.
G: 좋아. 그럼 종이에서 연필을 떼지 않고 그것을 그리는 것이 가능하니?
B: 시도해 볼게. 흠… 아니, 그게 어떻게 가능하니?
G: 음, 네 개의 빨간 점 중 한 곳에서 시작하면 돼.
B: 빨간 점 중에 아무 점이나 말하는 거야?
G: 응. 원을 먼저 그리고, 그 다음에 삼각형 두 개를 이렇게 그려. 아니면 이렇게 삼각형을 먼저 그릴 수도 있어.
B: 오, 이제 알겠어.

W: 안녕하세요. 아들을 위한 배낭을 찾고 있어요.
M: 아들이 몇 살인가요?
W: 아들은 다섯 살이에요.
M: 이것을 추천하고 싶네요.
W: 오, 이거 정말 귀엽네요.
M: 네, 그렇지 않나요? 펭귄과 같이 생긴 모자가 있어서 아이들이 좋아하죠.
W: 제가 세탁을 위해 모자를 분리하는 것도 가능한가요?
M: 물론이죠. 모자를 쉽게 분리했다가 다시 붙일 수도 있어요.
W: 훌륭해요. 이걸 살게요.

B: Wendy, 너 요즘 계속 지각하네. 무슨 일 있어?
G: 일찍 일어나고 싶은데, 그게 안 돼.
B: 네 엄마가 널 깨워 주시지 않니?
G: 엄마가 깨워주시긴 하는데, 바로 일어나지 않아. 인공지능 로봇이 있으면 좋겠어.
B: 인공지능 로봇?
G: 응. 내가 아침에 꼭 일어나도록 확인해 주고, 아침밥을 가져다주는 그런 로봇 말이야.
B: 그거 좋은 생각이야.

Listen & Speak 2 A-2

B: I'm _____ _____ _____ my uncle in Mexico.

G: What are you _____ _____ _____ _____, Mike?

B: I'll _____ _____ _____ _____ _____ at his house _____ he has a big _____ _____.

G: That's great. _____ you _____ _____?

B: No, _____ _____ _____ _____, but I can't. _____ I'll _____ _____ _____ a water walking ball _____.

G: A water walking ball? _____ _____ _____?

B: _____ a large ball. We _____ _____ it and _____ _____ the water.

G: That _____ _____ fun.

Real Life Talk

Bora: What _____ you _____, Jessie?

Jessie: I'm _____ Dr. Rebecca, _____ _____ _____.

Bora: Wow, that's _____.

Jessie: Thanks. I wish I _____ _____ _____ _____ like her.

Bora: Is it possible _____ _____ _____ _____ them, too?

Jessie: Yes. She can _____ your mind _____ _____ _____ _____.

Bora: That's very _____.

Jessie: What about you? Do you also _____ _____ _____ _____?

Bora: Sure. I love Sky X. I wish I _____ _____ _____ _____ _____.

Jessie: I like him, too. He can _____ _____ _____ _____.

Bora: Yes. He _____ _____ _____ in space.

Wrap Up 1

W: Hi, Tom. _____ _____ _____ _____ _____?

B: I'm _____ my drone.

W: Cool! _____ you _____ _____ it?

B: No, I'm not very good _____ _____, but I'm _____ _____.

W: _____ _____ _____, I _____ a sandwich restaurant. Is it _____ _____ _____ _____ _____ _____ with your drone?

B: No, it _____. But I think _____ _____ _____ _____ _____ one or two years.

W: _____ will _____ _____.

B: 나는 멕시코에 있는 삼촌을 방문할 계획이야.
G: 거기서 뭐 할 거야, Mike?
B: 삼촌이 큰 수영장을 가지고 계셔서 난 대부분의 시간을 삼촌 집에서 보낼 거야.
G: 멋지다. 너 수영 잘하니?
B: 아니, 잘했으면 좋겠는데, 못해. 그래서 대신 나는 물 위를 걷는 공을 가지고 놀 거야.
G: 물 위를 걷는 공? 그게 뭐야?
B: 그건 큰 공이야. 그 안에 들어가서 물 위를 걸으면 돼.
G: 그거 분명 재밌겠다.

Bora: Jessie야, 뭐 하고 있어?
Jessie: 내가 제일 좋아하는 슈퍼 영웅인 닥터 레베카를 그리고 있어.
Bora: 와, 훌륭해.
Jessie: 고마워. 나는 그녀처럼 사람들의 마음을 읽을 수 있으면 좋겠어.
Bora: 그녀가 사람들의 마음을 통제하는 것도 가능하니?
Jessie: 응. 그녀가 원하면 네 마음을 통제할 수 있어.
Bora: 그거 정말 멋지다.
Jessie: 너는 어때? 너도 좋아하는 슈퍼 영웅이 있니?
Bora: 물론. 나는 스카이 X를 좋아해. 스카이 X처럼 하늘을 날 수 있으면 좋겠어.
Jessie: 나도 그가 좋아. 그는 우주에서 숨 쉴 수도 있잖아.
Bora: 응. 그는 우주에서 뭐든 할 수 있어.

W: 안녕, Tom. 무엇을 하는 중이니?
B: 지금 드론을 날리고 있어요.
W: 멋지구나! 드론 조종을 잘하니?
B: 아니요, 전 지금은 별로 잘하지 못하지만 열심히 연습하고 있어요.
W: 네가 알다시피, 내가 샌드위치 가게를 운영하고 있잖아. 너는 네 드론으로 주문한 음식을 배달하는 것이 가능하니?
B: 아니요, 불가능해요. 하지만 1~2년 후에는 가능할 거라 생각해요.
W: 그러면 좋겠구나.

※ 다음 우리말에 맞도록 대화를 영어로 쓰시오.

Listen & Speak 1 A-1

G: _____

B: _____

G: _____
_____

B: _____

G: _____

B: _____

G: _____
_____

B: _____

G: 너 이걸 종이에 그릴 수 있겠니?
B: 물론이지. 가운데 지점으로부터 두 개의 삼각형을 그리면 돼. 그러고 나서 이렇게 원을 그리면 되지.
G: 좋아. 그럼 종이에서 연필을 떼지 않고 그것을 그리는 것이 가능하니?
B: 시도해 볼게. 흠… 아니, 그게 어떻게 가능하니?
G: 음, 네 개의 빨간 점 중 한 곳에서 시작하면 돼.
B: 빨간 점 중에 아무 점이나 말하는 거야?
G: 응. 원을 먼저 그리고, 그 다음에 삼각형 두 개를 이렇게 그려. 아니면 이렇게 삼각형을 먼저 그릴 수도 있어.
B: 오, 이제 알겠어.

Listen & Speak 1 A-2

W: _____

M: _____

W: _____

M: _____

W: _____

M: _____

W: _____

M: _____

W: _____

W: 안녕하세요. 아들을 위한 배낭을 찾고 있어요.
M: 아들이 몇 살인가요?
W: 아들은 다섯 살이에요.
M: 이것을 추천하고 싶네요.
W: 오, 이거 정말 귀엽네요.
M: 네, 그렇지 않나요? 펭귄과 같이 생긴 모자가 있어서 아이들이 좋아하죠.
W: 제가 세탁을 위해 모자를 분리하는 것도 가능한가요?
M: 물론이죠. 모자를 쉽게 분리했다가 다시 붙일 수도 있어요.
W: 훌륭해요. 이걸 살게요.

Listen & Speak 2 A-1

B: _____

G: _____

B: _____

G: _____

B: _____

G: _____

B: _____

B: Wendy, 너 요즘 계속 지각하네. 무슨 일 있어?
G: 일찍 일어나고 싶은데, 그게 안 돼.
B: 네 엄마가 널 깨워 주시지 않니?
G: 엄마가 깨워주시긴 하는데, 바로 일어나지 않아. 인공지능 로봇이 있으면 좋겠어.
B: 인공지능 로봇?
G: 응. 내가 아침에 꼭 일어나도록 확인해 주고, 아침밥을 가져다주는 그런 로봇 말이야.
B: 그거 좋은 생각이야.

Listen & Speak 2 A-2

B: _____

G: _____

B: _____

G: _____

B: _____

G: _____

B: _____

G: _____

B: 나는 멕시코에 있는 삼촌을 방문할 계획이야.

G: 거기서 뭐 할 거야, Mike?

B: 삼촌이 큰 수영장을 가지고 계셔서 난 대부분의 시간을 삼촌 집에서 보낼 거야.

G: 멋지다. 너 수영 잘하니?

B: 아니, 잘했으면 좋겠는데, 못해. 그래서 대신 나는 물 위를 걷는 공을 가지고 놀 거야.

G: 물 위를 걷는 공? 그게 뭐야?

B: 그건 큰 공이야. 그 안에 들어가서 물 위를 걸으면 돼.

G: 그거 분명 재밌겠다.

Real Life Talk

Bora: _____

Jessie: _____

Bora: _____

Jessie: _____

Bora: _____

Jessie: _____

Bora: _____

Jessie: _____

Bora: _____

Jessie: _____

Bora: _____

Bora: Jessie야, 뭐 하고 있어?

Jessie: 내가 제일 좋아하는 슈퍼 영웅인 닥터 레베카를 그리고 있어.

Bora: 와, 훌륭해.

Jessie: 고마워. 나는 그녀처럼 사람들의 마음을 읽을 수 있으면 좋겠어.

Bora: 그녀가 사람들의 마음을 통제하는 것도 가능하니?

Jessie: 응. 그녀가 원하면 네 마음을 통제할 수 있어.

Bora: 그거 정말 멋지다.

Jessie: 너는 어때? 너도 좋아하는 슈퍼 영웅이 있니?

Bora: 물론. 나는 스카이 X를 좋아해. 스카이 X처럼 하늘을 날 수 있으면 좋겠어.

Jessie: 나도 그가 좋아. 그는 우주에서 숨 쉴 수도 있잖아.

Bora: 응. 그는 우주에서 뭐든 할 수 있어.

Wrap Up 1

W: _____

B: _____

W: _____

B: _____

W: _____

B: _____

W: _____

W: 안녕, Tom. 무엇을 하는 중이니?

B: 지금 드론을 날리고 있어요.

W: 멋지구나! 드론 조종을 잘하니?

B: 아니요, 전 지금은 별로 잘하지 못하지만 열심히 연습하고 있어요.

W: 네가 알다시피, 내가 샌드위치 가게를 운영하고 있잖아. 너는 네 드론으로 주문한 음식을 배달하는 것이 가능하니?

B: 아니요, 불가능해요. 하지만 1~2년 후에는 가능할 거라 생각해요.

W: 그러면 좋겠구나.

※ 다음 우리말과 일치하도록 빈칸에 알맞은 것을 골라 쓰시오.

1 Who are the people who _____ the world? Do you think you are _____ young _____ be _____ of these people?

A. too   B. change   C. to   D. one

2 In the _____ stories you will meet three teenagers who _____ their ideas to _____ the world a better _____ .

A. following   B. place   C. used   D. make

A Robotic Hand from a Helpful Mind (Easton LaChappelle)

3 One day, _____ I was fourteen, I _____ _____ a little girl at a science _____ .

A. across   B. fair   C. came   D. when

4 She had a _____ hand _____ could only _____ and _____ .

A. open   B. robotic   C. close   D. that

5 I was _____ _____ the hand _____ _____ her 80,000 dollars!

A. cost   B. that   C. had   D. surprised

6 'I _____ she _____ a _____ robotic hand,' I thought to _____ .

A. myself   B. wish   C. better   D. had

7 _____ that, I started to make a _____ _____ and _____ robotic hand.

A. cheaper   B. with   C. much   D. better

8 After many _____ , finally, by _____ 3D printing technology, I was _____ to make a useful robotic hand for the _____ of only 300 dollars.

A. able   B. failures   C. price   D. using

9 I decided to _____ the designs and software for my 3D robotic hand _____ _____ for _____ .

A. others   B. share   C. free   D. with

10 Maybe someone can take _____ I have _____ and do _____ _____ with it.

A. useful   B. what   C. something   D. done

11 No _____ person can _____ the world, but we can _____ a better world by _____ together.

A. working   B. change   C. one   D. build

Headbands for Girls' Education (Mary Grace Henry)

12 'Why _____ many girls in Africa _____ to school I can? I wish they _____ go to school, too.'

A. as   B. can't   C. could   D. go

13 I _____ this _____ when I was twelve. I _____ that their families couldn't _____ it.

A. realized   B. thought   C. afford   D. had

14 I wondered _____ I _____ do _____ for those girls. Then I _____ an idea.

A. something   B. had   C. could   D. if

15 For my birthday, I _____ my parents to _____ me a _____ _____ .

A. sewing   B. asked   C. buy   D. machine

---

1 세상을 바꾸는 사람들은 누구인가? 여러분은 너무 어려서 이런 사람들 중 하나가 될 수 없다고 생각하나요?

2 다음 이야기에서 여러분은 세상을 더 나은 곳으로 만들기 위해 자신들의 아이디어를 사용한 세 명의 십 대들을 만날 겁니다.

돕는 마음으로부터 탄생한 로봇 손 (Easton LaChappelle)

3 내가 열네 살이었을 때, 어느 날 한 과학 박람회에서 어린 소녀를 우연히 만났다.

4 그녀는 겨우 접었다 펴지기만 하는 로봇 손을 가지고 있었다.

5 나는 그녀가 그 손에 8만 달러를 지불했다는 데 놀랐다!

6 '나는 그녀가 더 나은 로봇 손을 가질 수 있으면 좋겠어.'라고 마음속으로 생각했다.

7 나는 이런 생각을 가지고 더 싸고 좋은 로봇 손을 만들기 시작했다.

8 많은 실패 뒤 마침내 3D 프린트 기술을 사용해서 나는 단 300달러짜리의 유용한 로봇 손을 만들 수 있었다.

9 나는 내 3D 로봇 손의 디자인과 소프트웨어를 다른 사람들과 무료로 공유하기로 결심했다.

10 아마도 누군가는 내가 만든 것을 이용해 다른 유용한 것을 할 수 있을 것이다.

11 혼자 세상을 바꿀 수는 없지만, 함께 일 하면서 더 나은 세상을 만들 수 있다.

여학생 교육을 위한 머리띠 (Mary Grace Henry)

12 '아프리카의 많은 소녀들은 왜 나처럼 학교에 갈 수 없지? 나는 그들도 학교에 갈 수 있으면 좋을 텐데.'

13 내가 12살 때, 이런 생각을 했었다. 나는 그들의 가족이 그럴 금전적 여유가 없다는 것을 깨달았다.

14 나는 내가 그 소녀들을 위해서 어떤 것을 할 수 있을까 생각했다. 그때 아이디어가 떠올랐다.

15 나는 내 생일에 부모님께 재봉틀을 사 달라고 부탁드렸다.

16 They _____ me one, and I learned _____ to _____ headbands for _____.
    A. make   B. bought   C. myself   D. how

17 I _____ ten _____ and _____ them _____ my school.
    A. headbands   B. sold   C. created   D. at

18 Soon, I _____ money to _____ one girl in Africa to school. I couldn't _____ there.
    A. stop   B. send   C. enough   D. raised

19 I started a _____ to _____ girls in Africa _____ couldn't _____ to school.
    A. who   B. business   C. go   D. help

20 Thanks to the _____ of my business, I can _____ the school _____ for many poor girls in countries _____ Kenya and Uganda to go to school.
    A. fees   B. success   C. pay   D. like

21 I also _____ for their _____, _____, and pencils. Isn't it _____?
    A. amazing   B. pay   C. uniforms   D. textbooks

22 My _____ to you is to just do _____. When you see a _____, _____.
    A. need   B. advice   C. act   D. something

23 Start small, _____ little _____. Your warm _____ can change _____.
    A. steps   B. lives   C. taking   D. heart

Useless Corn Cobs as Useful Water Filters (Lalita Prasida)

24 As a young girl _____ in the countryside in India, I often _____ that the water around us was _____ _____.
    A. polluted   B. found   C. living   D. seriously

25 I wondered _____ I could _____ this problem. Then I _____ the idea to use corn cobs.
    A. on   B. hit   C. solve   D. how

26 _____ corn cobs _____ everywhere _____ my _____.
    A. village   B. useless   C. in   D. were

27 I thought that the small _____ in the corn cobs could filter _____ out of the _____ water.
    A. dirty   B. holes   C. polluted   D. matter

28 One day, I _____ up some dried cobs along the road, _____ them, and _____ them in a _____ of dirty water.
    A. placed   B. picked   C. bowl   D. washed

29 _____ a _____, I checked the water, and it looked _____.
    A. clearer   B. while   C. much   D. after

30 Then, _____ corn cobs that I had _____ _____ farmers, I built a _____ system.
    A. filtering   B. using   C. from   D. collected

31 My system _____ 70 to 80 percent of the _____ _____ the water.
    A. matter   B. removed   C. dirty   D. from

32 I hope my filtering system can _____ _____ all the lakes not _____ in my village but _____ in other areas.
    A. only   B. up   C. clean   D. also

16 그들은 재봉틀을 사 주셨고 나는 머리띠 만드는 법을 혼자 배웠다.

17 10개의 머리띠를 만들어 학교에서 팔았다.

18 나는 곧 아프리카에 있는 한 명의 소녀를 학교에 보낼 수 있는 충분한 자금을 모았다. 나는 거기서 멈출 수 없었다.

19 나는 학교에 갈 수 없는 아프리카의 소녀들을 돕기 위해 사업을 시작했다.

20 내 사업의 성공 덕분에 나는 케냐와 우간다 같은 나라에 있는 많은 가난한 소녀들이 학교에 갈 수 있게 수업료를 지불할 수 있다.

21 나는 또한 그들의 교과서와 교복, 연필을 위한 비용도 지불한다. 놀랍지 않은가?

22 나의 조언은 그냥 무엇이든 하라는 것이다. 필요성이 보인다면 행동하라.

23 작은 단계를 밟아가면서 작은 것부터 시작하라. 너의 따뜻한 마음이 삶을 바꿀 수 있다.

유용한 물 여과 장치로 쓰인 쓸모없는 옥수수 속대 (Lalita Prasida)

24 인도의 시골에 살고 있었던 어린 소녀인 나는 종종 내 주변에 있는 물이 심각하게 오염되어 있는 것을 발견했다.

25 나는 이 문제를 어떻게 해결할 수 있을지 궁금했다. 그때 나는 옥수수 속대를 이용해야겠다는 생각이 불현듯 떠올랐다.

26 내가 사는 마을에는 쓸모없는 옥수수 속대가 곳곳에 널려 있다.

27 나는 옥수수 속대의 작은 구멍들이 더러운 물질을 오염된 물 밖으로 걸러 낼 수 있을 거라고 생각했다.

28 어느 날 나는 길을 따라 마른 옥수수 속대를 주운 뒤, 그것들을 씻어서 더러운 물이 담긴 그릇에 넣었다.

29 잠시 뒤 물을 확인했는데 훨씬 더 맑게 보였다.

30 그러고 나서 나는 농부들로부터 모은 옥수수 속대를 이용하여 여과 장치를 만들었다.

31 내 장치는 물에서 **70~80%**의 더러운 물질을 제거했다.

32 나는 내 여과 장치가 내 마을뿐만 아니라 다른 지역에 있는 모든 호수를 깨끗하게 해 줄 수 있기를 희망한다.

※ 다음 우리말과 일치하도록 빈칸에 알맞은 것을 골라 쓰시오.

1 Who are the people _____ _____ the world? Do you think you are _____ _____ _____ _____ one of these people?

2 In the following stories you _____ _____ three teenagers who used their ideas _____ _____ the world a better place.

A Robotic Hand from a Helpful Mind (Easton LaChappelle)

3 One day, _____ I was fourteen, I _____ _____ a little girl _____ a _____ _____ .

4 She had a _____ hand _____ could only _____ and _____ .

5 I was _____ _____ the hand _____ _____ 80,000 dollars!

6 'I _____ she _____ a better robotic hand,' I _____ _____ _____ .

7 _____ that, I started to make _____ _____ _____ and _____ robotic hand.

8 After many _____ , finally, _____ _____ 3D printing technology, I _____ _____ _____ make a useful robotic hand _____ the _____ _____ only 300 dollars.

9 I decided _____ _____ the designs and software _____ my 3D robotic hand _____ _____ _____ _____ .

10 _____ someone can _____ _____ _____ _____ _____ and do _____ _____ _____ it.

11 _____ _____ person can _____ the world, but we can _____ a better world _____ _____ _____ .

Headbands for Girls' Education (Mary Grace Henry)

12 'Why _____ many girls in Africa _____ _____ _____ as I can? I wish they _____ _____ to school, too.'

13 I _____ _____ _____ when I was twelve. I _____ _____ their families _____ _____ it.

14 I wondered _____ _____ _____ _____ _____ for those girls. Then I _____ an idea.

---

1 세상을 바꾸는 사람들은 누구인가? 여러분은 너무 어려서 이런 사람들 중 하나가 될 수 없다고 생각하나요?

2 다음 이야기에서 여러분은 세상을 더 나은 곳으로 만들기 위해 자신들의 아이디어를 사용한 세 명의 십 대들을 만날 겁니다.

돕는 마음으로부터 탄생한 로봇 손 (Easton LaChappelle)

3 내가 열네 살이었을 때, 어느 날 한 과학 박람회에서 어린 소녀를 우연히 만났다.

4 그녀는 겨우 접었다 펴지기만 하는 로봇 손을 가지고 있었다.

5 나는 그녀가 그 손에 8만 달러를 지불했다는 데 놀랐다!

6 '나는 그녀가 더 나은 로봇 손을 가질 수 있으면 좋겠어.'라고 마음속으로 생각했다.

7 나는 이런 생각을 가지고 더 싸고 좋은 로봇 손을 만들기 시작했다.

8 많은 실패 뒤 마침내 3D 프린트 기술을 사용해서 나는 단 300달러짜리의 유용한 로봇 손을 만들 수 있었다.

9 나는 내 3D 로봇 손의 디자인과 소프트웨어를 다른 사람들과 무료로 공유하기로 결심했다.

10 아마도 누군가는 내가 만든 것을 이용해 다른 유용한 것을 할 수 있을 것이다.

11 혼자 세상을 바꿀 수는 없지만, 함께 일 하면서 더 나은 세상을 만들 수 있다.

여학생 교육을 위한 머리띠 (Mary Grace Henry)

12 '아프리카의 많은 소녀들은 왜 나처럼 학교에 갈 수 없을까? 나는 그들도 학교에 갈 수 있으면 좋을 텐데.'

13 내가 12살 때, 이런 생각을 했었다. 나는 그들의 가족이 그럴 금전적 여유가 없다는 것을 깨달았다.

14 나는 내가 그 소녀들을 위해서 어떤 것을 할 수 있을까 생각했다. 그때 아이디어가 떠올랐다.

15 For my birthday, I _____ my parents _____ _____ _____ _____ _____ _____.

16 They _____ _____ _____, and I learned _____ _____ _____ headbands _____ _____.

17 I created _____ _____ and sold _____ at my school.

18 Soon, I _____ _____ _____ to send one girl in Africa to school. I couldn't _____ there.

19 I started _____ _____ _____ _____ girls in Africa _____ couldn't _____ to school.

20 Thanks _____ _____ _____ of my business, I can pay the school _____ _____ many poor girls in countries _____ Kenya and Uganda _____ _____ _____.

21 I also _____ _____ their _____, _____, and pencils. _____ it _____?

22 My _____ to you _____ to just _____ _____. When you see _____ _____, _____.

23 Start _____, _____ little steps. Your _____ _____ can change _____.

Useless Corn Cobs as Useful Water Filters (Lalita Prasida)

24 _____ a young girl _____ in the countryside in India, I _____ _____ _____ the water _____ us was _____ _____.

25 I wondered _____ _____ _____ _____ this problem. Then I _____ _____ the idea _____ corn cobs.

26 _____ corn cobs _____ everywhere _____ my village.

27 I thought that _____ _____ _____ in the corn cobs _____ _____ out of the _____ water.

28 One day, I _____ _____ some dried cobs along the road, _____, and _____ them _____ _____ _____ dirty water.

29 _____ _____ _____, I checked the water, and _____ looked _____ _____.

30 Then, _____ corn cobs _____ I had _____ farmers, I _____ a _____ system.

31 My system _____ 70 to 80 percent of _____ _____ from the water.

32 I hope my _____ _____ can _____ all the lakes _____ in my village _____ _____ in _____.

※ 다음 문장을 우리말로 쓰시오.

1 Who are the people who change the world? Do you think you are too young to be one of these people?

➡ _____

2 In the following stories you will meet three teenagers who used their ideas to make the world a better place.

➡ _____

_____

A Robotic Hand from a Helpful Mind (Easton LaChappelle)

3 One day, when I was fourteen, I came across a little girl at a science fair.

➡ _____

4 She had a robotic hand that could only open and close.

➡ _____

5 I was surprised that the hand had cost her 80,000 dollars!

➡ _____

6 'I wish she had a better robotic hand,' I thought to myself.

➡ _____

7 With that, I started to make a much cheaper and better robotic hand.

➡ _____

8 After many failures, finally, by using 3D printing technology, I was able to make a useful robotic hand for the price of only 300 dollars.

➡ _____

9 I decided to share the designs and software for my 3D robotic hand with others for free.

➡ _____

10 Maybe someone can take what I have done and do something useful with it.

➡ _____

11 No one person can change the world, but we can build a better world by working together.

➡ _____

Headbands for Girls' Education (Mary Grace Henry)

12 'Why can't many girls in Africa go to school as I can? I wish they could go to school, too.'

➡ _____

13 I had this thought when I was twelve. I realized that their families couldn't afford it.

➡ _____

14 I wondered if I could do something for those girls. Then I had an idea.

➡ _____

15 For my birthday, I asked my parents to buy me a sewing machine.

➡ _____

16 They bought me one, and I learned how to make headbands for myself.

➡ _____

17 I created ten headbands and sold them at my school.

➡ _____

18 Soon, I raised enough money to send one girl in Africa to school. I couldn't stop there.

➡ _____

19 I started a business to help girls in Africa who couldn't go to school.

➡ _____

20 Thanks to the success of my business, I can pay the school fees for many poor girls in countries like Kenya and Uganda to go to school.

➡ _____

➡ _____

21 I also pay for their textbooks, uniforms, and pencils. Isn't it amazing?

➡ _____

22 My advice to you is to just do something. When you see a need, act.

➡ _____

23 Start small, taking little steps. Your warm heart can change lives.

➡ _____

Useless Corn Cobs as Useful Water Filters (Lalita Prasida)

24 As a young girl living in the countryside in India, I often found that the water around us was seriously polluted.

➡ _____

25 I wondered how I could solve this problem. Then I hit on the idea to use corn cobs.

➡ _____

26 Useless corn cobs were everywhere in my village.

➡ _____

27 I thought that the small holes in the corn cobs could filter dirty matter out of the polluted water.

➡ _____

28 One day, I picked up some dried cobs along the road, washed them, and placed them in a bowl of dirty water.

➡ _____

29 After a while, I checked the water, and it looked much clearer.

➡ _____

30 Then, using corn cobs that I had collected from farmers, I built a filtering system.

➡ _____

31 My system removed 70 to 80 percent of the dirty matter from the water.

➡ _____

32 I hope my filtering system can clean up all the lakes not only in my village but also in other areas.

➡ _____

※ 다음 괄호 안의 단어들을 우리말에 맞도록 바르게 배열하시오.

1 (are / who / people / the / change / who / world? / the // you / do / think / are / you / young / too / be / to / of / one / people? / these)
➡ _____

2 (the / in / stories / following / you / meet / will / teenagers / three / used / who / ideas / their / make / to / world / the / better / a / place.)
➡ _____

A Robotic Hand from a Helpful Mind (Easton LaChappelle)

3 (day, / one / I / when / fourteen, / was / came / I / across / little / a / girl / a / at / fair. / science)
➡ _____

4 (had / she / robotic / a / that / hand / could / open / only / close. / and)
➡ _____

5 (was / I / that / surprised / the / had / hand / cost / 80,000 / her / dollars!)
➡ _____

6 (wish / 'I / had / she / better / a / hand,' / robotic / thought / I / myself. / to)
➡ _____

7 (that, / with / started / I / make / to / much / a / and / cheaper / robotic / better / hand.)
➡ _____

8 (many / after / finally, / failures, / using / by / printing / 3D / technology, / was / I / to / able / a / make / robotic / useful / for / hand / price / the / only / of / dollars. / 300)
➡ _____

9 (decided / I / share / to / designs / the / software / and / my / for / robotic / 3D / with / hand / others / free. / for)
➡ _____

10 (someone / maybe / take / can / I / what / done / have / and / something / do / with / useful / it.)
➡ _____

11 (one / no / can / person / the / change / world, / we / but / build / can / world / better / a / by / together. / working)
➡ _____

Headbands for Girls' Education (Mary Grace Henry)

12 (can't / 'why / girls / many / Africa / in / to / go / as / school / can? / I // wish / I / could / they / to / go / too.' / school,)
➡ _____

13 (had / I / thought / this / I / when / twelve. / was // realized / I / their / that / couldn't / families / it. / afford)
➡ _____

14 (wondered / I / I / if / do / could / for / something / girls. / those // I / then / an / had / idea.)
➡ _____

15 (my / for / birthday, / asked / I / parents / my / buy / to / a / me / machine. / sewing)
➡ _____

16 (bought / they / one, / me / I / and / how / learned / make / to / myself. / headbands / for)
➡ _____

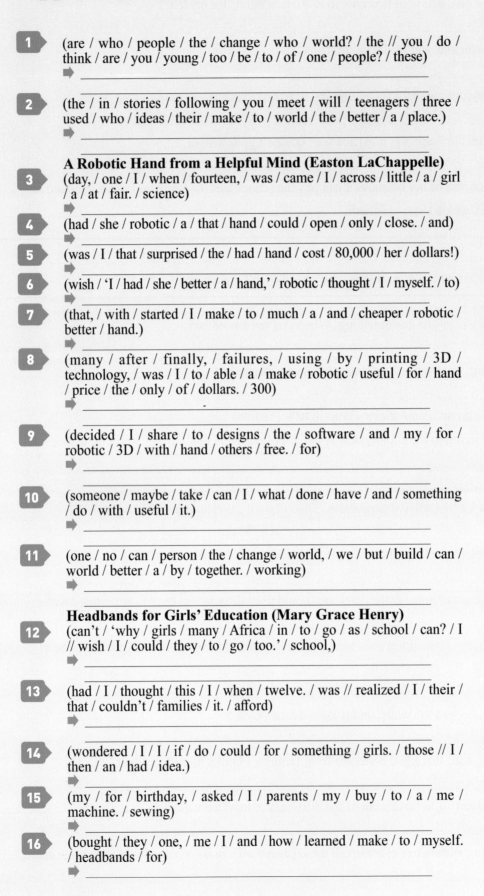

1 세상을 바꾸는 사람들은 누구인 가? 여러분은 너무 어려서 이런 사람들 중 하나가 될 수 없다고 생각하나요?

2 다음 이야기에서 여러분은 세상 을 더 나은 곳으로 만들기 위해 자신들의 아이디어를 사용한 세 명의 십 대들을 만날 겁니다.

돕는 마음으로부터 탄생한 로봇 손 (Easton LaChappelle)

3 내가 열네 살이었을 때, 어느 날 한 과학 박람회에서 어린 소녀를 우연히 만났다.

4 그녀는 겨우 접었다 펴지기만 하 는 로봇 손을 가지고 있었다.

5 나는 그녀가 그 손에 8만 달러를 지불했다는 데 놀랐다!

6 '나는 그녀가 더 나은 로봇 손을 가질 수 있으면 좋겠어.'라고 마음 속으로 생각했다.

7 나는 이런 생각을 가지고 더 싸고 좋은 로봇 손을 만들기 시작했다.

8 많은 실패 뒤 마침내 3D 프린트 기술을 사용해서 나는 단 300달 러짜리의 유용한 로봇 손을 만들 수 있었다.

9 나는 내 3D 로봇 손의 디자인과 소프트웨어를 다른 사람들과 무 료로 공유하기로 결심했다.

10 아마도 누군가는 내가 만든 것을 이용해 다른 유용한 것을 할 수 있을 것이다.

11 혼자 세상을 바꿀 수는 없지만, 함께 일 하면서 더 나은 세상을 만들 수 있다.

여학생 교육을 위한 머리띠 (Mary Grace Henry)

12 '아프리카의 많은 소녀들은 왜 나 처럼 학교에 갈 수 없지? 나는 그 들도 학교에 갈 수 있으면 좋을 텐데.'

13 내가 12살 때, 이런 생각을 했었 다. 나는 그들의 가족이 그럴 금전 적 여유가 없다는 것을 깨달았다.

14 나는 내가 그 소녀들을 위해서 어 떤 것을 할 수 있을까 생각했다. 그때 아이디어가 떠올랐다.

15 나는 내 생일에 부모님께 재봉 틀을 사 달라고 부탁드렸다.

16 그들은 재봉틀을 사 주셨고 나 는 머리띠 만드는 법을 혼자 배 웠다.

17 (created / I / headbands / ten / sold / and / at / them / school. / my)
➡

18 (I / soon, / enough / raised / to / money / one / send / girl / Africa / in / school. / to // couldn't / I / there. / stop)
➡

19 (started / I / business / a / help / to / in / girls / who / Africa / couldn't / to / school. / go)
➡

20 (to / thanks / success / the / my / of / business, / can / I / the / pay / fees / school / many / for / girls / poor / countries / in / Kenya / like / Uganda / and / go / to / school. / to)
➡

21 (also / I / for / pay / textbooks, / their / and / uniforms, / pencils. // it / amazing? / isn't)
➡

22 (advice / my / you / to / is / just / to / something. / do // you / when / a / see / act. / need,)
➡

23 (small, / start / little / taking / steps. // warm / your / can / heart / lives / change)
➡

Useless Corn Cobs as Useful Water Filters (Lalita Prasida)

24 (a / as / girl / young / living / the / in / countryside / India, / in / often / I / that / found / water / the / us / around / seriously / was / polluted.)
➡

25 (wondered / I / I / how / solve / could / problem. / this // I / then / on / hit / idea / the / use / to / cobs. / corn)
➡

26 (corn / useless / were / cobs / in / everywhere / village. / my)
➡

27 (thought / I / the / that / small / in / holes / the / cobs / corn / filter / could / matter / dirt / of / out / polluted / the / water.)
➡

28 (day, / one / picked / I / some / up / cobs / dried / along / road, / the / them, / washed / and / them / placed / a / in / of / bowl / water. / dirty)
➡

29 (a / after / while, / checked / I / water, / the / it / and / much / looked / clearer.)
➡

30 (using / then, / cobs / corn / I / that / collected / had / farmers, / from / built / I / a / system. / filtering)
➡

31 (system / my / 70 / removed / to / percent / 80 / of / dirty / the / from / matter / water. / the)
➡

32 (hope / I / filtering / my / can / system / clean / all / up / the / not / lakes / only / in / village / my / also / but / in / areas. / other)
➡

17 10개의 머리띠를 만들어 학교에서 팔았다.
18 나는 곧 아프리카에 있는 한 명의 소녀를 학교에 보낼 수 있는 충분한 자금을 모았다. 나는 거기서 멈출 수 없었다.
19 나는 학교에 갈 수 없는 아프리카의 소녀들을 돕기 위해 사업을 시작했다.
20 내 사업의 성공 덕분에 나는 케냐와 우간다 같은 나라에 있는 많은 가난한 소녀들이 학교에 갈 수 있게 수업료를 지불할 수 있다.
21 나는 또한 그들의 교과서와 교복, 연필을 위한 비용도 지불한다. 놀랍지 않은가?
22 나의 조언은 그냥 무엇이든 하라는 것이다. 필요성이 보인다면 행동하라.
23 작은 단계를 밟아가면서 작은 것부터 시작하라. 너의 따뜻한 마음이 삶을 바꿀 수 있다.
유용한 물 여과 장치로 쓰인 쓸모없는 옥수수 속대 (Lalita Prasida)
24 인도의 시골에 살고 있었던 어린 소녀인 나는 종종 내 주변에 있는 물이 심각하게 오염되어 있는 것을 발견했다.
25 나는 이 문제를 어떻게 해결할 수 있을지 궁금했다. 그때 나는 옥수수 속대를 이용해야겠다는 생각이 불현듯 떠올랐다.
26 내가 사는 마을에는 쓸모없는 옥수수 속대가 곳곳에 널려 있다.
27 나는 옥수수 속대의 작은 구멍들이 더러운 물질을 오염된 물 밖으로 걸러 낼 수 있을 거라고 생각했다.
28 어느 날 나는 길을 따라 마른 옥수수 속대를 주운 뒤, 그것들을 씻어서 더러운 물이 담긴 그릇에 넣었다.
29 잠시 뒤 물을 확인했는데 훨씬 더 맑게 보였다.
30 그리고 나서 나는 농부들로부터 모은 옥수수 속대를 이용하여 여과 장치를 만들었다.
31 내 장치는 물에서 70~80%의 더러운 물질을 제거했다.
32 나는 내 여과 장치가 내 마을뿐만 아니라 다른 지역에 있는 모든 호수를 깨끗하게 해 줄 수 있기를 희망한다.

※ 다음 우리말을 영어로 쓰시오.

1 세상을 바꾸는 사람들은 누구인가? 여러분은 너무 어려서 이런 사람들 중 하나가 될 수 없다고 생각하나요?

➡ _____

2 다음 이야기에서 여러분은 세상을 더 나은 곳으로 만들기 위해 자신들의 아이디어를 사용한 세 명의 십 대들을 만날 겁니다.

➡ _____

A Robotic Hand from a Helpful Mind (Easton LaChappelle)

3 내가 열네 살이었을 때, 어느 날 한 과학 박람회에서 어린 소녀를 우연히 만났다.

➡ _____

4 그녀는 겨우 접었다 펴지기만 하는 로봇 손을 가지고 있었다.

➡ _____

5 나는 그녀가 그 손에 8만 달러를 지불했다는 데 놀랐다!

➡ _____

6 '나는 그녀가 더 나은 로봇 손을 가질 수 있으면 좋겠어.'라고 마음속으로 생각했다.

➡ _____

7 나는 이런 생각을 가지고 더 싸고 좋은 로봇 손을 만들기 시작했다.

➡ _____

8 많은 실패 뒤 마침내 3D 프린트 기술을 사용해서 나는 단 300달러짜리의 유용한 로봇 손을 만들 수 있었다.

➡ _____
_____

9 나는 내 3D 로봇 손의 디자인과 소프트웨어를 다른 사람들과 무료로 공유하기로 결심했다.

➡ _____

10 아마도 누군가는 내가 만든 것을 이용해 다른 유용한 것을 할 수 있을 것이다.

➡ _____

11 혼자 세상을 바꿀 수는 없지만, 함께 일 하면서 더 나은 세상을 만들 수 있다.

➡ _____

Headbands for Girls' Education (Mary Grace Henry)

12 '아프리카의 많은 소녀들은 왜 나처럼 학교에 갈 수 없지? 나는 그들도 학교에 갈 수 있으면 좋을 텐데.'

➡ _____

13 내가 12살 때, 이런 생각을 했었다. 나는 그들의 가족이 그럴 금전적 여유가 없다는 것을 깨달았다.

➡ _____

14 나는 내가 그 소녀들을 위해서 어떤 것을 할 수 있을까 생각했다. 그때 아이디어가 떠올랐다.

➡ _____

15 나는 내 생일에 부모님께 재봉틀을 사 달라고 부탁드렸다.

➡ _____

16 그들은 재봉틀을 사 주셨고 나는 머리띠 만드는 법을 혼자 배웠다.

➡ _____

17 10개의 머리띠를 만들어 학교에서 팔았다.

➡ _____

18 나는 곧 아프리카에 있는 한 명의 소녀를 학교에 보낼 수 있는 충분한 자금을 모았다. 나는 거기서 멈출 수 없었다.

➡ _____

19 나는 학교에 갈 수 없는 아프리카의 소녀들을 돕기 위해 사업을 시작했다.

➡ _____

20 내 사업의 성공 덕분에 나는 케냐와 우간다 같은 나라에 있는 많은 가난한 소녀들이 학교에 갈 수 있게 수업료를 지불할 수 있다.

➡ _____

_____

21 나는 또한 그들의 교과서와 교복, 연필을 위한 비용도 지불한다. 놀랍지 않은가?

➡ _____

22 나의 조언은 그냥 무엇이든 하라는 것이다. 필요성이 보인다면 행동하라.

➡ _____

23 작은 단계를 밟아가면서 작은 것부터 시작하라. 너의 따뜻한 마음이 삶을 바꿀 수 있다.

➡ _____

Useless Corn Cobs as Useful Water Filters (Lalita Prasida)

24 인도의 시골에 살고 있었던 어린 소녀인 나는 종종 내 주변에 있는 물이 심각하게 오염되어 있는 것을 발견했다.

➡ _____

_____

25 나는 이 문제를 어떻게 해결할 수 있을지 궁금했다. 그때 나는 옥수수 속대를 이용해야겠다는 생각이 불현 듯 떠올랐다.

➡ _____

26 내가 사는 마을에는 쓸모없는 옥수수 속대가 곳곳에 널려 있다.

➡ _____

27 나는 옥수수 속대의 작은 구멍들이 더러운 물질을 오염된 물 밖으로 걸러 낼 수 있을 거라고 생각했다.

➡ _____

28 어느 날 나는 길을 따라 마른 옥수수 속대를 주운 뒤, 그것들을 씻어서 더러운 물이 담긴 그릇에 넣었다.

➡ _____

_____

29 잠시 뒤 물을 확인했는데 훨씬 더 맑게 보였다.

➡ _____

30 그러고 나서 나는 농부들로부터 모은 옥수수 속대를 이용하여 여과 장치를 만들었다.

➡ _____

31 내 장치는 물에서 70~80%의 더러운 물질을 제거했다.

➡ _____

32 나는 내 여과 장치가 내 마을뿐만 아니라 다른 지역에 있는 모든 호수를 깨끗하게 해 줄 수 있기를 희망한다.

➡ _____

※ 다음 우리말과 일치하도록 빈칸에 알맞은 말을 쓰시오.

Communication Task

1. A: I'm Sky X. I _____ _____.
2. B: Hi, Sky X. Nice _____ _____ _____.
3. C: I _____ I _____ _____ _____ you. _____ _____ _____ _____ _____ to fly to the moon?
4. A: _____.
5. D: Then _____ _____ _____ _____ _____ _____ to the sun?
6. A: No. That's _____.

1. A: 나는 스카에 X야. 나는 하늘을 날 수 있어.
2. B: 안녕, 스카이 X. 만나서 반가워.
3. C: 나는 너처럼 하늘을 날 수 있으면 좋겠어. 너는 달까지 날아가는 것이 가능하니?
4. A: 물론이지.
5. D: 그럼 너는 태양으로 여행하는 것이 가능하니?
6. A: 아니. 그건 불가능해.

Enjoy Writing

1. _____ Genie,
2. I have three wishes. _____ _____ _____ you can _____ _____ _____ _____ _____.
3. First, I _____ I _____ in Hawaii. Then I _____ _____ _____ _____ _____ _____.
4. Second, I _____ every Wednesday _____ a holiday. Then, I _____ _____ _____ _____ _____.
5. _____, _____ _____ _____ _____ _____ the president of Korea.
6. Then I would try hard to _____ _____ _____ _____ _____ _____ _____ _____ _____.
7. I don't know _____ _____ _____ _____ _____ _____, but _____ _____ you _____.
8. _____ _____, Sohee

1. Genie에게
2. 나는 세 가지 소원이 있다. 네가 나의 소원들을 모두 이루어 줄 수 있을지 궁금하다.
3. 첫 번째로, 나는 하와이에 살았으면 좋겠다. 그럼 하와이의 아름다운 해변에서 수영할 수 있을 것이다.
4. 두 번째로, 나는 모든 수요일이 휴일이었으면 좋겠다. 그럼 나는 더 편히 쉴 수 있을 것이다.
5. 마지막으로, 나는 한국의 대통령이었으면 좋겠다.
6. 그럼 나는 이 나라를 살기에 더 행복한 곳으로 만들기 위해 열심히 노력할 것이다.
7. 나는 네가 나를 도와줄 수 있을지 모르겠지만, 네가 할 수 있길 바란다.
8. 행운을 빌며, 소희가

After Your Read

1. _____ _____!
2. Easton _____ _____ _____ a girl's expensive robotic hand and wanted _____ _____ _____ _____ _____ _____ one.
3. Finally he made one _____ _____ _____ _____ and _____ _____ _____ his designs and software _____ _____.
4. Mary _____ she _____ _____ girls in Africa to school.
5. She _____ and _____ _____ _____.
6. Now she _____ _____ the school _____, textbooks, uniforms, and pencils of _____ _____ _____ _____ _____ _____ _____ _____.
7. Lalita wondered _____ _____ _____ _____ _____ _____.
8. _____ _____ _____ _____, she made _____ _____ _____.
9. It _____ 70 to 80 percent of _____ _____ _____ _____ _____.

1. 창의적인 십 대들!
2. Easton은 어떤 소녀의 비싼 로봇 손을 보고 놀라서, 더 싸고 좋은 로봇 손을 만들고 싶었다.
3. 마침내 그는 단 300달러짜리 로봇 손을 만들었고 그의 디자인과 소프트웨어를 무료로 나누기로 결심했다.
4. Mary는 아프리카 소녀들을 학교에 보낼 수 있기를 바랐다.
5. 그녀는 머리띠를 만들어 팔았다.
6. 이제 그녀는 아프리카의 많은 가난한 소녀들의 학비와 교과서, 교복 그리고 연필의 비용을 지불한다.
7. Lalita는 어떻게 물을 깨끗하게 할 수 있을지 궁금했다.
8. 그녀는 옥수수 속대를 이용해서 정수 장치를 만들었다.
9. 그 정수 장치는 오염된 물에서 70~80 퍼센트의 더러운 물질을 제거했다.

※ 다음 우리말을 영어로 쓰시오.

Communication Task

1. A: 나는 스카에 X야. 나는 하늘을 날 수 있어.
➡ _____

2. B: 안녕, 스카이 X. 만나서 반가워.
➡ _____

3. C: 나는 너처럼 하늘을 날 수 있으면 좋겠어. 너는 달까지 날아가는 것이 가능하니?
➡ _____

4. A: 물론이지.
➡ _____

5. D: 그럼 너는 태양으로 여행하는 것이 가능하니?
➡ _____

6. A: 아니. 그건 불가능해.
➡ _____

Enjoy Writing

1. Genie에게
➡ _____

2. 나는 세 가지 소원이 있다. 네가 나의 소원들을 모두 이루어 줄 수 있을지 궁금하다.
➡ _____

3. 첫 번째로, 나는 하와이에 살았으면 좋겠다. 그럼 하와이의 아름다운 해변에서 수영할 수 있을 것이다.
➡ _____

4. 두 번째로, 나는 모든 수요일이 휴일이었으면 좋겠다. 그럼 나는 더 편히 쉴 수 있을 것이다.
➡ _____

5. 마지막으로, 나는 한국의 대통령이었으면 좋겠다.
➡ _____

6. 그럼 나는 이 나라를 살기에 더 행복한 곳으로 만들기 위해 열심히 노력할 것이다.
➡ _____

7. 나는 네가 나를 도와줄 수 있을지 모르겠지만, 네가 할 수 있길 바란다.
➡ _____

8. 행운을 빌며, 소희가
➡ _____

After Your Read

1. 창의적인 십 대들!
➡ _____

2. Easton은 어떤 소녀의 비싼 로봇 손을 보고 놀라서, 더 싸고 좋은 로봇 손을 만들고 싶었다.
➡ _____

3. 마침내 그는 단 300달러짜리 로봇 손을 만들었고 그의 디자인과 소프트웨어를 무료로 나누기로 결심했다.
➡ _____

4. Mary는 아프리카 소녀들을 학교에 보낼 수 있기를 바랐다.
➡ _____

5. 그녀는 머리띠를 만들어 팔았다.
➡ _____

6. 이제 그녀는 아프리카의 많은 가난한 소녀들의 학비와 교과서, 교복 그리고 연필의 비용을 지불한다.
➡ _____

7. Lalita는 어떻게 물을 깨끗하게 할 수 있을지 궁금했다.
➡ _____

8. 그녀는 옥수수 속대를 이용해서 정수 장치를 만들었다.
➡ _____

9. 그 정수 장치는 오염된 물에서 70~80퍼센트의 더러운 물질을 제거했다.
➡ _____

※ 다음 영어를 우리말로 쓰시오.

01 necklace

02 piece

03 amount

04 beauty

05 whisper

06 couple

07 diamond

08 shocked

09 ball

10 worn

11 similar

12 whatever

13 fancy

14 admire

15 cry

16 lend

17 franc

18 huge

19 worth

20 invitation

21 ambassador

22 jeweler

23 replace

24 nearly

25 second job

26 jewelry

27 lie

28 borrow

29 certainly

30 look

31 run into

32 pay back

33 at once

34 call on

35 Do I know you?

36 spend+시간+동명사

37 It takes+목적어+
　　시간+to부정사

※ 다음 우리말을 영어로 쓰시오.

01 속삭이다, 귓속말을 하다 _____

02 프랑 (프랑스, 스위스 등의 화폐 단위) _____

03 거대한, 엄청난 _____

04 양, 액수 _____

05 무도회 _____

06 ~이든지, ~한 어떤 것이든 _____

07 확실히, 틀림없이 _____

08 존경하다, 칭찬하다 _____

09 목걸이 _____

10 한 개, 한 부분, 조각 _____

11 대사 _____

12 다이아몬드 _____

13 울다 _____

14 화려한 _____

15 충격을 받은 _____

16 거의 _____

17 ~의 가치가 있는 _____

18 초대, 초대장 _____

19 보석 상인 _____

20 아름다움, 미 _____

21 비슷한, 유사한 _____

22 빌리다 _____

23 보석류 _____

24 부부 _____

25 빌려주다 _____

26 (다른 사람 · 사물을) 대신하다 _____

27 부업 _____

28 거짓말 _____

29 지친 _____

30 보기, 눈길 _____

31 ~을 우연히 만나다 _____

32 절 아시나요? _____

33 즉시, 당장 _____

34 ~에게 청하다, 부탁하다 _____

35 갚다, 돌려주다 _____

※ 다음 영영풀이에 알맞은 단어를 <보기>에서 골라 쓴 후, 우리말 뜻을 쓰시오.

1 _____ : very tired: _____

2 _____ : two people who are married: _____

3 _____ : a quantity of something: _____

4 _____ : alike in many ways: _____

5 _____ : almost but not quite: _____

6 _____ : to take a place of: _____

7 _____ : surely, without doubt: _____

8 _____ : feeling very upset or surprised: _____

9 _____ : a large formal place where people dance: _____

10 _____ : a statement which you know is not true: _____

11 _____ : to let tears come from the eyes because of sadness, hurt, etc.: _____

12 _____ : hard, bright, precious stone which is clear and colorless: _____

13 _____ : a request to come to an event or somewhere: _____

14 _____ : to like and respect someone or something very much:

_____

15 _____ : to speak or say something very softly and low: _____

16 _____ : a diplomat of the highest rank who is the official representative of his or her country in another country: _____

보기			
whisper	amount	ambassador	similar
invitation	shocked	lie	replace
admire	worn	diamond	couple
ball	certainly	cry	nearly

※ 다음 우리말과 일치하도록 빈칸에 알맞은 것을 골라 쓰시오.

Scene 1

1 _____ _____ Mr. and Mrs. Loisel's home _____ _____ .

    A. in   B. is   C. Paris   D. this

2 _____ the home is _____ , Mrs. Loisel is _____ .

    A. nice   B. although   C. happy   D. not

3 She is young and _____ , and _____ a _____ _____ .

    A. fancier   B. pretty   C. wants   D. life

4 Mrs. Loisel: (*to* _____) Same old house and _____ dinners. I hate _____ here!

    A. boring   B. living   C. herself   D. same

5 Mr. Loisel: Matilda, I am _____ . Look _____ I _____ for you!

    A. what   B. got   C. have   D. home

6 Mrs. Loisel: _____ is _____ ?

    A. that   B. what

7 Mr. Loisel: An _____ to the Ambassador's Ball. I _____ to _____ to _____ it. Everybody wanted it.

    A. fight   B. invitation   C. get   D. had

8 Mrs. Loisel: (*crying*) _____ _____ I _____ it?

    A. would   B. why   C. want

9 Mr. Loisel: Matilda. _____ is _____ ?

    A. wrong   B. what

10 Mrs. Loisel: I have _____ to _____ to _____ a _____ party. I cannot go.

    A. fancy   B. nothing   C. such   D. wear

11 Mr. Loisel: _____ _____ sad. Here, I will give you 400 francs. _____ _____ a beautiful new dress.

    A. yourself   B. be   C. get   D. don't

Scene 2

12 Mr. Loisel: (_____ _____ *Matilda's new dress*) _____ , Matilda. Beautiful!

    A. amazing   B. at   C. looking

13 Mrs. Loisel: _____ is _____ _____ .

    A. right   B. something   C. not

14 Mr. Loisel: What _____ _____ _____ ?

    A. wrong   B. be   C. could

15 Mrs. Loisel: (*crying*) Oh, no. What am I _____ _____ ?

    A. to   B. going   C. do

장면 1

1 이곳은 파리의 Loisel 부부의 집이다.

2 그들의 집은 멋지지만, Loisel 부인은 행복하지 않다.

3 그녀는 젊고 예뻐서 더 화려하고 고급스러운 삶을 원한다.

4 Mrs. Loisel: (혼잣말로) 똑같은 낡은 집과 매일 같이 똑같은 지겨운 저녁 식사. 여기서 사는 게 너무 싫어!

5 Mr. Loisel: Matilda, 나 집에 왔어요. 내가 당신을 위해 무엇을 가져왔는지 봐요!

6 Mrs. Loisel: 뭐예요?

7 Mr. Loisel: 대사님이 여는 무도회 초대장이에요. 이걸 얻기 위해 엄청난 노력을 했던 말이에요. 모두가 갖고 싶어 했거든요.

8 Mrs. Loisel: (울면서) 내가 그걸 왜 갖고 싶겠어요?

9 Mr. Loisel: Matilda. 무슨 문제 있어요?

10 Mrs. Loisel: 그런 고급스러운 파티에 입고 갈 옷이 하나도 없는걸요. 못가요.

11 Mr. Loisel: 슬퍼하지 말아요. 자, 여기 400프랑을 줄게요. 아름다운 새 드레스를 사요.

장면 2

12 Mr. Loisel: (Matilda의 새 드레스를 보며) 멋져요, Matilda. 아름답군요!

13 Mrs. Loisel: 뭔가 제대로 맞지 않아요.

14 Mr. Loisel: 뭐가 안 맞을 수 있죠?

15 Mrs. Loisel: (울면서) 오, 안 돼. 어쩌면 좋아요?

16 Mr. Loisel: _____ _____ _____, Matilda?

A. is   B. what   C. it

17 Mrs. Loisel: I have no _____ to _____ with my beautiful dress. I will look _____ _____!

A. poor   B. jewelry   C. wear   D. so

18 Mr. Loisel: _____ _____ your friend, Mrs. Forestier. I am _____ she will _____ you some of her jewelry.

A. lend   B. call   C. sure   D. on

19 Mrs. Loisel: That is a good idea! _____ me _____ _____ _____.

A. once   B. let   C. at   D. go

Scene 3

20 Mrs. Forestier: Matilda, it is _____ nice _____ see you! What _____ you _____?

A. brings   B. so   C. here   D. to

21 Mrs. Loisel: We _____ _____ _____ the Ambassador's Ball.

A. invited   B. are   C. to

22 Mrs. Forestier: The Ambassador's Ball! That is _____! You _____ _____ _____.

A. wonderful   B. excited   C. be   D. must

23 Mrs. Loisel: Yes… And no. I am sad to _____ I have no _____. May I _____ something _____ you?

A. jewelry   B. from   C. say   D. borrow

24 Mrs. Forestier: Sure! _____ is _____ _____.

A. case   B. here   C. my

25 Mrs. Loisel: Wow, you have _____ _____ _____ _____!

A. wonderful   B. so   C. pieces   D. many

26 Mrs. Forestier: _____ _____ you _____.

A. whatever   B. like   C. choose

27 Mrs. Loisel: Would you _____ _____ this _____ _____? It is beautiful!

A. necklace   B. lend   C. diamond   D. me

28 Mrs. Forestier: _____! Now _____ _____ the ball.

A. go   B. certainly   C. enjoy

Scene 4

29 Matilda has a _____ _____. Everybody at the ball _____ her _____.

A. admires   B. perfect   C. beauty   D. evening

30 _____ _____ very late _____ the Loisels _____ the ball.

A. leave   B. it   C. when   D. is

31 Mr. Loisel: It was _____ a _____ _____. I am _____ tired.

A. night   B. such   C. long   D. so

16 Mr. Loisel: 뭐예요, 부인?

17 Mrs. Loisel: 이 아름다운 드레스에 어울릴 보석이 하나도 없어요. 내가 너무 불쌍해 보일 거예요!

18 Mr. Loisel: 당신 친구 Forestier 부인에게 부탁해 봐요. 그녀는 자신이 가진 보석을 분명히 빌려줄 거예요.

19 Mrs. Loisel: 그거 좋은 생각이에요! 지금 당장 가봐야겠어요.

장면 3

20 Mrs. Forestier: Matilda, 이렇게 보게 되어서 정말 좋아요! 무슨 일로 왔어요?

21 Mrs. Loisel: 우리 부부가 대사의 무도회에 초대되었어요.

22 Mrs. Forestier: 대사의 무도회라! 멋지네요! 당신은 분명 신났겠군요.

23 Mrs. Loisel: 네… 그리고 아니기도 해요. 말하기 슬프지만 난 보석이 없어요. 부인에게서 좀 빌릴 수 있을까요?

24 Mrs. Forestier: 물론이죠! 여기 내 보석함이에요.

25 Mrs. Loisel: 와, 부인은 정말 멋진 보석들이 많네요!

26 Mrs. Forestier: 원하는 것 아무거나 골라요.

27 Mrs. Loisel: 이 다이아몬드 목걸이를 빌려줄 수 있나요? 이거 정말 아름다워요!

28 Mrs. Forestier: 당연하죠! 자, 이제 가서 무도회를 즐겨요.

장면 4

29 Matilda는 완벽한 저녁을 보낸다. 무도회장에 있는 모든 사람들이 아름다운 그녀를 감탄하며 바라본다.

30 Loisel 부부는 아주 늦은 시간이 되어서야 무도회를 떠났다.

31 Mr. Loisel: 정말 길고 긴 밤이었어요. 정말 피곤해요.

32 Mrs. Loisel: But it was _____ _____. Do you know I _____ _____ the Ambassador?

    A. worth   B. with   C. it   D. danced

33 Mr. Loisel: I am glad you _____ _____, but I _____ to go to _____ in the morning.

    A. yourself   B. have   C. enjoyed   D. work

34 Mrs. Loisel: (_____ *in the mirror*) Just one _____ _____. (*shocked*) The necklace… It is _____!

    A. look   B. looking   C. gone   D. more

35 Mr. Loisel: What? Did you have it _____ _____ the _____?

    A. when   B. left   C. we   D. ball

36 Mrs. Loisel: Yes, I _____ _____. Please _____ _____ it!

    A. go   B. did   C. find   D. surely

37 Mr. Loisel _____ the _____.

    A. streets   B. searches

38 He _____ _____ the ball and _____ _____ to the police.

    A. goes   B. to   C. then   D. returns

39 When the _____ is not _____, Mr. Loisel tells Matilda _____ _____ to her friend.

    A. lie   B. necklace   C. found   D. to

40 Matilda tells Mrs. Forestier she _____ the _____ and would _____ it before _____ it.

    A. returning   B. broke   C. fix   D. necklace

41 The _____ needs time to _____ a _____ _____.

    A. similar   B. couple   C. one   D. find

Scene 5

42 Mr. Loisel: (*to the jeweler*) Excuse me? _____ _____ _____ _____ that diamond necklace?

    A. at   B. may   C. look   D. we

43 Mrs. Loisel: (_____) It is _____ the _____. We _____ have it!

    A. must   B. nearly   C. same   D. whispering

44 Mr. Loisel: _____ _____ is it?

    A. much   B. how

45 Jeweler: _____ _____.

    A. francs   B. 40,000

46 Mr. Loisel: _____ _____ 36,000?

    A. about   B. how

47 Mrs. Loisel: Please, we _____ _____ _____.

    A. need   B. really   C. it

48 Jeweler: Well, _____ … 36,000 _____.

    A. it   B. then   C. is

49 They do not _____ 36,000 francs. It is a _____ _____ money.

    A. amount   B. have   C. huge   D. of

50 _____ they _____ it.

    A. borrow   B. so

---

32 Mrs. Loisel: 그렇지만 충분히 가치가 있었어요. 당신, 제가 대사님과 춤춘 것을 아나요?

33 Mr. Loisel: 당신이 즐거웠다니 기쁘지만 나 아침에 출근해야 해요.

34 Mrs. Loisel: (거울을 보며) 한 번만 더 볼게요. (충격을 받고) 목걸이… 목걸이가 없어졌어요!

35 Mr. Loisel: 뭐라고요? 무도회를 떠날 때 걸고 있었소?

36 Mrs. Loisel: 네, 분명히 하고 있었는데. 가서 찾아 줘요!

37 Loisel 씨는 길거리를 수색한다.

38 그는 무도회장으로 되돌아가 본 다음 경찰서에도 간다.

39 목걸이가 발견되지 않자, Loisel 씨는 Matilda에게 그녀의 친구에게 거짓말을 하라고 한다.

40 Matilda는 Forestier 부인에게 목걸이를 망가뜨려서 돌려주기 전에 고쳐 주겠다고 말한다.

41 부부는 비슷한 것을 찾을 시간이 필요하다.

장면 5

42 Mr. Loisel: (보석상에게) 실례합니다. 저 다이아몬드 목걸이 좀 볼 수 있을까요?

43 Mrs. Loisel: (속삭이며) 거의 똑같아요. 저걸 꼭 사야만 해요!

44 Mr. Loisel: 이거 얼마인가요?

45 Jewler: 40,000프랑이에요.

46 Mr. Loisel: 36,000에 안 될까요?

47 Mrs. Loisel: 부탁드려요. 우린 이게 정말 필요하거든요.

48 Jewler: 음, 그럼… 36,000프랑에 하시죠.

49 그들은 36,000프랑이 없다. 그건 큰돈이다.

50 그래서 그들은 돈을 빌린다.

51 After _____ the necklace _____ Mrs. Forestier, the couple _____ ten years _____ back the money.

    A. spends   B. for   C. paying   D. buying

52 They _____ _____ a very small _____.

    A. to   B. move   C. place

53 Mr. Loisel gets a _____ _____. Matilda _____ clothes for _____.

    A. washes   B. second   C. others   D. job

54 Ten years of _____ work _____ Matilda _____ and _____.

    A. makes   B. hard   C. worn   D. old

55 After ten _____, Matilda _____ Mrs. Forestier _____ the street.

    A. into   B. on   C. years   D. runs

Scene 6

56 Mrs. Loisel: Mrs. Forestier, _____ _____.

    A. morning   B. good

57 Mrs. Forestier: _____ _____ _____ you?

    A. know   B. do   C. I

58 Mrs. Loisel: Yes, _____ _____ _____, Matilda.

    A. is   B. it   C. me

59 Mrs. Forestier: Oh, I _____ _____ it! You _____ so much.

    A. changed   B. believe   C. have   D. cannot

60 Mrs. Loisel: I _____ some _____ because of you.

    A. times   B. had   C. difficult   D. have

61 Mrs. Forestier: _____ me? _____ do you _____?

    A. mean   B. because   C. what   D. of

62 Mrs. Loisel: Do you _____ the diamond necklace you _____? Well, I _____ it.

    A. lent   B. remember   C. lost   D. me

63 Mrs. Forestier: But you _____ me.

    A. to   B. it   C. returned

64 Mrs. Loisel: No, I returned _____ one just _____ it. It took us ten years to _____ it.

    A. pay   B. another   C. like   D. for

65 Mrs. Forestier: You _____ a diamond necklace _____ _____ _____?

    A. to   B. bought   C. mine   D. replace

66 Mrs. Loisel: Yes.

67 Mrs. Forestier: Oh, my poor Matilda. Why _____ you come to me and tell me the _____? My diamond necklace was not _____. It was _____ only 500 francs!

    A. worth   B. truth   C. real   D. didn't

51 부부는 Forestier 부인에게 돌려줄 목걸이를 산 후 돈을 갚는 데 십 년이 걸린다.

52 그들은 아주 작은 곳으로 이사한다.

53 Loisel 씨는 부업을 구한다. Matilda는 다른 사람들을 위해 빨래를 해 준다.

54 10년 동안의 고된 일로 Matilda는 늙고 지쳤다.

55 십 년 후, Matilda는 Forestier 부인과 거리에서 마주친다.

장면 6

56 Mrs. Loisel: Forestier 부인, 좋은 아침이에요.

57 Mrs. Forestier: 제가 당신을 아나요?

58 Mrs. Loisel: 네, 저예요, Matilda.

59 Mrs. Forestier: 오, 믿을 수 없어요! 당신 너무 많이 변했어요.

60 Mrs. Loisel: 저는 당신 때문에 힘든 시간을 보냈거든요.

61 Mrs. Forestier: 나 때문에요? 무슨 말이에요?

62 Mrs. Loisel: 당신이 빌려준 목걸이 기억하죠? 음, 제가 그걸 잃어버렸어요.

63 Mrs. Forestier: 그런데 그거 나한테 돌려줬잖아요.

64 Mrs. Loisel: 아니요, 나는 당신 것과 똑같은 다른 목걸이를 돌려줬어요. 그 값을 치르느라 십 년이 걸렸어요.

65 Mrs. Forestier: 내 것을 대체하려고 다이아몬드 목걸이를 샀다고요?

66 Mrs. Loisel: 네, 맞아요.

67 Mrs. Forestier: 오, 가엾은 Matilda. 왜 내게 와서 사실을 말하지 않았어요? 그 다이아몬드 목걸이는 진품이 아니었어요. 그건 단돈 오백 프랑짜리였다고요!

※ 다음 우리말과 일치하도록 빈칸에 알맞은 것을 골라 쓰시오.

Scene 1

1 _____ _____ Mr. and Mrs. Loisel's home _____ _____.

2 _____ the home is _____, Mrs. Loisel is _____ _____.

3 She is young and pretty, _____ _____ a _____ _____.

4 Mrs. Loisel: (_____ _____) Same _____ _____ and same _____ dinners. I _____ _____ here!

5 Mr. Loisel: Matilda, I _____ _____. Look _____ I _____ _____ for you!

6 Mrs. Loisel: What is _____?

7 Mr. Loisel: An _____ _____ the Ambassador's Ball. I _____ _____ _____ _____ _____ _____. Everybody wanted it.

8 Mrs. Loisel: (*crying*) _____ _____ I want it?

9 Mr. Loisel: Matilda. What _____ _____?

10 Mrs. Loisel: I have _____ _____ _____ to _____ _____ _____ _____. I cannot go.

11 Mr. Loisel: _____ _____ sad. Here, I will _____ _____ 400 francs. _____ _____ a _____ _____ _____.

Scene 2

12 Mr. Loisel: (_____ _____ *Matilda's new dress*) _____, Matilda. Beautiful!

13 Mrs. Loisel: Something is _____ _____.

14 Mr. Loisel: _____ _____ _____ _____?

15 Mrs. Loisel: (*crying*) Oh, no. What am I _____ _____ _____?

장면 1

1 이곳은 파리의 Loisel 부부의 집이다.

2 그들의 집은 멋지지만, Loisel 부인은 행복하지 않다.

3 그녀는 젊고 예뻐서 더 화려하고 고급스러운 삶을 원한다.

4 Mrs. Loisel: (혼잣말로) 똑같은 낡은 집과 매일 같이 똑같은 지겨운 저녁 식사. 여기서 사는 게 너무 싫어!

5 Mr. Loisel: Matilda, 나 집에 왔어요. 내가 당신을 위해 무엇을 가져왔는지 봐요!

6 Mrs. Loisel: 뭐예요?

7 Mr. Loisel: 대사님이 여는 무도회 초대장이에요. 이걸 얻기 위해 엄청난 노력을 했단 말이에요. 모두가 갖고 싶어 했거든요.

8 Mrs. Loisel: (울면서) 내가 그걸 왜 갖고 싶겠어요?

9 Mr. Loisel: Matilda. 무슨 문제 있어요?

10 Mrs. Loisel: 그런 고급스러운 파티에 입고 갈 옷이 하나도 없는걸요. 못가요.

11 Mr. Loisel: 슬퍼하지 말아요. 자, 여기 400프랑을 줄게요. 아름다운 새 드레스를 사요.

장면 2

12 Mr. Loisel: (Matilda의 새 드레스를 보며) 멋져요, Matilda. 아름답군요!

13 Mrs. Loisel: 뭔가 제대로 맞지 않아요.

14 Mr. Loisel: 뭐가 안 맞을 수 있죠?

15 Mrs. Loisel: (울면서) 오, 안 돼. 어쩌면 좋아요?

16 Mr. Loisel: _____ _____ _____, Matilda?

17 Mrs. Loisel: I have _____ _____ _____ _____ with my _____ _____. I will look _____ _____!

18 Mr. Loisel: _____ _____ your friend, Mrs. Forestier. I am sure _____ _____ _____ _____ _____ some of her _____.

19 Mrs. Loisel: That is a good idea! _____ _____ _____ _____ _____.

Scene 3

20 Mrs. Forestier: Matilda, it is so nice _____ _____ you! _____ _____ _____ _____ _____?

21 Mrs. Loisel: We are _____ _____ the Ambassador's Ball.

22 Mrs. Forestier: The Ambassador's Ball! That is _____! You _____ _____ _____ _____.

23 Mrs. Loisel: Yes… And no. I am sad _____ _____ I have _____ _____. May I _____ _____ _____ _____ _____?

24 Mrs. Forestier: Sure! _____ _____ my _____.

25 Mrs. Loisel: Wow, you have _____ _____ _____!

26 Mrs. Forestier: Choose _____ _____ _____.

27 Mrs. Loisel: Would you _____ _____ _____ _____ _____? It is beautiful!

28 Mrs. Forestier: _____! Now _____ _____ _____ the ball.

Scene 4

29 Matilda has _____ _____ _____. Everybody at the ball _____ _____ _____.

30 _____ _____ very late _____ _____ _____ _____ the ball.

31 Mr. Loisel: It was _____ _____ _____ _____. I am so _____.

---

16 Mr. Loisel: 뭐예요, 부인?

17 Mrs. Loisel: 이 아름다운 드레스에 어울릴 보석이 하나도 없어요. 내가 너무 불쌍해 보일 거예요!

18 Mr. Loisel: 당신 친구 Forestier 부인에게 부탁해 봐요. 그녀는 자신이 가진 보석을 분명히 빌려줄 거예요.

19 Mrs. Loisel: 그거 좋은 생각이에요! 지금 당장 가봐야겠어요.

장면 3

20 Mrs. Forestier: Matilda, 이렇게 보게 되어서 정말 좋아요! 무슨 일로 왔어요?

21 Mrs. Loisel: 우리 부부가 대사의 무도회에 초대되었어요.

22 Mrs. Forestier: 대사의 무도회라! 멋지네요! 당신은 분명 신났겠군요.

23 Mrs. Loisel: 네… 그리고 아니기도 해요. 말하기 슬프지만 난 보석이 없어요. 부인에게서 좀 빌릴 수 있을까요?

24 Mrs. Forestier: 물론이죠! 여기 내 보석함이에요.

25 Mrs. Loisel: 와, 부인은 정말 멋진 보석들이 많네요!

26 Mrs. Forestier: 원하는 것 아무거나 골라요.

27 Mrs. Loisel: 이 다이아몬드 목걸이를 빌려줄 수 있나요? 이거 정말 아름다워요!

28 Mrs. Forestier: 당연하죠! 자, 이제 가서 무도회를 즐겨요.

장면 4

29 Matilda는 완벽한 저녁을 보낸다. 무도회장에 있는 모든 사람들이 아름다운 그녀를 감탄하며 바라본다.

30 Loisel 부부는 아주 늦은 시간이 되어서야 무도회를 떠났다.

31 Mr. Loisel: 정말 길고 긴 밤이었어요. 정말 피곤해요.

32 Mrs. Loisel: But _____ _____ _____ _____ . Do you know I _____ _____ the Ambassador?

33 Mr. Loisel: I am glad _____ _____ _____ , but I have to _____ _____ _____ in the morning.

34 Mrs. Loisel: (_____ _____ *the mirror*) Just one _____ _____ . (*shocked*) The necklace… It is gone!

35 Mr. Loisel: What? Did you have it _____ _____ _____ _____ _____ ?

36 Mrs. Loisel: Yes, I surely _____ . Please _____ _____ it!

37 Mr. Loisel _____ the streets.

38 He _____ _____ the ball and then _____ _____ the police.

39 When the necklace _____ _____ _____ , Mr. Loisel tells Matilda _____ _____ _____ her friend.

40 Matilda tells Mrs. Forestier she _____ the _____ and would _____ _____ before _____ _____ .

41 The couple needs time _____ _____ _____ _____ _____ .

Scene 5

42 Mr. Loisel: (*to the jeweler*) Excuse me? _____ _____ _____ _____ that diamond necklace?

43 Mrs. Loisel: (_____) It is _____ _____ _____ . We _____ _____ it!

44 Mr. Loisel: _____ _____ is it?

45 Jeweler: 40,000 _____ .

46 Mr. Loisel: _____ _____ 36,000?

47 Mrs. Loisel: Please, we _____ _____ _____ .

48 Jeweler: Well, then… 36,000 _____ _____ .

49 They _____ _____ _____ 36,000 francs. It is _____ _____ _____ _____ money.

50 So they _____ _____ .

---

32 Mrs. Loisel: 그렇지만 충분히 가치가 있었어요. 당신, 제가 대사님과 춤춘 것을 아나요?

33 Mr. Loisel: 당신이 즐거웠다니 기쁘지만 나 아침에 출근해야 해요.

34 Mrs. Loisel: (거울을 보며) 한 번만 더 볼게요. (충격을 받고) 목걸이… 목걸이가 없어졌어요!

35 Mr. Loisel: 뭐라고요? 무도회를 떠날 때 걸고 있었소?

36 Mrs. Loisel: 네, 분명히 하고 있었는데. 가서 찾아 줘요!

37 Loisel 씨는 길거리를 수색한다.

38 그는 무도회장으로 되돌아가 본 다음 경찰서에도 간다.

39 목걸이가 발견되지 않자, Loisel 씨는 Matilda에게 그녀의 친구에게 거짓말을 하라고 한다.

40 Matilda는 Forestier 부인에게 목걸이를 망가뜨려서 돌려주기 전에 고쳐 주겠다고 말한다.

41 부부는 비슷한 것을 찾을 시간이 필요하다.

장면 5

42 Mr. Loisel: (보석상에게) 실례합니다. 저 다이아몬드 목걸이 좀 볼 수 있을까요?

43 Mrs. Loisel: (속삭이며) 거의 똑같아요. 저걸 꼭 사야만 해요!

44 Mr. Loisel: 이거 얼마인가요?

45 Jewler: 40,000프랑이에요.

46 Mr. Loisel: 36,000에 안 될까요?

47 Mrs. Loisel: 부탁드려요, 우린 이게 정말 필요하거든요.

48 Jewler: 음, 그럼… 36,000프랑에 하시죠.

49 그들은 36,000프랑이 없다. 그건 큰돈이다.

50 그래서 그들은 돈을 빌린다.

51 After _____ the necklace _____ Mrs. Forestier, the couple _____ ten years _____ _____ the money.

52 They _____ _____ a very _____ _____ .

53 Mr. Loisel _____ _____ _____ _____ . Matilda _____ clothes _____ _____ .

54 Ten years of hard work _____ Matilda _____ and _____ .

55 After ten years, Matilda _____ _____ Mrs. Forestier _____ the street.

Scene 6

56 Mrs. Loisel: Mrs. Forestier, _____ _____ .

57 Mrs. Forestier: _____ _____ _____ _____ ?

58 Mrs. Loisel: Yes, _____ _____ _____ , Matilda.

59 Mrs. Forestier: Oh, I cannot _____ _____ ! You _____ _____ so much.

60 Mrs. Loisel: I _____ _____ some _____ _____ _____ _____ you.

61 Mrs. Forestier: Because of me? _____ _____ _____ ?

62 Mrs. Loisel: Do you remember the diamond necklace _____ _____ _____ ? Well, I _____ _____ .

63 Mrs. Forestier: But you _____ _____ to me.

64 Mrs. Loisel: No, I returned _____ _____ just _____ _____ . _____ _____ us ten years _____ _____ _____ _____ .

65 Mrs. Forestier: You _____ a diamond necklace _____ _____ _____ ?

66 Mrs. Loisel: Yes.

67 Mrs. Forestier: Oh, my poor Matilda. _____ _____ _____ to me and _____ _____ the truth? My diamond necklace _____ _____ _____ . It was _____ only 500 francs!

51 부부는 Forestier 부인에게 돌려줄 목걸이를 산 후 돈을 갚는 데 십 년이 걸린다.

52 그들은 아주 작은 곳으로 이사한다.

53 Loisel 씨는 부업을 구한다. Matilda는 다른 사람들을 위해 빨래를 해 준다.

54 10년 동안의 고된 일로 Matilda는 늙고 지쳤다.

55 십 년 후, Matilda는 Forestier 부인과 거리에서 마주친다.

장면 6

56 Mrs. Loisel: Forestier 부인, 좋은 아침이에요.

57 Mrs. Forestier: 제가 당신을 아나요?

58 Mrs. Loisel: 네, 저예요, Matilda.

59 Mrs. Forestier: 오, 믿을 수 없어요! 당신 너무 많이 변했어요.

60 Mrs. Loisel: 저는 당신 때문에 힘든 시간을 보냈거든요.

61 Mrs. Forestier: 나 때문에요? 무슨 말이에요?

62 Mrs. Loisel: 당신이 빌려준 목걸이 기억하죠? 음, 제가 그걸 잃어버렸어요.

63 Mrs. Forestier: 그런데 그거 나한테 돌려줬잖아요.

64 Mrs. Loisel: 아니요, 나는 당신 것과 똑같은 다른 목걸이를 돌려줬어요. 그 값을 치르느라 십 년이 걸렸어요.

65 Mrs. Forestier: 내 것을 대체하려고 다이아몬드 목걸이를 샀다고요?

66 Mrs. Loisel: 네, 맞아요.

67 Mrs. Forestier: 오, 가엾은 Matilda. 왜 내게 와서 사실을 말하지 않았어요? 그 다이아몬드 목걸이는 진품이 아니었어요. 그건 단돈 오백 프랑짜리였다고요!

※ 다음 문장을 우리말로 쓰시오.

Scene 1

1 This is Mr. and Mrs. Loisel's home in Paris.

➡ _____

2 Although the home is nice, Mrs. Loisel is not happy.

➡ _____

3 She is young and pretty, and wants a fancier life.

➡ _____

4 Mrs. Loisel: (*to herself*) Same old house and same boring dinners. I hate living here!

➡ _____

5 Mr. Loisel: Matilda, I am home. Look what I have got for you!

➡ _____

6 Mrs. Loisel: What is that?

➡ _____

7 Mr. Loisel: An invitation to the Ambassador's Ball. I had to fight to get it. Everybody wanted it.

➡ _____

8 Mrs. Loisel: (*crying*) Why would I want it?

➡ _____

9 Mrs. Loisel: Matilda. What is wrong?

➡ _____

10 Mrs. Loisel: I have nothing to wear to such a fancy party. I cannot go.

➡ _____

11 Mr. Loisel: Don't be sad. Here, I will give you 400 francs. Get yourself a beautiful new dress.

➡ _____

Scene 2

12 Mr. Loisel: (*looking at Matilda's new dress*) Amazing, Matilda. Beautiful!

➡ _____

13 Mrs. Loisel: Something is not right.

➡ _____

14 Mr. Loisel: What could be wrong?

➡ _____

15 Mrs. Loisel: (*crying*) Oh, no. What am I going to do?

➡ _____

16   Mr. Loisel: What is it, Matilda?

➡ _____

17   Mrs. Loisel: I have no jewelry to wear with my beautiful dress. I will look so poor!

➡ _____

18   Mr. Loisel: Call on your friend, Mrs. Forestier. I am sure she will lend you some of her jewelry.

➡ _____

19   Mrs. Loisel: That is a good idea! Let me go at once.

➡ _____

Scene 3

20   Mrs. Forestier: Matilda, it is so nice to see you! What brings you here?

➡ _____

21   Mrs. Loisel: We are invited to the Ambassador's Ball.

➡ _____

22   Mrs. Forestier: The Ambassador's Ball! That is wonderful! You must be excited.

➡ _____

23   Mrs. Loisel: Yes… And no. I am sad to say I have no jewelry. May I borrow something from you?

➡ _____

24   Mrs. Forestier: Sure! Here is my case.

➡ _____

25   Mrs. Loisel: Wow, you have so many wonderful pieces!

➡ _____

26   Mrs. Forestier: Choose whatever you like.

➡ _____

27   Mrs. Loisel: Would you lend me this diamond necklace? It is beautiful!

➡ _____

28   Mrs. Forestier: Certainly! Now go enjoy the ball.

➡ _____

Scene 4

29   Matilda has a perfect evening. Everybody at the ball admires her beauty.

➡ _____

30   It is very late when the Loisels leave the ball.

➡ _____

31   Mr. Loisel: It was such a long night. I am so tired.

➡ _____

32 Mrs. Loisel: But it was worth it. Do you know I danced with the Ambassador?

➡ _____

33 Mr. Loisel: I am glad you enjoyed yourself, but I have to go to work in the morning.

➡ _____

34 Mrs. Loisel: (*looking in the mirror*) Just one more look. (*shocked*) The necklace... It is gone!

➡ _____

35 Mr. Loisel: What? Did you have it when we left the ball?

➡ _____

36 Mrs. Loisel: Yes, I surely did. Please go find it!

➡ _____

37 Mr. Loisel searches the streets.

➡ _____

38 He returns to the ball and then goes to the police.

➡ _____

39 When the necklace is not found, Mr. Loisel tells Matilda to lie to her friend.

➡ _____

40 Matilda tells Mrs. Forestier she broke the necklace and would fix it before returning it.

➡ _____

41 The couple needs time to find a similar one.

➡ _____

Scene 5

42 Mr. Loisel: (*to the jeweler*) Excuse me? May we look at that diamond necklace?

➡ _____

43 Mrs. Loisel: (*whispering*) It is nearly the same. We must have it!

➡ _____

44 Mr. Loisel: How much is it?

➡ _____

45 Jeweler: 40,000 francs.

➡ _____

46 Mr. Loisel: How about 36,000?

➡ _____

47 Mrs. Loisel: Please, we really need it.

➡ _____

48 Jeweler: Well, then... 36,000 it is.

➡ _____

49 They do not have 36,000 francs. It is a huge amount of money.

➡ _____

50 So they borrow it.

➡ _____

51 After buying the necklace for Mrs. Forestier, the couple spends ten years paying back the money.

➡ _____

52 They move to a very small place.

➡ _____

53 Mr. Loisel gets a second job. Matilda washes clothes for others.

➡ _____

54 Ten years of hard work makes Matilda old and worn.

➡ _____

55 After ten years, Matilda runs into Mrs. Forestier on the street.

➡ _____

Scene 6

56 Mrs. Loisel: Mrs. Forestier, good morning.

➡ _____

57 Mrs. Forestier: Do I know you?

➡ _____

58 Mrs. Loisel: Yes, it is me, Matilda.

➡ _____

59 Mrs. Forestier: Oh, I cannot believe it! You have changed so much.

➡ _____

60 Mrs. Loisel: I have had some difficult times because of you.

➡ _____

61 Mrs. Forestier: Because of me? What do you mean?

➡ _____

62 Mrs. Loisel: Do you remember the diamond necklace you lent me? Well, I lost it.

➡ _____

63 Mrs. Forestier: But you returned it to me.

➡ _____

64 Mrs. Loisel: No, I returned another one just like it. It took us ten years to pay for it.

➡ _____

65 Mrs. Forestier: You bought a diamond necklace to replace mine?

➡ _____

66 Mrs. Loisel: Yes.

➡ _____

67 Mrs. Forestier: Oh, my poor Matilda. Why didn't you come to me and tell me the truth? My diamond necklace was not real. It was worth only 500 francs!

➡ _____

_____

※ 다음 괄호 안의 단어들을 우리말에 맞도록 바르게 배열하시오.

Scene 1

1 (is / this / Mrs. / and / Mr. / home / Loisel's / Paris. / in)
➡ _____

2 (the / although / is / home / nice, / Loisel / Mrs. / not / is / happy.)
➡ _____

3 (is / she / young / pretty, / and / wants / and / a / life. / fancier)
➡ _____

4 (Mrs. Loisel: / *herself*) / (*to* // old / same / and / house / boring / same / dinners. // hate / I / here! / living)
➡ _____

5 (Mr. Loisel: / Matilda, / am / I / home. // what / look / have / I / for / got / you!)
➡ _____

6 (Mrs. Loisel: / is / that? / what)
➡ _____

7 (Mr. Loisel: / invitation / an / the / to / Ball. / Ambassador's // had / I / fight / to / get / it. / to // wanted / everybody / it.)
➡ _____

8 (Mrs. Loisel: / (*crying*) / would / why / want / I / it?)
➡ _____

9 (Mr. Loisel: / Matilda. / is / what / wrong?)
➡ _____

10 (Mrs. Loisel: / have / I / to / nothing / wear / such / to / a / party. / fancy // cannot / I / go.)
➡ _____

11 (Mr. Loisel: / be / don't / sad. // I / here, / give / will / 400 / you / francs. // yourself / get / beautiful / a / dress. / new)
➡ _____

Scene 2

12 (Mr. Loisel: / (*looking / Matilda's / at / dress*) / *new* // Matilda, / Amazing, / Beautiful!)
➡ _____

13 (Mrs. Loisel: / is / something / right. / not)
➡ _____

14 (Mr. Loisel: / could / what / wrong? / be)
➡ _____

15 (Mrs. Loisel: / (*crying*) / no. / oh, // am / what / going / I / do? / to)
➡ _____

장면 1

1 이곳은 파리의 Loisel 부부의 집이다.

2 그들의 집은 멋지지만, Loisel 부인은 행복하지 않다.

3 그녀는 젊고 예뻐서 더 화려하고 고급스러운 삶을 원한다.

4 Mrs. Loisel: (혼잣말로) 똑같은 낡은 집과 매일 같이 똑같은 지겨운 저녁 식사. 여기서 사는 게 너무 싫어!

5 Mr. Loisel: Matilda, 나 집에 왔어요. 내가 당신을 위해 무엇을 가져왔는지 봐요!

6 Mrs. Loisel: 뭐예요?

7 Mr. Loisel: 대사님이 여는 무도회 초대장이에요. 이걸 얻기 위해 엄청난 노력을 했단 말이에요. 모두가 갖고 싶어 했거든요.

8 Mrs. Loisel: (울면서) 내가 그걸 왜 갖고 싶겠어요?

9 Mr. Loisel: Matilda. 무슨 문제 있어요?

10 Mrs. Loisel: 그런 고급스러운 파티에 입고 갈 옷이 하나도 없는걸요. 못가요.

11 Mr. Loisel: 슬퍼하지 말아요. 자, 여기 400프랑을 줄게요. 아름다운 새 드레스를 사요.

장면 2

12 Mr. Loisel: (Matilda의 새 드레스를 보며) 멋져요, Matilda. 아름답군요!

13 Mrs. Loisel: 뭔가 제대로 맞지 않아요.

14 Mr. Loisel: 뭐가 안 맞을 수 있죠?

15 Mrs. Loisel: (울면서) 오, 안 돼. 어쩌면 좋아요?

16 (Mr. Loisel: / is / what / it, / Matilda?)
➡ _____

17 (Mrs. Loisel: / have / I / jewelry / no / wear / to / my / with / dress. / beautiful // will / I / so / look / poor!)
➡ _____
_____

18 (Mr. Loisel: / on / call / friend, / your, / Forestier. / Mrs. // am / I / she / sure / will / you / lend / of / some / jewelry. / her)
➡ _____
_____

19 (Mrs. Loisel: / is / that's / a / idea! / good // me / let / at / go / once.)
➡ _____

Scene 3

20 (Mrs. Forestier: / Matilda, is / it / nice / so / see / you! / to // brings / what / here? / you)
➡ _____

21 (Mrs. Loisel: / are / we / to / invited / the / Ball. / Ambassador's)
➡ _____

22 (Mrs. Forestier: / Ambassador's / The / Ball! // is / that / wonderful! // must / you / excited. / be)
➡ _____

23 (Mrs. Loisel: / Yes... / no. / and // am / I / to / sad / say / have / I / jewelry. / no // I / may / something / borrow / you? / from)
➡ _____
_____

24 (Mrs. Forestier: / sure! // is / here / case. / my)
➡ _____

25 (Mrs. Loisel: / you / wow, / so / have / wonderful / many / pieces!)
➡ _____

26 (Mrs. Forestier: / whatever / chose / like. / you)
➡ _____

27 (Mrs. Loisel: / you / would / me / lend / this / necklace? // diamond // is / it / beautiful!)
➡ _____

28 (Mrs. Forestier: / certainly! // go / now / the / enjoy / ball.)
➡ _____

Scene 4

29 (has / Matilda / a / evening. / perfect // at / everybody / ball / the / her / admires / beauty.)
➡ _____
_____

30 (is / it / late / very / the / when / Loisels / the / leave / ball.)
➡ _____

31 (Mr. Loisel: / was / it / a / such / night. / long // am / I / tired. / so)
➡ _____

16 Mr. Loisel: 뭐예요, 부인?

17 Mrs. Loisel: 이 아름다운 드레스에 어울릴 보석이 하나도 없어요. 내가 너무 불쌍해 보일 거예요!

18 Mr. Loisel: 당신 친구 Forestier 부인에게 부탁해 봐요. 그녀는 자신이 가진 보석을 분명히 빌려줄 거예요.

19 Mrs. Loisel: 그거 좋은 생각이에요! 지금 당장 가봐야겠어요.

장면 3

20 Mrs. Forestier: Matilda, 이렇게 보게 되어서 정말 좋아요! 무슨 일로 왔어요?

21 Mrs. Loisel: 우리 부부가 대사의 무도회에 초대되었어요.

22 Mrs. Forestier: 대사의 무도회라! 멋지네요! 당신은 분명 신났겠군요.

23 Mrs. Loisel: 네… 그리고 아니기도 해요. 말하기 슬프지만 난 보석이 없어요. 부인에게서 좀 빌릴 수 있을까요?

24 Mrs. Forestier: 물론이죠! 여기 내 보석함이에요.

25 Mrs. Loisel: 와, 부인은 정말 멋진 보석들이 많네요!

26 Mrs. Forestier: 원하는 것 아무거나 골라요.

27 Mrs. Loisel: 이 다이아몬드 목걸이를 빌려줄 수 있나요? 이거 정말 아름다워요!

28 Mrs. Forestier: 당연하죠! 자, 이제 가서 무도회를 즐겨요.

장면 4

29 Matilda는 완벽한 저녁을 보낸다. 무도회장에 있는 모든 사람들이 아름다운 그녀를 감탄하며 바라본다.

30 Loisel 부부는 아주 늦은 시간이 되어서야 무도회를 떠났다.

31 Mr. Loisel: 정말 길고 긴 밤이었어요. 정말 피곤해요.

32 (Mrs. Loisel: / it / but / worth / was / it. // you / know / do / danced / I / the / with / Ambassador?)
➡ _____

33 (Mr. Loisel: / am / I / you / glad / yourself, / enjoyed / I / but / go / to / have / to / in / work / morning. / the)
➡ _____

34 (Mrs. Loisel: / in / (looking / mirror) / the // one / just / look. / more // (shocked) // necklace... / the // is it / gone!)
➡ _____

35 (Mr. Loisel: / what? / you / did / it / have / we / when / the / left / ball?)
➡ _____

36 (Mrs. Loisel: / I / yes, / did. / surely // go / please / it! / find)
➡ _____

37 (Loisel / Mr. / the / searches / streets.)
➡ _____

38 (returns / he / the / to / ball / and / goes / then / the / to / police.)
➡ _____

39 (the / when / is / necklace / found, / not / Loisel / Mr. / Matilda / tells / to / lie / friend. / her / to)
➡ _____

40 (Matilda / Mrs. / tells / Forestier / broke / she / necklace / the / and / fix / would / before / it / it. / returning)
➡ _____

41 (couple /the / time / needs / find / to / a / one. / similar)
➡ _____

Scene 5
42 (Mr. Loisel: / the / jeweler) / (to // me? / excuse // we / may / at / look / diamond / that / necklace?)
➡ _____

43 (Mrs. Loisel: / (whispering) / is / it / the / nearly / same. // must / we / it! / have)
➡ _____

44 (Mr. Loisel: / much / how / it? / is)
➡ _____

45 (Jeweler: / francs. / 40,000)
➡ _____

46 (Mr. Loisel: / about / how / 36,000?)
➡ _____

47 (Mrs. Loisel: / we / please, / need / really / it.)
➡ _____

48 (Jeweler: / then... / well, / it / 36,000 / is.)
➡ _____

49 (do / they / have / not / francs. / 36,000 // is / it / a / amount / huge / money. / of)
➡ _____

50 (they / so / it. / borrow)
➡ _____

32 Mrs. Loisel: 그렇지만 충분히 가치가 있었어요. 당신, 제가 대사님과 춤춘 것을 아나요?

33 Mr. Loisel: 당신이 즐거웠다니 기쁘지만 나 아침에 출근해야 해요.

34 Mrs. Loisel: (거울을 보며) 한 번만 더 볼게요. (충격을 받고) 목걸이… 목걸이가 없어졌어요!

35 Mr. Loisel: 뭐라고요? 무도회를 떠날 때 걸고 있었소?

36 Mrs. Loisel: 네, 분명히 하고 있었는데. 가서 찾아 줘요!

37 Loisel 씨는 길거리를 수색한다.

38 그는 무도회장으로 되돌아가 본 다음 경찰서에도 간다.

39 목걸이가 발견되지 않자, Loisel 씨는 Matilda에게 그녀의 친구에게 거짓말을 하라고 한다.

40 Matilda는 Forestier 부인에게 목걸이를 망가뜨려서 돌려주기 전에 고쳐 주겠다고 말한다.

41 부부는 비슷한 것을 찾을 시간이 필요하다.

장면 5

42 Mr. Loisel: (보석상에게) 실례합니다. 저 다이아몬드 목걸이 좀 볼 수 있을까요?

43 Mrs. Loisel: (속삭이며) 거의 똑같아요. 저걸 꼭 사야만 해요!

44 Mr. Loisel: 이거 얼마인가요?

45 Jewler: 40,000프랑이에요.

46 Mr. Loisel: 36,000에 안 될까요?

47 Mrs. Loisel: 부탁드려요. 우린 이게 정말 필요하거든요.

48 Jewler: 음, 그럼… 36,000프랑에 하시죠.

49 그들은 36,000프랑이 없다. 그건 큰돈이다.

50 그래서 그들은 돈을 빌린다.

51 (buying / after / necklace / the / Mrs. / for / Forestier, / couple / the / ten / spends / paying / years / the / back / money.)
➡ _____

52 (move / they / to / very / a / place. / small)
➡ _____

53 (Loisel / Mr. / a / gets / job. / second // washes / Matilda / for / clothes / others.)
➡ _____

54 (years / ten / hard / of / makes / work / old / Matilda / worn. / and)
➡ _____

55 (ten / after / years, / runs / Matilda / into / Forestier / Mrs. / the / on / street.)
➡ _____

Scene 6

56 (Mrs. Loisel: / Forestier, / Mrs. / morning. / good)
➡ _____

57 (Mrs. Forestier: / I / do / you? / know)
➡ _____

58 (Mrs. Loisel: / it / yes, / me, / is / Matilda.)
➡ _____

59 (Mrs. Forestier: / I / oh, / believe / cannot / it! // have / you / so / changed / much.)
➡ _____

60 (Mrs. Loisel: / have / I / some / had / times / difficult / of / because / you.)
➡ _____

61 (Mrs. Forestier: / of / because / me? // do / what / mean? / you)
➡ _____

62 (Mrs. Loisel: / you / do / the / remember / diamond / you / necklace / me? / lent // I / well, / it. / lost)
➡ _____

63 (Mrs. Forestier: / you / but / it / returned / to / me.)
➡ _____

64 (Mrs. Loisel: / I / no, / another / returned / just / one / it. / like // took / it / ten / us / to / years / for / pay / it.)
➡ _____

65 (Mrs. Forestier: / bought / you / diamond / a / necklace / replace / to / mine?)
➡ _____

66 (Mrs. Loisel: / yes.)
➡ _____

67 (Mrs. Forestier: / my / oh, / Matilda. / poor // didn't / why / come / you / me / to / and / me / tell / truth? / the // diamond / my / was / necklace / real. / not // was / it / only / worth / francs! / 500)
➡ _____
_____

51 부부는 Forestier 부인에게 돌려줄 목걸이를 산 후 돈을 갚는 데 십 년이 걸린다.

52 그들은 아주 작은 곳으로 이사한다.

53 Loisel 씨는 부업을 구한다. Matilda는 다른 사람들을 위해 빨래를 해 준다.

54 10년 동안의 고된 일로 Matilda는 늙고 지쳤다.

55 십 년 후, Matilda는 Forestier 부인과 거리에서 마주친다.

장면 6

56 Mrs. Loisel: Forestier 부인, 좋은 아침이에요.

57 Mrs. Forestier: 제가 당신을 아나요?

58 Mrs. Loisel: 네, 저예요, Matilda.

59 Mrs. Forestier: 오, 믿을 수 없어요! 당신 너무 많이 변했어요.

60 Mrs. Loisel: 저는 당신 때문에 힘든 시간을 보냈거든요.

61 Mrs. Forestier: 나 때문에요? 무슨 말이에요?

62 Mrs. Loisel: 당신이 빌려준 목걸이 기억하죠? 음, 제가 그걸 잃어버렸어요.

63 Mrs. Forestier: 그런데 그거 나한테 돌려줬잖아요.

64 Mrs. Loisel: 아니요, 나는 당신 것과 똑같은 다른 목걸이를 돌려줬어요. 그 값을 치르느라 십 년이 걸렸어요.

65 Mrs. Forestier: 내 것을 대체하려고 다이아몬드 목걸이를 샀다고요?

66 Mrs. Loisel: 네, 맞아요.

67 Mrs. Forestier: 오, 가엾은 Matilda. 왜 내게 와서 사실을 말하지 않았어요? 그 다이아몬드 목걸이는 진품이 아니었어요. 그건 단돈 오백 프랑짜리였다고요!

※ 다음 우리말을 영어로 쓰시오.

Scene 1

1 이곳은 파리의 Loisel 부부의 집이다.

➡ _____

2 그들의 집은 멋지지만, Loisel 부인은 행복하지 않다.

➡ _____

3 그녀는 젊고 예뻐서 더 화려하고 고급스러운 삶을 원한다.

➡ _____

4 Mrs. Loisel: (혼잣말로) 똑같은 낡은 집과 매일 같이 똑같은 지겨운 저녁 식사. 여기서 사는 게 너무 싫어!

➡ _____

5 Mr. Loisel: Matilda, 나 집에 왔어요, 내가 당신을 위해 무엇을 가져왔는지 봐요!

➡ _____

6 Mrs. Loisel: 뭐예요?.

➡ _____

7 Mr. Loisel: 대사님이 여는 무도회 초대장이에요. 이걸 얻기 위해 엄청난 노력을 했단 말이에요. 모두가 갖고 싶어 했거든요.

➡ _____

8 Mrs. Loisel: (울면서) 내가 그걸 왜 갖고 싶겠어요?

➡ _____

9 Mr. Loisel: Matilda. 무슨 문제 있어요?

➡ _____

10 Mrs. Loisel: 그런 고급스러운 파티에 입고 갈 옷이 하나도 없는걸요. 못가요.

➡ _____

11 Mr. Loisel: 슬퍼하지 말아요. 자, 여기 400프랑을 줄게요. 아름다운 새 드레스를 사요.

➡ _____

Scene 2

12 Mr. Loisel: (Matilda의 새 드레스를 보며) 멋져요, Matilda. 아름답군요!

➡ _____

13 Mrs. Loisel: 뭔가 제대로 맞지 않아요.

➡ _____

14 Mr. Loisel: 뭐가 안 맞을 수 있죠?

➡ _____

15 Mrs. Loisel: (울면서) 오, 안 돼. 어쩌면 좋아요?

➡ _____

16 Mr. Loisel: 뭐예요, 부인?

➡ _____

17 Mrs. Loisel: 이 아름다운 드레스에 어울릴 보석이 하나도 없어요. 내가 너무 불쌍해 보일 거예요!

➡ _____

18 Mr. Loisel: 당신 친구 Forestier 부인에게 부탁해 봐요. 그녀는 자신이 가진 보석을 분명히 빌려줄 거예요.

➡ _____

19 Mrs. Loisel: 그거 좋은 생각이에요! 지금 당장 가봐야겠어요.

➡ _____

Scene 3

20 Mrs. Forestier: Matilda, 이렇게 보게 되어서 정말 좋아요! 무슨 일로 왔어요?

➡ _____

21 Mrs. Loisel: 우리 부부가 대사의 무도회에 초대되었어요.

➡ _____

22 Mrs. Forestier: 대사의 무도회라! 멋지네요! 당신은 분명 신났겠군요.

➡ _____

23 Mrs. Loisel: 네… 그리고 아니기도 해요. 말하기 슬프지만 난 보석이 없어요. 부인에게서 좀 빌릴 수 있을까요?

➡ _____

24 Mrs. Forestier: 물론이죠! 여기 내 보석함이에요.

➡ _____

25 Mrs. Loisel: 와, 부인은 정말 멋진 보석들이 많네요!

➡ _____

26 Mrs. Forestier: 원하는 것 아무거나 골라요.

➡ _____

27 Mrs. Loisel: 이 다이아몬드 목걸이를 빌려줄 수 있나요? 이거 정말 아름다워요!

➡ _____

28 Mrs. Forestier: 당연하죠! 자, 이제 가서 무도회를 즐겨요.

➡ _____

Scene 4

29 Matilda는 완벽한 저녁을 보낸다. 무도회장에 있는 모든 사람들이 아름다운 그녀를 감탄하며 바라본다.

➡ _____

30 Loisel 부부는 아주 늦은 시간이 되어서야 무도회를 떠났다.

➡ _____

31 Mr. Loisel: 정말 길고 긴 밤이었어요. 정말 피곤해요.

➡ _____

32 Mrs. Loisel: 그렇지만 충분히 가치가 있었어요. 당신, 제가 대사님과 춤춘 것을 아나요?

➡ _____

33 Mr. Loisel: 당신이 즐거웠다니 기쁘지만 나 아침에 출근해야 해요.

➡ _____

34 Mrs. Loisel: (거울을 보며) 한 번만 더 볼게요. (충격을 받고) 목걸이… 목걸이가 없어졌어요!

➡ _____

35 Mr. Loisel: 뭐라고요? 무도회를 떠날 때 걸고 있었소?

➡ _____

36 Mrs. Loisel: 네, 분명히 하고 있었는데. 가서 찾아 줘요!

➡ _____

37 Loisel 씨는 길거리를 수색한다.

➡ _____

38 그는 무도회장으로 되돌아가 본 다음 경찰서에도 간다.

➡ _____

39 목걸이가 발견되지 않자, Loisel 씨는 Matilda에게 그녀의 친구에게 거짓말을 하라고 한다.

➡ _____

40 Matilda는 Forestier 부인에게 목걸이를 망가뜨려서 돌려주기 전에 고쳐 주겠다고 말한다.

➡ _____

41 부부는 비슷한 것을 찾을 시간이 필요하다.

➡ _____

Scene 5

42 Mr. Loisel: (보석상에게) 실례합니다. 저 다이아몬드 목걸이 좀 볼 수 있을까요?

➡ _____

43 Mrs. Loisel: (속삭이며) 거의 똑같아요. 저걸 꼭 사야만 해요!

➡ _____

44 Mr. Loisel: 이거 얼마인가요?

➡ _____

45 Jewler: 40,000프랑이에요.

➡ _____

46 Mr. Loisel: 36,000에 안 될까요?

➡ _____

47 Mrs. Loisel: 부탁드려요, 우린 이게 정말 필요하거든요.

➡ _____

48 Jewler: 음, 그럼… 36,000프랑에 하시죠.

➡ _____

49 그들은 36,000프랑이 없다. 그건 큰돈이다.

➡ _____

50 그래서 그들은 돈을 빌린다.

➡ _____

51 부부는 Forestier 부인에게 돌려줄 목걸이를 산 후 돈을 갚는 데 십 년이 걸린다.

➡ _____

52 그들은 아주 작은 곳으로 이사한다.

➡ _____

53 Loisel 씨는 부업을 구한다. Matilda는 다른 사람들을 위해 빨래를 해 준다.

➡ _____

54 10년 동안의 고된 일로 Matilda는 늙고 지쳤다.

➡ _____

55 십 년 후, Matilda는 Forestier 부인과 거리에서 마주친다.

➡ _____

Scene 6

56 Mrs. Loisel: Forestier 부인, 좋은 아침이에요.

➡ _____

57 Mrs. Forestier: 제가 당신을 아나요?

➡ _____

58 Mrs. Loisel: 네, 저예요, Matilda.

➡ _____

59 Mrs. Forestier: 오, 믿을 수 없어요! 당신 너무 많이 변했어요.

➡ _____

60 Mrs. Loisel: 저는 당신 때문에 힘든 시간을 보냈거든요.

➡ _____

61 Mrs. Forestier: 나 때문에요? 무슨 말이에요?

➡ _____

62 Mrs. Loisel: 당신이 빌려준 목걸이 기억하죠? 음, 제가 그걸 잃어버렸어요.

➡ _____

63 Mrs. Forestier: 그런데 그거 나한테 돌려줬잖아요.

➡ _____

64 Mrs. Loisel: 아니요, 나는 당신 것과 똑같은 다른 목걸이를 돌려줬어요. 그 값을 치르느라 십 년이 걸렸어요.

➡ _____

65 Mrs. Forestier: 내 것을 대체하려고 다이아몬드 목걸이를 샀다고요?

➡ _____

66 Mrs. Loisel: 네, 맞아요.

➡ _____

67 Mrs. Forestier: 오, 가엾은 Matilda. 왜 내게 와서 사실을 말하지 않았어요? 그 다이아몬드 목걸이는 진품이 아니었어요. 그건 단돈 오백 프랑짜리였다고요!

➡ _____

_____

영어 기출 문제집

적중100

정답 및 해설

시사 | 박준언

중 **3**

적중100

영어 기출 문제집

적중100

2학기

정답 및 해설

시사 | 박준언

중 3

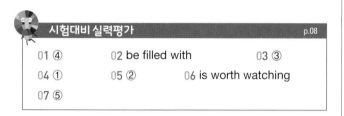

Have Fun with Art!

01 ④	02 be filled with	03 ③
04 ①	05 ②	06 is worth watching
07 ⑤		

01 • '대학은 우리가 구체적인 과목에 대한 지식을 배우는 곳이다.'
• '학생들은 주어진 주제로 찬반 토론을 벌였습니다.' '과목, 주
제'라는 의미를 가지는 단어는 'subject'가 맞다.

02 '흥미롭게도, 이 도서관은 종이로 된 책 대신에 전자책으로 가득
찰 것입니다.' <영영풀이> '비어 있는 공간에 어떤 물질을 넣다'
의 의미로 'be filled with'가 적절하다.

03 (A) '아테네가 민주주의의 발생지라는 것은 당연하다.'라는 의
미로 'no wonder'가 '~은 (별로) 놀랄 일이 아니다'의 의미로
적절하다. 'as well'은 '또한'의 의미이다. (B) '불가리아'라는
이름은 유럽에서 가장 오래된 나라 이름으로 여겨진다. '~로 여
겨지다'는 'be regarded as'가 적절하다.

04 '오랜 시간 동안 변화 없이 한 무리의 사람들 또는 사회에서 지
속되어 온 관습이나 행동 방식을 따르거나 속해 있는'의 의미로
'traditional(전통적인)'이 적절하다.

05 '어떤 식으로든 장식되지 않은; 아무것도 추가하지 않은'의 의미
로 'plain(평범한)'이 적절하다.

06 'be worth+동명사' 형태로 '~할 만한 가치가 있다'는 뜻이다.
'watch'를 동명사 'watching'으로 바꾸어야 한다.

07 ⑤의 '포함하다-제외하다'는 반의어 관계이고, 나머지는 유의어
관계이다. ①은 '만들다, 창조하다', ②는 '생생한, 활기찬', ③은
'흔한, 평범한', ④는 '운영하다'라는 의미이다.

01 (1) goods   (2) meaning   (3) amazing   (4) creative

02 plain, Plain, plain

03 (1) performances   (2) Back then

    (3) pay attention to   (4) break down

04 (1) boring, 지루한   (2) practice, 연습하다

    (3) cone, 원뿔

01 (1) 가격은 상품에 표시되어 있다. (2) 태극기에는 수많은 역
사와 의미가 담겨 있다. / '의미'라는 명사로 사용되기 때문에
'meaning'이 적절하다. (3) 말은 놀라운 동물입니다. 그들은 아

름답고, 강하며, 영리합니다. / 동사 'amaze'를 'animals'를 수
식하는 형용사로 '놀라운'의 의미를 가진 'amazing'으로 바꾸
어 준다. (4) 창의적인 사람은 흥미로운 아이디어를 생각하는 능
력을 가지고 있습니다. / 명사 'person'을 수식해야 하므로 동사
'create'의 형용사 'creative'가 적절하다.

02 • 우리 짐은 갈색이고 장식이 없습니다. • 평원과 사막이 수목이
울창한 해안지대의 산맥과 태평양 연안에까지 뻗쳐 있었다. • 그
들은 평범한 얼굴보다는 아름다운 얼굴을 보기를 좋아합니다. /
'plain'은 명사로 '평원, 평야', 형용사로 '보통의, 평범한, 수수한'
의 의미를 가지고 있다.

03 (1) performance: 공연 (2) back then: 그 당시에 (3) pay
attention to: ~에 주의를 기울이다 (4) break down: 부수다, 분
해하다

04 (1) 재미있거나 흥미롭지 않은 (2) 어떤 것에 숙련되기 위해 그
것을 규칙적으로 또는 반복적으로 하거나 연주하다 (3) 평평한,
둥근 또는 타원형의 기초와 점이 형성될 때까지 좁아지는 꼭대
기를 가진 형태

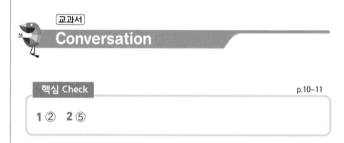

교과서 Conversation

1 ②   2 ⑤

교과서 대화문 익히기

1 T   2 F   3 F   4 T

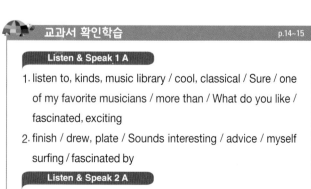

교과서 확인학습

Listen & Speak 1 A

1. listen to, kinds, music library / cool, classical / Sure / one
of my favorite musicians / more than / What do you like /
fascinated, exciting

2. finish / drew, plate / Sounds interesting / advice / myself
surfing / fascinated by

Listen & Speak 2 A

1. The other day, play / how did you like / main

characters, performance, fantastic / as well / a little
boring / should see / Only if, a lot of
2. how do you like / a lot / What do you like most /
learning different drawing skills, What / painting
skills, with / work, creative / practice a lot

Real Life Talk

didn't you / special / How did you like / fantastic / was
fascinated by / creativity / No wonder, one of the
greatest painters, What else / a gift shop, were printed
/ anything / How do you like / looks great on

Wrap Up 1

festival, didn't / performed / How did you like / special
guest, called / heard / performance / No wonder

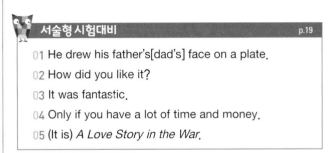

시험대비 기본평가   p.16

01 How do you like   02 ④   03 ③
04 ②

01 'How do you like ~?'는 '~은 어때?'라는 뜻으로 어떤 것에
   대해 만족하는지 아니면 불만족하는지 묻는 표현이다.
02 '~에 매료되다, ~에 관심이 있다'는 표현이 적절하다. ④번은 '~
   에 만족하다'라는 의미가 되려면 'be satisfied with'를 사용해
   야 한다.
03 빈칸 다음의 대답으로 보아, 빈칸에는 축제가 어땠는지 묻는 말
   이 적절하다.
04 'How do you like ~?'는 어떤 것에 대해 만족하는지 아니면
   불만족하는지 묻는 표현이다.

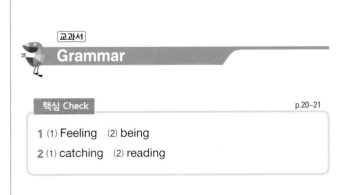

시험대비 실력평가   p.17~18

01 ②, ④   02 ①   03 ④   04 ②
05 She likes classical music.
06 ②   07 ④
08 how do you like your art class?
09 She thought it was very creative.
10 were fascinated by

01 빈칸 다음의 Andy가 한 말로 보아 만족이나 불만족을 묻는 표
   현이 적절하다.
02 Bora는 미술관에 가지 않았다.
03 며칠 전에 연극을 봤다는 말에 → (C) 그 연극이 어땠는지 묻고
   → (D) 주인공들이 좋았고, 그들의 연기가 훌륭했다는 말을 하
   고 → (A) 이야기도 또한 좋았는지 묻는 말에 → (B) 그것은
   약간 지루했다는 말을 하는 것이 자연스럽다.

04 '오페라의 유령'이라는 노래에 관한 대화 내용이므로 ②가 가장
   적절하다.
05 질문: Sandy는 어떤 종류의 음악을 좋아하는가?
06 'one of+복수 명사'이므로 'musicians'가 되어야 한다.
07 ④번은 '축제는 어땠니?'라는 물음에, B가 '그것에 관해 들어봤
   어. 가수가 유명해.'라고 말하는 것은 자연스럽지 못하다.
08 어떤 것에 대해 만족하는지 아니면 불만족하는지 묻는 표현인
   'How do you like ~?'를 이용한다.
09 질문: Claire는 Allen의 작품에 관해 어떻게 생각했는가?
10 '~에 매료되다'라는 의미로 동사 'fascinate'를 과거분사
   'fascinated'로 바꾸어 준다.

서술형 시험대비   p.19

01 He drew his father's[dad's] face on a plate.
02 How did you like it?
03 It was fantastic.
04 Only if you have a lot of time and money.
05 (It is) *A Love Story in the War.*

01 질문: Jim은 미술 과제로 무엇을 그렸는가? / Jim의 롤 모델
   은 그의 아버지이므로 my role model을 his father 또는 his
   dad로 바꾼다.
02 Andy의 대답 'It was fantastic!'으로 보아 빈칸에는 샤갈 전
   시회에 대해 어떤지 묻는 말이 오는 것이 자연스럽다.
03 질문: Andy는 Chagall 전시회를 어떻게 생각했는가?
04 '~해야만'의 의미로 'Only if+주어+동사 -'를 사용한다.
05 질문: 소년이 본 연극의 제목은 무엇인가?

교과서
Grammar

핵심 Check   p.20~21

1 (1) Feeling   (2) being
2 (1) catching   (2) reading

시험대비 기본평가   p.22

01 ⑤   02 ④   03 ②
04 (1) working   (2) paying attention to
   (3) crying

01 부사절을 분사구문으로 바꿀 때, 주어가 같으면 주어를 생략하고 분사를 쓴다.

02 'be worth V-ing'를 활용한다. worth에서 파생된 같은 의미의 다양한 표현도 익혀두는 것이 좋다.

03 두 문장을 하나로 만들어 보면 'As[While] Billy watched the emotional scenes, she was moved.'가 된다. ②가 분사구문으로 적절한 답이다. ① 과거분사 부적절 ③ 수동태형 부적절 ④ '접속사+주어'가 있을 때는 분사구문 불가능 ⑤ 의미상 '양보'의 접속사 Though 부적절

04 동명사의 관용적 표현들과 관련된 문제들이다. 'be worth V-ing'에서 동명사를 수동형으로 쓰지 않는 것에 유의한다.

01 ⑤	02 ①	03 ②	04 ④
05 ②	06 Changed → Changing		07 ③
08 ③	09 ③	10 ②	

11 Cartoons not being regarded as an art form at that time

12 Wanting everyone to enjoy his art   13 ①

14 ④   15 ③   16 ⑤

01 'be worth'는 V-ing(동명사)를 받는다. 'be worthy of V-ing[being p.p.]'로도 표현 가능하며, 'It is worth paying attention to ~' 형태로도 쓸 수 있다.

02 동명사의 관용적 표현에 관련된 문제이다. 'can't help'는 V-ing(동명사)를 받는다. 'can't but V(동사원형)', 'can't help but V(동사원형)'로도 표현 가능하며, 'have no choice but to V' 형태로도 쓸 수 있다.

03 부사절을 써서 영작하면, 'When people saw familiar images in art exhibitions, they found them refreshing.'이 된다. ②가 부사절을 분사구문으로 적절히 전환했다.

04 부사절을 써서 영작하면, 'Although pop art looks plain, it is filled with meaning.'이 된다. ④는 looks를 looking으로 적절하게 표현한 분사구문 앞에 접속사 Although를 덧붙였다.

05 각 문장을 해석하면, (1) '세계 역사와 문화 발전에 관한 책들은 읽을 가치가 있다.', (2) '그 집은 최소 50만 달러의 가치가 있음에 틀림없다.'이다, 명사나 동명사를 목적어로 받으며, '가치'의 의미를 가진 것은 worth이다.

06 '흔한 물건들을 놀라운 예술로 변모시키면서'(능동의 분사 구문)이므로 Changing으로 고치는 것이 적절하다.

07 ③의 knowing은 '현재분사'로 쓰였다. 'Brian은 그의 친구들이 참여하지 않을 것을 알고 그 계획을 포기했다.' 나머지는 모두 동명사이다. ① '그 작가의 책들은 알 가치가 없다.' ② '미래의 우리의 삶이 어떻게 될지 알 수 없다.' ④ '주변에 한국인들이 거의 살지 않기 때문에, 우리는 그녀를 알 수밖에 없다.' ⑤ '그녀의 문제가 불안감에서 왔다는 것을 알아도 소용없었다.'

08 내용상 Though의 역접 관계가 아닌, As 또는 Because 등과 같은 이유를 나타내는 접속사가 적절하다.

09 'be worth'는 V-ing(동명사)를 받는다. 'be worthy of V-ing[being p.p.]'로도 표현 가능하며, 'It is worth seeing and collecting the works ~' 형태도 가능하다.

10 <보기>는 '약간 평범하고 흔해보일지라도, 팝 아트는 수많은 의미로 가득 차 있다.'는 뜻으로, ② '11년간 마드리드에서 살아왔지만, Angella는 여전히 스페인어를 잘 못한다.'는 문장과 함께 '양보'의 의미인 '역접'으로 사용되었다. ① '조건' ③ '이유' ④ '이유' 또는 '시간' ⑤ '이유'

11 주어진 우리말의 부사절을 표현하면, 'Though cartoons were not regarded as an art form at that time,'이고, 종속절과 주절의 주어가 달라, 독립분사구문으로 Cartoons를 문두에 쓰고, 분사구문 앞에 부정어 not을 쓰면 'Cartoons not being regarded as ~' 형태가 된다.

12 주어진 우리말의 부사절을 표현하면, 'As he wanted everyone to enjoy his art,'이고, 접속사와 주어를 생략하고 Wanting으로 표현하면, 적절한 답이 된다.

13 모든 문장이 'be worth V-ing'이다. 일반적으로 '주어가 V할 가치가 있다'는 뜻인데, 주어는 V-ing의 대상이다. ①은 '팝 아트는 주목할 만한 가치가 있다.'라는 문장인데, pay attention은 전치사 to가 동반되어야 대상을 취할 수 있다. 그러므로 문미에 to를 추가하는 것이 적절하다.

14 동명사의 관용적 표현들이 사용된 문장들이다. ④는 '엎질러진 우유를 보며 우는 것은 소용없다.'라는 문장으로 'It is no use V-ing'일 때, crying이 맞는 표현이고, 'of no use'가 쓰였을 때는 'to V'를 쓰는 것이 적절하다.

15 'be worth'는 V-ing(동명사)를 취한다. 'be worthy of V-ing(being p.p.)'와 뜻이 같고, 'It is worth V-ing', 또는 'It is worth while V-ing(또는 to V)' 형태로도 표현 가능하다.

16 '내가 가장 좋아하는 시인이 쓰는 글은 세 번 읽을 가치가 있다.'라는 문장이다. ⑤는 '시인이 쓰는 글' 또는 '시인에 의해 쓰여진 글'이 아닌, '내가 가장 좋아하는 시'이므로 주어의 성격이 다르고, be worth 뒤의 동명사도 수동형으로 썼기 때문에 어법상 틀린 문장이다.

01 (1) visiting (2) checking (3) seeing (4) buying
   (5) laughing (6) laugh (7) laugh (8) to laugh
   (9) advertising (10) knowing (11) to know
   (12) carrying (13) prepare (14) preparing

02 (1) Being able to turn common objects into amazing art
   (2) Believing that art should be easy, pop artists broke
   (3) There not being any friends left around here
   (4) Finding his subjects in magazines and stores

03 (1) Gloria's mom couldn't help drinking the sour beverage to save her.
   (2) The expensive TV set was worth paying for.
   (3) It was no use fixing the ceiling unless the water problem is resolved.
   (4) Those men were busy preparing for the awards ceremony.
   (5) Pop art is worth paying attention to.

04 (1) As Andy Warhol wanted to show that art is something you see every day, he made many copies of his works.
   (2) Using daily images in a creative way, you can make a work of art for everyone.
   (3) When seeing familiar images in art exhibitions, people found them refreshing.
   (4) Using common images and everyday items, pop art looks plain.
   (5) Though[Although] looking plain, pop art is filled with meaning that art should be easy to understand. 또는 Looking plain, pop art is filled with meaning that art should be easy to understand.
   (6) Wanting everyone to enjoy his art, a pop artist set[sets] up his works in outdoor places.
   (7) Though cartoons were not regarded as an art form at that time, Roy Lichtenstein used them in making his works.

01 동명사의 관용적 표현에 관련된 문제이다. 다양한 동명사의 관용적 표현들을 알아두어야 한다. 'be worth V-ing = be worthy of V-ing[being p.p.] = It be worth V-ing'이며, 'can't help V-ing = can't but V(동사원형) = can't help but V(동사원형) = have no choice but to V'이다. 'It is no use V-ing = It is useless[of no use] to V', 'There is no V-ing = It is impossible to V'이다.

02 분사구문으로 시작하는 문장들이다. 각 분사구문의 원래의 부사

절을 쓰면, (1) 'As they were able to turn common objects into amazing art', (2) 'Since[As] they believed that art should be easy', (3) 'As[Since, Because] there were not any friends left around here', (4) 'While he was finding his subjects in magazines and stores'이다. (3)은 주절과 종속절의 주어가 다르므로 유도부사 there를 문두에 쓴 독립분사구문이다.

03 'be worth V-ing'를 포함한 다양한 동명사의 관용적 표현들과 같은 의미의 다른 표현들을 많이 숙지하는 것이 좋다. 문제의 조건에서 가장 짧은 형태의 문장을 영작하는 것이 조건이므로, (3)의 경우 of no use를 useless로 바꾸면 단어들의 수가 더 줄어들겠지만 동명사를 받을 수 없음에 유의한다.

04 어법상 어색한 것을 '한 단어'로 고치거나 이동하라고 언급한 문제의 조건에 유의한다. (1) 접속사 As가 있으므로, wanting을 wanted로 고친다. 동사가 과거 시제임에 유의. 주절과 종속절의 주어가 같으므로 As만을 생략하는 것은 불가능하다. (2) Use → Using (3) seen → seeing (4) Used → Using (5) 구조는 접속사가 있는 분사구문 형태이나, 의미상 Because가 어색하다. 역접의 접속사 Though 또는 Although로 바꾸든가, 생략하는 것이 적절하다. (6) 분사구문이 양쪽에 나온 형태이다. 주절에 setting을 동사 set로 바꾸는 것이 적절하다. (현재시제로 보고 sets라고 해도 무방하다.) (7) 부사절과 종속절의 주어가 다른데, 독립분사구문 형태를 쓰려면 접속사가 없어야 한다. 그러나 Though를 생략해도, being not의 순서가 좋지 않아서, 차라리 being을 동사 were로 고쳐 부사절을 만든다.

교과서
Reading

확인문제   p.28

1 T   2 T   3 F   4 F

확인문제   p.29

1 T   2 F   3 T   4 F

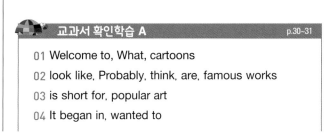

교과서 확인학습 A   p.30~31

01 Welcome to, What, cartoons
02 look like, Probably, think, are, famous works
03 is short for, popular art
04 It began in, wanted to

05 Instead of, traditional, turned, to

06 used, from, advertising

07 familiar images, them refreshing

08 become truly popular

09 that, too, to understand

10 By using, changed that thought

11 Using, looks plain. In other words, artistic

12 worth paying attention to, is filled with

13 famous pop artists

14 famous for, ability, able to change, into amazing

15 is called, found, subjects in

16 is made up

17 Another work shows, made, copies

18 copies of his works, to show that, you see

19 another, who made, fun

20 sculptures of everyday items

21 In the beginning, created, made of, soft materials

22 For example, cloth to make, huge sculptures, such as

23 Wanting, to enjoy, set up, outdoor

24 ran, inside, to sell, were fun goods

25 used, in his works, were, painted, lively colors

26 included, were, regarded as

27 However, differently, himself, Why, they not

28 broke down, between, and, by adding

29 believed, should be, Anyone, create, enjoy

30 creating, pop art

31 By using, in, make, for, the most important lesson

교과서 확인학습 B
p.32~33

1 Welcome to the Pop Art Exhibition! What do you see? Paintings of soup cans? Big cartoons?

2 Do they look like art works? Probably not, but think again. They are all famous works of pop art.

3 Pop is short for popular. So pop art means popular art, or art for people.

4 It began in the 1950s in America. Pop artists at that time wanted to create something fun and easy.

5 Instead of difficult traditional art works, they turned their eyes to popular culture.

6 They used images from TV, comic books, magazines, and advertising.

7 When people saw familiar images in art exhibitions, they found them refreshing.

8 Since then, pop art has become truly popular.

9 People thought that art was too difficult to understand.

10 By using daily images and bright colors, pop artists changed that thought.

11 Using common images, pop art looks plain. In other words, it doesn't look artistic.

12 But it is still worth paying attention to. Although it looks plain, it is filled with meaning.

13 Let's learn about some famous pop artists.

14 They became famous for their special artistic ability. They were able to change common objects into amazing art.

15 Andy Warhol is called the King of Pop Art. He found his subjects in magazines and stores.

16 One of his famous works is made up of pictures of Marilyn Monroe, the American actor.

17 Another work shows cans of soup. He made many copies of these works.

18 Why did he make copies of his works? He wanted to show that art is something you see every day.

19 Claes Oldenburg is another pop artist who made art fun.

20 He made sculptures of everyday items, such as a hamburger, cookies, and a brush.

21 In the beginning, he created soft sculptures. They were made of plastic, paper, and other soft materials.

22 For example, he used cloth to make toilets. Later, he made huge sculptures of daily items, such as an ice cream cone.

23 Wanting everyone to enjoy his art, he set up his works in outdoor places.

24 He also ran a store inside his studio to sell his works. For him, artistic works were fun goods for people.

25 Roy Lichtenstein used cartoons in his works. They were large and painted in lively colors.

26 He even included speech balloons in his paintings. Back then, cartoons were not regarded as an art form.

27 However, Roy Lichtenstein thought differently. He asked himself, 'Why are they not?'

28 Then Roy Lichtenstein broke down the wall between high art and popular culture by adding cartoons to art.

29 Pop artists believed art should be easy. Anyone can create and enjoy art.

30 How about creating a work of pop art today?

31 By using daily images in a creative way, you can make a work of art for everyone. This is the most important lesson from pop art.

시험대비 실력평가
p.34~37

01 cartoon

02 They used images from TV, comic books, magazines, and advertising.

03 ③ 04 ④

05 He is called the King of Pop Art. 06 ④

07 ②

08 He wanted everyone to enjoy his art.

09 ③ 10 [C]–[B]–[A] 11 ③

12 ②

13 Pop artists believed art should be easy.

14 ④ 15 ⑤ 16 It began in 1950s.

17 ②, ④ 18 ④ 19 ④

20 He found his subjects in magazines and stores.

21 ③

22 He created soft sculptures in the beginning.

23 ④ 24 ⑤ 25 cartoons

26 He added cartoons to art. 27 ⑤

01 신문이나 잡지에 나오는 익살스러운 그림 혹은 연속적인 그림은 '만화(cartoon)'이다.

02 팝 아트 작가들은 텔레비전, 만화책, 잡지 및 광고에 나오는 이미지들을 사용했다.

03 사람들은 예술이 너무 어려워서 이해할 수 없는 것으로 생각했었다.

04 Andy Warhol이 자신의 작품들의 사본을 많이 만들었다고 말한 후 사본을 많이 만든 이유를 묻는 말이 들어가는 것이 자연스럽다.

05 그는 팝 아트의 왕이라 불린다.

06 글쓴이는 팝 아트는 여전히 주목할 만한 가치가 있다고 하였다.

07 Claes Oldenburg는 부드러운 조각품을 만들었다고 말하며 재료를 언급하고, 변기를 만들기 위해 천을 사용했다고 좀 더 자세히 말하고 있으므로 예시를 이끄는 For example이 가장 적절하다.

08 Claes Oldenburg는 모든 사람이 그의 작품을 보고 즐기기를 원했다.

09 Claes Oldenburg는 일상적인 물품들의 조각을 만든 예술가로, 초기에 플라스틱이나 종이, 그리고 다른 부드러운 재료들로 조각품을 만들었고, 나중에는 일상 물품의 거대한 조각품을 만들었다

고 하였으므로 ③번이 그의 작품에 해당한다고 볼 수 있다.

10 Roy Lichtenstein은 작품에 만화를 사용했는데 [C] 당시에 만화는 예술 형식으로 여겨지지 않음 [B] 하지만 Roy Lichtenstein는 다르게 생각하고 만화가 왜 예술로 간주되지 않는지 의문을 품음 [A] 만화를 예술에 첨가함으로써 Roy Lichtenstein는 순수 예술과 대중문화 사이의 벽을 허물음

11 be regarded as: ~라고 여겨지다

12 글의 내용은 누구나 예술 작품을 만들고 즐길 수 있다는 의미이다. 따라서 ②번이 가장 적절하다.

13 팝 아티스트들은 예술이 쉬워야 한다고 믿었다.

14 (A)는 '작품'이라는 의미로 쓰이고 있다. ① 일하다 ② 작동하다 ③ 일, 직장 ④ 작품 ⑤ 효과가 있다

15 팝 아티스트들은 일상적인 이미지를 사용하였다.

16 팝 아트는 1950년대에 시작됐다.

17 팝 아트는 일상적인 이미지와 밝은 색을 사용하여 만들어지며, 팝 아트의 의미는 사람들을 위한 예술이라고 하였으므로 ②, ④번이 가장 적절하다.

18 Andy Warhol의 작품들로 미루어 보아 흔한 대상을 놀라운 예술로 바꾸었다고 말하는 것이 자연스럽다. 따라서 ④번을 common이라고 쓰는 것이 적절하다.

19 수프 통조림으로 팝 아트 작품을 만든 예시가 나와 있다.

20 Andy Warhol은 잡지와 상점에서 주제를 찾았다.

21 예시로 이어지고 있는 것은 일상적인 물품들이다.

22 Claes Oldenburg는 초기에 부드러운 조각품을 만들었다고 하였다.

23 Claes Oldenburg는 변기를 만들기 위해서 천을 사용했다.

24 밑줄 친 (A)는 목적어로 사용된 재귀대명사이다. ⑤번은 강조 용법으로 사용되었다.

25 만화를 가리키는 말이다.

26 Roy Lichtenstein은 만화를 예술에 첨가하였다.

27 ⑤ Roy Lichtenstein은 순수 예술과 대중문화 사이의 벽을 허물었다. built → broke down

서술형 시험대비
p.38~39

01 It means popular art or art for people.

02 popular culture, difficult traditional art works

03 미술 전시회에서 친숙한 이미지를 보고 사람들이 그것들이 신선하다는 걸 알게 되었을 때

04 By using daily images and bright colors, pop artists changed people's thought toward art.

05 It's because it uses common images.

06 They were able to change common objects into amazing art.

01 팝 아트란 대중 예술 또는 사람들을 위한 예술이라는 뜻이다.

02 1950년대에, 미국의 팝 아티스트들은 전통 예술 작품보다는 대중문화에 흥미가 있었다.

03 앞 문장의 상황을 가리키는 말이다.

04 팝 아티스트들은 일상적인 이미지와 밝은 색을 씀으로써 예술을 향한 사람들의 생각을 바꾸었다.

05 팝 아트가 평범해 보이는 이유는 흔한 이미지를 사용하기 때문이다.

06 몇 명의 유명한 팝 아트 작가들은 흔한 대상을 놀라운 예술로 바꿀 수 있었다.

07 Andy Warhol의 유명한 작품 중 하나는 미국 배우인 Marilyn Monroe의 사진으로 구성되어 있다. 그 작품 외에도, 그는 쉽게 구할 수 있는 흔한 대상을 사용하여 예술작품을 만들었다.

08 '예술'이 '재미있는' 것이므로 목적격보어로 형용사 fun을 쓰는 것에 유의한다. 여기에서 쓰인 동사 make는 5형식 동사이다. '또 다른 하나'를 말할 때는 'another'를 사용하며, '예술을 재미있게 만들었던'이 '작가'를 수식하므로 관계대명사를 활용하여 문장을 완성한다.

09 원인을 나타내는 분사구문이므로 Because 혹은 As를 써서 같은 의미의 절을 완성할 수 있다.

10 부드러운 조각품을 만들기 위해서 Claes Oldenburg는 플라스틱, 종이, 그리고 다른 부드러운 재료들을 사용하였다.

11 Roy Lichtenstein의 그림은 생기 넘치는 색들로 그려졌다고 하였다.

12 '왜 만화는 예술로 간주되지 않을까?'라는 의미이다.

13 앞 문장을 가리키는 말이다.

영역별 핵심문제

p.41~45

01 unfamiliar　02 ④　　03 ②　　04 ⑤

05 be made up of　　06 ④　　07 ③

08 How do you like your food?

09 ③　　10 ④　　11 ④

12 I have an interest in your drawing.　13 ③

14 ④

15 (1) works were[are] worth seeing

(2) was so busy watching the show that

16 ⑤　　　17 ③　　　18 ④

19 Pop is short for popular. 20 ③

21 People thought that art was too difficult to understand.　　22 ④　　　23 ⑤

24 He included speech balloons in his paintings.

25 ③

26 The writer liked the story of the movie.

27 ⑤

01 반의어 관계이다. 활기 없는-활기 넘치는 : 친숙한-낯선

02 (A) 나는 텐트를 설치할 괜찮은 장소를 알고 있어. (B) 그들은 나에게 떠나라고 했다. 다시 말해서, 나는 해고되었다.

03 독창적이고 특이한 아이디어를 생산하거나 사용하는 능력

04 전통적 스타일이나 형식, 또는 오랜 기간에 걸쳐 개발된 방법에 기초하고, 지속적인 가치가 있는 것으로 여겨지는

05 be made up of: ~로 구성되다

06 ④번은 '나는 에릭 칼 특별전이라는 전시회에 갔습니다.'라는 말로 'exhibition'은 '전시회'라는 의미이다.

07 '대중음악의 신나는 리듬이 정말 좋아.'라는 대답으로 보아 ③번이 가장 적절하다.

08 어떤 것에 대해 만족하는지 아니면 불만족하는지 묻는 표현인 'How do you like ~?'를 사용한다.

09 주어진 문장이 '너는 미술관에서 또 무엇을 봤니?'라는 뜻이므로 ③번에 들어가는 것이 자연스럽다.

10 Andy가 왜 티셔츠를 구입했는지는 대화에서 언급되어 있지 않다.

11 이것은 내가 가장 소중히 여기는 거라는 말에 → (D) '그건 머그컵이 아니니?'라고 묻고 → (B) '응'이라고 답을 하며 7년 동안 사용해 왔다는 말에 → (A) 놀라움을 표현하고 → (C) 머그컵이 어떤지 물어보고 → (E) 좋아 보인다는 말을 하는 것이 자연스럽다.

12 관심을 표현하는 말로 'be fascinated by', 'have an interest in', 'be interested in', 'be into' 등을 사용하여 표현할 수 있다.

13 ③의 meeting은 현재분사이다. 나머지는 모두 동명사로 사용되었다.

14 There가 있는 '독립분사구문'이다. 해석을 해보면 '비록 만화가 예술에 속할 수 없다는 오해가 있었지만, 몇몇 팝 아티스트들은 만화를 사용함으로써 훌륭한 예술작품들을 만들었다.'라는 내용이다. 부사구와 주절이 역접 관계이므로, '조건'이나 '이유'가 아닌, '양보'임을 알 수 있다. '양보'의 접속사 Though가 쓰인 ④

가 적절하다.

15 동명사의 관용적 용법을 활용하는 문제이다. (1) '세계적으로 유명한 팝 아티스트 Florentijn Hofman의 작품들은 볼 만한 가치가 있었다.'는 문장이다. works가 복수이므로 'was → were'로 고쳐 넣고, 동명사 visiting을 활용한다. were 대신 are를 써도 좋다. (2) '민준이는 쇼를 보느라 너무 바빠서 전화를 받을 수 없었다.'는 문장이다. be busy V-ing를 활용 'watch → watching'으로 고쳐 단어를 배열한다.

16 분사구문의 부정은 not을 분사 앞에 쓴다. 접속사를 쓸 경우, 접속사 뒤에 주어가 오면 분사구문은 쓸 수 없으므로 ①은 안 된다. ②, ④는 내용이 반대가 되고, ③은 not의 위치가 틀렸다.

17 '작년에 뉴욕에서 열린 Andy Warhol의 작품전은 방문할만한 가치가 있었다.'라는 문장이다. '주어+be worth V-ing'에서 주어가 V-ing의 의미상 목적어가 될 때, V-ing 뒤에 추가로 목적어를 쓰지 않는다.

18 모두 팝 아티스트들을 지칭하지만 ④번은 일반 사람들을 가리키는 말이다.

19 'pop'은 'popular(대중적인)'의 줄임말이라고 하였다.

20 팝 아트 작가들은 재미있고 쉬운 것을 만들고 싶어 했다고 하였으므로 ③번이 글의 내용과 일치한다.

21 사람들은 예술이 너무 어려워서 이해할 수 없는 것으로 생각했었다.

22 그 당시에 만화는 예술 형식으로 여겨지지 않았지만 Roy Lichtenstein는 다르게 생각하였다고 말하고 그의 남다른 생각이 이어지는 것이 자연스럽다.

23 일상적인 이미지를 창의적인 방식으로 사용함으로써 모든 사람을 위한 예술 작품을 만들 수 있고 이것이 바로 팝 아트의 가장 중요한 교훈이라고 하였다.

24 Roy Lichtenstein은 자신의 작품에 말풍선을 넣었다.

25 관계대명사 that은 계속적 용법으로 쓰일 수 없다. 따라서 who라고 쓰는 것이 적절하다.

26 글쓴이는 영화의 이야기가 마음에 들었다고 하였다.

27 영화를 보는 데 얼마만큼의 시간을 소요했는지는 위 글을 읽고 답할 수 없다.

단원별 예상문제
p.46~49

01 popularity 02 ④ 03 ① 04 ②
05 Was the story good as well? 06 boring
07 ⑤
08 I prefer pop music to classical music.
09 ④ 10 ④ 11 ① 12 ②
13 ②, ④ 14 ①, ④ 15 ③
16 They are famous for their special artistic ability.
17 ⑤ 18 ⑤

19 He set up his works in outdoor places.
20 ③
21 magazines and stores, sculptor, cartoons

01 '형용사-명사' 관계다. 창의적인-창의성 : 인기 있는-인기

02 어떤 사람이 특정한 상황에서 당신이 무엇을 해야 하는지 또는 어떻게 행동해야 하는지에 대해 당신에게 제안하는 의견

03 만족이나 불만족에 대해 묻는 표현으로 'How do you like ~?'를 사용한다. 'What'을 'How'로 바꾸어야 한다.

04 Bora가 'Andy 야, 너 미술관에 갔었지, 그렇지 않니?'라고 묻는 것으로 보아 미술관에서 이야기하고 있지 않다는 것을 알 수 있다.

05 'as well'은 문장 끝에서 '또한'의 의미로 사용된다.

06 '재미있거나 흥미롭지 않은'의 의미로 'boring'이 적절하다.

07 음악 도서관에서 얼마나 많은 종류의 음악을 들을 수 있는지는 언급되어 있지 않다.

08 'like A more than B'는 'B보다 A를 더 좋아한다'라는 의미로 'prefer A to B'로 바꾸어 쓸 수 있다.

09 주어와 목적어가 동일할 때는 재귀대명사를 사용한다. 'me'를 'myself'로 고친다.

10 종속절이 주절보다 앞선 시제이므로, 완료분사구문이 필요하며 준동사의 부정은 not을 앞에 쓰는 것이므로, Not having been invited로 시작하는 ④가 적절하다.

11 동명사의 관용적 용법 중 'be worth V-ing'에서 동명사는 능동형으로 써야 한다. 단, be worthy of V-ing는 수동형 동명사 being p.p.가 좋다.

12 동명사의 관용적 용법 중 'can't help V-ing = can't but V(동사원형) = can't help but V(동사원형) = have no choice but to V'와 관련된 문제이다. ② crying → cry

13 'be worth V-ing = be worthy of V-ing[being p.p.] = It be worth V-ing' ② to buy → buying ④ 'worth of being visited'에서 worth → worthy 또는 of being visited → visiting

14 앞선 문장과 같은 맥락의 문장을 연결하는 것이므로 '다시 말해서' 혹은 '즉'이라는 의미의 연결어가 들어가는 것이 적절하다.

15 밑줄 친 (B)는 '주제'라는 의미로 쓰였다. ① 과목 ② 피실험자 ③ 주제 ④ ~될 수 있는 ⑤ 주어

16 그들은 특별한 예술적인 능력으로 유명해졌다고 하였다.

17 Andy Warhol의 또 다른 작품으로 수프 통조림들을 보여준다고 하였으므로 ⑤번이 옳다.

18 Claes Oldenburg는 일상적인 물품들을 주제로 삼았다. 따라서 ⑤번은 적절하지 않다.

19 Claes Oldenburg는 자신의 작품을 실외에 설치했다.

20 답변은 팝 아트에 관한 설명이 주를 이루고 있으므로 ③번이 가장 적절하다.

21 Andy Warhol은 잡지와 상점에서 주제를 찾는 것을 좋아했고, Claes Oldenburg는 훌륭한 조각가였으며, Roy Lichtenstein은 그의 그림에 만화를 사용한 것으로 유명했다.

서술형 실전문제 p.50~51

01 (A) fascinated   (B) painters   (C) were
02 (2) I was fascinated by its design.
03 (1) Though other people laughing at cartoons,
　　(2) Using common everyday objects and images,
04 the island in the East Sea, is worth protecting
05 There is no knowing how long the
06 (1) It having rained heavily the day before,
　　(2) Strictly speaking,
　　(3) Exhausted from a series of overtime work,
　　(4) Finding the kitty the old lady had lost,
07 Pop art began in America in 1950s.
08 Pop artists at that time wanted to create something fun and easy.
09 familiar images
10 (A) touching   (B) Watching   (C) moved
11 He went to his friend's house to watch a movie.

01 (A): '~에 매료되다'라는 의미로 'be fascinated by'를 사용한다. (B) 'one of the 최상급+복수 명사'로 단수인 'painter'를 복수명사로 바꾸어 준다. (C) 주어가 복수 명사인 'Famous works'이므로 복수 동사 'were'가 적절하다.

02 밝은 색깔이 아니라 디자인에 매료되었다고 소개하고 있다.

03 분사구문을 배열하는 문제이다. 각각 (1) '양보', (2) '이유'의 부사절을 분사구문으로 만든 것이다.

04 동명사의 관용적 용법 'be worth V-ing'를 활용한 문장이다.

05 동명사의 관용적 용법 'there is no V-ing'를 활용한 문장이다. 'V하는 것은 불가능하다.'라는 뜻이다.

06 (1) 원래의 부사절에서 비인칭 주어 it이 있으므로, 'It having rained'와 같이 독립분사구문 형태로 표현하는 것이 적절하다. (2) 비인칭 독립분사구문이므로, 문 두에 People을 쓸 필요가 없다. (3) 수동이므로 Exhausting을 Exhausted로 고쳐야 한다. (4) 능동이므로 Found → Finding이 적절하다.

07 팝 아트는 1950년대에 미국에서 시작되었다.

08 -thing으로 끝나는 부정대명사는 형용사가 뒤에서 수식하는 것에 유의하여 답한다.

09 사람들이 전시회에서 본 친숙한 이미지들을 가리키는 말이다.

10 감정을 유발할 때에는 현재분사를, 감정을 느낄 때에는 과거분사

를 쓰며, (B)는 주절의 주어가 분사구문의 주어와 같으므로 생략되었다. 따라서 내가 감동적인 장면을 본 것이므로 현재분사를 쓰는 것이 적절하다. (A)에 moving, (C)에 touched라고 써도 좋다.

11 글쓴이는 영화를 보러 친구 집에 갔다고 하였다.

창의사고력 서술형 문제 p.52

|모범답안|

01 ① Playing the guitar, she composed a song.
　② Holding something in her mouth, she is lying on the bed.
　③ Walking in the bird park, he talked to the parrot.
　④ Watching TV, he didn't hear the phone ringing.

02 Last Saturday / the concert hall / a musical / *You and Me* / my favorite actor was in it / the songs and dances / about a girl who invited her best friends to her birthday party / about their friendship / The main character was / sang many beautiful songs / fantastic / Singing along to the songs during the performance, excited

01 단어들을 적절히 조합하여 내용과 어법에 맞게 영작한 답이면 된다.

단원별 모의고사 p.53~57

01 ⑤　　02 familiar　　03 ③　　04 ④
05 ③　　06 ④　　07 ④
08 I drew myself surfing in the sea.　09 ②
10 I couldn't take my eyes off it.　11 ②
12 ③　　13 ③　　14 ④
15 (1) used everyday items
　(2) If they watch the pop artist making
　(3) she got interested in the film
　(4) Though she was unhealthy
16 ②　　17 (C)-(B)-(A)
18 But it is still worth paying attention to.　19 ④
20 ③
21 It's because he wanted to show that art is something you see every day.
22 other → another　　23 ④　　24 ⑤
25 He ran a store inside his studio to sell his works.

01 ⑤번은 'original(원본)'에 관한 설명이다. 'copy(복사본)'의 영어 설명은 'something that has been made to be

exactly like something else(다른 것과 똑같도록 만들어진 것)'이다.

02 유의어 관계이다. 조언, 충고 : 친숙한

03 '누군가 또는 어떤 것 대신에'의 의미로 'instead of'가 적절하다.

04 ④번은 책을 읽었다는 말에 대해 B가 그것을 혼자 시청했다고 답하는 것은 어색하다.

05 앞의 말에 동의할 때 사용하는 말로 '놀랄 일이 아니다.'라는 'No wonder.'가 적절하다.

06 (d)의 'them'은 'things like umbrellas, cups, and backpacks'를 가리킨다.

07 미술 과제에 관한 대화이므로 ④번이 가장 적절하다.

08 주어와 목적어가 동일할 때 재귀대명사를 목적어 자리에 사용한다.

09 대화의 흐름상 연극이 어땠는지 묻는 말이 적절하다.

10 'can't take A off B': 'B에서 A를 떼지 못하다'

11 ①, ④는 주절과 종속절의 주어가 다르므로, 분사구문의 주어를 쓴다. 날씨를 나타내는 '독립분사구문'은 주어 It을 쓴다. ③, ⑤는 반대로 주절과 종속절의 주어가 같으므로, 주어를 분사구문 앞에 쓸 필요가 없다. ① Drawing → My sister drawing ③ The structures observed → Observed ④ Not snowing → It not snowing ⑤ Maggy memorizing → Memorizing

12 동명사의 관용적 용법 'be worth V-ing'와 관련된 문제이다. 'be worthy of V-ing[being p.p.] = It be worth V-ing' 모두 같은 의미이며, ③과 같이 be worth가 있을 때는 능동형으로 visiting을 쓴다. be worthy of가 있을 때는 being visited 가능하다.

13 동명사의 관용적 용법 중 'can't help V-ing'와 관련된 문제이다. 'can't but V(동사원형) = can't help but V(동사원형) = have no choice but to V' 모두 같은 의미를 나타낸다. ③ crying → cry

14 ④ 부사절로 고치면, 'As there were no coins left'이다. 주어가 다르므로, 유도부사 there는 생략할 수 없다. 'Being no coins left → There being no coins left'가 적절하다.

15 각 문장의 분사구문은, (1) '양태'(그가 일상의 물건들을 사용하듯이) (2) '조건'(그 팝 아티스트가 그림을 제작하는 것을 본다면) (3) '이유'(그 영화에 흥미를 느껴서) (4) '양보'(건강하지 않은데도 불구하고) 등이다. 각각에 맞는 접속사와 대명사를 활용하는 것에 유의한다.

16 위 글은 팝 아트의 의미와 팝 아트가 어떻게 발전하게 되었는지

에 관한 글이다. 따라서 ②번이 가장 적절하다.

17 (C)의 그 당시는 1950년대를 의미한다. 전통 예술 작품 대신 대중문화로 눈을 돌렸다고 하였으므로 (B)에서 대중문화에 해당하는 텔레비전, 만화책 등이 제시가 되고, 사람들의 반응이 나온 후 (A)에서 그때부터 팝 아트는 정말 유명해졌다고 말하는 순서가 가장 자연스럽다.

18 be worth Ving: V할 가치가 있다, pay attention to: ~에 주목하다

19 팝 아트는 평범해 보일지라도 의미로 가득 차 있다고 하였다.

20 위 글은 Andy Warhol의 작품에 관한 설명이므로 Marilyn Monroe가 그 당시에 미국에서 가장 사랑받았던 배우이며 이른 나이에 죽었다는 문장은 글의 흐름상 어색하다.

21 Andy Warhol은 예술은 매일 보는 것임을 보여 주고 싶었기 때문에 자신의 작품 사본을 많이 만들었다.

22 other+복수명사, another+단수명사

23 빈칸 뒤에 other soft materials의 예가 오므로 ④ '예를 들면'이 적절하다.

24 (A)는 to부정사의 부사적 용법 중 목적(~하기 위해서)으로 쓰였다. ①, ③ 형용사적 용법 ② 진주어 ④ 동사의 목적어 ⑤ 부사적 용법 중 목적

25 Claes Oldenburg는 작품 판매를 위해 작업실 안에 상점을 운영하였다.

You Can Do It, Too

시험대비 실력평가
p.62

01 ③	02 afford	03 ②	04 ③
05 ⑤	06 ⑤		

01 주어진 단어는 반의어 관계에 있다. 따라서 ③번이 적절하다. ①, ④ 매우 귀중한, ② 귀중한, ⑤ 돈이 드는, 비싼

02 '어떤 것을 할 수 있다'는 '~할 여유가 되다(afford)'이다.

03 ① 그 연설자는 논의를 위한 몇 가지 진지한 주제를 제안함으로써 끝냈다. by Ving: V함으로써 ② 그는 사람들의 삶을 더 편안하게 만들어줄 새로운 방법을 생각해 냈다. hit on: ~을 생각해 내다 ③ 당신의 노력 덕분에, 우리는 이 프로젝트를 가까스로 끝낼 수 있었습니다. ④ 매주 그들은 노래를 만들고 함께 연주하기 위해서 만난다. ⑤ 당신은 그녀가 그것을 공짜로 해주리라고 기대할 순 없어요.

04 ① 우리가 이 물건들을 집안에 두는 것은 쓸모가 없어. useless: 쓸모없는 ② 정부는 이민을 통제하려고 시도한다. control: 조종하다, 통제하다 ③ 사람들은 쓰레기로 환경을 오염시킨다. pollute: 오염시키다 ④ 필터가 물속의 모든 오염물질들을 제거하는 것은 아니다. remove: 제거하다, 없애다 ⑤ 우리는 그가 살아 있는지 죽었는지 모른다. whether: ~인지 아닌지

05 thanks to: ~ 덕분에, look forward to ~ing: ~하기를 고대하다

06 모두 '동사-명사'의 관계이지만 attempt는 동사와 명사의 형태가 같으며 attemption이라는 단어는 존재하지 않는다.

서술형 시험대비
p.63

01 (1) coin　(2) control　(3) business　(4) cost
　　(5) for free
02 fair
03 (1) pollution　(2) limitation　(3) beautiful
04 (1) We can collect things like shoes and clothes that people no longer need.
　　(2) The entrance fee is $10 for adults.
　　(3) Sam rides a bike not to pollute the air.
05 (A) to　(B) by　(C) for
06 success

01 (1) 나는 중국 동전 하나를 가지고 있어. (2) 너는 너의 소비를 통

제하는 방법을 배울 필요가 있어. (3) 그녀는 언젠가 자신의 사업체를 가지길 원해요. (4) 나는 그것이 전부 5달러만 들었다는 것을 믿을 수 없어요. (5) 사람들이 무료로 일을 해 주길 기대할 수는 없다.

02 fair는 '박람회'라는 의미 외에도 형용사로 '공정한, 타당한'이라는 의미를 갖는다.

03 (1), (2) 동사에 어미 '-tion'을 붙여서 명사가 된 것이다. pollute의 명사형은 pollution으로 만들 수 있다. (3) 명사에 어미 '-ful'을 붙여서 형용사가 된 것으로, beauty의 형용사형은 beautiful이다.

04 각각 (1) '모으다' (2) '요금' (3) '오염시키다'라는 말이 빠져 있으므로 collect, fee, pollute를 써서 문장을 완성하다.

05 (A) look forward to Ving: ~을 고대하다, think to oneself: 마음속으로 생각하다 (B) by Ving: V함으로써, by oneself: 혼자서, 혼자 힘으로 (C) pay for: ~을 지불하다, blame A for B: A를 B라는 이유로 비난하다

06 '목적 또는 목표의 성취'는 '성공'이다.

교과서 Conversation

핵심 Check
p.64~65

1 Is it possible for her to control them, too?
2 she can drive the truck
3 I wish I lived in a big city.

교과서 대화문 익히기

Check(√) True or False
p.66

1 F　2 T　3 F　4 F

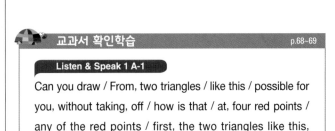

교과서 확인학습
p.68~69

Listen & Speak 1 A-1

Can you draw / From, two triangles / like this / possible for you, without taking, off / how is that / at, four red points / any of the red points / first, the two triangles like this, triangles first / I get it

Listen & Speak 1 A-2

looking for, for / How old / five years old / to recommend / so / isn't it, that looks like, love it / for me to take, off / ake it off, put it back / wonderful, take it

Listen & Speak 2 A-1

you have been late for, wrong / wake up early, can't / wake you up / does, right away. I wish, could / An AI robot / that could make sure, give me breakfast / great

Listen & Talk 2 A-2

planning to visit / going to do there / spend most of my time, because, swimming pool / Can, swim well / I wish I could, have fun with, instead / What is that / It's, go inside, walk on / must be

Real Life Talk

are, doing / drawing, my favorite superhero / great / could read people's minds / for her to control / if she wants to / cool / have any favorite superheroes / could fly like him / even breathe in / can do anything

Wrap Up 1

What are you doing / flying / Are, good at / right now, practicing hard / As you know, run / for you to deliver orders / isn't, it will be possible in / That, be great

시험대비 기본평가   p.70

01 (A) Is it possible for you   (B) Is it possible for you
02 ③   03 ③
04 I could have an AI robot.

01 달이나 태양까지 날아가는 것이 가능한지 묻는 말이므로 가주어 it과 의미상의 주어 'for+목적격'을 적절히 이용하여 문장을 완성할 수 있다.

02 가능을 묻는 표현인 'Is it possible for ~ to V?'는 'Is it likely that 주어 can V ~?'로 바꾸어 쓸 수 있다.

03 Wendy는 계속해서 지각을 하고 있으므로, 일찍 일어나고 싶지만 그렇게 안 된다는 의미가 자연스럽다.

04 이어지는 대화 내용으로 보아 Wendy는 인공지능 로봇이 있으면 좋겠다는 바람의 말을 했음을 알 수 있다.

시험대비 실력평가   p.71~72

01 ③   02 ④   03 (D)–(A)–(C)–(E)–(B)
04 ②
05 It is because she can't wake up early.

06 I wish I could invent a time machine.   07 ⑤
08 ②   09 ③   10 ③   11 ④
12 Can you deliver orders with your drone?

01 가능성을 묻는 말에 긍정으로 답하고 있으므로 ③번이 적절하다.

02 종이에서 연필을 떼지 않고 그림을 그릴 때 빨간 점 중에서 아무 점에서 시작해도 된다고 하였다.

03 일찍 일어나고 싶지만 그럴 수 없다는 말에 (D) 엄마가 깨워주시지 않느냐고 묻고 (A) 엄마가 깨워주시지만 자신이 바로 일어나지 않는다며, 인공지능 로봇이 있으면 좋겠다는 소망을 말함 (C) 인공지능 로봇이냐고 되묻자 (E) 그것을 원하는 이유를 설명하고 (B) 이 말에 좋은 생각이라고 답하는 순서가 자연스럽다.

04 ⓐ는 '최근에'라는 말이다. 따라서 ②번이 적절하다.

05 Wendy는 일찍 일어날 수 없어서 지각한 것이다.

06 이어지는 말로 보아 A는 타임머신을 발명하고 싶다는 소망을 나타냈음을 알 수 있다.

07 스마트폰을 가지고 있다면 친구들에게 메시지를 보낼 것이라는 내용이 가장 적절하다.

08 밑줄 친 부분은 가능성을 묻는 말이다. 따라서 ②번이 적절하다.

09 모자를 더 큰 것으로 교환할 수 있냐고 묻는 말에 긍정으로 대답하고 그럴 수 있을 것 같지 않다는 말이 이어지고 있으므로 어색한 대화이다.

10 hardly는 '거의 ~하지 않는'이라는 의미의 부사이다. hard는 형용사와 부사의 형태가 같으므로 'I'm practicing hard'라고 쓰는 것이 적절하다.

11 여자는 Tom이 드론으로 샌드위치 배달을 할 수 있는지 묻고 있으므로 ④번이 글의 내용과 일치한다.

12 가능을 묻는 말이므로 'Can you ~?'로 표현할 수 있다.

서술형 시험대비   p.73

01 Is it possible for you to draw this on the paper?
02 to draw it without taking your pencil off the paper
03 (1) 원을 먼저 그리고 그 다음에 삼각형 두 개를 그린다.
    (2) 삼각형 두 개를 먼저 그리고 원을 그린다.
04 I wish I could keep calm and pass the time.
    I wish I could create a shelter.
    I wish I could wait for help.
    I wish I could find food.
05 It is possible for Dr. Rebecca to read people's

minds and control them.
06 Bora's favorite superhero is Sky X.

01 가능성을 묻는 표현이므로 'Is it possible ~?'로 물을 수 있으며 to부정사의 의미상 주체로 'for+목적격'을 이용할 수 있다.

02 연필을 떼지 않고 그것을 그리는 것을 의미하는 말이다.

03 원을 먼저 그린 후 삼각형 두 개를 그리거나, 삼각형 두 개를 먼저 그린 후 원을 그리는 두 가지 방법이 제시되어 있다.

04 바람이나 소원을 말할 때 'I wish'를 써서 나타낼 수 있다. 해석: 내가 차분함을 유지하며 시간을 보낼 수 있으면 좋겠어. 내가 피신처를 만들 수 있다면 좋겠어. 내가 도움을 기다릴 수 있으면 좋겠어. 내가 음식을 찾을 수 있으면 좋겠어.

05 닥터 레베카는 사람들의 마음을 읽고 조종하는 것이 가능하다.

06 보라가 가장 좋아하는 슈퍼 영웅은 스카이 X이다.

교과서
Grammar

핵심 Check   p.74~75

1 (1) lived   (2) were[was]   (3) could
2 (1) if   (2) whether

시험대비 기본평가   p.76

01 (1) can → could   (2) has → had
   (3) work → worked   (4) may might
02 ④   03 ④   04 ③

01 모든 문장이 가정법이라는 조건이 주어졌고, 구조는 '가정법 과거' 형태이므로, 조건절의 동사를 과거시제로, 주절의 조동사도 과거형이 적절하다.

02 세 문장 모두 '~인지 아닌지' 여부를 나타내는 명사절로서 접속사가 들어가는 자리이다. 문두 또는 바로 다음에 or not이 오는 경우 if는 불가능하므로, whether가 적절하다.

03 I wish 가정법 문장이다. 주절에 '동사의 과거형' 또는 '조동사 과거+동사원형'의 구조가 오는 답을 선택하는 것이 적절하다.

04 명사절 접속사 if를 찾는 문제이다. ①, ②, ④, ⑤는 모두 조건의 부사절 접속사로 쓰였다.

시험대비 실력평가   p.77~79

01 ④   02 ⑤   03 ③
04 I don't know if you can help me.
05 I wish I were the President of the United States.
06 David asked me whether there was a bathroom
07 If I were the girl, I would give up.   08 ④
09 ②   10 ③   11 ②   12 ⑤
13 ②   14 ④   15 ⑤   16 ④

01 'I wish 가정법 과거' 문장에서 주절에는 '동사의 과거형' 또는 '조동사의 과거+동사원형'이 온다. will make → would make 또는 made가 적절하다.

02 ⑤ 가정법 문장이라면 can을 could로, 직설법 문장이라면 pushed를 push로 쓰는 것이 적절하다.

03 간접의문문을 이끄는 명사절 접속사 if는 whether와 달리 'or not'을 바로 붙여서 쓸 수 없다.

04 의문사가 없을 때 간접의문문은 if로 시작한다. 주절의 I don't know에 맞는 if 이하를 적절히 배열한다.

05 'I wish 가정법' 문장에서 '~라면 좋을 텐데'라는 뜻을 나타낼 때, 주절에는 'were'가 온다.

06 의문사가 없을 때 간접의문문은 whether로 시작한다. 주절의 어순은 'whether+주어+동사'인데, 유도부사 there가 오는 문장은 'there+동사+주어'가 바른 어순이 된다.

07 가정법 과거 시제의 문장이다. If절에 과거동사 were를 쓰고, 주절에 조동사의 과거형 would를 쓴다.

08 ④만 조건의 부사절 접속사이며, 나머지는 모두 간접의문문을 이끄는 명사절 접속사이다.

09 ②를 제외한 나머지는 모두 가정법의 주절에서 쓰이는 조동사이다. ②의 could는 can의 과거시제이다.

10 ③만 조건의 부사절을 이끄는 접속사이다. 나머지는 모두 간접의문문의 명사절을 이끈다.

11 '~가 없다면'이라는 가정법 표현은 'If there were no ~'로 나타내며, without 또는 'If it were not for ~'로 대체할 수 있고, 이 경우 if를 생략해서 'were it not for ~'로 표현 가능하다. ② is → were

12 'I wish 가정법 과거'는 직설법 현재 시제의 반대 의미이므로, 직설법의 couldn't make를 can't make로 고치는 것이 적절하다.

13 ① 직설법으로는, 'Vanessa의 동생이 휴대폰이 없어서 한 대 갖고 싶어 한다.'는 내용인데, 가정법으로는 '갖고자 한다면 얻을 수 있다'가 되어 의미가 다르다. ③ 직설법과 같은 뜻이 되려면, 가정법 과거완료 시제가 필요하다. ④ 가정법과 직설법에 모두

not이 있어서 뜻이 반대된다. ⑤ 직설법으로 '비가 억수같이 와서 가족 모두가 집에 있었다.'는 내용인데, 가정법은 '비가 억수같이 온다면, 모든 가족이 집에 머무르지 않을 텐데.'가 되어 어색하다.

14 의문사가 없는 의문문의 간접의문문을 이끄는 명사절 접속사 if/whether를 적절히 사용하여, 동사 ask의 목적어 자리에 쓰고, 내용상 can의 과거시제 could를 활용한 ④가 정답이다. ① '소녀가 로봇 손을 만들어 달라고 부탁했다.'가 되어, 우리말과 일치하지 않는다. ②, ③ 접속사 that을 쓰는 경우는 '~인지'라는 의사를 묻기보다 '~이라는 것'이라는 사실과 관계될 때 쓴다. ⑤ 접속사 whether는 올바르지만, could make는 '만들 수 있는지'라는 뜻이고, made는 '만들었는지'가 되어 뜻이 같지 않다.

15 ① can → could ② can → could ③ will → would ④ is → could be

16 (A)와 (C)는 'I wish 가정법' 형태이다. 주절에 동사 또는 조동사의 과거형을 쓴다. (B)는 가정법 과거 문장이고, 주절에 조동사의 과거형 would가 적절하다.

01 (1) I wish I could pay the school fees for many poor girls to
  (2) I wish the small holes in the corn cobs could filter
  (3) I wish the girl I met at a science fair had
  (4) the villagers helped me, I could build

02 (1) I asked myself that night if I could solve the problem of the polluted water.
  (2) Tony wasn't sure if[whether] he could make it but he decided to try.
  (3) Whether Jane will follow her heart or not is important in her life.
  (4) Even her closest friends doubted whether she could do something for the girls in Africa.
  (5) Most people in my town are wondering if it will rain next week.
  (6) Sean couldn't decide whether to reject the job offer or not.
  (7) The researchers want to know if[whether] my filtering system can clean up all the lakes not only in my village but also in other areas.

03 (1) But for   (2) If it were not for
  (3) Were it not for
  (4) As there is her invention, the town does

04 (1) Matilda wondered if she could borrow something from Mrs. Forestier.
  (2) Matilda asked Mrs. Forestier if she would lend her that diamond necklace.

05 wish the poor girls in Africa could go

06 wish I sang well like

07 Ask Mike if Susan speaks Korean.

08 Gloria was not sure if her baby was hungry or sad.

01 'I wish 가정법', 'If절의 가정법 과거' 등에 유의하여, 주어진 단어들을 적절히 배열한다.

03 '그녀의 발명이 없다면, 마을은 수질 오염 문제로 고통을 겪을 텐데.'라는 내용으로 직설법으로 표현하면, '그녀의 발명이 있어서, 마을은 수질 오염 문제로 고통을 겪지 않는다.'가 된다. 가정법 과거를 전제로, 'Without = But for = If it were not for = Were it not for'를 기억해 두는 것이 좋다.

04 간접의문문을 이끄는 명사절 접속사 if를 사용하여, 대화의 내용 (1) 'Matilda는 Mrs. Forestier로부터 뭔가를 빌릴 수 있을지 궁금해 했다.'와, (2) 'Matilda는 Mrs. Forestier에게 그 다이아몬드 목걸이를 빌려줄 것인지 물어봤다.'에 알맞게 바른 어순으로 배열한다.

05 '아프리카의 가난한 소녀들이 학교에 갈 수 없기 때문에, 나는 안타깝게 느껴졌다.'라는 직설법 문장을 가정법으로 표현하면, '아프리카의 가난한 소녀들이 학교에 갈 수 있으면 좋을 텐데.'가 된다. 'I wish 가정법'을 활용하되, can't가 could로 바뀌는 것에 유의하여 영작한다.

06 '가수인 나의 할아버지처럼 노래를 잘하면 좋을 텐데.'라는 의미가 되도록 I wish 가정법에 동사 과거형 sang을 활용한다.

07 Susan이 3인칭 단수임에 유의하여, 적절하게 영작한다. 간접의문문의 어순은 'if+주어+동사'임에 유의한다.

08 '확신할 수 없었다'는 내용으로 보아, 과거시제와 not이 쓰였음을 알 수 있다. 시제에 유의하여, 적절히 영작한다.

교과서
Reading

확인문제   p.82
1 T   2 T   3 F

확인문제   p.83
1 F   2 T   3 F

01 who change, too young to be

02 will meet, to make

03 when, came across, at, fair

04 robotic, that, open, close

05 surprised that, had cost her

06 wish, had, to myself

07 a much cheaper, better

08 failures, by using, was able to, for, of

09 to share, for, with others for free

10 take what I have done, something useful

11 No one, change, build, by working

12 can't, go to school, could go

13 had this thought, realized that, afford

14 if I could do something, had

15 asked, buy me a sewing machine

16 bought me one, how to make

17 ten headbands, them

18 raised enough money, stop

19 a business, who, go

20 to the success, fees for, like, to go to school

21 pay for, textbooks, uniforms, amazing

22 advice, is, do something, a need, act

23 small, taking, lives

24 As, living, often found that, seriously polluted

25 how I could solve, hit on, to use

26 Useless, were, in

27 the small holes, could filter dirty matter, polluted

28 picked, washed them, placed, in a bowl of

29 After a while, it, much clearer

30 using, that, collected from, filtering

31 removed, the dirty matter

32 filtering system, clean up, not only, but also

1 Who are the people who change the world? Do you think you are too young to be one of these people?

2 In the following stories you will meet three teenagers who used their ideas to make the world a better place.

3 One day, when I was fourteen, I came across a little girl at a science fair.

4 She had a robotic hand that could only open and close.

5 I was surprised that the hand had cost her 80,000 dollars!

6 'I wish she had a better robotic hand,' I thought to myself.

7 With that, I started to make a much cheaper and better robotic hand.

8 After many failures, finally, by using 3D printing technology, I was able to make a useful robotic hand for the price of only 300 dollars.

9 I decided to share the designs and software for my 3D robotic hand with others for free.

10 Maybe someone can take what I have done and do something useful with it.

11 No one person can change the world, but we can build a better world by working together.

12 'Why can't many girls in Africa go to school as I can? I wish they could go to school, too.'

13 I had this thought when I was twelve. I realized that their families couldn't afford it.

14 I wondered if I could do something for those girls. Then I had an idea.

15 For my birthday, I asked my parents to buy me a sewing machine.

16 They bought me one, and I learned how to make headbands for myself.

17 I created ten headbands and sold them at my school.

18 Soon, I raised enough money to send one girl in Africa to school. I couldn't stop there.

19 I started a business to help girls in Africa who couldn't go to school.

20 Thanks to the success of my business, I can pay the school fees for many poor girls in countries like Kenya and Uganda to go to school.

21 I also pay for their textbooks, uniforms, and pencils. Isn't it amazing?

22 My advice to you is to just do something. When you see a need, act.

23 Start small, taking little steps. Your warm heart can change lives.

24 As a young girl living in the countryside in India, I often found that the water around us was seriously polluted.

25 I wondered how I could solve this problem. Then I hit on the idea to use corn cobs.

26 Useless corn cobs were everywhere in my village.

27 I thought that the small holes in the corn cobs could filter dirty matter out of the polluted water.

28 One day, I picked up some dried cobs along the

road, washed them, and placed them in a bowl of dirty water.

29 After a while, I checked the water, and it looked much clearer.

30 Then, using corn cobs that I had collected from farmers, I built a filtering system.

31 My system removed 70 to 80 percent of the dirty matter from the water.

32 I hope my filtering system can clean up all the lakes not only in my village but also in other areas.

시험대비 실력평가
p.88~91

01 the people who change the world 02 ②

03 ④ 04 ⑤

05 He used 3D printing technology. 06 ③

07 Because their families couldn't afford it.

08 afford 09 ⑤

10 Useless Corn Cobs as Useful Water Filters

11 ④ 12 ④ 13 ⑤ 14 ②

15 It's because the girl's robotic hand had cost her 80,000 dollars. 16 ④ 17 to go

18 ② 19 (D)—(B)—(A)—(C) 20 ⑤

21 ④

22 The small holes in the corn cobs could filter dirty matter out of the polluted water.

23 ③

24 주변에 있는 물이 심각하게 오염되어 있는 것

25 ③

01 세상을 바꾸는 사람들을 의미하는 말이다.

02 세상을 더 나은 곳으로 만들기 위해 자신들의 아이디어를 사용한 세 명의 십대들을 만날 것이라고 하였으므로 ②번이 가장 적절하다.

03 글쓴이는 자신이 발명한 로봇 손 디자인을 다른 사람들과 무료로 공유했다고 하였다. 따라서 혼자 세상을 바꿀 수는 없지만 함께 일하면서 더 나은 세상을 만들 수 있다고 말하는 것이 자연스럽다.

04 많은 실패 뒤에 마침내 300달러짜리의 유용한 로봇 손을 만들었고 이 로봇 손의 디자인과 소프트웨어를 다른 사람들과 무료로 공유하기로 결심했다는 것이 적절하다.

05 글쓴이는 3D 프린트 기술을 이용하여 로봇 손을 만들었다.

06 ③번 뒤에 나오는 대명사 They와 one이 가리키는 것은 주어진 문장의 my parents와 a sewing machine이다.

07 아프리카의 많은 소녀들이 학교를 갈 수 없는 이유는 그들의 가족

들에게 금전적 여유가 없기 때문이었다.

08 무언가에 돈을 지불할 만큼 충분한 돈을 가지고 있는 것은 밑줄 친 '~할 여유가 되다(afford)'이다.

09 글쓴이는 머리띠를 10개 만들어 학교에서 팔았다고 하였다.

10 위 글은 쓸모없는 옥수수 속대로 유용한 물 여과 장치를 만든 이야기이다.

11 과거동사의 병렬이므로 placed라고 쓰는 것이 적절하다.

12 Lalita는 농부들로부터 옥수수 속대를 모았다.

13 빈칸에는 비교급을 강조하는 부사(구) much, still, even, far, a lot이 들어갈 수 있다. very는 원급을 강조한다.

14 글쓴이가 만든 3D 로봇 손의 디자인과 소프트웨어를 의미한다.

15 소녀가 로봇 손에 8만 달러를 지불했다는 말에 글쓴이는 놀랐다고 하였다.

16 Easton은 겨우 접었다 펴지기만 하는 로봇 손에 8만 달러를 지불한 소녀를 돕고 싶은 마음에 로봇 손을 만들기 시작했다.

17 for many poor girls in countries like Kenya and Uganda라는 의미상의 주어가 존재하므로 to부정사형으로 쓰는 것이 적절하다.

18 이어지는 내용과 글 전체의 내용은 행동을 하라는 것이다. 따라서 act가 가장 적절하다.

19 (D) 아프리카 소녀들이 학교에 갈 수 없는 이유가 궁금함 (B) 가족들에게 금전적인 여유가 없기 때문임을 알게 되고, 소녀들을 돕기 위한 아이디어를 떠올려 부모님에게 재봉틀을 사달라고 말함 (A) 재봉틀로 머리띠를 만들어 한 명의 소녀를 도움 (C) 여러 소녀들을 돕기 위해 사업을 시작함

20 Mary는 아프리카의 가난한 소녀들을 돕기 위해 머리띠를 만들어 파는 아이디어를 떠올렸다.

21 주어진 문장의 the water는 글쓴이가 옥수수 속대를 넣은 더러운 물을 지칭한다. 따라서 ④번에 들어가는 것이 가장 적절하다.

22 옥수수 속대의 작은 구멍들이 더러운 물질을 오염된 물 밖으로 걸러 낼 수 있었다.

23 (A)는 '~로(서)'라는 의미로 쓰인 전치사이다. ① ~이기 때문에 ② ~처럼, ~같이 ③ ~로(서) ④ ~하는 대로 ⑤ ~하다시피

24 Lalita가 살고 있는 주변의 물이 심각하게 오염된 문제를 의미한다.

25 옥수수 속대에는 좁은 하나의 구멍이 아니라 작은 구멍들이 있다.

서술형 시험대비
p.92~93

01 He met her at a science fair.

02 소녀가 더 나은 로봇 손을 가질 수 있으면 좋겠다는 생각

03 He was able to make a useful robotic hand for the price of only 300 dollars.

04 We can build a better world by working together.

05 cheap → expensive, foot → hand, sell → share

06 She asked her parents to buy her a sewing machine.

07 the school fees, their textbooks, uniforms, and pencils, to go to school

08 My advice to you is to just do something.

09 clearer

10 She lived in the countryside in India.

11 She decided to use corn cobs to filter water.

12 Her system removed 70 to 80 percent of the dirty matter from the water.

13 (1) If I were an inventor, I could make cheaper and more convenient robotic arms.

(2) If Jake weren't wearing the skirt, he would not look like a school girl.

(3) If there were a pen, I could write or draw a thing right now.

(4) If Henry had the violin, it would be easy for him to perform the songs.

14 whether to study in England or Canada 15 ①

16 ②　　　17 ⑤　　　18 ④　　　19 ②

20 Do you think you are so young that you can't be one of these people?

21 She paid 80,000 dollars for it.　　　22 ⑤

23 ⑤

24 The small holes in the corn cobs could filter dirty matter out of the polluted water.

25 ③　　　　26 ⑤

27 I don't know if you can help me, but I hope you can.

01 Easton은 한 과학 박람회에서 어린 소녀를 만났다고 하였다.

02 앞 문장에서 Easton이 마음속으로 생각했던 것을 가리키는 말이다.

03 Easton은 3D 프린트 기술을 사용해서 단 300달러짜리의 유용한 로봇 손을 만들 수 있었다.

04 혼자 세상을 바꿀 수는 없지만, 함께 일하면서 더 나은 세상을 만들 수 있다고 하였다.

05 소녀는 비싼 로봇 손을 가지고 있었고 Easton은 자신의 디자인과 소프트웨어를 무료로 공유하기로 결심하였다.

06 Mary는 부모님께 자신의 생일에 재봉틀을 사 달라고 부탁드렸다.

07 사업의 성공 덕분에 Mary는 케냐와 우간다 같은 나라에 있는 많은 가난한 소녀들이 학교에 갈 수 있게 수업료를 지불할 뿐만 아니라 교과서와 교복, 연필을 위한 비용도 지불할 수 있다.

08 조언은 셀 수 없으므로 단수 취급하며, '무엇이든 하라는 것'이므로 to just do something이라고 쓰는 것이 적절하다.

09 물이 더 깨끗해져 있었다고 말하는 것이 자연스러우며, 비교급 강조 부사 much가 있으므로 clearer라고 쓰는 것이 가장 적절하다.

10 그녀는 인도의 시골에 살고 있었다.

11 물을 걸러내기 위해 Lalita는 옥수수 속대를 사용하기로 결정하였다.

12 Lalita의 여과장치는 물에서 70~80%의 더러운 물질을 제거하였다.

영역별 핵심문제　　　p.95~99

01 ⑤　　　02 ④　　　03 ②　　　04 ④

05 ④　　　06 ⑤

07 Is it possible for you to swim well?

08 Because his uncle has a big swimming pool.

09 ③　　　10 ④　　　11 ③　　　12 ④

01 모두 '동사-명사'의 관계이지만, ⑤번은 ment라는 단어는 존재하지 않는다. ① 참가하다 – 참가 ② 느끼다 – 느낌 ③ 빛나다 – 빛 ④ (정보를) 알아내다, 알리다 – 정보 ⑤ mention: 언급

02 '~할 여유가 있다'는 의미로 쓰이는 단어는 afford이다.

03 hit on: ~을 생각해 내다, come across: 우연히 마주치다, By Ving: V함으로써

04 <보기>에서 쓰인 fair는 '박람회'라는 의미이다. ①, ③ 공정한 ② 상당한, 제법 큰 ④ 박람회 ⑤ (날씨가) 맑은

05 대답에서 '너는 원하는 무엇이든 될 수 있다'고 답하는 것으로 보아, 말하는 이의 가능성에 관해 묻는 말이 들어가는 것이 적절하다.

06 사막에서 살 수 있으면 좋겠다는 말에 동감을 표현하면서 아주 위험해 보인다고 말하고 있으므로 어색하다.

07 가능성을 묻는 말이므로 'Is it possible ~?'을 이용할 수 있으며 to부정사의 의미상의 주체로 'for+목적격'을 명시해야 한다.

08 Mike의 삼촌이 큰 수영장을 가지고 계셔서 Mike는 대부분의 시간을 삼촌 집에서 보낼 것이라고 하였다.

09 수영을 잘 못하기 때문에 물 위를 걷는 공을 가지고 놀 것이라고 말하는 것이 자연스럽다.

10 Mike가 삼촌의 집에서 얼마나 머무를지는 대화에 나와 있지 않다.

11 동사 asked의 목적어가 되는 명사절로서, 뒤의 or not과 호응하는 것은 whether뿐이다. if를 사용해야 할 경우에는 or not을 문미로 보내면 가능하다. ① if or not 불가능 ② however는 명사절을 이끌 수 없다. ④ could I는 어순 부적절 ⑤

succeeded → could succeed

12 주어 역할의 명사절을 이끄는 접속사가 필요하다. Though, As 등은 부사절을 이끌기 때문에 부적절하고, 내용상 '학생이 A를 받을지 여부는 중요하지 않다'는 것이므로, whether가 맞다. if 는 문두에서 명사절을 이끌 수 없다.

13 직설법 현재 문장을 가정법으로 바꿀 때, 종속절에는 동사의 과거형을, 주절에는 '조동사의 과거형+동사원형'을 쓰는 것에 유의하여, 문장을 전환한다. (4)에서 'it is not easy'는 가정법으로 바꿀 때, 조동사 would를 활용하고, 내용이 반대가 되므로 'it would be easy'로 바뀌는 것에 유의한다.

14 윤호는 영국에서 공부할지 캐나다에서 공부할지 결정할 수 없었다.

15 ①은 조건문의 부사절을 만드는 접속사로 쓰였다. 나머지는 모두 의문사가 없는 간접의문문을 이끄는 명사절 접속사이다.

16 우리말은 'I wish 가정법'에 해당한다. 조동사의 과거형 could 를 활용하되, 어순과 내용에 유의한다.

17 우리말은 '가정법 과거시제'를 의미한다. 가정법 과거에 맞게 동사의 과거형을 쓰되, 이 예문의 경우 비인칭 주어 it과 동사의 과거형 rained를 사용하는 것에 유의한다.

18 <보기>의 if는 가정법 과거 시제의 부사절을 이끄는 종속접속사로 쓰였다. ④를 제외하면, 모두 간접의문문의 명사절을 이끄는 접속사로서 '~인지'라는 뜻이다.

19 (B) 과학 박람회에서 로봇 손을 가진 소녀를 만남 (A) 소녀가 더 나은 로봇 손을 가지길 바라며 로봇 손을 만들기 시작하고, 3D 프린트 기술을 사용하여 만듦 (C) 자신이 만든 로봇 손의 디자인과 소프트웨어를 다른 사람들과 무료로 공유하기로 결심함

20 '너무 ~해서 …할 수 없는'이라는 의미로 쓰이는 'too ~ to V'는 'so ~ that S can't V'와 같다.

21 소녀는 로봇 손에 8만 달러를 지불했다고 하였다.

22 Easton은 3D 로봇 손의 디자인과 소프트웨어를 다른 사람들과 무료로 공유하기로 결심하였다. 따라서 ⑤번이 글의 내용과 일치한다.

23 ⑤번에 이어지는 글쓴이의 여과장치는 주어진 문장의 a filtering system을 의미한다.

24 Lalita는 옥수수 속대의 작은 구멍들이 더러운 물질을 오염된 물 밖으로 걸러낼 수 있을 것이라고 생각했다.

25 Lalita는 여과 장치를 만들기 위해 옥수수 속대를 사용하였다.

26 'live in a happier place'이므로 'to live in'으로 쓰는 것이 적절하다.

27 know의 목적어로 '~인지 아닌지'로 해석되는 명사절 접속사 if 혹은 whether를 쓰는 것에 유의한다.

단원별 예상문제   p.100~105

01 ⑤   02 ③   03 (1) useless (2) robotic
04 Is it possible for you to solve the puzzle?
05 (E)–(B)–(A)–(C)–(D)   06 ③   07 ④
08 ③   09 I would like to fly like him.
10 ②   11 ①, ③   12 ④   13 ④
14 (1) if he is going to come back here
　 (2) if she had breakfast with the man
　 (3) if anyone has seen my teacher's book on the bench
　 (4) if the professor and her students can come on time for dinner
　 (5) if there are any clothes for us to give out to the poor villagers
　 (6) if it will be cloudy the day after tomorrow
15 ③   16 ②   17 ④
18 wish I were[was] as tall as Jordan
19 Bob knew Judy's SNS address, he would visit her SNS
20 it not been for 3D printing technology, I wouldn't have been able to make a useful robotic hand for the price of only 300 dollars
21 (1) if it is going to rain today
　 (2) if she can wash the parrot
　 (3) if she got a cleaner's license
　 (4) if anyone will come to see her
　 (5) if there is anything left to eat
　 (6) if Becky has washed her before
22 (1) is → were[was] (2) are → were
　 (3) have → had (4) is → were[was]
　 (5) be → have been (6) can → could
23 (1) Peter's girl friend asked him if he really loved her.
　 (2) Easton was not sure if he could make her a better dress.
　 (3) Mary asked her parents if they would buy her a sewing machine for her birthday.
24 ②   25 ④   26 ③
27 She started a business to help girls in Africa who couldn't go to school.
28 ⑤번 → warm   29 ③
30 She hopes her filtering system can clean up all the lakes not only in her village but also in other areas.
31 ④

01 '실로 꿰매다'는 '바느질하다(sew)'이다.
02 get together는 '만나다, 모이다'라는 의미이다.

03 (1) 그녀는 최선을 다했지만, 소용없었다. 하지만 그녀는 포기하지 않았다. (2) Sue는 최근에 로봇 진공청소기를 샀어. 그것은 멋져 보여.

04 가능을 묻는 표현은 'Is it possible to V ~?'이며, to부정사의 의미상 주어로 'for+목적격'을 써서 나타낼 수 있다.

05 무엇을 하고 있느냐는 물음에 (E) 드론을 날리고 있다고 말함 (B) 드론 조종을 잘하는지 묻자 (A) 지금은 별로 잘하지 못하지만 열심히 연습하고 있다고 함 (C) 드론으로 샌드위치 배달을 할 수 있느냐는 물음에 (D) 불가능하다고 답하며 1~2년 후에는 가능할 것이라고 말함

06 아들을 위한 배낭을 구매하고 있으므로 대화가 벌어지는 장소는 쇼핑몰이 가장 적절하다.

07 모두 배낭을 지칭하는 말이지만 ④번은 가주어 it이다.

08 배낭에 붙어 있는 모자는 세탁을 위해 분리하는 것이 가능하다고 하였다.

09 소망을 표현하는 말은 'would like to V'이다.

10 가능을 묻는 말이므로 ②번이 적절하다. 의미상의 주어가 'for her'로 제시되고 있으므로 that절에서 주어를 she로 쓰는 것에 유의한다.

11 ② next Monday가 있으므로, 미래시제이다. 간접의문문의 명사절에서 미래시제는 will을 써야 한다. ④ 부사 last weekend는 과거시제이다. will come → came ⑤ 'if or not'은 쓰지 않는다. or not을 삭제 또는 문장 끝에 두거나 if 대신에 whether를 쓰는 것이 적절하다.

12 I wish 가정법 문장에서 조동사는 과거형으로 쓴다.

13 '직설법 현재'를 가정법으로 고치면 '가정법 과거'가 된다. If절에 '과거동사(be동사일 경우 were 또는 was)'를, 주절에 '조동사 과거+동사원형'을 쓰되, 직설법과 반대되도록 쓰는 것에 유의한다.

14 의문사 없는 간접의문문의 명사절을 이끄는 접속사 if를 활용하는 문제이다. 수와 시제, 어순 등에 유의한다.

15 ① doesn't → didn't ② can see → could see ④ can → could ⑤ follows → followed

16 ① work → worked ③ had helped → helped, can → could ④ know → knew ⑤ will → would

17 ① is the rumor → the rumor is ② depend → depends ③ did Mr. Parker make → Mr. Parker made ⑤ that → whether

18 직설법에서 'Jordan만큼 키가 크고 싶다'고 했으므로, 가정법으로는 'Jordan처럼 키가 크면 좋을 텐데'를 표현하는 'I wish 가정법'이 적절하다.

19 직설법 문장을 해석해 보면, 'Bob이 Judy의 SNS 주소를 모르고 있고, 그녀의 SNS를 방문하고 싶어한다.'이므로, 가정법 과

거시제 'Bob이 Judy의 SNS 주소를 안다면 그녀의 SNS를 방문할 텐데.'라고 표현하는 것이 적절하다.

20 직설법에서 '300달러 가격에 유용한 로봇 손을 만들 수 있었고, 그것은 3D 프린팅 기술 때문이었다.'라고 했으므로, 가정법 과거완료시제 '3D 프린팅 기술이 없었더라면, 로봇 손을 만들 수 없었을 것이다.'라고 표현하는 것이 적절하다. 원래는 'If it had not been for'와 같이 해야 하나, Had가 문두에 있으므로, If가 생략된 형태인 'Had it not been for'로 종속절을 만들고, 주절에는 '조동사과거+have+p.p.' 형태를 쓰는 것에 유의한다.

21 그림에 등장하는 모든 생각은 의문사가 없는 의문문이다. 간접의문문으로 전환할 때, if 또는 whether를 사용하되, 문제의 조건에서 whether는 쓸 수 없다고 했으므로 if를 이용하여, 수와 시제에 맞추되, (3)과 같은 경우 과거시제에 맞게 if절에 과거 동사 got을 쓰는 것 등에 유의한다.

22 문제에서 각 문장이 가정법이라고 했으므로, (1), (2), (3), (4)에 나온 'if절' 또는 'I wish' 뒤의 동사를 과거형으로 쓴다. be동사는 were로 고친다. 주어가 3인칭 단수이거나 1인칭일 경우 was를 쓸 수도 있다. (5) 내용상 과거시제이므로 '가정법 과거완료'로 표현한다. 가정법 과거완료의 주절에는 '조동사+have+p.p.'를 쓴다. (6) and를 기준으로 동사원형 병렬 구조이므로, 조동사만 고친다. can → could

23 기본적으로 간접의문문으로 전환할 때, 시제와 대명사, 수 일치, 부사구 등에 유의하도록 한다.

24 글의 내용은 아프리카 소녀들이 교육을 받을 수 있도록 돕고자 한 글쓴이의 노력이다. 따라서 ②번이 가장 적절하다.

25 빈칸 (B)에는 전치사 for가 들어간다. 사람의 성질을 나타내는 형용사 뒤에는 'of+목적격'으로 to부정사의 의미상 주어를 나타낸다.

26 글쓴이는 아프리카 소녀들이 학교에 갈 수 있도록 머리띠를 만들어 팔았고, 이로 인하여 많은 소녀들을 학교에 보낼 수 있게 되었다고 하였다. 따라서 ③번이 가장 적절하다.

27 Mary가 사업을 시작한 이유는 학교에 갈 수 없는 아프리카 소녀들을 돕기 위해서였다.

28 타인을 돕는 행동에 관해 말하고 있으므로 '따뜻한 마음이 삶을 바꿀 수 있다'고 말하는 것이 자연스럽다.

29 밑줄 친 (A)는 불완전한 절을 이끄는 목적격 관계대명사이다. 모두 명사절 접속사로 쓰였지만 ③번은 전치사 at의 목적어가 빠져 있으므로 관계대명사 that이다.

30 Lalita는 자신의 여과 장치가 자신의 마을뿐만 아니라 다른 지역에 있는 모든 호수를 깨끗하게 해 줄 수 있기를 희망한다.

31 Lalita가 만든 여과 장치는 물에서 70~80%의 더러운 물질을 제거했다고 하였다. 따라서 완전히 깨끗한 물을 만들 수는 없었다.

01 read people's minds

02 Dr. Rebecca is Jessie's favorite superhero.

03 Sky X can fly and do anything in space.

04 (1) I lived in Hawaii
  (2) I were[was] the president of Korea
  (3) I had a million dollars
  (4) every Wednesday were[was] a holiday

05 ④, ④ I don't know if what the professor wrote is worth reading.

06 how I could solve this problem

07 It was to use corn cobs.

08 Useless corn cobs were everywhere in Lalita's village.

09 air → water, leaves → cobs, moved → removed

10 if (또는 whether)

11 I wish I lived in Hawaii.

---

01 'I wish+주어+과거동사'는 소망을 나타내는 표현으로, 주로 현재의 사실과 반대되는 상황을 나타낼 때 쓴다. 따라서 Jessie는 닥터 레베카와 달리 사람들의 마음을 읽을 수 없다는 의미이다.

02 Jessie가 가장 좋아하는 슈퍼 영웅은 닥터 레베카이다.

03 Sky X는 하늘을 날 수 있고 우주에서 무엇이든 할 수 있다고 하였다.

04 'I wish 가정법' 문장에서, 주절에 '동사의 과거형' 또는 '조동사 과거+동사원형'의 구조가 오도록 영작한다.

05 의문사가 없는 간접의문을 이끄는 접속사 if 뒤에 that절이 왔는데, 불완전할 경우 what을 생각할 필요가 있다. if 뒤에 쓰인 'what the professor wrote'가 명사절 주어이다. 해석해 보면 '나는 교수님이 쓴 것이 읽을 가치가 있는지 모른다.'가 된다. 그러므로 that → what이 적절하다.

06 간접의문문의 어순은 '의문사+주어+동사'임에 유의하여 답한다.

07 오염된 물을 깨끗하게 만들기 위해 Lalita가 생각해 낸 아이디어는 옥수수 속대를 사용하는 것이었다.

08 Lalita의 마을에는 쓸모없는 옥수수 속대가 어디에나 있었다.

09 Lalita는 심각하게 오염된 물을 깨끗하게 만들기 위해 옥수수 속대를 이용하여 오염 물질의 70~80%를 제거하였다.

10 '~인지 아닌지'라는 의미로 불확실한 명사절을 이끌 때 쓰는 접속사 if 또는 whether가 적절하다.

11 'I wish ~'는 '~하면 좋을 텐데'라는 의미로 현재 사실과 반대되거나 이룰 수 없는 일에 대한 아쉬움을 나타낼 때 쓰인다.

|모범답안|

01 for you to fly to the moon /
  for you to travel to the sun

02 ② If I had a puppy, I would walk it every day.
  ③ If it weren't raining, I could go backpacking.
  ④ If Sam stayed longer, I would make some pizza for him.

03 I had a million dollars / help all the children who can't afford to go to school / I were a famous singer / I would be on TV and my grandma would be happy / I were a bird / I could fly all around the world

---

02 가정법 과거시제의 조건절과 함께 주절에 조동사 과거형을 적절히 이용하여 어법에 맞게 쓰면 정답.

01 ④   02 ②   03 pollute

04 She looks forward to meeting you tomorrow.

05 ④   06 (D)–(B)–(C)–(A)

07 Can I take the cap off for washing?

08 ④   09 wish I could   10 ④, ⑤

11 She wakes Wendy up.   12 ④   13 ④

14 ③   15 ②   16 ④   17 ⑤

18 ③

19 He decided to share the designs and software for his 3D robotic hand with others for free.

20 ⑤   21 ②

22 I wish they could go to school, too.   23 ②

24 She started a business to help them.   25 ④

---

01 ① pay for: ~을 지불하다 ② thank A for B: A에게 B라는 이유로 고마워하다 ③ for oneself: 스스로 ④ hit on: (생각을) 떠올리다 ⑤ for free: 공짜로

02 소망을 표현하는 말이므로 ②번이 가장 적절하다.

03 유의어 관계에 있는 단어이다. 따라서 '오염시키다'라는 의미로 쓰이는 pollute를 쓸 수 있다.

04 look forward to Ving: V하기를 고대하다

05 come across는 '우연히 만나다'라는 의미로 'to meet or find by chance'로 풀이될 수 있다.

06 (D) 한국어를 배운지 얼마나 되었는지 물음 (B) 한 달 동안 배워 왔다고 답함 (C) 한국어를 읽는 것이 가능한지 물음 (A) 읽을 수는 있지만 말하는 것은 아직 미숙하다고 답함

07 세탁을 위해 모자를 분리하는 것이 가능한지를 묻는 표현이다. 따라서 'Can 주어 V ~?'로 표현할 수 있다.

08 ④ 가방이 무엇으로 만들어졌는지는 위 대화를 읽고 알 수 없다.

09 수영을 잘하냐고 묻는 말에 '아니'라고 답하며 '그렇지만 할 수

없다'는 말이 이어지고 있으므로 '아니, 잘했으면 좋겠는데, 못해.'라고 말하는 것이 자연스럽다.

10 모두 일찍 일어나고 싶다는 소망을 나타내는 말이지만, ④번은 일찍 일어나길 몹시 기다린다는 표현이며 ⑤번은 항상 일찍 일어나는 습관을 나타내는 말이다.

11 Wendy의 어머니는 그녀를 깨워준다고 하였다.

12 소망을 나타내는 표현과 가능성을 나타내는 표현은 같지 않다. ④번은 'I want to have ~' 혹은 'I'd like to have ~' 등으로 표현할 수 있다.

13 when은 ⓐ와 ⓑ에 넣으면 무리가 없으나, ⓒ에는 내용상 부적절하다. whether는 ⓑ에 적절하지 않다. 따라서, 세 개의 빈칸에 공통으로 가능한 것은 if 뿐이다.

14 ③ 'Mary가 버스를 놓친다면, 지각하지 않았을 것이다.'라는 문장은 어법과 의미에서 모두 어색하다. 가정법을 적절히 적용하여 고치면, 'If Mary missed the bus, she would be late for work.'가 된다.

15 주어진 문장은 '연경이 컨디션이 좋으면, 다른 선수들보다 두 배의 스파이크 공격을 해낼 텐데.'라는 가정법 과거 문장이다. 직설법으로는 반대의 현재시제이므로, As가 이끄는 종속절과 주절에 모두 현재시제가 있는 ②가 정답이다. '연경이 컨디션이 좋지 않아서, 두 배의 공격을 해내지 않는다.'

16 보기에 주어진 could는 가정법의 주절에 사용된 can의 과거시제형이다. ④는 공손한 질문을 위한 조동사이다.

17 보기에 주어진 if는 간접의문문의 명사절을 이끄는 접속사이다. ⑤번을 제외한 나머지 모두 같은 역할이다. ⑤번은 조건의 부사절을 만드는 if가 쓰였다.

18 주어진 문장의 that이 의미하는 것은 소녀가 더 나은 로봇 손을 가지기를 바라는 Easton의 생각이다. 따라서 ③번이 가장 적절하다.

19 Easton은 자신이 만든 3D 로봇 손 디자인과 소프트웨어를 다른 사람들과 무료로 공유하기로 결심했다.

20 혼자서 세상을 바꿀 수는 없다는 의미이므로 '세상이 한 사람에 의해 바뀔 수는 없다'는 ⑤번이 가장 적절하다.

21 Easton은 과학 박람회에서 우연히 한 소녀를 만났다.

22 현실과 반대되는 상황을 가정하는 가정법이므로 'I wish'가 이끄는 절은 과거시제임에 유의하자.

23 자신이 소녀들을 위해서 어떤 것을 할 수 있을까 생각했다는 의미이다. 불확실한 절을 이끄는 접속사는 if이다.

24 Mary는 학교에 갈 수 없는 아프리카 소녀들을 돕기 위해 사업을 시작하였다.

25 Mary는 자신의 이웃이 아닌 아프리카에 있는 소녀들을 돕고 있다.

The Necklace

Reading

확인문제 p.116

1 T 2 F 3 T 4 F

확인문제 p.117

1 F 2 F 3 T

확인문제 p.118

1 T 2 F 3 F 4 F 5 T

확인문제 p.119

1 T 2 T 3 F 4 T 5 F 6 T

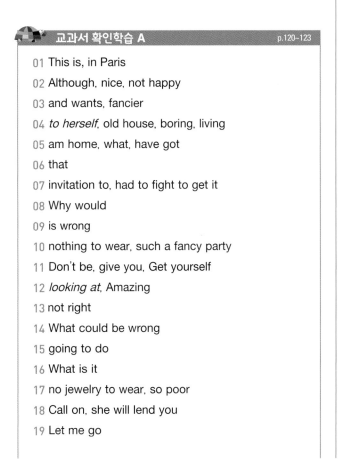

교과서 확인학습 A p.120~123

01 This is, in Paris

02 Although, nice, not happy

03 and wants, fancier

04 *to herself*, old house, boring, living

05 am home, what, have got

06 that

07 invitation to, had to fight to get it

08 Why would

09 is wrong

10 nothing to wear, such a fancy party

11 Don't be, give you, Get yourself

12 *looking at*, Amazing

13 not right

14 What could be wrong

15 going to do

16 What is it

17 no jewelry to wear, so poor

18 Call on, she will lend you

19 Let me go

20 to see, What brings you here

21 invited to

22 wonderful, excited

23 to say, no jewelry, borrow something from you

24 Here is

25 so many wonderful pieces

26 whatever you like

27 lend me this diamond necklace

28 Certainly, go enjoy

29 a perfect evening, admires her beauty

30 It is, when the Loisels leave

31 such a long night

32 it was worth it, danced with

33 you enjoyed yourself

34 *looking in*, more look.

35 when we left the ball

36 did, go find

37 searches

38 returns to, goes to

39 is not found, to lie to

40 broke, fix it, returning it

41 to find a similar one

42 May we look at

43 *whispering*, nearly the same

44 How much

45 francs

46 How about

47 really need it

48 it is

49 do not have, a huge amount of

50 borrow it

51 buying, for, spends, paying

52 move to

53 gets a second job,washes, for

54 makes, old, worn

55 runs into, on

56 good morning

57 Do I know you

58 it is me

59 believe it, have changed

60 have had, difficult times

61 What do you mean

62 you lent me, lost it

63 returned it

64 another one, like it, It, to pay for it

65 bought, to replace

67 Why didn't you come, tell me, was not real, worth

1 This is Mr. and Mrs. Loisel's home in Paris.

2 Although the home is nice, Mrs. Loisel is not happy.

3 She is young and pretty, and wants a fancier life.

4 Mrs. Loisel: (*to herself*) Same old house and same boring dinners. I hate living here!

5 Mr. Loisel: Matilda, I am home. Look what I have got for you!

6 Mrs. Loisel: What is that?

7 Mr. Loisel: An invitation to the Ambassador's Ball. I had to fight to get it. Everybody wanted it.

8 Mrs. Loisel: (*crying*) Why would I want it?

9 Mr. Loisel: Matilda. What is wrong?

10 Mrs. Loisel: I have nothing to wear to such a fancy party. I cannot go.

11 Mr. Loisel: Don't be sad. Here, I will give you 400 francs. Get yourself a beautiful new dress.

12 Mr. Loisel: (*looking at Matilda's new dress*) Amazing, Matilda. Beautiful!

13 Mrs. Loisel: Something is not right.

14 Mr. Loisel: What could be wrong?

15 Mrs. Loisel: (*crying*) Oh, no. What am I going to do?

16 Mr. Loisel: What is it, Matilda?

17 Mrs. Loisel: I have no jewelry to wear with my beautiful dress. I will look so poor!

18 Mr. Loisel: Call on your friend, Mrs. Forestier. I am sure she will lend you some of her jewelry.

19 Mrs. Loisel: That is a good idea! Let me go at once.

20 Mrs. Forestier: Matilda, it is so nice to see you! What brings you here?

21 Mrs. Loisel: We are invited to the Ambassador's Ball.

22 Mrs. Forestier: The Ambassador's Ball! That is wonderful! You must be excited.

23 Mrs. Loisel: Yes··· And no. I am sad to say I have no jewelry. May I borrow something from you?

24 Mrs. Forestier: Sure! Here is my case.

25 Mrs. Loisel: Wow, you have so many wonderful pieces!

26 Mrs. Forestier: Choose whatever you like.

27 Mrs. Loisel: Would you lend me this diamond necklace? It is beautiful!

28 Mrs. Forestier: Certainly! Now go enjoy the ball.

29 Matilda has a perfect evening. Everybody at the ball admires her beauty.

30 It is very late when the Loisels leave the ball.

31 Mr. Loisel: It was such a long night. I am so tired.

32 Mrs. Loisel: But it was worth it. Do you know I danced with the Ambassador?

33 Mr. Loisel: I am glad you enjoyed yourself, but I have to go to work in the morning.

34 Mrs. Loisel: (*looking in the mirror*) Just one more look. (*shocked*) The necklace... It is gone!

35 Mr. Loisel: What? Did you have it when we left the ball?

36 Mrs. Loisel: Yes, I surely did. Please go find it!

37 Mr. Loisel searches the streets.

38 He returns to the ball and then goes to the police.

39 When the necklace is not found, Mr. Loisel tells Matilda to lie to her friend.

40 Matilda tells Mrs. Forestier she broke the necklace and would fix it before returning it.

41 The couple needs time to find a similar one.

42 Mr. Loisel: (*to the jeweler*) Excuse me? May we look at that diamond necklace?

43 Mrs. Loisel: (*whispering*) It is nearly the same. We must have it!

44 Mr. Loisel: How much is it?

45 Jeweler: 40,000 francs.

46 Mr. Loisel: How about 36,000?

47 Mrs. Loisel: Please, we really need it.

48 Jeweler: Well, then... 36,000 it is.!

49 They do not have 36,000 francs. It is a huge amount of money.

50 So they borrow it.

51 After buying the necklace for Mrs. Forestier, the couple spends ten years paying back the money.

52 They move to a very small place.

53 Mr. Loisel gets a second job. Matilda washes clothes for others.

54 Ten years of hard work makes Matilda old and worn.

55 After ten years, Matilda runs into Mrs. Forestier on the street.

56 Mrs. Loisel: Mrs. Forestier, good morning.

57 Mrs. Forestier: Do I know you?

58 Mrs. Loisel: Yes, it is me, Matilda.

59 Mrs. Forestier: Oh, I cannot believe it! You have changed so much.

60 Mrs. Loisel: I have had some difficult times because of you.

61 Mrs. Forestier: Because of me? What do you mean?

62 Mrs. Loisel: Do you remember the diamond necklace you lent me? Well, I lost it.

63 Mrs. Forestier: But you returned it to me.

64 Mrs. Loisel: No, I returned another one just like it. It took us ten years to pay for it.

65 Mrs. Forestier: You bought a diamond necklace to replace mine?

66 Mrs. Loisel: Yes.

67 Mrs. Forestier: Oh, my poor Matilda. Why didn't you come to me and tell me the truth? My diamond necklace was not real. It was worth only 500 francs!

서술형 실전문제 p.128~131

01 (1) admire (2) ball (3) replace (4) invitation

02 ②   **03** ⑤

04 (1) (h)uge (2) (n)early (3) look

05 ④

06 (1) I had to fight to get the invitation to the Ambassador's Ball.
  (2) I have nothing to wear to such a fancy party.
  (3) I am sad to say I have no jewelry.
  (4) Matilda was sorry to lie to her friend.
  (5) The couple needs time to find a similar necklace.
  (6) It took us ten years to pay for the necklace.

07 to pay → paying

08 The necklace was worth only 500

09 He has got an invitation to the Ambassador's Ball.

10 It is because she has nothing to wear to such a fancy party.

11 He gives her 400 francs.

12 I am sure she will lend you some of her jewelry.

13 a new dress, jewelry to wear

14 Choose whatever you like.

15 jewelry

16 She is visiting Mrs. Forestier because she wants to borrow her jewelry.

17 yourself

18 Matilda's beauty is admired at the ball.

19 He tells her to lie to her friend.

20 They move to a very small place. Mr. Loisel gets a second job and Matilda washes clothes for others.

21 Ten years of hard work makes Matilda look old and worn.

22 They pay 36,000 francs to pay for it.

---

01 (1) admire: 존경하다, 칭찬하다. 당신은 그가 그 상황에 대처한 방식을 존경해야 해요. (2) ball: 무도회. 그는 가면을 쓰고 무도회에 간다. (3) replace: ~을 대신하다. 많은 산업에서 기계가 인간 노동을 대신하게 되었다. (4) invitation: 초대, 초대장. 제가 안타깝게도 당신의 친절한 초대를 받아들일 수가 없습니다.

02 ②의 영영풀이는 quality의 영영풀이이다. ① certainly: 확실히, 틀림없이, 그럼요. 확실히, 의심 없이. ② amount: 양, 액수. 어떤 것의 양. ③ jewelry: 보석류. 반지나 목걸이 같은 옷이나 몸에 걸치는 장식물. ④ cry: 울다 · 슬픔, 아픔 등 때문에 눈에서 눈물이 나오게 하다. ⑤ ambassador: 대사. 다른 나라에서 자신의 나라의 공식적인 대표인 가장 높은 지위의 외교관

03 call on: 요청하다, ① respect: 존경하다 ② delay: 연기하다 ③ recommend: 추천하다 ④ invite: 초대하다

04 (1) huge: 거대한, 엄청난 (2) nearly: 거의 (3) look: 보기, 눈길

05 (A) call on: 요청하다. 그것은 일본에게 계획을 취소할 것을 요청했다. take on: 떠맡다, 고용하다 (B) pay back: 갚다, 돌려주다. 나는 내년까지 빚을 못 갚을 것 같아. take back: 취소[철회]하다

06 'to부정사'가 들어가는 다양한 문장들이다. 각각 (1) to부정사의 '부사적' 용법 중 '목적(~하기 위해서)'이다. (2) to부정사의 '형용사적' 용법으로, '앞의 명사를 수식'하고 있다. (3), (4) to부정사의 '부사적' 용법 중 '감정의 원인, 이유'이다. (5) to부정사의 '형용사적' 용법으로 쓰였다. (6) to부정사의 '명사적' 용법으로 사용되었고, 가주어-진주어 구문이다. '주어'로 쓰였다.

07 동사 'spend'는 목적어로 '시간, 노력, 돈' 등을 받고, 관용적으로 동명사가 와서 '~하느라 시간, 돈 등을 사용하다'라는 뜻을 가지고 있다. '그 돈을 갚느라 10년을 보낸다.'는 문장이므로, to pay를 paying으로 고치는 것이 적절하다.

09 Loisel 씨는 아내 Matilda를 위해 대사님이 여는 무도회 초대장을 가지고 왔다.

10 Loisel 부인이 무도회에 갈 수 없다고 말한 이유는 그런 고급스러운 파티에 입고 갈 옷이 하나도 없기 때문이다.

12 be sure (that) ~: ~을 확신하다

13 해석: Matilda는 새 드레스를 가졌지만, 그녀는 그것에 어울릴 보석이 없기 때문에 여전히 만족하지 못한다.

14 whatever는 복합관계대명사로 불완전한 절을 이끌며 주절 내에서 명사 역할을 한다. 이 문장의 경우 choose의 목적어를 이끌고 있다.

15 보석을 의미하는 말이다.

16 Loisel 부인이 Forestier 부인을 방문 중인 이유는 목걸이를 빌리고 싶어서이다.

17 주어와 목적어가 같을 때, 목적어로 재귀대명사를 쓴다. 이를 재귀대명사의 재귀적 용법이라고 부른다.

18 무도회에서 모든 사람들이 아름다운 Matilda를 감탄하며 바라본다고 하였다.

19 Loisel 씨는 목걸이가 발견되지 않자 Matilda에게 그녀의 친구에게 거짓말을 하라고 한다.

20 두 사람은 아주 작은 곳으로 이사 가서 Loisel 씨는 부업을 구하고 Matilda는 다른 사람들을 위해 빨래를 해준다.

21 10년 동안의 고된 일은 Matilda를 늙고 지쳐 보이게 만든다.

22 두 사람은 다이아몬드 목걸이에 36,000프랑을 지불한다.

단원별 예상문제 p.132~138

01 reading　　02 into

03 (1) worn　(2) once　(3) similar　(4) shocked

04 (1) (d)ifferent　(2) (h)uge　(3) (a)dmire

05 (r)eplace

06 It takes me an hour to walk there and back.

07 years of hard work makes Matilda old and worn

08 ⑤　　　　09 ④　　　　10 ③

11 (1) Whoever comes to this village

　(2) whoever tries to make fool of good people

　(3) whatever he has in his hands　　12 ①

13 needs time to find a similar diamond necklace

14 ②　　　　15 ④

16 He had to fight to get it. 17 ③　　18 ④

19 ⑤번 → did 20 ⑤　　　21 ④　　　22 ③

23 The couple needs time to find a similar necklace.

24 Matilda tells Mrs. Forestier she broke the necklace and would fix it before returning it.

25 excited　　26 ⑤

27 What brings you here?　28 ③　　29 go

30 It is because she has no jewelry to wear with her beautiful dress.

31 ⑤

32 It is because they have to pay back the money they borrowed.　　33 ⑤

34 It takes ten years for the couple to pay back the money.

35 on purpose → accidentally　　36 ②

37 ④　　　　38 ⑤

39 It was worth only 500 francs.

40 Matilda가 Forestier 부인의 목걸이를 잃어버렸다는 것

01 • worth: ~의 가치가 있는(형용사이지만 전치사처럼 쓰여, 뒤에 명사, 대명사, 동명사 등이 옴). 그의 책들 중 극히 소수만이 읽을 가치가 있다. • spend 돈·시간 ~ing: 돈·시간 등을 ~하는 데 보내다. 나는 거의 매일 도서관에서 책을 읽으면서 보낸다.

02 • run into: ~을 우연히 만나다. 나는 우연히 옛 친구를 만났다. • fall into: ~에 빠지다. 돌고래는 깊이 잠들 수가 없다.

03 (1) worn: 지친. 우리 좀 앉을까? 난 너무 지쳤어. (2) at once: 당장. 당장 가는 것이 상책이다. (3) similar: 비슷한, 유사한. 다른 사람들도 비슷한 문제를 겪어 왔다. (4) shocked: 충격을 받은. 그 소식을 들었을 때 충격을 받았어요.

04 (1) 반의어 관계이다. borrow: 빌리다, lend: 빌려주다, similar: 비슷한, 유사한, different: 다른, 상이한 (2) 반의어 관계이다. deep: 깊은, shallow: 얕은, tiny 아주 작은, huge 거대한, 엄청난 (3) 동의어 관계이다. replace: ~을 대신하다, substitute: ~을 대신하다, 대리하다, respect 존경하다, admire 존경하다

05 replace: ~을 대신하다. 어떤 것이 엄마의 사랑과 관심을 대신할 수 있을까?

06 it takes+목적어+시간+to부정사: (목적어)가 ~하는 데 (시간)이 걸리다

07 '10년'은 'ten years'이다. 또한, 주어가 '10년'이라는 '단위'를 말하고, 현재시제이므로 make를 makes로 고치는 것이 적절하고, '늙고 수척해진'이라는 표현은 'old and worn'이므로 wear를 worn으로 고쳐서 알맞게 배열한다.

08 보기의 'to 부정사'는 '형용사'적 용법으로 쓰여서 '앞의 명사를 수식'한다. ⑤번의 'to부정사'도 같은 역할이다. ① '부사적' 용법 '감정의 원인' ②, ③ '부사적' 용법 '목적' ④ '부사적' 용법 '형용사 수식' 09 소망을 표현하는 말은 'would like to V'이다.

10 보기의 'to 부정사'는 '부사적' 용법으로 쓰여서 '감정의 원인'을 나타낸다. ③번의 'to 부정사'는 명사적 용법이다. ①, ④ '부사적' 용법-'목적'(~하기 위해서) ② '부사적' 용법 '감정의 원인' ⑤ '부사적' 용법-'판단의 근거'

12 ①은 '현재분사'이다. 해석하면, 그 왕자는 찢어진 드레스에 울고 있는 소녀를 두고 떠났다.라는 뜻이다. 나머지는 모두 '동명사'로 사용되었다. 특히 ②, ⑤는 전치사의 목적어로 쓰였고, ③, ④는 동명사의 관용적 용법으로 'spend+시간+V-ing', 'have difficult times V-ing' 등으로, 꼭 암기하는 것이 좋다.

13 '필요하다'라는 우리말로 보아 '현재시제'임을 알 수 있다. 동사 need를 needs로 형태 변화하는 것에 유의하여, 'to부정사'가 명사 뒤에서 '수식'하는 형태로 영작한다.

14 일반적으로 that이 관계대명사 목적격으로 사용되었을 경우와, 명사절로서 목적어를 이끄는 접속사로 사용되었을 경우 생략 가능하다. ②는 It ~ that 강조구문으로 사용되었고, 문맥상 when으로 바꿀 수는 있으나, 생략은 불가능하다. ①과 ⑤는 명사절 목적어를 이끄는 접속사이며, ③, ④는 관계대명사의 목적격이다.

15 관계대명사 what은 불완전한 절을 이끌며 주절에서 명사 역할을 한다. ④번의 문장은 완전한 절을 이끌고 있으므로 명사절 접속사 that이 들어가는 것이 적절하다.

16 Loisel 씨는 초대장을 얻어 내기 위해 싸워야 했다고 하였다.

17 이어지는 대화에서 Loisel 씨가 아내에게 옷을 살 돈을 주겠다고 말하고 있으므로 ③번이 가장 적절하다.

18 Matilda는 자신의 삶이 지루하고 즐길만한 것이 아니라고 생각한다. Matilda는 이곳에서 살기 싫다는 말을 남편에게 한 것이 아니라 혼잣말로 한다.

19 'I surely had it when we left the ball.'을 받아주는 문장이므로 'I surely did.'라고 쓰는 것이 적절하다. 일반동사의 대동사는 do(es), did를 쓴다.

20 밑줄 친 ⓐ는 '수리하다, 고치다'라는 의미로 쓰였다. ① 준비[주선]하다 ② (음식을) 준비하다, 마련하다 ③ (움직이지 않게) 고정시키다 ④ (날짜, 시간, 양 등을) 정하다 ⑤ 수리하다, 고치다

21 Loisel 씨는 아내가 즐거웠다고 말하자 기쁘다고 말했다.

22 Matilda는 대사와 춤을 추며 즐거운 시간을 보냈지만 목걸이가 사라진 것을 알고 초조해하고 있다. 따라서 ③번이 가장 적절하다.

23 부부는 비슷한 것을 찾을 시간이 필요하다고 하였다.

24 Matilda는 Forestier 부인에게 목걸이를 망가뜨려서 돌려주기 전에 고쳐 주겠다고 말한다.

25 감정을 느낄 때는 과거분사를 쓰는 것이 적절하다.

26 마땅한 보석이 없으므로 빌려달라고 요청하는 말이 가장 자연스럽다. lend: ~을 빌려주다, borrow: ~을 빌리다

27 무슨 일로 왔느냐는 물음을 사물을 주어로 하여 표현할 수 있다.

28 Loisel 부인과는 달리 Forestier 부인에게는 많은 보석이 있다.

29 사역동사의 목적격 보어로 동사원형이 쓰인다.

30 Matilda는 아름다운 드레스에 어울릴 보석이 하나도 없어서 자신이 불쌍해 보일 것이라고 한다.

31 드레스에 어울릴 보석이 하나도 없다는 이유로 슬퍼하는 부인에게 Loisel 씨는 친구 Forestier 부인에게 가서 보석을 빌려달라는 부탁을 해 보라고 제안하고, 이에 부인은 지금 당장 가봐야겠다고 말하고 있으므로 ⑤번이 가장 적절하다.

32 빌린 돈을 갚아야 했기 때문에 두 사람은 아주 작은 곳으로 이사한다고 하였다.

33 Matilda를 늙고 지쳐 보이게 만든 것은 10년 동안의 고된 일이다.

34 커플이 Forestier 부인에게 돌려줄 목걸이를 산 후 돈을 갚는 데 십 년이 걸린다.

35 Matilda는 Forestier 부인을 우연히 만난다고 하였다. '우연히'는 accidentally, by accident, by chance로 표현할 수 있다.

36 이어지는 대화의 내용으로 미루어보아 Matilda가 10년 동안 힘든 시간을 보내어 외모에 많은 변화가 있었기 때문에 Mrs. Forestier가 그녀를 알아볼 수 없음을 알 수 있다.

37 모두 Matilda가 Forestier 부인에게서 빌린 목걸이를 가리키는 말이지만, ④번은 Matilda가 부인에게 사준 목걸이를 가리키는 말이다.

38 밑줄 친 (B)는 to부정사의 부사적 용법 중 목적으로 쓰였다. ① 형용사적 용법 ② 명사적 용법 중 진주어 ③ 명사적 용법 중 주어 ④ 명사적 용법 중 목적어 ⑤ 부사적 용법 중 목적 (~하기 위해서)

39 Forestier 부인의 목걸이는 500프랑이었다.

40 Matilda가 Forestier 부인의 목걸이를 잃어버렸다는 것을 뜻한다.

교과서 파헤치기

Lesson 8

단어 TEST Step 1   p.02

01 상품, 제품   02 아마

03 주제, 과목, 실험대상자   04 거대한, 큰

05 대중적인, 인기 있는   06 포함하다, 넣다

07 능력   08 전통적인   09 보통의, 평범한

10 활기 넘치는, 생생한   11 원뿔, 원뿔형 물체

12 주인공   13 전시회   14 접시

15 실외의   16 열, 발열   17 광고

18 연기, 공연   19 흔한, 평범한, 공통의

20 창의력   21 친숙한   22 예술 작품

23 특수효과   24 창의적인   25 교훈

26 예술적인   27 복사본   28 운영하다

29 화려한   30 클래식의, 고전적인 31 신선한, 참신한

32 조각품   33 장식   34 ~의 가치가 있는

35 ~로 구성되다   36 설치하다   37 요전 날, 며칠 전

38 ~로 여겨지다   39 다시 말해서, 즉   40 ~ 대신에

41 ~에 주의를 기울이다   42 ~을 부수다

43 ~로 눈길을 돌리다

단어 TEST Step 2   p.03

01 popular   02 artistic   03 boring
04 plate   05 advertising   06 exhibition
07 colorful   08 familiar   09 sculpture
10 performance   11 creative   12 lively
13 fever   14 creativity   15 truly
16 worth   17 common   18 toilet
19 goods   20 ability   21 art work
22 huge   23 include   24 probably
25 refreshing   26 lesson   27 main character
28 traditional   29 outdoor   30 decoration
31 plain   32 run   33 cone
34 special effects 35 be made of   36 in other words
37 break down   38 be regarded as
39 pay attention to 40 change A into B
41 be short for   42 be made up of 43 the other day

단어 TEST Step 3   p.04

1 boring, 지루한   2 plain, 평범한

3 popular, 대중적인, 인기 있는   4 performance, 연기

5 ability, 능력   6 creativity, 창의력   7 decoration, 장식

8 practice, 연습하다   9 familiar, 친숙한   10 cone, 원뿔

11 advice, 충고   12 classical, 클래식의, 고전적인

13 include, 포함하다   14 sculpture, 조각품

15 traditional, 전통적인   16 exhibition, 전시회

대화문 TEST Step 1   p.05~06

Listen & Speak 1 A

1. listen to, kinds, music library / cool, listen to classical / Sure, classical music / one of my favorite musicians, about / more than classical music / What do you like / fascinated by, exciting

2. finish, art homework / drew, plate / Sounds interesting / advice, did, draw / myself surfing / fascinated by your drawing

Listen & Speak 2 A

1. The other day, play / how did you like / main characters, actors', performance, fantastic / as well / a little boring, pretty good / should see / Only if, a lot of

2. how do you like / a lot, class / What do you like most / learning different drawing skills, What / painting skills, with / work last time, thought, creative / practice a lot

Real Life Talk

didn't you / special / How did you like / fantastic, was fascinated by, paintings, creativity / No wonder, one of the greatest painters, What else / a gift shop, Famous works, were printed / anything / How do you like / looks great on

Wrap Up 1

festival, didn't / A lot of, performed / How did you like / special guest, called / heard, famous / performance / No wonder

대화문 TEST Step 2   p.07~08

Listen & Speak 1 A

1. B: Sandy, you can listen to many kinds of music in this music library.

   G: That's cool, Bob. Can I listen to classical music?

B: Sure. Do you like classical music?

G: Yes, Beethoven is one of my favorite musicians. How about you?

B: I like pop music more than classical music.

G: I see. What do you like most about pop music?

B: I'm really fascinated by its exciting rhythms.

2. G: Jim, did you finish your art homework?

B: Yes. I drew the face of my role model on a plate.

G: Sounds interesting. Who is your role model?

B: My dad. He always gives me good advice. Who did you draw, Amy?

G: Well, I drew myself surfing in the sea.

B: Wonderful! I'm fascinated by your drawing.

G: Thank you.

Listen & Speak 2 A

1. B: The other day I watched a play, *A Love Story in the War*.

G: Oh, how did you like the play?

B: I liked the main characters. The actors' performances were fantastic.

G: Was the story good as well?

B: No. It was a little boring, but the music was pretty good.

G: So, do you think I should see it?

B: Only if you have a lot of time and money.

2. B: Caire, how do you like your art class?

G: It's great. I learn a lot in the class.

B: What do you like most about it?

G: I enjoy learning different drawing skills. What about you, Allen?

B: I also like the class. I learn good painting skills. I love painting with many colors.

G: Oh, I saw your work last time. I thought it was very creative.

B: Thanks. I practice a lot.

Real Life Talk

Bora: Andy, you went to the art museum, didn't you?

Andy: Yes. They had a special Chagall exhibition.

Bora: How did you like it?

Andy: It was fantastic! I was fascinated by the colors in his paintings and his creativity.

Bora: No wonder. He was one of the greatest painters ever. What else did you see in the museum?

Andy: I went to a gift shop and saw things like umbrellas, cups, and backpacks. Famous works of art were printed on them.

Bora: Did you buy anything?

Andy: Yes. I bought this T-shirt. How do you like it?

Bora: It looks great on you.

Andy: Thank you.

Wrap Up 1

B: Cindy, you went to the music festival, didn't you?

G: Yes. A lot of famous musicians performed there.

B: How did you like the festival?

G: It was fantastic! I really liked the special guest. Do you know the band called *the Brothers*?

B: Oh, I've heard about them. The singer is famous.

G: Yes. His performance was great.

B: No wonder.

본문 TEST Step 1 p.09~10

01 Welcome, Exhibition, Paintings, cartoons

02 Probably, think, famous works

03 short, so, popular art

04 began, create something, easy

05 Instead, traditional, works, turned

06 used, from, magazines, advertising

07 familiar images, exhibitions, refreshing

08 Since, become truly popular

09 that, too, to understand

10 using, bright, changed, thought

11 common, plain, words, artistic

12 worth paying attention, filled

13 Let's learn, famous, artists

14 famous, ability, change, objects

15 called, found, subjects in

16 famous, made up, actor

17 Another, made, copies, works

18 copies, works, show, something

19 another, who made, fun

20 sculptures, everyday items, brush

21 beginning, created, made, materials

22 cloth, huge sculptures, as

23 Wanting, set up, outdoor

24 ran, inside, sell, goods

25 used, works, painted, lively

26 included, were, regarded as

27 However, differently, himself, Why

28 broke down, between, adding

29 believed, should, Anyone, create

30 creating, work, pop art

31 using, creative, important lesson

01 Welcome to, Exhibition, What, cartoons

02 look like, Probably, think, are, famous works

03 is short for popular, popular art

04 It began in, wanted to, something fun

05 Instead of, traditional, turned, to popular culture

06 used, from, advertising

07 familiar images, art exhibitions, them refreshing

08 Since, become truly popular

09 that, too, to understand

10 By using, bright colors, changed that thought

11 Using, looks plain. In other words, artistic

12 worth paying attention to, looks plain, is filled with

13 Let's, famous pop artists

14 famous for, ability, able to change common objects into amazing

15 is called, found, subjects in

16 is made up

17 Another work shows, made, copies, works

18 copies of his works, to show that, you see

19 another, who made, fun

20 sculptures of everyday items, such as, brush

21 In the beginning, created soft sculptures, made of, soft materials

22 For example, cloth to make, huge sculptures, daily items, such as

23 Wanting, to enjoy, set up, outdoor

24 ran, inside, to sell, were fun goods

25 used, in his works, were, painted, lively colors

26 included, Back then, were, regarded as

27 However, differently, himself, Why, they not

28 broke down, between, and, by adding

29 believed, should be, Anyone, create, enjoy

30 creating, pop art

31 By using, in, creative way, make, for, the most important lesson

1 팝 아트 전시회에 온 것을 환영한다! 무엇이 보이는가? 수프 통조림들을 모아 놓은 그림? 커다란 만화 그림?

2 그것들이 예술 작품처럼 보이는가? 아마 그렇게 보이지 않겠지만, 다시 생각해 봐라. 그것들은 모두 유명한 팝 아트 작품들이다.

3 'pop'은 'popular(대중적인)'의 줄임말이다. 그래서 팝 아트는 대중 예술 또는 사람들을 위한 예술이라는 뜻이다.

4 팝 아트는 1950년대 미국에서 시작됐다. 그 당시 팝 아트 작가들은 재미있고 쉬운 것을 만들고 싶어 했다.

5 어려운 전통 예술 작품 대신 그들은 대중문화로 눈을 돌렸다.

6 그들은 텔레비전, 만화책, 잡지 및 광고에 나오는 이미지들을 사용했다.

7 미술 전시회에서 친숙한 이미지들을 봤을 때 사람들은 그것들이 신선하다는 걸 알게 되었다.

8 그때부터 팝 아트는 정말 유명해졌다.

9 사람들은 예술이 너무 어려워서 이해할 수 없는 것으로 생각했었다.

10 일상적인 이미지와 밝은 색을 씀으로써, 팝 아트 작가들은 그러한 관점을 바꿨다.

11 흔한 이미지를 사용하기 때문에 팝 아트는 평범해 보인다. 즉, 팝 아트는 예술적으로 보이지 않는다.

12 하지만 여전히 주목할 만한 가치가 있다. 평범해 보일지라도 그것은 의미로 가득 차 있다.

13 몇 명의 유명한 팝 아트 작가들에 대해 알아보자.

14 그들은 특별한 예술적인 능력으로 유명해졌다. 그들은 흔한 대상을 놀라운 예술로 바꿀 수 있었다.

15 Andy Warhol은 팝 아트의 왕이라 불린다. 그는 잡지와 상점에서 주제를 찾았다.

16 그의 유명 작품들 중 하나는 미국 배우인 Marilyn Monroe의 사진으로 구성되어 있다.

17 또 다른 작품은 수프 통조림들을 보여준다. 그는 이 작품들의 사본을 많이 만들었다.

18 그는 왜 작품의 복사본을 만들었나? 그는 예술은 여러분이 매일 보는 것임을 보여 주고 싶어 했다.

19 Claes Oldenburg는 예술을 재미있게 만들었던 또 다른 팝 아트 작가이다.

20 그는 햄버거와 쿠키, 붓 같은 일상적인 물품들의 조각품을 만들었다.

21 초기에 그는 부드러운 조각품을 만들었다. 그것들은 플라스틱, 종이, 그리고 다른 부드러운 재료들로 만들어졌다.

22 예를 들어서 그는 변기를 만들기 위해 천을 사용했다. 나중에 그는 아이스크림콘 같은 일상 물품의 거대한 조각품을 만들었다.

23 그는 모든 사람이 그의 작품을 보고 즐기기를 원했기 때문에 그의 작품들을 실외에 설치했다.

24 그는 작품 판매를 위해 그의 작업실 안에 상점을 운영하기도 했다. 그에게 예술적인 작품들은 사람들을 위한 재미있는 제품이었다.

25 Roy Lichtenstein은 그의 작품에 만화를 사용했다. 그것들은 크고 생기 넘치는 색들로 그려졌다.

26 그는 심지어 그의 작품에 말풍선을 넣었다. 그 당시에 만화는 예술 형식으로 여겨지지 않았다.

27 하지만 Roy Lichtenstein은 다르게 생각했다. 그는 스스로에게 '왜 만화는 예술로 간주되지 않을까?'라고 물었다.

28 만화를 예술에 첨가함으로써 Roy Lichtenstein은 순수

예술과 대중문화 사이의 벽을 허물었다.

29 팝 아트 작가들은 예술은 쉬워야 한다고 믿었다. 누구나 예술을 만들 수 있고, 즐길 수 있다.

30 오늘 팝 아트 작품 하나를 만들어 보는 것은 어떤가?

31 일상적인 이미지를 창의적인 방식으로 사용함으로써, 모든 사람을 위한 예술 작품을 만들 수 있다. 이것이 팝 아트의 가장 중요한 교훈이다.

1 Welcome to the Pop Art Exhibition! What do you see? Paintings of soup cans? Big cartoons?

2 Do they look like art works? Probably not, but think again. They are all famous works of pop art.

3 Pop is short for popular. So pop art means popular art, or art for people.

4 It began in the 1950s in America. Pop artists at that time wanted to create something fun and easy.

5 Instead of difficult traditional art works, they turned their eyes to popular culture.

6 They used images from TV, comic books, magazines, and advertising.

7 When people saw familiar images in art exhibitions, they found them refreshing.

8 Since then, pop art has become truly popular.

9 People thought that art was too difficult to understand.

10 By using daily images and bright colors, pop artists changed that thought.

11 Using common images, pop art looks plain. In other words, it doesn't look artistic.

12 But it is still worth paying attention to. Although it looks plain, it is filled with meaning.

13 Let's learn about some famous pop artists.

14 They became famous for their special artistic ability. They were able to change common objects into amazing art.

15 Andy Warhol is called the King of Pop Art. He found his subjects in magazines and stores.

16 One of his famous works is made up of pictures of Marilyn Monroe, the American actor.

17 Another work shows cans of soup. He made many copies of these works.

18 Why did he make copies of his works? He wanted to show that art is something you see every day.

19 Claes Oldenburg is another pop artist who made

art fun.

20 He made sculptures of everyday items, such as a hamburger, cookies, and a brush.

21 In the beginning, he created soft sculptures. They were made of plastic, paper, and other soft materials.

22 For example, he used cloth to make toilets. Later, he made huge sculptures of daily items, such as an ice cream cone.

23 Wanting everyone to enjoy his art, he set up his works in outdoor places.

24 He also ran a store inside his studio to sell his works. For him, artistic works were fun goods for people.

25 Roy Lichtenstein used cartoons in his works. They were large and painted in lively colors.

26 He even included speech balloons in his paintings. Back then, cartoons were not regarded as an art form.

27 However, Roy Lichtenstein thought differently. He asked himself, 'Why are they not?'

28 Then Roy Lichtenstein broke down the wall between high art and popular culture by adding cartoons to art.

29 Pop artists believed art should be easy. Anyone can create and enjoy art.

30 How about creating a work of pop art today?

31 By using daily images in a creative way, you can make a work of art for everyone. This is the most important lesson from pop art.

Project Step 1

1. want to make with
2. Why don't we
3. Let's build, like
4. How about drawing
5. let's give, some paper cups

Enjoy Writing B

1. The Best Musical, My Life
2. Last Saturday, to watch a musical
3. The title of the musical
4. because, in it
5. songs, dances of the musical
6. a girl who invited her best friends
7. talked about their friendship

8. main character, many beautiful songs

9. Singing along to, during the performance, excited

10. worth watching

Enjoy Writing B

1. Movie That Moved

2. went to, to watch a movie

3. The title of the movie, because my friend recommended

4. story of the movie, a brave man who tried to find

5. The main character, was played by, who

6. emotional scenes, moved

7. was really worth watching

구석구석지문 TEST Step 2   p.20

Project Step 1

1. A: What do you want to make with these paper cups?

2. B: Why don't we make a tower?

3. C: Wonderful! Let's build a tower like the Leaning Tower of Pisa.

4. D: How about drawing something on the cups?

5. B: Sounds great. First, let's give everyone some paper cups.

Enjoy Writing B

1. The Best Musical of My Life

2. Last Saturday I went to the concert hall to watch a musical.

3. The title of the musical was *You and Me*.

4. I watched it because my favorite actor was in it.

5. I liked the songs and dances of the musical.

6. The story was about a girl who invited her best friends to her birthday party.

7. They talked about their friendship.

8. The main character was Sophie. She sang many beautiful songs. It was fantastic.

9. Singing along to the songs during the performance, I was excited.

10. The musical was really worth watching.

Enjoy Writing B

1. A Movie That Moved Me

2. Last Saturday I went to my friend's house to watch a movie.

3. The title of the movie was *My Son*. I watched it because my friend recommended it.

4. I liked the story of the movie. The story was about a brave man who tried to find his lost son.

5. The main character was John. He was played by the actor Roy Jones, who was fantastic.

6. It was touching. Watching the emotional scenes, I

---

was moved.

7. The movie was really worth watching.

단어 TEST Step 1 p.21

01 ~할 여유가 되다 02 사업 03 옥수수 속대
04 여과장치, 필터; 여과하다, 거르다 05 수집하다
06 발명(품) 07 유용한 08 편안한, 여유 있는
09 꿰매다, 바느질하다
10 통제하다, 조절하다, 조정하다 11 재봉틀
12 쓸모없는, 소용없는 13 체계, 장치
14 성냥 15 값이 들다 16 시골
17 오염시키다 18 입장료 19 삼각형
20 머무르다 21 실패 22 박람회
23 (지금을) 모으다 24 요금 25 제거하다
26 성공 27 대통령, 회장, 총재 28 ~인지 (아닌지)
29 단계 30 추천하다 31 오염
32 깨닫다, 인식하다 33 십 대(= teen) 34 머리띠
35 ~을 생각해 내다 36 우연히 마주치다 37 ~ 덕분에
38 스스로 39 A를 B로 바꾸다 40 무료로
41 지불하다 42 마음속으로 생각하다
43 A 뿐만 아니라 B도

단어 TEST Step 2 p.22

01 pollution 02 afford 03 realize
04 stay 05 business 06 collect
07 success 08 remove 09 cost
10 relaxed 11 fair
12 sewing machine 13 fee
14 countryside 15 entrance fee 16 filter
17 corn cob 18 useless 19 failure
20 whether 21 match 22 sew
23 pollute 24 raise 25 control
26 teenager 27 recommend 28 triangle
29 useful 30 invention 31 president
32 system 33 inventor 34 step
35 pay for 36 thanks to 37 for oneself
38 think to oneself
39 change A into B 40 come across
41 for free 42 get together
43 not only A but also B

단어 TEST Step 3 p.23

1 robotic, 로봇식의 2 sew, 꿰매다, 바느질하다
3 afford, ~할 여유가 되다 4 cost, 값이 들다
5 success, 성공 6 for free, 무료로 7 coin, 동전
8 come across, 우연히 마주치다
9 hit on, ~을 생각해 내다 10 business, 사업
11 pollute, 오염시키다 12 software, 소프트웨어
13 fair, 박람회 14 headband, 머리띠
15 control, 통제하다, 조정하다 16 match, 성냥

대화문 TEST Step 1 p.24~25

Listen & Speak 1 A-1

Can you draw, on / From, two triangles, draw, circle, like this / possible for you, without taking, off / how is that possible / at, four red points / any of the red points / first, the two triangles like this, triangles first / I get it

Listen & Speak 1 A-2

looking for, for / How old / five years old / to recommend / so cute / isn't it, that looks like, so, love it / for me to take, off, washing / take it off, put it back / wonderful, take it

Listen & Speak 2 A-1

you have been late for, lately, wrong / wake up early, can't / wake you up / does, right away, I wish, could / An AI robot / that could make sure, got up, give me breakfast / great

Listen & Talk 2 A-2

planning to visit / going to do there / spend most of my time, because, swimming pool / Can, swim well / I wish I could, So, have fun with, instead / What is that / It's, go inside, walk on / must be

Real Life Talk

are, doing / drawing, my favorite superhero / great / could read people's minds / for her to control / control, if she wants to / cool / have any favorite superheroes / could fly like him / even breathe in space / can do anything

Wrap Up 1

What are you doing / flying / Are, good at / right now, practicing hard / As you know, run, possible for you to deliver orders / isn't, it will be possible in / That, be great

대화문 TEST Step 2 p.26~27

Listen & Speak 1 A-1

G: Can you draw this on the paper?
B: Sure. From the middle point, I draw two triangles.

Then I draw the circle, like this.

G: Good. Now, is it possible for you to draw it without taking your pencil off the paper?

B: I'll try. Hmm... No, how is that possible?

G: Well, start at one of the four red points.

B: Do you mean any of the red points?

G: Yes. Draw the circle first and then the two triangles like this. Or you can draw the triangles first, like this.

B: Oh, now I get it.

Listen & Speak 1 A-2

W: Hi. I'm looking for a backpack for my son.

M: How old is your son?

W: He is five years old.

M: I want to recommend this one.

W: Oh, it's so cute.

M: Yes, isn't it? It has a cap that looks like a penguin, so kids love it.

W: Is it possible for me to take the cap off for washing?

M: Sure. You can easily take it off and put it back on.

W: That's wonderful. I'll take it.

Listen & Speak 2 A-1

B: Wendy, you have been late for school a lot lately. What's wrong?

G: I want to wake up early, but I just can't.

B: Doesn't your mom wake you up?

G: She does, but I don't get up right away. I wish I could have an AI robot.

B: An AI robot?

G: Yes. I mean one that could make sure I got up and give me breakfast in the morning.

B: That sounds great.

Listen & Speak 2 A-2

B: I'm planning to visit my uncle in Mexico.

G: What are you going to do there, Mike?

B: I'll spend most of my time at his house because he has a big swimming pool.

G: That's great. Can you swim well?

B: No, I wish I could, but I can't. So I'll have fun with a water walking ball instead.

G: A water walking ball? What is that?

B: It's a large ball. We go inside it and walk on the water.

G: That must be fun.

Real Life Talk

Bora: What are you doing, Jessie?

Jessie: I'm drawing Dr. Rebecca, my favorite superhero.

Bora: Wow, that's great.

Jessie: Thanks. I wish I could read people's minds like her.

Bora: Is it possible for her to control them, too?

Jessie: Yes. She can control your mind if she wants to.

Bora: That's very cool.

Jessie: What about you? Do you also have any favorite superheroes?

Bora: Sure. I love Sky X. I wish I could fly like him.

Jessie: I like him, too. He can even breathe in space.

Bora: Yes. He can do anything in space.

Wrap Up 1

W: Hi, Tom. What are you doing?

B: I'm flying my drone.

W: Cool! Are you good at it?

B: No, I'm not very good right now, but I'm practicing hard.

W: As you know, I run a sandwich restaurant. Is it possible for you to deliver orders with your drone?

B: No, it isn't. But I think it will be possible in one or two years.

W: That will be great.

본문 TEST Step 1   p.28~29

01 change, too, to, one
02 following, used, make, place
03 when, came across, fair
04 robotic, that, open, close
05 surprised that, had cost
06 wish, had, better, myself
07 With, much cheaper, better
08 failures, using, able, price
09 share, with others, free
10 what, done, something useful
11 one, change, build, working
12 can't, go, as, could
13 had, thought, realized, afford
14 if, could, something, had
15 asked, buy, sewing machine
16 bought, how, make, myself
17 created, headbands, sold, at
18 raised enough, send, stop
19 business, help, who, go
20 success, pay, fees, like,
21 pay, textbooks, uniforms, amazing

22 advice, something, need, act

23 taking, steps, heart, lives

24 living, found, seriously polluted

25 how, solve, hit on

26 Useless, were, in, village

27 holes, dirty matter, polluted

28 picked, washed, placed, bowl

29 After, while, much clearer

30 using, collected from, filtering

31 removed, dirty matter from

32 clean up, only, also

본문 TEST Step 2   p.30~31

01 who change, too young to be

02 will meet, to make

03 when, came across, at, science fair

04 robotic, that, open, close

05 surprised that, had cost her

06 wish, had, thought to myself

07 With, a much cheaper, better

08 failures, by using, was able to, for, price of

09 to share, for, with others for free

10 Maybe, take what I have done, something useful with

11 No one, change, build, by working together

12 can't, go to school, could go

13 had this thought, realized that, couldn't afford

14 if I could do something, had

15 asked, to buy me a sewing machine

16 bought me one, how to make, for myself

17 ten headbands, them

18 raised enough money, stop

19 a business to help, who, go

20 to the success, fees for, like, to go to school

21 pay for, textbooks, uniforms, Isn't, amazing

22 advice, is, do something, a need, act

23 small, taking, warm heart, lives

24 As, living, often found that, around, seriously polluted

25 how I could solve, hit on, to use

26 Useless, were, in

27 the small holes, could filter dirty matter, polluted

28 picked up, washed them, placed, in a bowl of

29 After a while, it, much clearer

30 using, that, collected from, built, filtering

31 removed, the dirty matter

32 filtering system, clean up, not only, but also, other areas

본문 TEST Step 3   p.32~33

1 세상을 바꾸는 사람들은 누구인가? 여러분은 너무 어려서 이런 사람들 중 하나가 될 수 없다고 생각하나요?

2 다음 이야기에서 여러분은 세상을 더 나은 곳으로 만들기 위해 자신들의 아이디어를 사용한 세 명의 십 대들을 만날 겁니다.

3 내가 열네 살이었을 때, 어느 날 한 과학 박람회에서 어린 소녀를 우연히 만났다.

4 그녀는 겨우 접었다 펴지기만 하는 로봇 손을 가지고 있었다.

5 나는 그녀가 그 손에 8만 달러를 지불했다는 데 놀랐다!

6 '나는 그녀가 더 나은 로봇 손을 가질 수 있으면 좋겠어.'라고 마음속으로 생각했다.

7 나는 이런 생각을 가지고 더 싸고 좋은 로봇 손을 만들기 시작했다.

8 많은 실패 뒤 마침내 3D 프린트 기술을 사용해서 나는 단 300 달러짜리의 유용한 로봇 손을 만들 수 있었다.

9 나는 내 3D 로봇 손의 디자인과 소프트웨어를 다른 사람들과 무료로 공유하기로 결심했다.

10 아마도 누군가는 내가 만든 것을 이용해 다른 유용한 것을 할 수 있을 것이다.

11 혼자 세상을 바꿀 수는 없지만, 함께 일 하면서 더 나은 세상을 만들 수 있다.

12 '아프리카의 많은 소녀들은 왜 나처럼 학교에 갈 수 없지? 나는 그들도 학교에 갈 수 있으면 좋을 텐데.'

13 내가 12살 때, 이런 생각을 했었다. 나는 그들의 가족이 그럴 금전적 여유가 없다는 것을 깨달았다.

14 나는 내가 그 소녀들을 위해서 어떤 것을 할 수 있을까 생각했다. 그때 아이디어가 떠올랐다.

15 나는 내 생일에 부모님께 재봉틀을 사 달라고 부탁드렸다.

16 그들은 재봉틀을 사 주셨고 나는 머리띠 만드는 법을 혼자 배웠다.

17 10개의 머리띠를 만들어 학교에서 팔았다.

18 나는 곧 아프리카에 있는 한 명의 소녀를 학교에 보낼 수 있는 충분한 자금을 모았다. 나는 거기서 멈출 수 없었다.

19 나는 학교에 갈 수 없는 아프리카의 소녀들을 돕기 위해 사업을 시작했다.

20 내 사업의 성공 덕분에 나는 케냐와 우간다 같은 나라에 있는 많은 가난한 소녀들이 학교에 갈 수 있게 수업료를 지불할 수 있다.

21 나는 또한 그들의 교과서와 교복, 연필을 위한 비용도 지불한다. 놀랍지 않은가?

22 나의 조언은 그냥 무엇이든 하라는 것이다. 필요성이 보인다면 행동하라.

23 작은 단계를 밟아가면서 작은 것부터 시작하라. 너의 따뜻한

24 마음이 삶을 바꿀 수 있다.

24 인도의 시골에 살고 있었던 어린 소녀인 나는 종종 내 주변에 있는 물이 심각하게 오염되어 있는 것을 발견했다.

25 나는 이 문제를 어떻게 해결할 수 있을지 궁금했다. 그때 나는 옥수수 속대를 이용해야겠다는 생각이 불현듯 떠올랐다.

26 내가 사는 마을에는 쓸모없는 옥수수 속대가 곳곳에 널려 있다.

27 나는 옥수수 속대의 작은 구멍들이 더러운 물질을 오염된 물 밖으로 걸러 낼 수 있을 거라고 생각했다.

28 어느 날 나는 길을 따라 마른 옥수수 속대를 주운 뒤, 그것들을 씻어서 더러운 물이 담긴 그릇에 넣었다.

29 잠시 뒤 물을 확인했는데 훨씬 더 맑게 보였다.

30 그리고 나서 나는 농부들로부터 모은 옥수수 속대를 이용하여 여과 장치를 만들었다.

31 내 장치는 물에서 70~80%의 더러운 물질을 제거했다.

32 나는 내 여과 장치가 내 마을뿐만 아니라 다른 지역에 있는 모든 호수를 깨끗하게 해 줄 수 있기를 희망한다.

---

1 Who are the people who change the world? Do you think you are too young to be one of these people?

2 In the following stories you will meet three teenagers who used their ideas to make the world a better place.

3 One day, when I was fourteen, I came across a little girl at a science fair.

4 She had a robotic hand that could only open and close.

5 I was surprised that the hand had cost her 80,000 dollars!

6 'I wish she had a better robotic hand,' I thought to myself.

7 With that, I started to make a much cheaper and better robotic hand.

8 After many failures, finally, by using 3D printing technology, I was able to make a useful robotic hand for the price of only 300 dollars.

9 I decided to share the designs and software for my 3D robotic hand with others for free.

10 Maybe someone can take what I have done and do something useful with it.

11 No one person can change the world, but we can build a better world by working together.

12 'Why can't many girls in Africa go to school as I can? I wish they could go to school, too.'

13 I had this thought when I was twelve. I realized that their families couldn't afford it.

14 I wondered if I could do something for those girls. Then I had an idea.

15 For my birthday, I asked my parents to buy me a sewing machine.

16 They bought me one, and I learned how to make headbands for myself.

17 I created ten headbands and sold them at my school.

18 Soon, I raised enough money to send one girl in Africa to school. I couldn't stop there.

19 I started a business to help girls in Africa who couldn't go to school.

20 Thanks to the success of my business, I can pay the school fees for many poor girls in countries like Kenya and Uganda to go to school.

21 I also pay for their textbooks, uniforms, and pencils. Isn't it amazing?

22 My advice to you is to just do something. When you see a need, act.

23 Start small, taking little steps. Your warm heart can change lives.

24 As a young girl living in the countryside in India, I often found that the water around us was seriously polluted.

25 I wondered how I could solve this problem. Then I hit on the idea to use corn cobs.

26 Useless corn cobs were everywhere in my village.

27 I thought that the small holes in the corn cobs could filter dirty matter out of the polluted water.

28 One day, I picked up some dried cobs along the road, washed them, and placed them in a bowl of dirty water.

29 After a while, I checked the water, and it looked much clearer.

30 Then, using corn cobs that I had collected from farmers, I built a filtering system.

31 My system removed 70 to 80 percent of the dirty matter from the water.

32 I hope my filtering system can clean up all the lakes not only in my village but also in other areas.

Communication Task

1. can fly
2. to meet you
3. wish, could fly like, Is it possible for you
4. Sure
5. is it possible for you to travel
6. impossible

Enjoy Writing

1. To
2. I wonder if, make my wishes come true
3. wish, lived, could swim at a beautiful beach
4. wish, were, could he more relaxed
5. Finally, I wish I were
6. make my country a happier place to live in
7. if you can help me, I hope, can
8. Best Let's

After Your Read

1. Creative Teens
2. was surprised at, to make a cheaper and better
3. fo only 300 dollars, decided to share, for free
4. wished, could send
5. made, sold headbands
6. pays for, fees, many poor school girls in Africa
7. how she could clean the water
8. Using corn cobs, a filtering system
9. removed, the dirty matter from the water

6. Then I would try hard to make my country a happier place to live in.
7. I don't know if you can help me, but I hope you can.
8. Best Let's, Sohee

After Your Read

1. Creative Teens!
2. Easton was surprised at a girl's expensive robotic hand and wanted to make a cheaper and better one.
3. Finally he made one fo only 300 dollars and decided to share his designs and software for free.
4. Mary wished she could send girls in Africa to school.
5. She made and sold headbands.
6. Now she pays for the school fees, textbooks, uniforms, and pencils of many poor school girls in Africa.
7. Lalita wondered how she could clean the water.
8. Using corn cobs, she made a filtering system.
9. It removed 70 to 80 percent of the dirty matter from the water.

Communication Task

1. A: I'm Sky X. I can fly.
2. B: Hi, Sky X. Nice to meet you.
3. C: I wish I could fly like you. Is it possible for you to fly to the moon?
4. A: Sure.
5. D: Then is it possible for you to travel to the sun?
6. A: No. That's impossible.

Enjoy Writing

1. To Genie,
2. I have three wishes. I wonder if you can make my wishes come true.
3. First, I wish I lived in Hawaii. Then I could swim at a beautiful beach.
4. Second, I wish every Wednesday were a holiday. Then, I could he more relaxed.
5. Finally, I wish I were the president of Korea.

단어 TEST Step 1 — p.40

01 목걸이　02 한 개, 한 부분, 조각
03 양, 액수　04 아름다움, 미
05 속삭이다, 귓속말을 하다　06 부부
07 다이아몬드　08 충격을 받은　09 무도회
10 지친　11 비슷한, 유사한
12 ~이든지, ~한 어떤 것이든　13 화려한
14 존경하다, 칭찬하다, 감탄하며 바라보다　15 울다
16 빌려주다　17 (프랑스, 스위스 등의 화폐 단위) 프랑
18 거대한, 엄청난　19 ~의 가치가 있는　20 초대, 초대장
21 대사　22 보석 상인
23 (다른 사람·사물을) 대신하다　24 거의
25 부업　26 보석류　27 거짓말
28 빌리다　29 확실히, 틀림없이　30 보기, 눈길
31 ~을 우연히 만나다　32 갚다, 돌려주다
33 즉시, 당장　34 ~에게 청하다, 부탁하다
35 절 아시나요?　36 ~하는 데 (시간)이 걸리다
37 (목적어)가 ~하는 데 (시간)을 소비하다

단어 TEST Step 2 — p.41

01 whisper　02 franc　03 huge
04 amount　05 ball　06 whatever
07 certainly　08 admire　09 necklace
10 piece　11 ambassador　12 diamond
13 cry　14 fancy　15 shocked
16 nearly　17 worth　18 invitation
19 jeweler　20 beauty　21 similar
22 borrow　23 jewelry　24 couple
25 lend　26 replace　27 second job
28 lie　29 worn　30 look
31 run into　32 Do I know you?
33 at once　34 call on　35 pay back

단어 TEST Step 3 — p.42

1 worn, 지친　2 couple, 부부　3 amount, 양, 액수
4 similar, 비슷한, 유사한　5 nearly, 거의
6 replace, ~을 대신하다　7 certainly, 확실히, 틀림없이
8 shocked, 충격을 받은　9 ball, 무도회　10 lie, 거짓말
11 cry, 울다　12 diamond, 다이아몬드
13 invitation, 초대, 초대장
14 admire, 존경하다, 칭찬하다, 감탄하며 바라보다

15 whisper, 속삭이다, 귓속말을 하다
16 ambassador, 대사

본문 TEST Step 1 — p.43~46

01 This is, in Paris
02 Although, nice, not happy
03 pretty, wants, fancier life
04 herself, same boring, living
05 home, what, have got
06 What, that
07 invitation, had, fight, get
08 Why would, want
09 What, wrong
10 nothing, wear, such, fancy
11 Don't be, Get yourself
12 looking at, Amazing
13 Something, not right
14 could be wrong
15 going to do
16 What is it
17 jewelry, wear, so poor
18 Call on, sure, lend
19 Let, go at once
20 so, to, brings, here
21 are invited to
22 wonderful, must be excited
23 say, jewelry, borrow, from
24 Here, my case
25 so many wonderful pieces
26 Choose whatever, like
27 lend me, diamond necklace
28 Certainly, go enjoy
29 perfect evening, admires, beauty
30 It is, when, leave
31 such, long night, so
32 worth it, danced with
33 enjoyed yourself, have, work
34 looking, more look, gone
35 when we left, ball
36 surely did, go find
37 searches, streets
38 returns to, then goes
39 necklace, found, to lie
40 broke, necklace, fix, returning
41 couple, find, similar one

42 May we look at

43 *whispering*, nearly, same, must

44 How much

45 40,000 francs

46 How about

47 really need it

48 then, it is

49 have, huge amount of

50 So, borrow

51 buying, for, spends, paying

52 move to, place

53 second job, washes, others

54 hard, makes, old, worn

55 years, runs into, on

56 good morning

57 Do I know

58 it is me

59 cannot believe, have changed

60 have had, difficult times

61 Because of, What, mean

62 remember, lent me, lost

63 returned it to

64 another, like, pay for

65 bought, to replace mine

67 didn't, truth, real, worth

01 This is, in Paris

02 Although, nice, not happy

03 and wants, fancier life

04 *to herself*, old house, boring, hate living

05 am home, what, have got

06 that

07 invitation to, had to fight to get it

08 Why would

09 is wrong

10 nothing to wear, such a fancy party

11 Don't be, give you, Get yourself, beautiful new dress

12 *looking at*, Amazing

13 not right

14 What could be wrong

15 going to do

16 What is it

17 no jewelry to wear, beautiful dress, so poor

18 Call on, she will lend you, jewelry

19 Let me go at once

20 to see, What brings you here

21 invited to

22 wonderful, must be excited

23 to say, no jewelry, borrow something from you

24 Here is, case

25 so many wonderful pieces

26 whatever you like

27 lend me this diamond necklace

28 Certainly, go enjoy

29 a perfect evening, admires her beauty

30 It is, when the Loisels leave

31 such a long night, tired

32 it was worth it, danced with

33 you enjoyed yourself, go to work

34 *looking in*, more look.

35 when we left the ball

36 did, go find

37 searches

38 returns to, goes to

39 is not found, to lie to

40 broke, necklace, fix it, returning it

41 to find a similar one

42 May we look at

43 *whispering*, nearly the same, must have

44 How much

45 francs

46 How about

47 really need it

48 it is

49 do not have, a huge amount of

50 borrow it

51 buying, for, spends, paying back

52 move to, small place

53 gets a second job, washes, for others

54 makes, old, worn

55 runs into, on

56 good morning

57 Do I know you

58 it is me

59 believe it, have changed

60 have had, difficult times because of

61 What do you mean

62 you lent me, lost it

63 returned it

64 another one, like it, It took, to pay for it

65 bought, to replace mine

67 Why didn't you come, tell me, was not real, worth

39

1 이곳은 파리의 Loisel 부부의 집이다.

2 그들의 집은 멋지지만, Loisel 부인은 행복하지 않다.

3 그녀는 젊고 예뻐서 더 화려하고 고급스러운 삶을 원한다.

4 Mrs. Loisel: (혼잣말로) 똑같은 낡은 집과 매일 같이 똑같은 지겨운 저녁 식사. 여기서 사는 게 너무 싫어!

5 Mr. Loisel: Matilda, 나 집에 왔어요. 내가 당신을 위해 무엇을 가져왔는지 봐요!

6 Mrs. Loisel: 뭐예요?

7 Mr. Loisel: 대사님이 여는 무도회 초대장이에요. 이걸 얻기 위해 엄청난 노력을 했단 말이에요. 모두가 갖고 싶어 했거든요.

8 Mrs. Loisel: (울면서) 내가 그걸 왜 갖고 싶겠어요?

9 Mr. Loisel: Matilda. 무슨 문제 있어요?

10 Mrs. Loisel: 그런 고급스러운 파티에 입고 갈 옷이 하나도 없는걸요. 못가요.

11 Mr. Loisel: 슬퍼하지 말아요. 자, 여기 400프랑을 줄게요. 아름다운 새 드레스를 사요.

12 Mr. Loisel: (Matilda의 새 드레스를 보며) 멋져요, Matilda. 아름답군요!

13 Mrs. Loisel: 뭔가 제대로 맞지 않아요.

14 Mr. Loisel: 뭐가 안 맞을 수 있죠?

15 Mrs. Loisel: (울면서) 오, 안 돼. 어쩌면 좋아요?

16 Mr. Loisel: 뭐예요, 부인?

17 Mrs. Loisel: 이 아름다운 드레스에 어울릴 보석이 하나도 없어요. 내가 너무 불쌍해 보일 거예요!

18 Mr. Loisel: 당신 친구 Forestier 부인에게 부탁해 봐요. 그녀는 자신이 가진 보석을 분명히 빌려줄 거예요.

19 Mrs. Loisel: 그거 좋은 생각이에요! 지금 당장 가봐야겠어요.

20 Mrs. Forestier: Matilda, 이렇게 보게 되어서 정말 좋아요! 무슨 일로 왔어요?

21 Mrs. Loisel: 우리 부부가 대사의 무도회에 초대되었어요.

22 Mrs. Forestier: 대사의 무도회라! 멋지네요! 당신은 분명 신났겠군요.

23 Mrs. Loisel: 네… 그리고 아니기도 해요. 말하기 슬프지만 난 보석이 없어요. 부인에게서 좀 빌릴 수 있을까요?

24 Mrs. Forestier: 물론이죠! 여기 내 보석함이에요.

25 Mrs. Loisel: 와, 부인은 정말 멋진 보석들이 많네요!

26 Mrs. Forestier: 원하는 것 아무거나 골라요.

27 Mrs. Loisel: 이 다이아몬드 목걸이를 빌려줄 수 있나요? 이거 정말 아름다워요!

28 Mrs. Forestier: 당연하죠! 자, 이제 가서 무도회를 즐겨요.

29 Matilda는 완벽한 저녁을 보낸다. 무도회장에 있는 모든 사람들이 아름다운 그녀를 감탄하며 바라본다.

30 Loisel 부부는 아주 늦은 시간이 되어서야 무도회를 떠났다.

31 Mr. Loisel: 정말 길고 긴 밤이었어요. 정말 피곤해요.

32 Mrs. Loisel: 그렇지만 충분히 가치가 있었어요. 당신, 제가 대사님과 춤춘 것을 아나요?

33 Mr. Loisel: 당신이 즐거웠다니 기쁘지만 나 아침에 출근해야 해요.

34 Mrs. Loisel: (거울을 보며) 한 번만 더 볼게요. (충격을 받고) 목걸이… 목걸이가 없어졌어요!

35 Mr. Loisel: 뭐라고요? 무도회를 떠날 때 걸고 있었소?

36 Mrs. Loisel: 네, 분명히 하고 있었는데. 가서 찾아 줘요!

37 Loisel 씨는 길거리를 수색한다.

38 그는 무도회장으로 되돌아가 본 다음 경찰서에도 간다.

39 목걸이가 발견되지 않자, Loisel 씨는 Matilda에게 그녀의 친구에게 거짓말을 하라고 한다.

40 Matilda는 Forestier 부인에게 목걸이를 망가뜨려서 돌려주기 전에 고쳐 주겠다고 말한다.

41 부부는 비슷한 것을 찾을 시간이 필요하다.

42 Mr. Loisel: (보석상에게) 실례합니다. 저 다이아몬드 목걸이 좀 볼 수 있을까요?

43 Mrs. Loisel: (속삭이며) 거의 똑같아요. 저걸 꼭 사야만 해요!

44 Mr. Loisel: 이거 얼마인가요?

45 Jewler: 40,000프랑이에요.

46 Mr. Loisel: 36,000에 안 될까요?

47 Mrs. Loisel: 부탁드려요, 우린 이게 정말 필요하거든요.

48 Jewler: 음, 그럼… 36,000프랑에 하시죠.

49 그들은 36,000프랑이 없다. 그건 큰돈이다.

50 그래서 그들은 돈을 빌린다.

51 부부는 Forestier 부인에게 돌려줄 목걸이를 산 후 돈을 갚는 데 십 년이 걸린다.

52 그들은 아주 작은 곳으로 이사한다.

53 Loisel 씨는 부업을 구한다. Matilda는 다른 사람들을 위해 빨래를 해 준다.

54 10년 동안의 고된 일로 Matilda는 늙고 지쳤다.

55 십 년 후, Matilda는 Forestier 부인과 거리에서 마주친다.

56 Mrs. Loisel: Forestier 부인, 좋은 아침이에요.

57 Mrs. Forestier: 제가 당신을 아나요?

58 Mrs. Loisel: 네, 저예요, Matilda.

59 Mrs. Forestier: 오, 믿을 수 없어요! 당신 너무 많이 변했어요.

60 Mrs. Loisel: 저는 당신 때문에 힘든 시간을 보냈거든요.

61 Mrs. Forestier: 나 때문에요? 무슨 말이에요?

62 Mrs. Loisel: 당신이 빌려준 목걸이가 기억하죠? 음, 제가 그걸 잃어버렸어요.

63 Mrs. Forestier: 그런데 그거 나한테 돌려줬잖아요.

64 Mrs. Loisel: 아니요, 나는 당신 것과 똑같은 다른 목걸이를 돌려줬어요. 그 값을 치르느라 십 년이 걸렸어요.

65 Mrs. Forestier: 내 것을 대체하려고 다이아몬드 목걸이를 샀다고요?

66 Mrs. Loisel: 네, 맞아요.

67 Mrs. Forestier: 오, 가엾은 Matilda. 왜 내게 와서 사실을 말하지 않았어요? 그 다이아몬드 목걸이는 진품이 아니었어요. 그건 단돈 오백 프랑짜리였다고요!

1 This is Mr. and Mrs. Loisel's home in Paris.

2 Although the home is nice, Mrs. Loisel is not happy.

3 She is young and pretty, and wants a fancier life.

4 Mrs. Loisel: (to herself) Same old house and same boring dinners. I hate living here!

5 Mr. Loisel: Matilda, I am home. Look what I have got for you!

6 Mrs. Loisel: What is that?

7 Mr. Loisel: An invitation to the Ambassador's Ball. I had to fight to get it. Everybody wanted it.

8 Mrs. Loisel: (crying) Why would I want it?

9 Mr. Loisel: Matilda. What is wrong?

10 Mrs. Loisel: I have nothing to wear to such a fancy party. I cannot go.

11 Mr. Loisel: Don't be sad. Here, I will give you 400 francs. Get yourself a beautiful new dress.

12 Mr. Loisel: (looking at Matilda's new dress) Amazing, Matilda. Beautiful!

13 Mrs. Loisel: Something is not right.

14 Mr. Loisel: What could be wrong?

15 Mrs. Loisel: (crying) Oh, no. What am I going to do?

16 Mr. Loisel: What is it, Matilda?

17 Mrs. Loisel: I have no jewelry to wear with my beautiful dress. I will look so poor!

18 Mr. Loisel: Call on your friend, Mrs. Forestier. I am sure she will lend you some of her jewelry.

19 Mrs. Loisel: That is a good idea! Let me go at once.

20 Mrs. Forestier: Matilda, it is so nice to see you! What brings you here?

21 Mrs. Loisel: We are invited to the Ambassador's Ball.

22 Mrs. Forestier: The Ambassador's Ball! That is wonderful! You must be excited.

23 Mrs. Loisel: Yes… And no. I am sad to say I have no jewelry. May I borrow something from you?

24 Mrs. Forestier: Sure! Here is my case.

25 Mrs. Loisel: Wow, you have so many wonderful pieces!

26 Mrs. Forestier: Choose whatever you like.

27 Mrs. Loisel: Would you lend me this diamond necklace? It is beautiful!

28 Mrs. Forestier: Certainly! Now go enjoy the ball.

29 Matilda has a perfect evening. Everybody at the ball admires her beauty.

30 It is very late when the Loisels leave the ball.

31 Mr. Loisel: It was such a long night. I am so tired.

32 Mrs. Loisel: But it was worth it. Do you know I danced with the Ambassador?

33 Mr. Loisel: I am glad you enjoyed yourself, but I have to go to work in the morning.

34 Mrs. Loisel: (looking in the mirror) Just one more look. (shocked) The necklace… It is gone!

35 Mr. Loisel: What? Did you have it when we left the ball?

36 Mrs. Loisel: Yes, I surely did. Please go find it!

37 Mr. Loisel searches the streets.

38 He returns to the ball and then goes to the police.

39 When the necklace is not found, Mr. Loisel tells Matilda to lie to her friend.

40 Matilda tells Mrs. Forestier she broke the necklace and would fix it before returning it.

41 The couple needs time to find a similar one.

42 Mr. Loisel: (to the jeweler) Excuse me? May we look at that diamond necklace?

43 Mrs. Loisel: (whispering) It is nearly the same. We must have it!

44 Mr. Loisel: How much is it?

45 Jeweler: 40,000 francs.

46 Mr. Loisel: How about 36,000?

47 Mrs. Loisel: Please, we really need it.

48 Jeweler: Well, then… 36,000 it is.l

49 They do not have 36,000 francs. It is a huge amount of money.

50 So they borrow it.

51 After buying the necklace for Mrs. Forestier, the couple spends ten years paying back the money.

52 They move to a very small place.

53 Mr. Loisel gets a second job. Matilda washes clothes for others.

54 Ten years of hard work makes Matilda old and worn.

55 After ten years, Matilda runs into Mrs. Forestier on the street.

56 Mrs. Loisel: Mrs. Forestier, good morning.

57 Mrs. Forestier: Do I know you?

58 Mrs. Loisel: Yes, it is me, Matilda.

59 Mrs. Forestier: Oh, I cannot believe it! You have changed so much.

60 Mrs. Loisel: I have had some difficult times because of you.

61 Mrs. Forestier: Because of me? What do you mean?

62 Mrs. Loisel: Do you remember the diamond necklace you lent me? Well, I lost it.

63 Mrs. Forestier: But you returned it to me.

64 Mrs. Loisel: No, I returned another one just like it. It took us ten years to pay for it.

65 Mrs. Forestier: You bought a diamond necklace to replace mine?

66 Mrs. Loisel: Yes.

67 Mrs. Forestier: Oh, my poor Matilda. Why didn't you come to me and tell me the truth? My diamond necklace was not real. It was worth only 500 francs!

MEMO

적중100

영어 기출 문제집

정답 및 해설

시사 | 박준언